RESEARCH ON
Altruism & Love

RESEARCH ON
Altruism & Love

An Annotated Bibliography of
Major Studies in Psychology,
Sociology, Evolutionary Biology,
and Theology

Edited by Stephen G. Post,
Byron Johnson,
Michael E. McCullough, and
Jeffrey P. Schloss

TEMPLETON FOUNDATION PRESS
Philadelphia and London

Templeton Foundation Press
Five Radnor Corporate Center, Suite 120
100 Matsonford Road
Radnor, Pennsylvania 19087
www.templetonpress.org

Designed and typeset by Kachergis Book Design
Printed by Versa Press, Inc.

LIBRARY OF CONGRESS CATALOGING-IN-PUBLICATION DATA
Research on altruism and love : an annotated bibliography of major
    studies in psychology, sociology, evolutionary biology, and theology /
    edited by Stephen G. Post . . . [et al.].
       p.   cm.
    Includes bibliographical references.
    ISBN 1–932031–32–4 (pbk. : alk. paper)
    1. Love—Bibliography.   2. Altruism—Bibliography.   I. Post, Stephen
Garrard, 1951—
    Z5865 .R47 2003
    [BJ1474]
    016.177′7—dc21
                                                2003001844

Printed in the United States of America
03 04 05 06 07   10 9 8 7 6 5 4 3 2 1

The man who foolishly does me wrong, I will return to him the protection of my most ungrudging love.
　　　—*Buddha*

Kind speech and forgiveness is better than alms followed by injury.
　　　—*Qur'an*

Spread love everywhere you go: first of all in your own house. Give love to your children, to your wife or husband, to a next door neighbor. . . . Let no one ever come to you without leaving better and happier. Be the living expression of God's kindness; kindness in your face, kindness in your eyes, kindness in your smile, kindness in your warm greeting.
　　　—*Mother Teresa*

God is love, and those who abide in love abide in God, and God abides in them.
　　　—*1 John*

Kindness in words creates confidence
Kindness in thinking creates profoundness
Kindness in giving creates love.
　　　—*Lao-tzu*

To do justice, to love kindness, and to walk humbly with your God.
　　　—*Micah*

Sooner or later, all the peoples of the world will have to discover a way to live together in peace, and thereby transform this pending cosmic elegy into a creative psalm of brotherhood. . . . The foundation of such a method is love.
　　　—*Martin Luther King Jr.*

A coward is incapable of exhibiting love; it is the prerogative of the brave.
　　　—*Mohandes K. Gandhi*

Contents

RESEARCH ON
Altruism & Love

Introduction

Stephen G. Post, Byron Johnson,
Michael E. McCullough, and Jeffrey P. Schloss

*T*he love on which we focus here is thankful for the very existence of others, shows concern for them, and attends to their various needs while seeking nothing in return. An unselfish, enduring, disinterested benevolence extending to all humanity, such love constitutes a perennial moral and spiritual ideal. This "pure unlimited love" is often said to be the sum of all virtue, and it is identified with the very essence of divine nature across the great religious cultures of the world.[1] While this ideal of love is indeed high and challenging, many everyday people act in remarkably compassionate ways and respond generously to the neediest as well as to those who are near and dear. Dostoyevsky, for example, found inspiration in the kind generosity of the Russian people. There are also those exemplars of unlimited love who inspire the world.

Selfishness, unfeeling arrogance, and hatred cause us to doubt the existence of this love, either in a rudimentary form within evolved human nature, or as a higher creative energy in which human participation is possible. We come to believe the saying, "Scratch an altruist, and watch an egoist bleed." We read Sartre's descriptions of "the look" of manipulation, which he saw as underlying every human interaction. We read the ethical egoists such as Ayn Rand and Friedrich Nietzsche, who tell us that even if there are genuinely altruistic motives in human nature, these should be entirely repressed lest the recipient of helping behavior become slothful. Much evolutionary biology places the strictest burden of proof on the proposition that humans are capable of any authentic benevolence toward humanity in general, and even parental love is deemed to be tainted by underlying "selfish genes." The social sciences, too, have taught us not to believe the human narrative of remarkably helping behavior that we see and hear and read about daily.

So it is that we come to lose confidence in benevolent motivations and detect underneath every ostensible act of unrequited generosity the supposedly ubiquitous shadow of self-interest. But does science really support this pessimistic view of the base metal of human nature? Or are our benevolent impulses genuine, not just with regard to the nearest and dearest, but even to the neediest? Might it be the case that in the generous giving of self lies the unsought-for discovery of a more fulfilled self? These are questions of such importance that they deserve the most balanced and unbiased scientific analysis.[2]

Scientific skepticism regarding genuine love for others is in tension with the remarkable human narrative of benevolent behavior. This narrative of love is itself a source of empirical insight. While not amenable to the application of strict scientific methods, the many biographies and autobiographies of lives lived more for the sake of all humanity than for self (and its proximate interests) are themselves a form of data. In the broad terms of Aristotelian epistemology, we should remain connected to the narrative of human helping behavior, whether in the aftermath of 9/11 or in routine acts of good neighbors, or in the remarkable lives of great saints of love in our time and in history. And this narrative, taken at face value, indicates that we are often surprisingly generous creatures. After all, it may be impossible for science to absolutely prove the existence of an internal motivational state like genuine benevolence, and yet even a casual perusal of local, national, and international human events indicates that people do amazingly good and compassionate things for others without expecting or requiring anything in return. But there is probably something fashionable in academics about being systematically skeptical of genuine benevolence while easily accepting the proposition that all human action springs from egoism. Fashions come and go.

Scientific questions about the substrate of human nature and its evolved benevolent impulses, coupled with broad observations about the narrative of human experience, still leave the human scope of thought on unlimited love incomplete. From early in the history of human cultures, we have raised metaphysical—or "Big Picture"—questions about the meaning of love in the drama of human destiny. Is love for others the only lasting source of meaning and purpose in life? Does such love follow the grain of the universe? Is God love? Is love the ultimate ethical ideal? This third aspect of human reflection on unlimited love is often the least scientific, although "Big Picture" questions about love in the universe should, we believe, be scientifically informed.

So it is that this annotated bibliography moves from scientific studies to the stories of human generosity, and to works of philosophy and theology about the place of love in the drama of an unfolding universe. We begin with scientific presentations of the important studies on other-regarding love in positive psychology (Bono and McCullough), love and altruism from sociology (Johnson, Fantuzzo, and Siegel), and evolutionary biology of altruistic motives and behavior (Kniffin, Wilson, and Schloss). But because it is imprudent to lose sight of the narrative of human experience, we turn to the lives of people who have manifested the works of love, although none would be so presumptuous as to think that they were perfectly loving (Emma Post). These narratives point to the traditions of perennial human reflection on unselfish love as essential to divine nature and as in mysterious ways available to us by participation. Thus, a final chapter focuses on theological, philosophical, and ethical speculation about divine and human love (Oord). Each chapter begins with an introduction on the significance of its content for the topic of unlimited love.

Such a highly integrative annotated bibliography will be reader-friendly in its tone and range. Whether the reader is primarily interested in science, biography, metaphysics, or ethics, we hope that he or she will work through this volume as a whole. If we succeed in encouraging such integrative learning and reflection, then we will have fulfilled our purpose.[3]

Before concluding this brief introduction, the reader deserves a broad definition of unlimited love, which is merely a creative linguistic transposition of *agape,* the ancient Greek word for love of all people and that is associated with God's exceptionless love for humanity:

The essence of love is to affectively affirm and to gratefully delight in the well-being of others; the essence of unlimited love is to extend this form of love to all others in an enduring fashion. In addition to being understood as the highest form of virtue, Unlimited Love is often deemed a Creative Presence underlying and integral to all reality. Participation in Unlimited Love is considered the fullest experience of spirituality, giving rise to inner peace and kindness, as well as to active works of love. Depending on the circumstances of others, unlimited love is expressed in a number of ways, including empathy and understanding, generosity and kindness, compassion and care, altruism and self-sacrifice, celebration and joy, and forgiveness and justice. In all these manifestations, unlimited love acknowledges for all others the absolutely full significance that, because of egoism or hatred, we otherwise acknowledge only for ourselves.

The reader also deserves a definition of *altruism,* a word different from love and yet related to it, which appears in this book title as well. It is a modern secular scientific concept whose sacred counterpart is *agape* love, although it lacks the emotional intonation of love. Both are other-regarding by definition and imply generous self-giving. Theologians' hesitancy to engage in dialogue with the science of altruism is understandable because altruism emerged as a decidedly secular concept within the nineteenth-century domain of scientific positivism, the view that science would eventually replace religion by substituting empirical reason for faith and superstition. Yet the positivist view has not withstood the facts of the twentieth century, which demonstrated that the influence of religion would rise rather than fall in a scientific world.

The term *altruism,* which derives from the Latin alter ("the other"), means literally "other-ism." It was created by the French sociologist Auguste Comte (1798–1857) to displace terms burdened by a theological history. It was suggested by a French legal expression, "le bien d'autrui" (the good of others). Comte viewed the subordination of altruism to egoism as the source of human evil, and he was neither a psychological nor an ethical egoist.

One need not endorse the secular humanistic tone of "altruism" to appreciate the scientific studies indicating the extent to which human nature manifests altruistic motives and behaviors. If there are any continuities or, perhaps better said, any points of correspondence or convergence, between human nature and unlimited love, it is science that must describe the base material of evolved human nature; this will require exploration of the forms of "altruism" in the human repertoire. If Unlimited Love is the ultimate reality that underlies the universe, one would expect to find some hint of it in human nature, just as one would wish to better understand how it is that Unlimited Love seems to break into the lives of many people who have gone on to become servants of all humanity.

Scientific progress in our understanding of love and unlimited love is absolutely crucial to meaningful dialogue and sustained public interest. Just as human beings endeavor to understand and harness the power of the wind, the atom, and gravity, they can make progress in understanding and facilitating the energies of unlimited love. Before we can move forward in the science of unlimited love, it is necessary to have some inventory of existing knowledge. [4]

Notes

1. Sir John Templeton, *Pure Unlimited Love* (Philadelphia: Templeton Foundation Press, 2000).

2. Stephen G. Post, Lynn G. Underwood, Jeffrey P. Schloss, and William B. Hurlbut, eds., *Altruism and Altruistic Love: Science, Philosophy, and Religion in Dialogue* (New York: Oxford University Press, 2002).

3. For a model of integrated science on altruistic love, see Pitirim A. Sorokin, *The Ways and Power of Love: Types, Factors, and Techniques of Moral Transformation,* with a foreword by S. G. Post (1954; Philadelphia: Templeton Foundation Press, 2002).

4. For a fuller exposition on the meaning of unlimited love, see Stephen G. Post, *Unlimited Love: Altruism, Compassion, Service* (Philadelphia: Templeton Foundation Press, 2003).

CHAPTER 1

Research on Other-Regarding Virtues, 1998–2002

Giacomo Bono and Michael E. McCullough

*I*n 2002, Shelley Kilpatrick and Mike McCullough's annotated bibliography of over seventy peer-reviewed articles on altruistic and prosocial behavior was published in *Altruistic Love: Science, Philosophy, and Religion in Dialogue.* Kilpatrick and McCullough provided summaries of and commentaries upon articles—mostly from the 1980s and 1990s, but also including some classics from previous decades—in which investigators explored altruism and prosocial behavior in many different forms, involving many different types of people from all walks of life.

Kilpatrick and McCullough's (2002) annotated bibliography included articles that had been published as recently as 1998. As 1998 was not that long ago, perhaps it seems too early to be revising their recent effort. However, the literature has grown so substantially in this short time that it seems worthwhile to offer a brief update. Science progresses most rapidly when the existing knowledge base is disseminated to innovators who can take that knowledge to the next step. And in light of the goal of the Institute for Research on Unlimited Love (IRUL) to stimulate high-quality scientific research, an update seems warranted. Herein we summarize more than three dozen exciting studies of other-regarding virtues and behavior that have appeared in the psychological literature between 1998 and 2002. The present annotated bibliography is noticeably slimmer than was Kirkpatrick and McCullough's, but the goals and focus are similar.

Our approach for locating these studies was straightforward: We performed a series of electronic searches of the PsycInfo database for research articles that were published from 1998 to 2002. These electronic searches led us to published research articles in psychology and related social sciences that touch on a broad range of other-regarding virtues (e.g., cooperation, altruism, forgiveness, generosity, kindness, and humility). We included only empirical articles, omitting review articles and conceptual articles.

To imply that our selection process was scientific, or even very systematic, would perhaps be disingenuous. Although we tried to concentrate on what we thought were the most exciting recent developments in the social-scientific study of other-regarding virtues, we also followed our noses, selecting studies that drew us in. No doubt, our noses led us away from many good studies. We gravitated toward studies, to mention only a handful of categories, that addressed: the evolutionary and genetic substrates of altruistic behavior (Korchmaros & Kenny, 2001; Krueger, Hicks, & McGue, 2001); the personality traits and psychological processes that are involved in choosing among social strategies that are cooperative rather than self-serving (e.g., Boone, et al., 2002; De Bruin & Van Lange, 1999a, 1999b; De Cremer & Van Lange, 2001; Koole, Jager, van de Berg, Vlek, & Hofstee, 2001), developmental studies examining the manifestations of other-regarding sentiments and prosocial behavior at specific points in the life course (e.g., Eisenberg, et al., 2002; Kakavoulis, 1998; Midlarsky, Kahana, Corley, Nemeroff, & Schonbar, 1999; Silverstein, Conroy, Wang, Giarusso, & Bengtson, 2002); social-psychological studies on processes related to love and commitment (Gonzaga, Keltner, Londahl, & Smith, 2001; Finkel, Rusbult, Kumashiro, & Hannon, 2002), studies on factors that diminish prejudice (Gaertner, et al., 1999); even studies that offer direction for designing interventions in the "real world" that can help to encourage other-regarding virtues and behavior (e.g., Kim & Webster, 2001; Perrine & Heather, 2000). The studies included herein varied in objectives from the most basic and theoretical (e.g., Macy & Skvoretz, 1998) to the utterly practical (Perrine & Heather, 2000).

Some of the studies that interested us the most demonstrate the occasional folly of selfishness and the ironically self-serving value of some of the other-regarding virtues. Witvliet, Ludwig, and Vander Laan's (2001) demonstration of the physiological strain that results from entertaining grudges and thoughts of revenge toward transgressors is a warning that overindulging the dark appetite for "balancing the scales" can exact a toll on the person who keeps the books and tries to collect the debts. By focusing on thoughts of empathy and forgiveness for the transgressor, one can avoid these physiological surcharges. Sheldon, Sheldon, and Osbaldiston (2000) explored the notion that people who make a priority of humanistic values—cooperation, self-acceptance, and community contribution—tend to form friendships with each other in the real world, whereas people who value individual materialistic advancement, attractiveness, and fame also tend to aggregate. Without "suckers to exploit," Sheldon and colleagues show us, groups composed of people who are oriented toward the self-serving values flounder in tasks that require teamwork, whereas groups composed of people who prioritize the more humanistic values speed ahead. By cooperating with their own kind, groups of cooperators compete better against other groups. By competing with their own kind, groups of competitors compete much worse against other groups (cf. Macy & Skvoretz, 1998).

There are other ironic stories to be told from the articles reviewed herein. Kelln and Ellard's (1999) study shows that forgiving someone for a transgression, instead of being "selfless," has a gift-like quality that, rather than working against the forgiver's self-interest, actually works for the forgiver by creating bonds of indebtedness. Put plainly, forgiven people want to do a good turn to those who have forgiven them. In a similar vein, Silverstein, Conroy, Wang, Giarusso, and Bengtson (2002) demonstrated that parents who make major investments of time, affection, and even money in their children get returns on these investments later in life in the form of emotional and tangible social support. By caring for others—whether the "others" are strangers or the closest of kin— we actually build bonds of indebtedness and fidelity.

Are these bonds of indebtedness and fidelity the fibers out of which true community can be fashioned, or are they chains? Or both? The answer to this question may be, in part, a matter for more empirical work, but it may also be a matter of taste, or a matter of one's *vision* for how society *should be* constructed and how people *should* relate to one another—matters that science cannot arbitrate. If choosing how to improve social relations and society is a matter of taste or vision, then which vision should we prefer? After all, every social structure has its pathologies. Feudal systems have no lack of indebtedness and fidelity, but would any of us choose for ourselves a feudal societal system without knowing in advance who our lord would be? And who has not had the experience of being forced by a teacher or supervisor to work in a group that clearly performed worse, not better, than the sum of its individual parts?

Clearly, neither a return to a feudal system of obligation and correlated prerogatives, nor a headlong plunge into warm-and-fuzzy but uncritical groupishness, is a wise way forward for human society. Still, for the social critic who thinks we need more cooperation, indebtedness, and fidelity, discoveries like those in the studies we review here may seem like a tonic from which our society could benefit.

 Ashton, M. C., Paunonen, S. V., Helmes, E., & Jackson D. N. (1998). **Kin altruism, reciprocal altruism, and the Big Five personality factors.** *Evolution and Human Behavior, 19*(4), 243–255.

Objective: Identify personality characteristics associated with kin altruism and reciprocal altruism, and relate those characteristics to the Big Five personality dimensions.

Design: Nonexperimental questionnaire.

Setting: University of Western Ontario, London, Ontario, Canada.

Participants: A total of 118 (69 female, 49 men; median age = 19) introductory psychology students volunteered to participate for course credit.

Assessment of Predictor Variables: Participants completed a questionnaire containing forty adjective minimarkers of the Big Five personality factors

(Saucier, 1994), which represent the four quadrants of the Agreeableness and Emotional Stability factor plane (e.g., patient, peaceful, tolerant and critical, demanding and irritable, respectively).

Assessment of Outcome Variables: Altruism was measured in several ways. Participants completed two self-report measures, the Jackson Personality Inventory-Revised (JPI-R; Jackson, 1994), which measures general altruistic behavior, and a questionnaire that measures four positive personality characteristics (e.g., feeling sorry for, worrying about, being closely attached to one's relatives, and being closely attached to one's friends) and four negative ones (e.g., tendency to suspect deceit from, become angry at, retaliate against, and hesitate to forgive other people) that are presumed to be related to both kin and reciprocal altruism. These items were aggregated into an Empathy/Attachment scale and Forgiveness/Nonretaliation scale (alphas = .73 and .75, respectively). Two versions of a money allocation task similar to a decomposed game procedure used by Kramer, McClintock, and Messick (1986) were used to measure kin and reciprocal altruism. Participants were to choose between two combinations ($125 for the participant and $75 for the other or $150 for the participant and $50 for the other) that would be hypothetically allotted to themselves and to a person who was described as uncooperative toward them (in the reciprocal version) and to someone with whom they had a long friendship and much in common (in the kin version).

Main Results: The personality traits involving empathy and attachment facilitated kin altruism, and personality traits involving forgiveness and nonretaliation facilitated reciprocal altruism. Moreover, the Empathy/Attachment and Forgiveness/Nonretaliation dimensions were found to be nearly orthogonal to each other. While the first traits fell roughly in the middle of the high Agreeableness/low Emotional Stability quadrant, the second traits fell roughly in the middle of the high Agreeableness/high Emotional quadrant.

Conclusion: Empathy and Attachment personality traits are related to kin altruism, while Forgiveness and Nonretaliatory traits are related to reciprocal (nonkin) altruism. The former appear to be related to high Agreeableness and low Emotional Stability, while the latter appear to be related to high Agreeableness and high Emotional. The importance of Agreeableness, the authors contend, lies in the interpersonal communication skills required for people to assess how another person (related or not) is likely to treat them. Moreover, negative emotions may energize kin altruism by facilitating feelings of empathy and attachment toward kin or they may discourage reciprocal altruism by facilitating anger and resentment toward exploitative individuals.

Commentary: This research found important relationships between personality and the two types of altruism recognized by ethologists and behavioral ecologists, altruism toward kin and toward nonkin.

Correspondence: Michael C. Ashton, Department of Psychology, University of Western Ontario, London, Ontario, Canada; email: mcashton@julian.uwo.ca.

🕮 Batson C. D., & Ahmad, N. (2001). Empathy-induced altruism in a prisoner's dilemma II: What if the target of empathy has defected? *European Journal of Social Psychology, 31*(1), 25–36.

Objective: To determine if empathy can motivate people to cooperate in a one-trial prisoner's dilemma, even when one knows that the interaction partner has already defected. This study seeks to rule out explanations that empathy-induced altruism can lead to cooperation because of expectations that the other will cooperate in return and because of anticipated guilt from defecting if the other were to cooperate.

Design: An experiment using a sequential, one-trial prisoner's dilemma involving three conditions (no communication, low empathy, high empathy).

Setting: University of Kansas, Lawrence.

Participants: Sixty undergraduate women enrolled in introductory psychology courses.

Assessment of Manipulated Variables: Individual participants were randomly assigned to one of the three conditions. They were led to believe they were exchanging something of value with another participant who remained anonymous (there actually was no other participant). The exchange involved cards worth a specified number of tickets in a raffle for a $30.00 gift certificate at any store. Participants received a note allegedly from the other participant (describing a relationship breakup and her need to be cheered up) and were instructed to read the note objectively or empathetically (i.e., using a well-validated procedure for enhancing empathy) or they were not given a note at all.

Assessment of Outcome Variables: After receiving a description of the payoff outcomes regarding the exchange, participants were given three red cards (valued at +5, +5, or –5 raffle tickets) and told that the other participant received three similarly valued blue cards. The payoff was as follows. A combination of two +5 cards, one red and one blue, was worth double the face value (20 tickets), and a negative total was worth zero tickets. They were then given an envelope containing a red card that the "other participant" ostensibly gave them (always a –5 card) in which they were to put the card they chose to give to the other participant. This was the main dependent variable—indicating cooperation if they gave a +5 card or defection if they gave a –5 card. Afterwards, participants were given a questionnaire containing ratings (on a seven-point scale) about different feelings and perceptions regarding the exchange (e.g., lucky, thankful, or hurt).

Main Results: Rate of cooperation was low in both the no-communication and low-empathy condition, but significantly higher in the high-empathy condition. The effect of empathy on defection was not mediated by attributions but by induced empathy for the interaction partner.

Conclusion: Even when an individual experiencing a particular need in a particular situation has already defected in a social dilemma (making the cost to the helper clear), empathy-induced altruism can still be a potent motivator to help this person.

Commentary: This research refines the picture outlined by the previous study by providing more convincing evidence that altruism is a strong prosocial motive that can lead to cooperative behavior in social dilemmas. Indeed, it is distinct from morality motives to the degree that we can cooperate not out of outcomes we expect or prospective expectations of guilt we may have for defecting on a cooperative partner; and despite knowledge that an interaction partner has defected on us already, we can display cooperative behavior in the face of complete cost. Although this experiment involved a relatively innocuous cost with low stakes (less probability of winning a raffle), research should investigate if costs involving higher stakes lead to different outcomes.

Correspondence: C. Daniel Batson, Department of Psychology, University of Kansas, Lawrence; email: dbatson@ukansas.edu.

Batson, C. D., Ahmad, N., Yin, J., Bedell, S. J., Johnson, J. W., Templin, C. M., & Whiteside, A. (1999, January). Two threats to the common good: Self-interested egoism and empathy-induced altruism. *Personality and Social Psychology Bulletin, 25*(1), 3–16.

Objective: To assess the power of self-interested egoism and empathy-induced altruism as threats to the common good, and to investigate if anticipated social evaluation will inhibit the former but not the latter.

Design: Two experiments, employing a one-trial resource-allocation dilemma with no face-to-face contact. Experiment 1 employed a 1×3 design, and experiment 2 employed a 2×3 design.

Setting: University of Kansas, Lawrence.

Participants: Participants for both experiments were undergraduates enrolled in introductory psychology courses. There were 90 participants in the first experiment and 120 in the second (both males and females).

Assessment of Manipulated Variables: In both experiments individual participants were given a chance to allocate scarce resources (i.e., raffle tickets) either to an individual in the allocation group or to the whole group. Allocations to the whole group gained 50 percent value, benefiting everyone equally, while allocations to an individual kept the same value and benefited only that individual at the expense of the common good. In experiment 1, participants were randomly assigned to one of three conditions in which their allocation decisions were made privately (an egoistic condition where they could give to themselves or the whole group, an altruism condition where they were asked to empathetically read a note allegedly from another participant that described a relationship breakup and the need to be cheered up, and a baseline condition where they were asked to read the same note objectively). In experiment 2, the same three conditions were employed, but a public allocation condition (whereby all participants' allocation decisions would be known) was added to each.

Assessment of Outcome Variables: The main dependent measure in both experiments was allocation of the raffle tickets. Afterwards, participants also completed a final questionnaire about reasons for and reactions to their allocation decisions. Manipulation checks showed that all independent variables were effective.

Main Results: In experiment 1, self-interested egoism and empathy-induced altruism both significantly reduced allocation to the group to similar degrees, compared to the baseline condition. Also, analyses of the questionnaire data showed that participants in the egoism and empathy conditions were more concerned with individual welfare (i.e., themselves or the needy other), that participants in the baseline condition were more concerned for the welfare of the group, and that the egoism and altruism participants were less likely to allocate to the group than the baseline participants. In experiment 2, the private conditions showed a similar pattern, but when participants thought that their allocation decisions would be public, they inhibited self-interested egoism but not altruism even though they also felt less moral about allocating to the individual rather than the group.

Conclusion: These experiments provide evidence that in addition to self-interest, altruism can also lead individuals to make decisions against the common good. Also, it appears that the prospect of social sanctions restrains people from acting on egoism but not on altruism. This may be because there are clear and strong social norms/sanctions against acting on self-interest at the expense of common interest but that is not so with altruism.

Commentary: This research indicates that empathy-induced altruism can be a threat against the common interest which is unique from self-interested egoism, and that investigating both will provide a fuller picture of the complexity of people's motives during social dilemmas. Further, altruism may go against the common good while seeming benign or benevolent.

Correspondence: C. Daniel Batson, Department of Psychology, University of Kansas; email: dbatson@ukansas.edu.

⫷ Batson, C. D., Chang, J., Orr, R., & Rowland, J. (2002). Empathy, attitudes, and action: Can feeling for a member of a stigmatized group motivate one to help the group? *Personality and Social Psychology Bulletin, 28*(2), 1656–1666.

Objective: To test if inducing empathy for a member of a stigmatized group improves attitudes toward a group as well as increases helping of the group.

Design: Experiment in which participants were induced to feel minimal empathy for a target person, lots of empathy for a target person, or lots of empathy for a fictional person.

Setting: University of Kansas, Lawrence.

Participants: A total of fifty-four introductory psychology students (36 women, 18 men) participated for course credit.

Assessment of Manipulated Variables: Participants were led to believe that they were participating in a project to get student feedback for how a student action committee should spend community outreach funds. First they were given information about four worthwhile community programs and then they were given information about an additional program for drug addicts (it was made clear that funds to the latter program would take away from funds to the former programs). Participants were instructed to listen to a tape of an alleged interview by a journalism major of a twenty-two-year-old man serving a seven-year sentence in the local penitentiary for possession and sales of heroin so that they could better decide how funds should be spent. In the interview, the man spoke about how he became addicted to heroin, how he began to steal and deal to support the addiction, about his arrest, about his life in prison, and about his plans to turn his life around for the better. The story also made it clear that the man would not benefit from any funds given to the drug program. Two empathy conditions were manipulated by having participants either listen to the interview objectively or empathically according to Stotland's method (1969). A third condition involved empathetically listening to the interview, except that the interview was previously described as fictitious, based on a journalism major's actual observations of the lives of heroin addicts.

Assessment of Outcome Variables: After listening to the interview, participants completed a questionnaire containing manipulation check items. Then they were given a community outreach budget recommendation form in which they were to indicate how much money should be allocated to the drug addiction program (no allocation, $1000, $2000, etc., up to a maximum of $8000 allowable for a program allocation). This was the main dependent variable. Participants were then given another questionnaire designed to measure attitudes toward people addicted to hard drugs. Items had participants rate on nine-point scales how much they agreed or disagreed with statements (e.g., "people addicted to hard drugs lack self-control and inner strength") or whether they felt positive or negative about "people addicted to hard drugs."

Main Results: Participants induced to feel empathy for a "real" addict reported more positive attitudes about people with hard drug addictions compared to those not induced to feel empathy. Empathic participants also recommended that more funds be allocated to the drug program (i.e., they helped more), compared to objective participants. Moreover, it was found that the effect of empathy on helping was mediated by attitudes toward hard drug addicts. Finally, participants who empathized with a fictional character showed a similar pattern to those who empathized with a "real" character.

Conclusion: Positive attitudes evoked by empathy for a stigmatized group can lead to increased helping of that group, even though it is known that the target in need would not benefit from the help. It appears that care evoked by empathy felt for a member of a stigmatized group can generalize to the group and stimulate motivation to benefit the group as whole.

Commentary: These results reveal the practical value of using empathy as a technique for creating more positive responses toward the troubled lives of the stigmatized. Not only can empathy help foster more positive attitudes toward stigmatized groups, but it can help shape people's helping behavior toward those groups as well.

Correspondence: C. Daniel Batson, Department of Psychology, University of Kansas; email: dbatson@ukansas.edu.

 Batson C. D., & Moran, T. (1999). Empathy-induced altruism in a prisoner's dilemma. *European Journal of Social Psychology,* 29(7), 909–924.

Objective: To investigate if empathy can motivate people to cooperate in a one-trial prisoner's dilemma and if framing the dilemma in terms of a business transaction (as opposed to a social transaction) will reduce cooperation in the absence of empathy.

Design: A 3 (no communication, low empathy, high empathy) × 2 (social dilemma, business dilemma) factorial experiment using a one-trial prisoner's dilemma methodology.

Setting: University of Kansas, Lawrence.

Participants: Sixty undergraduate women enrolled in introductory psychology courses.

Assessment of Manipulated Variables: Individual participants were randomly assigned to one of the six conditions in which they were led to believe they were exchanging something of value with another participant (who was actually fictitious). The exchange was either framed as a social exchange or a business transaction, involving a card worth a specified number of tickets in a raffle for a $30.00 gift certificate at any store. Participants received a note allegedly from the other participant (describing a relationship breakup and her need to be cheered up) and were instructed to read the note objectively or empathetically, or they were not given a note at all.

Assessment of Outcome Variables: Participants were given three cards (worth +5, +5, or –5) and a description of the payoff outcomes regarding the exchange. The main dependent variable included the choice of card they gave to the "other participant"—either a +5 card (indicating cooperation) or a –5 card (indicating defection). Afterwards, participants were given an envelope containing the card the "other participant" ostensibly gave them (always the –5 card) and a questionnaire containing ratings (on a seven-point scale) about different feelings and perceptions regarding the exchange (e.g., lucky, thankful, or hurt).

Main Results: Rate of cooperation was low in the no-communication/business and low-empathy/business conditions, moderate in the no-communication/social and low-empathy/social conditions, and high in the high-empathy/social and high-empathy/business conditions. Overall cooperation was also greater in the social exchange than the business exchange condition, indicating that moral motivation may be involved in social exchange but exempt in business exchange.

Conclusion: Empathy for a particular individual experiencing a particular need in a particular situation was found to be a potent motivator to help this person in a social dilemma, even if it was at a cost, and this difference was not due to lack of interest in the outcome of the exchange, changed expectations about the other's cooperativeness, or to differential information about the other's need. Moreover, those who cooperated (and lost everything) were relatively upset, unhappy, and dissatisfied, indicating that altruistic empathy coexisted with, rather than substituted, self-interest.

Commentary: This research shows that altruism can be a prosocial motive in social dilemmas that is distinct from morality, with its own goals, psychological antecedents, and behavioral consequences. As well, it seems a business transaction framework is not strong enough to completely extinguish empathy-induced altruism, but it does attenuate it.

Correspondence: C. Daniel Batson, Department of Psychology, University of Kansas; email: dbatsonukansas.edu.

🐌 Boone, C., de Brabander, B., Carree, M., de Jong, G., van Olffen, W., & van Witteloostuijn, A. (2002). Locus of control and learning to cooperate in a prisoner's dilemma game. *Personality and Individual Differences, 32*(5), 929–946.

Objective: To examine if people with an internal locus of control are more astute in learning to cooperate in a social dilemma than people with an external locus of control.

Design: Two experiments using a standard prisoner's dilemma game (PDG) methodology.

Setting: University of Groningen, the Netherlands.

Participants: A total of 182 students participated in the experiments as part of a course.

Assessment of Manipulated Variables: For each experiment five different PDGs were presented to subjects in a fixed order. The PDGs concerned an oligopoly pricing problem in which participants could set a low price (i.e., make a competitive choice) or set a high price (make a cooperative choice). The first two PDGs involved making twelve one-time choices in a row against a fictitious party (this served as a baseline cooperation measure), and the last three involved repeated interaction with a partner. Locus of control, the independent variable, was measured using Rotter's scale (1966). Reliability was adequate (Cronbach alpha = .65). This procedure was followed for both experiments, but participants were put in different dyads for both experiments to find out whether learning takes place irrespective of the partner with whom the participants interact.

Assessment of Outcome Variables: The dependent variable was cooperation, as measured by counting the total number of cooperative choices in each game.

Main Results: In the first experiment, individuals with an external locus of control were on average less cooperative than those with internal and intermediate levels of control, but this difference disappeared by the final game and in the entire second experiment.

Conclusion: Results suggest that the underlying reason for the observed differences between the external and internal locus of control individuals was related to differences in the capacity to learn: externals were slower to learn that cooperation is instrumental to furthering self-interest than internals were.

Commentary: Though this research utilized a sample skewed toward internal locus of control, its findings imply that experience can weaken the impact of locus of control on cooperative behavior.

Correspondence: Christophe Boone, Faculty of Economics and Business Administration, Maastricht University, Maastricht, the Netherlands.

Carlo, G., Allen, J. B., & Buhman, D. C. (1999). **Facilitating and disinhibiting prosocial behaviors: The nonlinear interaction of trait perspective taking and trait personal distress on volunteering.** *Basic and Applied Social Psychology, 21*(3), 189–197.

Objective: To examine if there are multiplicative relations of trait personal distress, trait sympathy, and trait perspective-taking on volunteering.

Design: Nonexperimental questionnaires administered in two sessions (six weeks apart).

Setting: State University of New York–Geneseo.

Participants: A total of 182 introductory psychology students (121 females, 61 males) who participated for course credit.

Assessment of Predictor Variables: In the first session, participants completed a packet of randomly ordered trait questionnaires that included three subscales from Davis's (1983) multidimensional measures of trait empathy. Subscales had participants rate on seven-point scales the degree to which certain statements about sympathy, perspective taking, and personal distress described them. Sample items include: "I often have tender, concerning feelings, for people less fortunate than me" (sympathy), "I try to look at everybody's side of a disagreement before I make a decision" (perspective taking), and "In emergency situations, I feel anxious and ill-at-ease" (personal distress). Reliabilities were good (Cronbach alphas = .73, .79, and .80). Social desirability was also measured (Crown & Marlowe, 1964; alpha = .78).

Assessment of Outcome Variables: The dependent variable was intent to volunteer, which was measured in the second session. A representative from a local volunteer organization at the university presented participants with an opportunity to volunteer time in one or more areas (e.g., aging, handicapped services, tutoring poor or disadvantaged students, crisis management for battered women, and youth services for abused children). Participants received a volunteer form that asked if they would be interested in volunteering, if so how many one-hour sessions they would be willing to volunteer (from one or two sessions to nineteen or more).

Main Results: As expected, there was a nonlinear interaction between trait personal distress and trait perspective-taking in the prediction of intent to volunteer. As perspective-taking increased, intent to volunteer increased, but only at low levels of personal distress. Females were also more likely to volunteer than men. Trait sympathy was not related to volunteering.

Conclusion: Results suggest that trait perspective-taking (but not sympathy) is strongly and positively related to volunteering when levels of personal distress are low but unrelated when personal distress is moderate or high.

Commentary: This research shows that multiplicative models of prosocial-related traits should be used for predicting prosocial behavior such as volunteering. The finding that trait sympathy was not related to volunteering—a finding that goes against much previous research—coupled with the finding that both egoistic traits (distress) and other-oriented traits (perspective-taking) may function concurrently in predicting prosocial behavior suggests indeed that prosocial behavior may be best explained in terms of nonlinear models of prosocial traits.

Correspondence: Gustavo Carlo, Department of Psychology, University of Nebraska–Lincoln; email: gcarlo@unlinfo.unl.edu.

&ᚹ De Bruin, E. N. M., & Van Lange, P. A. M. (1999a). **The double meaning of a single act: Influences of the perceiver and the perceived on cooperative behaviour.** *European Journal of Personality,* 13(3), 165–182.

Objective: To investigate how individual differences in social value orientation influence inferences drawn from the intelligence and morality information of a target person in a social dilemma.

Design: An experiment using a mixed-motive interdependence dilemma for two people.

Setting: Free University Amsterdam, the Netherlands.

Participants: A total of 164 students were recruited through a university newspaper advertisement.

Assessment of Manipulated Variables: Participants' social value orientation (SVO; McClintock, 1972) was assessed through a series of nine decomposed games involving a choice between a prosocial, an individualistic, and a competitive option. They were classified as one of the three if they responded with that option at least six times, resulting in 77 prosocials, 42 individualists, and 25 competitors. SVO was a between-subjects factor. Participants were then engaged in decision-making tasks involving choices between options that would affect how many points they and an interdependent would get. They were given four points (worth 50 Dutch cents to them and 100 to the target) and told that the same was so for the target. They were also told that they would receive some information about each partner before having to decide how many points to give and that for each decision they would be paired with another partner. Morality and intelligence of the partners were manipulated as within-subjects variables, by presenting participants with descriptively moral or immoral and intelligent or unintelligent targets—descriptions established through pretesting.

Assessment of Outcome Variables: Participants were asked how many of the four points they expected a target to give them in the social dilemma task (expected cooperation) and how many points they gave to the target (own cooperation).

Main Results: People found morality information to be greater in predictive utility than intelligence information when determining their expectations about a target's cooperative or uncooperative behavior and their decisions to cooperate or not with that target. Differential interpretations also varied by SVO. Unlike prosocials, proselfs (i.e., individualists and competitors) expected more cooperation from unintelligent than intelligent others. They also were less likely than prosocials to display cooperation when they expected it from the target. On the other hand, prosocials displayed more cooperation toward a moral target than toward an immoral one, and this difference was greater for prosocials than proselfs. People overall expected higher levels of cooperation than they were willing to display, but proselfs exhibited this bias toward relative benefit more than prosocials.

Conclusion: It appears that perceivers first attend to the moral information when forming impressions of targets. Prosocials attend to only this information in their decisions to reciprocate any cooperation they expect (though they expect more cooperation than they display). However, proselfs additionally attend to intelligence information and reciprocate even less cooperation than they expect, compared to prosocials. Therefore, evidence was found for the multifaceted nature of behavioral information in cooperation during social dilemmas.

Commentary: This research investigates the role of key factors underlying impression formation and resulting cooperative behavior in social dilemmas—social and intellectual attractiveness—and how people of different social value orientations use this information in determining their impressions and decisions to help others.

Correspondence: Ellen De Bruin, Department of Psychology, Free University of Amsterdam, the Netherlands; email: enm.de.bruin@psy. vu.nl.

      De Bruin, E. N. M., & Van Lange, P. A. M. (1999b). Impression forma-
tion and cooperative behavior. *European Journal of Social Psychology, 29,* 305–
328.

Objective: To examine the roles of morality versus intelligence information
and of positive versus negative information in people's impression formation of
an interdependent other, in their expectations for the other's cooperative or
noncooperative intentions, and in their decision to cooperate or not in return.

Design: Two experiments using a mixed-motive interdependence dilemma
for two people.

Setting: Free University Amsterdam, the Netherlands.

Participants: A total of 125 students (81 females and 44 males) for study 1
and 164 students (99 females and 65 males) for study 2 were recruited through
university newspaper advertisements.

Assessment of Manipulated Variables: For both experiments, participants
engaged in decision-making tasks involving choices between options that
would affect how many points they and an interdependent other (here called a
target) would get. They were given four points (worth 50 Dutch cents to them
and 100 to the target) and told that the same was so for the target. They were
also told that they would receive some information about each partner before
having to decide how many points to give and that for each decision they would
be paired with a new partner. Morality and intelligence of the partners were
manipulated as within-subjects variables, by presenting participants with descriptively moral or immoral and intelligent or unintelligent and neutral behaviors of the target—descriptions established through pretesting. In study 1 targets' morality and intelligence information were presented separately, but in
study 2 they were presented in combination.

Assessment of Outcome Variables: Participants were asked how many of the
four points they expected a target to give them in the social dilemma task (expected cooperation), how confident they were about this, and how many points
they gave to the target (own cooperation). Another dependent measure included number of target descriptions they recalled.

Main Results: In study 1, compared to intelligence information, morality
information led to more positive global impressions, increased expected cooperation from the target and confidence in these expectations, increased cooperation with the target, and better recall of target descriptions. Negativity effects
were also found for both types of information; there were greater differences in
global impression and expected and displayed cooperation levels between immoral and neutral targets than between moral and neutral ones, and there were
greater differences in global impression and displayed cooperation levels between unintelligent and neutral targets than between intelligent and neutral
ones. Finally, participants increased their relative benefit when it concerned unintelligent, moral, and neutral targets. In addition to yielding similar findings,

study 2 also showed the dominant influence of morality over intelligence by revealing that moral/unintelligent targets were evaluated and approached more favorably than immoral/intelligent targets.

Conclusion: These two experiments show that morality information plays a greater role than intelligence information in impressions, expectations of cooperation, confidence in such expectations, and in the amount of cooperation that people exhibit toward an interaction partner. Morality information is also recalled better than intelligence information. Impressions are better and expected and displayed cooperation are greater when a partner is seen as relatively moral, while impressions are better and displayed cooperation is greater when a partner is seen as unintelligent.

Commentary: The results of these studies enhance our understanding of impression formation processes and the consequences they have on cooperation in a two-person social dilemma. Specifically, they reveal how people try to maximize gain and minimize loss when confronting interaction partners who differ in morality and intelligence. Moral targets may be more appealing because people seem to be more ready to conclude that a moral person is intelligent (or that an immoral one is unintelligent), but not the opposite.

Correspondence: Ellen De Bruin, Department of Psychology, Free University of Amsterdam, the Netherlands; email: enm.de.bruin@psy. vu.nl.

⋘ De Cremer, D., & Van Lange, P. A. M. (2001). **Why prosocials exhibit greater cooperation than proselfs: The roles of social responsibility and reciprocity.** *European Journal of Personality, 15*(1, SpecIssue), S5–S18.

Objective: To investigate if prosocials' and proselfs' different behavioral reactions are linked to social responsibility and reciprocity.

Design: Study 1 employed a public-goods dilemma experiment, while study 2 employed a modified public-goods dilemma.

Setting: Maastricht University, the Netherlands.

Participants: Participants in study 1 consisted of sixty-three undergraduate students (mean age = 18.5 years) for class credit. In study 2, fifty-five undergraduate students volunteered to participate.

Assessment of Manipulated Variables: For both studies, a between-subjects independent variable, social value orientation (SVO; McClintock, 1972), was assessed through a series of nine decomposed games involving a choice between a prosocial, an individualistic, and a competitive option. Participants were classified as one of the three if they responded with that option at least six times, resulting in approximately 58 percent prosocials, 20 percent individualists, and 10 percent competitors. In study 1, they were then engaged in a social dilemma in which they were given 30 points (no value specified) and were to decide between contributing to the common good or to themselves (they were told the total amount contributed would then be doubled and split equally among all members, regardless of their contribution). In study 2, they were then engaged in a social dilemma in which they and a partner were given four chips each (worth 25 Dutch cents each to themselves and 50 cents each to the other). Reciprocity made up a second independent variable in this study. Participants were told their partner gave them either one chip or three chips (low- or high-cooperation conditions).

Assessment of Outcome Variables: The dependent variables in study 1 were degree of social responsibility for the public good (rated on a seven-point scale) and amount of points they were willing to contribute to the public good. The dependent variable in study 2 was the amount of chips given to the partner.

Main Results: Study 1 showed that prosocials gave more to the public good than proselfs and that this was due in part to the greater sense of social responsibility that proselfs exhibited. Study 2 showed that another motivational process underlies the increased cooperation of prosocials over proselfs, a strong desire to restore equality in outcomes (i.e., reciprocity). Thus, results from both studies provide support for Van Lange's (1999) integrative model of the complex interaction objectives of prosocials and proselfs.

Conclusion: Findings from both studies indicate that individuals with prosocial value orientations pursue interdependence goals of maximizing their own outcomes, maximizing the joint outcomes, and achieving equality in the outcomes. The latter two motives do not seem to motivate individuals with proself value orientations, and these are two reasons why they do not cooperate as much as prosocial individuals do.

Commentary: A major strength of this research is that it identifies key social psychological variables underlying the cooperative behavior of individuals with prosocial value orientations that have been empirically overlooked. Prosocials are more motivated than proselfs by social responsibility (i.e., concern for others' outcomes) and by reciprocity (i.e., concern for equality in outcomes). Future research efforts should employ field methods and examine specific circumstances under which social responsibility and reciprocity will be of importance so as to test the generalizability of these findings.

Correspondence: D. De Cremer, Department of Psychology, Maastricht University, the Netherlands; email: d.decremer@psychology.unimaas.nl.

Dixon D. J., & Abbey, S. E. (2000). **Religious altruism and organ donation.** *Psychosomatics: Journal of Consultation Liaison Psychiatry, 41*(5), 407–411.

Objective: To investigate religiously based altruism in renal transplantation through two case studies.

Design: Two case reports that outline the difficulties/prejudice two kidney donors faced when they conceptualized their charitable offers exclusively in terms of their religious beliefs and not in terms of kinship or emotional intimacy with the intended recipients.

Setting: Toronto, Canada.

Participants: Two individuals (one female, one male), one a member of a Christian church and the other a member of a Catholic church, who donated their kidneys out of faith-based altruism.

Assessment of Predictor Variables: Neither donor had a biological relationship or close emotional connection with the recipient, and religion was the framework by which the idea to donate was conceived and fostered. As a result, these two cases forced clinicians to directly assess serious, risky altruism that was based on a belief in God.

Assessment of Outcome Variables: The reactions provoked in the staff that handled these two cases.

Main Results: Three main trends were observed in the negative reactions of the staff to the two donors. First, the donors encountered unapologetic cynicism with respect to the notion that their religious affiliation, faith, and prayer could help resolve previous abuse or emotional issues in their life. Second, the staff exhibited objections toward the donors' motives and dismissed their religiosity as pathological for failing to make charity dependent on genetic proximity. Third, staff (especially in the first case) can exhibit prejudices toward certain denominations by replacing rigorous assessment of the case with disparaging caricatures inferred from the denomination.

Conclusion: Despite growing psychiatric research attesting to the benefits of religious involvement in mental health outcomes, these two cases show that there is still a lack of sensitivity toward unrelated organ donors and that conceptualizations of altruism are unduly restricted by an overvaluing of biological kinship and undervaluing of religious motivation.

Commentary: These case studies show that actual instances of altruism that are based solely on meaningful, caring relationships may prove unsettling for clinicians and may meet with prejudices about "religious pathology" rather than with accurate assessment that appreciates the complexity of ways in which solidarity with humanity can be conceived and expressed.

Correspondence: David J. Dixon, Department of Psychiatry, Toronto General Hospital, University Health Network, Toronto, Ontario, Canada.

   🐛 Eisenberg, N., Guthrie, I. K., Cumberland, A., Murphy, B. C., Shepard, S. A., Zhou, Q., & Carlo, G. (2002). **Prosocial development in early adulthood: A longitudinal study.** *Journal of Personality and Social Psychology, 82*(6), 993–1006.

Objective: To examine consistencies in prosocial personality and prosocial moral judgments as well as interrelations among them across time.

Design: A longitudinal experiment was conducted.

Setting: Tempe, Arizona.

Participants: Participants were recruited when they were preschoolers. The longitudinal cohort consisted of sixteen men and sixteen women (all Euro-

American, except for two Hispanics) from the community who were tested every other year for a total of twelve times (from ages 4 to 26 years).

Assessment of Predictor Variables: Utilizing observations, participants' and friends' reports, participant interviews, and parental reports, various measures of prosocial behavior and empathy related responding were assessed throughout the first nine testing times (e.g., observed prosocial behavior in preschool and measures of charity/volunteer helping as well as moral behavior at later times in participants' lives). Alphas for all measures ranged from .67 to .90, with most being around .80.

Assessment of Outcome Variables: At T10 through T12 various aspects of prosocial personality were measured through self-reports and friends' reports (e.g., empathy related-responding, social responsibility, care orientation, and moral behavior, which included subscales of consideration of others and suppression of aggression). Alphas ranged from .76 to .92. Also, prosocial moral reasoning was assessed through interviews at T10 and T12 and through objective measures at T11 (with alphas ranging from .68 to .98).

Main Results: Strong evidence was obtained for the presence of a prosocial personality disposition. Specifically, self-reported prosocial dispositions at ages 21–22 and 25–26 were found to often be related to self-reports of empathy, sympathy, and prosocial behavior, even as far as up to sixteen years earlier. Some measures of self-reported prosociality were related to mothers' reports of their children's helping behavior in adolescence and to friends' reports of prosocial dispositions up to four years earlier. Friends' reports of participants' prosociality at T10 and T12 were related to some measures of prosociality years earlier (up to ten years earlier for empathy). Finally, self-reported prosociality and prosocial moral judgment were positively related to prosocial behavior observed in preschool.

Conclusion: The data provide convincing evidence that prosocial dispositions emerge by late childhood and remain steady into adulthood and their seeds can be observed early in childhood. The results linking self-reports to reports from mothers and peers provide longitudinal evidence for the validity of self-report measures of prosocial dispositions and extend previous research findings linking prosocial moral judgment to individual differences in perspective taking, sympathy, and moral behavior by revealing the stability of these relationships (i.e., they remain the same across time).

Commentary: The continuity in the association between prosocial moral judgment and prosocial responding in late adolescence and into adulthood suggests that other-oriented cognitions and emotions may foster prosocial moral judgment and vice versa. Thus, this research is significant because the results outline the developmental picture of prosocial behavior. They also imply that the more moral reasoning is steeped in values and/or mature perspective-taking as people age, the more it can be expected that moral judgment will become intimately tied to prosocial emotions, cognitions, and actions.

Correspondence: Nancy Eisenberg, Department of Psychology, Arizona State University, Tempe, AZ 85287; email: Nancy.Eisenberg@asu.edu.

✎ Engel, G., Olson, K. R., & Patrick, C. (2002). **The personality of love: Fundamental motives and traits related to components of love.** *Personality and Individual Differences, 32*(5), 839–853.

Objective: To examine the relationship between two aspects of personality, fundamental motives and the Five Factor traits, and the three components of love, intimacy, passion, and commitment.

Design: Nonexperimental questionnaires.

Setting: Midwestern American university.

Participants: A total of 126 psychology students (36 females, 90 males; mean age = 20.3 years) who were involved in close relationships with someone of the opposite sex participated in the study for course credit.

Assessment of Predictor Variables: In the first testing session participants completed the NEO PI-R Form S (Costa & McCrae, 1992), which measures the five fundamental trait domains and thirty facets of personality.

Assessment of Outcome Variables: Students who were involved in relationships were asked to participate in a separate testing session. They completed the Sternberg Triangular Love Scale (Sternberg, 1998), which measures the degree of intimacy, passion, and commitment experienced toward a relationship partner, the Reiss Profile (Reiss & Havercamp, 1998), which measures fundamental human motives (e.g., personal and family relationships, sports, and achievement of happiness), and the Relationship Assessment Scale (RAS; Hendrick, 1988), which measures relationship satisfaction. All items in these measures used Likert-scale ratings.

Main Results: With respect to love and the Big Five traits, Conscientiousness positively predicted both males' and females' intimacy and passion but only males' commitment, the facet of deliberation positively predicted females' passion but not males', and males' commitment was predicted positively by Assertiveness and negatively by Vulnerability. With respect to love and motives, the Idealism motive positively predicted all three aspects of love for males (and only correlated with passion for females), the Tranquility motive negatively predicted males' intimacy and passion, the Acceptance motive and the Independence motive were negatively associated with females' passion, the Saving motive negatively predicted males' intimacy and passion, the Romance motive positively predicted females' passion and commitment, and the Power motive negatively predicted males' intimacy and commitment. With respect to the role of relationship satisfaction, Conscientiousness positively predicted males' and females' relationship satisfaction and love, there was a negative association between relationship satisfaction and the motive of Vengeance for females, Extraversion positively predicted females' relationship satisfaction, the motive of Idealism positively predicted males' relationship satisfaction, and the motives of Tranquility and Physical Activity negatively predicted males' relationship satisfaction.

Conclusion: Results suggest that individuals who have a strong desire for intimacy, passion, or commitment in their relationships may seek associated personality characteristics in potential partners, and that selecting appropriate relationship partners is important because personality is related to both love and relationship satisfaction.

Commentary: Though this research included mainly young participants who were not in very long-term (or marital) relationships and used only self-report methods, it did find important relationship between personality, relationship satisfaction, and love. The results have implications for premarital counselors, and they outline areas where future research can investigate important causal mechanisms between personality and love.

Correspondence: Kenneth R. Olson, Department of Psychology, Fort Hays State University, Hays, KS; email: kolson@fhsu.edu.

◄◌ Finkel, E. J., Rusbult, C. E., Kumashiro, M., & Hannon, P. A. (2002). **Dealing with betrayal in close relationships: Does commitment promote forgiveness?** *Journal of Personality and Social Psychology, 82*(6), 956–974.

Objective: To test if commitment motivates forgiveness and explore why it might.

Design: Three studies were conducted. The first was experimental, using a priming procedure to manipulate commitment and then assessing reactions to hypothetical betrayals; the second was a cross-sectional survey; and, the third was a nonexperimental interaction record study that tracked participants' responses to betrayal events over a two-week period.

Setting: University of North Carolina at Chapel Hill.

Participants: Undergraduate students enrolled in introductory psychology classes who were in dating relationships for at least one month were used for all three studies. Both males and females participated. Numbers ranged from 78 to 155 participants.

Assessment of Manipulated and Predictor Variables: In the first study, commitment to one's relationship partner was manipulated by having participants first answer questions designed to activate thoughts about dependence and commitment or thoughts about independence and lack of commitment. In the second study, participants were asked to describe a partner's previous violation of their expectations, how they reacted to it, and when it occurred; and they also completed a questionnaire designed to measure immediate and delayed reactions to the event, degree of commitment using the Investment Model Scale (IMS; Rusbult, Martz, and Agnew, 1998), and possible confounding variables. The independent variables in this study were time (immediate vs. delayed reactions), participant sex, and commitment level. In study 3, participants were asked to describe betrayals that occurred during a two-week period and their reactions to them and complete a similar questionnaire, which additionally measured three components proposed to comprise commitment—intent to persist, long-term orientation, and psychological attachment (Arriaga & Agnew, in press).

Assessment of Outcome Variables: For the first study, participants completed the IMS, read descriptions of twelve hypothetical acts of betrayal (e.g., "your partner lies to you about something important") and responded to four questions for each scenario measuring forgiveness vis-à-vis how much they would use exit (e.g., seeking vengeance), neglect (e.g., giving the partner the cold shoulder), voice (e.g., suggesting that the partners discuss the issue), and loyalty strategies (e.g., continuing to support the partner despite the dissatisfaction) in response to the dissatisfaction using nine-point Likert scales (Rusbult, 1993). The dependent variables in studies 2 and 3 were behavioral tendencies, cognitive interpretations, and emotional reactions. Most measures displayed acceptable to high levels of reliability.

Main Results: Participants in study 1 exhibited lower exit and neglect and greater voice and loyalty when high commitment was primed, compared to when low commitment was primed, and this effect was marginally mediated by subjective commitment. Also females used more voice strategy in response to the hypothetical betrayal. In study 2, immediate reactions to betrayal were more negative overall than delayed reactions were. Participants who were relatively more committed reported more negative immediate emotions as well as more positive delayed emotions. They also reported more benign interpretations of the betrayal and more positive behavioral tendencies. In study 3, it was found that individuals who intended to persist and remain dependent on their relationships were more likely to forgo vengeance to maintain their commitment. Studies 2 and 3 showed that the commitment-forgiveness association did not differ as a function of either severity of the incident or strength of the betrayal. Study 3 further showed that broader temporal or interpersonal concerns (i.e., long-term orientation and psychological attachment) did not contribute to the commitment-forgiveness association; rather, it was intent to persist and remain dependent on the relationship that increased one's chances of forgiving.

Conclusion: The results from all three studies reveal positive associations of commitment with interpersonal forgiveness. In particular, the commitment-forgiveness association appears to rest mainly on positive cognitive appraisals of betrayals (extent to which one discounts internal causes and identifies extenuating circumstances). Moreover, it seems the temporal properties of forgiveness are such that commitment leads people to experience more negative immediate reactions to norm violations but more prorelationship appraisals and behaviors as time passes.

Commentary: The interdependence-based model upon which these three studies are based extends our understanding of forgiveness by showing: that violations of relationship-relevant norms appear to be distinct threats to a couple's well-being, that prosocial motivation may be embodied not just in properties of individuals but in properties of dyads (and groups) as well, that increasing the salience of commitment-related thoughts can increase motivation to forgive, and that use of interdependence-based analyses, which emphasize causes and consequences of interaction, can help identify key obstacles to reconciliation following betrayal. Moreover, the use of different methods to converge on these results and consistent evidence refuting socially desirable responding lend strength to this research.

Correspondence: Eli J. Finkel, Department of Psychology, Carnegie Mellon University, Pittsburgh, PA; email: eli@andrew.cmu.edu.

 Gaertner, S. L., Dovidio, J. F., Rust, M. C., Nier, J. A., Banker, B. S., Ward, C. M., Mottola, G. R., & Houlette, M. (1999). Reducing intergroup bias: Elements of intergroup cooperation. *Journal of Personality and Social Psychology, 76*(3), 388–402.

Objective: To examine the potentially independent contributions of interaction and common fate and the processes by which these elements reduce intergroup prejudice and contribute to cooperation.

Design: Experiment in which Democrats and Republicans are brought into interaction with each other. A 3 (interaction: full, partial, or none) × 2 (common fate: yes, no) design was used.

Setting: A New England university.

Participants: A total of 576 college students (288 females, 288 males) participated for course credit. Pretesting conducted earlier identified half of them as Republicans and half as Democrats.

Assessment of Manipulated Variables: Participants were first divided into two three-person groups (Democrats and Republicans) and engaged in the winter survival problem (Johnson & Johnson, 1975), which was designed to increase the salience of their memberships in these three-person groups. They were then engaged in another problem that was designed to distinguish the two political ideologies. They were to come up with the best solution for reducing the U.S. budget deficit by prioritizing six spending programs (e.g., social security, national defense, education) and six tax-hikes (e.g., personal income tax, inheritance, gasoline tax). Participants were told that their solution would be evaluated against that of a bipartisan team of economic experts. The interaction independent variable was manipulated as follows: those in the full interaction condition were to reach a single consensus solution to the problem, those in the partial interaction were to arrive at separate solutions but report to the other group portions of their solution, and those in the no interaction condition simply arrived at a solution without interacting with the other group. Common fate was manipulated by having groups compete for a shared outcome of $10 per person or for independent outcomes of $10 per person.

Assessment of Outcome Variables: Participants were given postexperimental questionnaires. Besides manipulation checks, they contained measures of processes proposed to mediate the relationship between the elements of intergroup cooperation and bias, which included monetary reinforcement, ratings of how cooperative and competitive the two groups were, ratings of how much each of the three outgroup members were seen as individuated and personalized, and measures of participants' conceptual representations of the aggregate (e.g., "Which description best characterizes your impression of all you currently participating in this experiment? It felt most like one group, two subgroups within a group, two separate groups or separate individuals") as well as to what degree (1 = not at all to 7 = very much) it felt like each of these representations (Gaertner, Mann, Murrell, & Dovidio 1989; Gaertner, Mann, Dovidio, Murrell, & Pomare, 1990). Having more one-group or two-subgroups-within-a-group representations ratings is supposed to reflect degree of common ingroup identity (Gaertner, Dovidio, & Bachman, 1996). Intergroup bias was also measured with evaluative rating scales (Gaertner et al., 1989, 1990) in which participants rated on seven-point scales each of the five other participants in terms of likableness, cooperativeness, trustworthiness, and value. Pleasantness of facial expression was also observed as a less reactive measure of intergroup bias for participants in full interaction condition (interrater reliability = .78).

Main Results: Both common fate and interaction were effectively manipulated. Full interaction led to higher levels of perceived common fate than partial or no interaction, and common fate was equally effective across all interaction conditions (i.e., the independent variables did not interact). Increased interaction led to greater perceptions of how much the groups were communicating, how much the other group revealed about themselves, and how much the groups cooperated with each other (and no main or interaction effects of common fate on any of the measures were found).

With respect to the effects of the independent variables on intergroup bias, full and partial interaction led to higher evaluation ratings than did no interaction, and ingroup members were evaluated more positively than outgroup members across the common fate and interaction conditions. Ingroup bias was lowest in the full interaction conditions, followed by partial interaction, and then the no interaction conditions (no main or interaction effects on ingroup bias emerged). Interaction helped reduce bias even in the absence of common fate. This was primarily because the attractiveness of outgroup members is enhanced by the presence of any amount of interaction, but full interaction also diminished ingroup bias by reducing the evaluation of ingroup members more, compared to partial interaction (no effects of common fate emerged). Measures of facial affect showed that common fate increased positive reactions to out-group members.

With respect to how intergroup interaction reduced bias, perceptions of cooperating versus competing, of how much outgroup members revealed about themselves, and of common ingroup identity (more one-group and two-subgroup representations, and fewer separate group ones) were all mediators of this effect. Moreover, cognitive representations of the aggregate contributed above and beyond the other mediators in the causal relation between inter-group interaction and intergroup bias.

Conclusion: Common fate and interaction are independent components of intergroup cooperation, and both can help reduce intergroup bias, but only in-teraction was found to cause reductions in bias independently in this experi-ment. Common fate seems to reduce bias in automatic facial affect, though, which could feasibly have longer-term effects on intergroup relations. Inter-group interaction seems to reduce bias mainly through decategorization and re-categorization processes, which can occur with even minimal levels of interac-tion.

Commentary: This research sheds much-needed light on the processes in-volved in two key elements of cooperation, common fate and intergroup inter-action, and provides a picture of how these two variables help reduce bias. The findings are important for theoretical and practical reasons. Comprehending the processes by which these two elements operate is crucial for understanding how prejudice can be reduced, and this will allow agents of social change to bet-ter increase favorable intergroup attitudes in realization of this goal.

Correspondence: Samuel L. Gaertner, Department of Psychology, Universi-ty of Delaware, Newark, DE; email: gaertner@udel.edu.

⚓ Gonzaga, G. C., Keltner, D., Londahl, E. A., & Smith, M. D. (2001). **Love and the commitment problem in romantic relations and friendship.** *Jour-nal of Personality and Social Psychology, 81*(2), 247–262.

Objective: To test if the experience of love motivates approach-related be-havior, has a distinct signal, and correlates with commitment-enhancing behav-ior when relationships are threatened.

Design: Three experiments were conducted, one that examined interac-tions that generated love and tested the bond of romantic partners, a second that presented video clips of affiliation and sexual cues to naïve observers to ex-amine if nonverbal displays of love and desire are distinct, and a third study that observed opposite-sex best-friend interactions and examined if love correlates with approach and commitment related outcomes and has a distinct display.

Setting: A large Midwestern university, a large Western university, and a large Western high school.

Participants: Sixty heterosexual, college-aged couples involved in romantic relationships for at least six months participated for $20.00 in study 1, forty undergraduates (17 males and 23 females) participated for research credit in study 2, and sixteen opposite-sex-friend ninth-grade pairs and seventeen opposite-sex-friend twelfth-grade pairs were selected for their closeness to participate in study 3.

Assessment of Manipulated Variables: In study 1, romantic partners engaged in positive self-disclosure to generate love and in discussions about conflict (Levenson & Gottman, 1983) and teasing interactions (Keltner, Young, Heerey, Oemig, & Monarch, 1998) that tested their commitment. In study 2, video clips of four sexual cues (lip licks, lip puckers, touching the lips with the hands, and tongue protrusions) and four affiliation cues (head nods, Duchenne smiles, gesticulation, and forward leans) drawn from the videotaped interactions used in the first study were presented to observers. Similar to the first study, study 3 had opposite-sex friends engage in interactions designed to generate liking (e.g., discussions of the beginnings and benefits of the friendship).

Assessment of Outcome Variables: For study 1, participants' standing on the Big Five personality traits (John, Donahue, & Kentle, 1991) and relational commitment were measured. The main dependent measures included: participants' ratings (on eight-point Likert scales) of the degree to which they and their partners felt certain emotions (e.g., amusement, anger, anxiety, concern, desire, fear, happiness, and love) following each interaction, participants' ratings of the degree to which they and their partners perceived trust (on eight-point Likert scales) during conflict following the conflict discussion (e.g., fair, honest, openminded, forgiving, and cooperative), coding of affiliation cues (Ekman & Friesen, 1978), coding of constructive versus destructive conflict resolution (Heyman, Weiss, & Eddy, 1995), and coding of teasing interaction. Alpha levels ranged from .67 to .80, and coding of affiliation and teasing had 78.3 percent and 86 percent interjudge agreement. Study 2 participants were asked to decide whether targets were feeling love or desire based on the video clips from the first study. In the third study, participants rated the degree to which they and their partners felt certain emotions, and affiliation cues were coded (70.6% interjudge agreement).

Main Results: Study 1 showed, above and beyond the influence of personality traits related to increased intimacy, that momentary experiences of love correlated with approach-related states (desire and sympathy), that four affiliation cues correlated with self- and partner reports of love, and that the experience and display of love correlated with commitment-enhancing behaviors (constructive conflict resolution) and perceptions of trust when the relationship was threatened. The third study found similar patterns with respect to liking among adolescent, opposite-sex friends. Study 2 revealed that affiliation cues nonverbally communicate love (and not desire) to outside observers.

Conclusion: Together, these three studies demonstrate that the momentary experience and display of love (and liking) motivate approach, distinctly signal love instead of desire, and enhance commitment-related behaviors and perceptions in different contexts where relationships are threatened.

Commentary: This research helps to revise our understanding of heterosexual, romantic love by indicating that it is related to pleasure and approach rather than to reductions of distress as previous research had suggested, by showing how love promotes attachment processes, and by demonstrating that love is a "basic" emotion that serves a commitment function and is consistent with evolutionary theories suggesting that it may increase the ability of offspring to survive.

Correspondence: Gian C. Gonzaga, Department of Psychology, University of California, Berkeley, California; email: zaga@uclink4.berkeley.edu.

✑ Healy, K. (2000). **Embedded altruism: Blood collection regimes and the European Union's donor population.** *American Journal of Sociology, 105*(6), 1633–1657.

Objective: To investigate how blood donation may vary as a function of different blood collection regimes (in Europe) and explore factors related to how altruism is embedded in institutions.

Design: Analysis of data from a large survey on blood donation patterns throughout the European Union (EU).

Setting: Princeton University, Princeton, NJ.

Data-Set: The Eurobarometer (Reif & Marlier, 1996) is a survey carried out through multistage, national probability samples through the twelve member states of the EU. It contains data on blood donation across Europe (540 variables and 19,477 cases). In particular, respondents were asked about their opinions regarding the handling and collecting of blood and plasma, their reasons for donating and not donating, their knowledge about blood and plasma, and their attitudes about buying and selling blood.

Assessment of Independent Variables: Characteristics of individual donors (sex, age, education, income, whether or not one is networked with blood-transfusion recipients, and church attendance), which were recoded from the Eurobarometer survey, and institutional environments (the kind of collection system a country operates, the presence of a volunteer donor group in a country, and the presence of a commercial plasma operation in which individual suppliers are paid for plasma), which were coded from interview data detailed in Hagen's (1993) Council of Europe white paper.

Assessment of Outcome Variables: Whether or not respondents had given blood in the last year and whether or not they had ever given blood.

Main Results: A series of logistic regressions demonstrated that blood donation was more likely among males and younger individuals (than females and older individuals); that higher education and income increased the odds of ever having donated; and that knowing transfusion recipients increased the odds of donating in the last year, and especially increased the odds of ever having donated. With respect to institutional effects, state regimes were found to have more people who ever donate, but Red Cross regimes had more regular donors (i.e., church-attending individuals who may be involved in other volunteer activities), suggesting that more committed donor pools are made up of people who regularly attend church. Also, the presence of volunteer donor organizations in a country significantly increased the likelihood of donations, but only for those who are already likely to give and only for men (not women).

Conclusion: This study showed that how blood supply systems are organized affects how much blood is collected, from whom it is collected, and how blood donation is characterized (i.e., like/unlike other forms of giving). Collection regimes appear to produce both opportunities to give and differing donor populations.

Commentary: This study showed the range of organizational variation in EU blood collection and showed how it can effect blood donation, depicting blood giving as more than the just result of individual altruists, but the result of different institutional characteristics as well.

Correspondence: Kiernan Healy, Department of Sociology, Princeton University, Princeton, NJ 08544-1010; email: kjhealy@princeton.edu.

&Q Hertel, G., Neuhof, J., Theuer, T., & Kerr, N. L. (2000). **Mood effects on cooperation in small groups: Does positive mood simply lead to more cooperation?** *Cognition and Emotion, 14*(4), 441–472.

Objective: To examine if mood influences processes of decision-making rather than (or in addition to) influencing the level of cooperation by increasing heuristic processing when people feel good or secure and increasing systematic processing when people feel bad or insecure.

Design: Two experiments were conducted, one that varied the feeling states and one that varied the sense of security of participants before and during a simulated group conflict within a chicken dilemma structure.

Setting: University of Giessen, Germany.

Participants: Eighty female education students participated in study 1 and another eighty participated in study 2. They participated in a game by way of computers in groups of four without directly interacting with each other.

Assessment of Manipulated Variables: Both experiments were similar, except the first had mood as an independent variable and the second had subjective security (subjective evaluation of a situation is supposed to be a crucial mediator of mood effects). Mood was manipulated by showing short films (about four minutes) that induced either a good or bad mood (the effectiveness of each film was established through pilot testing) before the game part of the experiments. Security was manipulated by telling participants one of two things: 1) that the purpose of the experiment would not be revealed until the end, that something unforeseen, be it positive or negative, would happen during the game, and that they might be watched behind one-way mirrors (insecurity); or 2) that every part of the experiment would be explained in time and that it was all right just to follow whatever they thought was right during the game (security). This procedure was also established through pilot testing. The game involved a taxi enterprise in which participants were to decide how much time they should invest in driving (more driving increased collective gain, less driving increased individual gain). Points gained during the game could be cashed in for up to $6 afterwards. The second independent variable, descriptive social norms, was manipulated during the game by telling participants that former subjects either invested six hours (cooperation) or three hours (competition) of driving per week (this manipulation was strengthened in study 2 with the use of seven or two hours). The third independent variable, current behavior of the other group members, made up a within-subjects variable that was manipulated by giving false feedback that depicted others as being cooperative or competitive.

Assessment of Outcome Variables: The main dependent variable was number of hours invested in driving for the taxi enterprise (i.e., cooperation) throughout the trials. Each driver had to decide how much out of nine possible hours to invest per week (each trial made up a week). Each hour driven for the enterprise was doubled so that it amounted to two points (two hours worth of driving time) for common gain, which was then divided equally among all four participants, whereas each hour not driven for the enterprise amounted to one point (one hour of driving time) for individual gain. They were also told that everybody had to maintain a minimum level of investment to keep their licenses to drive (i.e., to maintain the common enterprise) and that they would receive feedback about the average amount of time the others gave collectively.

Main Results: Results from study 1 provided evidence that mood had no simple direct effect on cooperation but rather it had an effect on how persons decided to cooperate. Positive mood produced relatively high ratings of subjective security and more heuristic processing or use of consensus or reciprocity heuristics (as reflected by short decision latencies and strong tendencies to imitate others), while negative mood produced low ratings of subjective security and more systematic processing (as indicated by longer decision latencies). Unlike participants with a good mood, those with a bad mood decreased investment for the common when others cooperated sufficiently but increased investment when others' cooperation was critically low and threatened survival of the common. Results from study 2 replicated the patterns of study 1, showing that it is through subjective evaluation of the situation that mood affects decision-making.

Conclusion: This research shows that mood indirectly influences cooperative behavior by affecting the way people arrive at decisions to help. When people are in a good mood they feel more secure and tend to use consensus and reciprocity heuristics to mimic social norms. Thus they cooperate by simply following descriptive norms. However, when people are in a bad mood they feel insecure and think more systematically and rationally about the maintenance of the common and cooperate when it is more crucial.

Commentary: These two experiments show that feeling states affect decision-making processes and that the link between mood and helping is more complex than the simple assumption that good mood increases helping, as findings from much research have suggested. Therefore, this research broadens our understanding of how mood effects cooperation in interactive social dilemmas.

Correspondence: Guido Hertel, Universität Kiel, Institute fur Psychologie, Kiel, Germany; email: hertel@psychologie.uni-kiel.de.

❧   Holmes, J. G., Miller, D. T., & Lerner, M. J. (2002). Committing altruism under the cloak of self-interest: The exchange fiction. *Journal of Experimental Social Psychology, 38*(2), 144–151.

Objective: To test if framing the act of helping a charitable organization in terms of an economic transaction leads to greater willingness to contribute than when it is presented as an act of charity.

Design: Two field experiments were conducted. In the first, experimenters approached participants and asked if they would assist a charity by making a financial contribution either through a direct donation or through the purchase of decorative candles. The second experiment was similar, except in addition to varying the way the contribution was framed, it also varied the degree to which the exchange was purported to be a bargain.

Setting: Florida Atlantic University, FL.

Participants: There were eighty-eight participants in the first experiment and one hundred participants in the second experiment, half males and half females.

Assessment of Manipulated Variables: Need of actual charity organizations (with slightly modified names) was portrayed as low, moderate, or high in the first experiment and as either low or high in the second experiment. Both experiments also manipulated the framing of the contribution as a donation or an exchange, with the exchange involving the purchase of a candle. However, the second experiment included two baseline donation conditions and pricing conditions that describe the exchange as being a bargain, fair, or altruistic (more expensive so as to provide donation to the organization).

Assessment of Outcome Variables: The amount of money contributed to the organization was the dependent variable in both experiments.

Main Results: In experiment 1, high levels of need (with respect to the charity) significantly increased contributions over low need in the exchange condition but not in the donation condition, supporting the notion that compassionate behavior can be increased when it is disguised as an economic transaction. In experiment 2, the exchange framework elicited higher contributions than the donation framework only in the high-need condition. Also, contributions were higher in the bargain price condition than in the altruistic price condition.

Conclusion: The results showed that people are more willing to act on compassion when there is some self-interested justification for the behavior. People may inhibit unambiguous acts of helping to avoid internal conflicts, obligations to future requests for help, or violations of individualist cultural norms that discourage unconditional acts of helping.

Commentary: These experiments show that helping behavior can be increased by framing the behavior in a way that allows people to see themselves as altruistic but not unconditionally so. Thus, adding self-interest appeals to charity causes may provide additional incentive to help by providing an excuse to act.

Correspondence: John Holmes, Department of Psychology, University of Waterloo, Ontario, Canada; email: jholmes@watarts.uwaterloo.ca.

⁂ Kakavoulis, A. (1998). **Early childhood altruism: How parents see prosocial behavior in their young children.** *Early Child Development and Care, 140,* 115–126.

Objective: To investigate the variety of ways children between the ages of 0 and 6 express altruism and in particular try to depict the feelings and actions that make up typical altruistic behavior during this period of development.

Design: A naturalistic approach in which parent questionnaires were content analyzed.

Setting: University of Crete, Greece.

Participants: Out of 234 parents (mostly mothers) who had a minimum level of education and children in childcare or nursery schools that were sent questionnaires, 216 returned them completed. Questionnaires regarding 286 children from Athens and Crete (109 boys, 117 girls; ages ranging from 40 days to 7 years) were obtained, with most of them (70%) being between ages 2 and 4.

Assessment of Predictor Variables: Parents completed questionnaires that asked them to write about one or more (up to five) episodes of spontaneous love they had observed their children exhibit toward them or others in their environment by describing their children's prosocial behavior and noting the sex of their child and age for each episode. This yielded a total of 358 valid episodes (57.9% described one episode, 26.9% described two, 9.2% three, 3.7% four, and 2.3% described five episodes).

Assessment of Outcome Variables: Content analysis was conducted on the questionnaires for each year of age. Frequencies and percentages of prosocial behaviors were also calculated to determine different expressions across the age groups. In particular the qualitative data were coded for targets of altruism and type of altruistic feelings and behaviors (emotions and acts related to solidarity with others).

Main Results: Results showed that from the age of a few months on, children begin showing altruistic feelings and behaviors. Mothers and family members (collectively) were the recipients of most of this behavior, followed by grandmothers, other children, grandfathers, fathers, relatives, newborns, children in need, persons in need, cousins, teachers, and babies to be born (among females only). Children displayed twenty different altruistic feelings (from most frequent to least): love, compassion, affection, empathy, joy, nostalgia, sensitiveness, interest, understanding, enthusiasm, attachment, admiration, longing, repentance, respect, distress, fear, astonishment, anguish, and grief. They displayed an even greater variety of altruistic actions—as many as forty-five (e.g., helping, comforting one in distress, embracing, sharing, petting, kissing, crying for someone, protecting/defending someone were among the most frequent, while caring, giving gifts, keeping one company, cooperating, recruiting help, and holding one's seat were among the less frequent behaviors).

Conclusion: Children begin showing altruism as early as a few months, but a variety of expressions emerge between ages 3 and 5. They extend altruism mostly to loved persons (parents and family members), but it can be expressed toward anyone in distress as well.

Commentary: Though the reliability of the results is questionable (e.g., exclusive use of parental reports may present bias for such socially desirable behavior, no interjudge reliability figures for codes were reported), this research yielded a greater variety of altruistic feelings and behaviors than has been found in the current literature and it outlines specific feelings and actions that can be useful for educational contexts in which altruism can be fostered.

Correspondence: Alexandros K. Kakavoulis, University of Crete, Greece.

Kelln, B. R. C., & Ellard, J. H. (1999, July). **An equity theory analysis of the impact of forgiveness and retribution on transgressor compliance.** *Personality and Social Psychology Bulletin, 25*(7), 864–872.

Objective: To test an equity conceptualization of interpersonal forgiveness. Specifically, the study was designed to test if thinking of forgiveness as an unsolicited gift will increase the perceived debt of the transgressor to the victim and if retribution will reduce the perceived debt.

Design: An experiment in which participants are made to think they broke expensive electronic equipment during an ostensible memory study.

Setting: University of Calgary, Alberta, Canada.

Participants: A total of seventy-five male undergraduate students were recruited from introductory psychology courses (mean age = 18.6) and paid $4.00 for participating.

Assessment of Manipulated Variables: The independent variable was the reaction of the experimenter to the participant's transgression. The experimenter reacted with forgiveness, retribution, both, or neither. There was also a control condition in which no equipment was broken.

Assessment of Outcome Variables: The dependent variable was number of envelopes (out of a total of 50) the participant volunteered to deliver for the experimenter ostensibly as part of another study. Participants also completed a questionnaire that measured affective states (guilt in particular) throughout the study. Finally, at the end of the study they completed another questionnaire containing ratings (on nine-point Likert scales) about their liking for the experimenter and the study.

Main Results: Participants in the transgression conditions felt more guilt compared to those in the control condition. Those in the forgiveness-only condition complied with the experimenter's request the most ($M = 18.08$, $SD = 4.35$), followed by those in the neither forgiveness nor retribution condition ($M = 11.46$, $SD = 6.08$), then by those in the retribution and forgiveness condition ($M = 9.27$, $SD = 5.38$), then by those in the control condition ($M = 9.13$, $SD = 5.89$), and those in the retribution-only condition displayed the least compliance ($M = 7.29$, $SD = 6.33$) This pattern was not attributable to liking for the experimenter or the study.

Conclusion: It appears that participants volunteered to help more in the forgiveness-only condition because the unsolicited gift of forgiveness from the experimenter added to the guilt they felt following the transgression. Thus, increased compliance helped restore equity in the situation.

Commentary: This research explores an area that has been neglected by the research on forgiveness—how forgiveness influences transgressors' behavior. Results suggest that forgiveness may have beneficial effects on relationships simply because forgiveness can engage equity concerns in transgressors and thereby motivate them to reciprocate positively toward victims.

Correspondence: John H. Ellard, Department of Psychology, the University of Calgary, Alberta, Canada; email: ellard@acs.ucalgary.ca.

Kim, S. H., & Webster, J. M. (2001). Getting competitors to cooperate: A comparison of three reciprocal strategies. *Representative Research in Social Psychology*, 25, 9–19.

Objective: To examine which reciprocal strategy—a permissive tit-for-tat (TFT), a standard TFT, or a punitive TFT—is most effective in getting competitors to cooperate.

Design: A two-person prisoner's dilemma game experiment involving all three strategies.

Setting: University of Kentucky, Lexington.

Participants: A total of 147 students (77 females, 70 males) participated for course credit.

Assessment of Manipulated Variables: Participants were first asked to respond to five different two-person PDGs, which were used to measure value orientation (cooperator or competitor). Then they were seated at a computer and engaged in forty trials of a two-person PDG. They were assigned to a permissive TFT, standard TFT, or punitive TFT condition, and were told how many points they earned after trials were completed (which could be cashed in for up to $3 of school supplies). After the trials, participants completed a questionnaire that had them rate (on seven-point Likert scales) how exploitative the other person was, how predictable the other person's choices were, and how well their expectations of the other person's choice were met.

Assessment of Outcome Variables: The main dependent variable was the mean proportion of cooperative choice over forty trials.

Main Results: Though all three TFT strategies were similar for inducing cooperation from cooperators, the standard TFT was more effective overall than either punitive or permissive TFT. It induced as much cooperation from cooperators as it did from competitors.

Conclusion: Results were consistent with the findings made in Axelrod's computer tournaments (1994). That is, one-for-one reciprocal strategies (standard TFT) help induce similar amounts of cooperation with both competitive and cooperative opponents. It may well be that standard TFT does not always bring more payoff compared to the opponent, but on the whole it helps people get along well with a variety of strategies, be they exploitative or forgiving ones.

Commentary: This research provides evidence in support of the utility of standard TFT in inducing the most amount of cooperation in an interdependence situation, especially if it is not clear which strategy should be used or if nothing is known about opponents' values.

Correspondence: Sung Hee Kim, Department of Psychology, University of Kentucky, Lexington, KY; email: shkimoo@pop.uky.edu.

Koole, S. L., Jager, W., van den Berg, A. E., Vlek, C. A. J., & Hofstee, W. K. B. (2001). On the social nature of personality: Effects of extraversion, agreeableness, and feedback about collective resource use on cooperation in a resource dilemma. *Personality and Social Psychology Bulletin, 27*(3), 289–301.

Objective: To investigate how individual differences in Extraversion and Agreeableness affect cooperation in a social dilemma.

Design: The study used a computerized resource dilemma paradigm whereby participants shared access to a common pool of resources with others (in a simulation) and were given experimental feedback that the resource was being sustained or overused.

Setting: University of Groningen, the Netherlands.

Participants: A total of seventy-two first-year psychology students participated for a chance to win a prize (i.e., a compact-disc player or a $30 compact-disc voucher).

Assessment of Manipulated Variables: There were two independent variables, participants' Extraversion and Agreeableness scores, which were obtained as part of a personality research program, and feedback that their resource use was sustainable or rapidly depleting the source after each of twelve consecutive resource use decisions.

Assessment of Outcome Variables: The main dependent variable was participants' resource use throughout the resource dilemma simulation.

Main Results: Results showed that people who were high in Extraversion and low in Agreeableness generally took more from the common resource and that people who were low in Extraversion and high in Agreeableness were more complex in their resource use decisions. They reciprocated others' cooperation when resource use was sustainable and reduced their use when the common resource was threatened. These relationships were moderated by the situational variables of collective cooperation and severity of threat to the common resource, indicating the situated nature of the influence of personality on cooperation.

Conclusion: Results demonstrate that cooperatively oriented individuals are more sensitive to situational contingencies than less cooperatively oriented individuals and confirm that psychological mechanisms to cooperate are in part domain-specific and dependent on eliciting context.

Commentary: This research adds to previous research on social dilemmas and processes that lead people to act in self-interest or self-sacrifice. It indicates that when conflict between individual and collective interest is high, Extraversion and Agreeableness can explain a substantial amount of variation in cooperative behavior.

Correspondence: Sander L. Koole, Department of Social Psychology, Free University Amsterdam, Amsterdam; email: sl.koole@psy.vu.nl.

⟐   **Korchmaros, J. D., & Kenny, D. A. (2001). Emotional closeness as a mediator of the effect of genetic relatedness on altruism.** *Psychological Science,* *12*(3), 262–265.

Objective: To increase understanding of altruism by testing a model that includes both proximate and ultimate causes and that integrates findings from social and evolutionary psychology.

Design: Questionnaire experiment with hypothetical scenarios using a round-robin design.

Setting: University of Connecticut, Storrs.

Participants: Twenty-nine undergraduate students enrolled in introductory psychology (12 male and 17 female).

Assessment of Predictor Variables: Participants were asked to provide information about family members, such as name, relationship (or genetic relatedness), age, and emotional closeness (on seven-point Likert scales).

Assessment of Outcome Variables: Participants who provided information on at least five family members later read hypothetical scenarios in which every possible pairing of their five family members faced the same life-or-death dilemma. Only they could save their family members, and giving help would cost great risk, possibly injury to themselves. They were to indicate which family member they would more likely help, how certain they were of this decision (on four-point Likert scales), and the likelihood that they would respond similarly if asked again to respond to the same dilemma. Responses were combined into eight-point willingness-to-help scores, which were then computed into a single willingness-to-help score for each target. This was done so that family member could be used as the unit of analysis. Reliability of the willingness-to-help scores was .92, indicating that participants were more willing to help some family members over others.

Main Results: Using family member as the unit of analysis, effects of genetic-relatedness and age on altruism were found to vary by participant. Thus mediational analyses with multilevel modeling (to account for variance due to family member and to participant) were conducted. Genetic relatedness was found to predict altruistic willingness, and this effect was mediated by emotional closeness, which accounted for 33 percent of the relationship.

Conclusion: Results provided support for inclusive fitness theory (Hamilton, 1964) by showing that genetic relatedness (i.e., a distal cause) contributes to the prediction of altruistic willingness, and they revealed that emotional closeness (i.e., a proximate cause) is one of the psychological mechanisms that have evolved to help guide altruistic behavior. Thus it seems people do not just calculate costs and benefits in altruism toward kin but interdependence concerns of emotional closeness as well.

Commentary: This simple study showed how social psychological and evolutionary theory can be applied toward a fuller understanding of altruism and establishes a way to test models with yet other proximate causes. The results suggest that genetic relatedness combined with emotional closeness increases the inclusive fitness of genes that phenotypically result in altruism and that this is what may make altruism evolutionarily adaptive.

Correspondence: Josephine D. Korchmaros, Department of Psychology, University of Connecticut, Storrs, CT 06269-1020; email: jojokor@yahoo. com.

 Krueger, R. F., Hicks, B. M., & McGue, M. (2001). **Altruism and antisocial behavior: Independent tendencies, unique personality correlates, distinct etiologies.** *Psychological Science, 12*(5), 397–402.

Objective: To investigate if altruism and antisocial behavior make up opposite ends of a single dimension or if they can coexist in a person, if the two stem from the same or distinct personality correlates, and if the two have the same or distinct etiologies. Overall aim is to explore relationships between altruism and antisocial behavior.

Design: Nonexperimental survey using a behavior genetic design.

Setting: Minnesota.

Participants: Participants were male twins born between 1961 and 1964, who made up the youngest cohort enrolled in the Minnesota Twin Registry. Three different questionnaires were sent to participants. A sample of 673 participants was obtained (average age = 33), with 170 being monozygotic twins, 106 being dizygotic twins, and 121 being individuals whose twin did not participate.

Assessment of Predictor Variables: First, participants completed the Multidimensional Personality Questionnaire (MPQ; Tellegen, 2000), which consisted of eleven scales measuring positive emotionality (well-being, social potency, social closeness, achievement, and absorption), negative emotionality (stress reaction, alienation, and aggression), and constraint (control, harm-avoidance, and traditionalism). The MPQ has shown good reliability (Cronbach alphas range from .77 to .88). Second, they completed a self-report questionnaire of antisocial behavior that consisted of measures from the Short-Nye Self-Report Delinquency Items and the Seattle Self-Report Instrument (see Hindelang, Hirschi, & Weis, 1981) as well as the Clark Self-Report List of Deviant Behavior (Clark & Tifft, 1966). Items measured (on four-point Likert scales) frequency of engagement in a variety of antisocial behavior that spans a range of common and rare behaviors and a range of seriousness (inquiring about theft, illegal behavior involving drugs and alcohol, force, and miscellaneous vice). Third, they completed a self-report questionnaire of altruism that consisted of items adapted from the Self-Report Altruism Scale (Rushton, Chrisjohn, & Fekken, 1981) and additional items intended to expand the scope of altruistic actions. Items measured (on four-point Likert scales) frequency of altruistic behavior toward friends, acquaintances, strangers, and organizations.

Assessment of Outcome Variables: The questionnaire measuring antisocial behavior had good reliability (Cronbach's alpha = .89), as did the questionnaire measuring altruistic behavior (Cronbach's alpha = .90). Individuals from complete twin pairs were assigned weights of 0.5 to correct for nonindependence of observations and to reflect the number of independent observations used in the phenotypic analyses.

Main Results: A zero-order correlational approach, a correlational approach controlling for acquiescence, and a latent correlational approach (using confirmatory factor analysis) to account for random measurement error all demonstrated that antisocial behavior and altruistic behavior were independent behavioral tendencies. Four groups of items made up the antisocial behavior tendency (e.g., theft, drug-alcohol, force, and vice) and another four made up the altruistic behavioral tendency (e.g., friends, acquaintances, strangers, and organizations). Biometric models fit to twin data showed that individual differences in antisocial behavior were linked to genes and unique environments (i.e., nonfamilial), while individual differences in altruism were linked to both shared and unique environments. Finally, antisocial behavior was found to be associated with aggression, lack of control, and lack of harm avoidance, whereas altruistic behavior was found to be associated with social potency, social closeness, absorption, and lack of aggression.

Conclusion: Results indicate that antisocial behavior and altruistic behavior are independent tendencies, which also have distinct etiologies and personality correlates. Antisocial behavior was linked to sources of genes and unique environments and traits of negative emotionality and lack of constraint, while altruistic behavior was linked to sources of shared and unique environments and traits of positive emotionality.

Commentary: Though these findings are limited to male subjects, self-report indices, contemporaneous data, and to a specific behavioral operationalization of altruism, they answer fundamental questions about antisociality and altruism. This research shows the utility of combining an epidemiological sampling strategy with personality and differential psychology, it builds on a growing body of research attesting to the coexistence of desirable and undesirable qualities in human functioning, and it has practical implications for the design of interventions to increase altruism and decrease antisociality.

Correspondence: Robert Krueger, Department of Psychology, University of Minnesota, Minneapolis, MN 55455-0344; email: kruego38@tc.umn. edu.

Macy, M. W., & Skvoretz, J. (1998). The evolution of trust and cooperation between strangers: A computational model. *American Sociological Review,* 63(5), 638–660.

Objective: To test if embedded social ties (e.g., tight congregations or neighborhoods) facilitate the coordination of effective trust conventions and if nonembedded encounters (e.g., between random strangers) diffuse such conventions across the population.

Design: A computer simulation experiment that models a series of prisoner dilemma games (PDG) involving embedded and nonembedded relationships to show how trust and cooperation can evolve without formal or informal social controls.

Setting: Cornell University, Ithaca, NY, and University of South Carolina, Spartanburg, SC.

Participants: Data from two populations are used. Each population consists of 1000 players who play PD with nine neighbors and 990 strangers (Frank, 1988; Orbell & Dawes, 1991).

Assessment of Manipulated Variables: The experiment involves three structural manipulations: the relative cost of exiting the PDG, neighborhood size, and embeddedness of the interaction (i.e., extent to which players' interaction with prospective partners is limited to players' neighborhood).

Assessment of Outcome Variables: Levels of trust and cooperation between neighbors and between strangers for the two populations are measured using a genetic algorithm that tracks reproductive fitness (i.e., a function of cumulative payoffs in repeated PDG) relative to other players in the computational ecology. This relative-fitness index determines the probability that each strategy will propagate (i.e., when two mated strategies recombine continually so as to refresh the heterogeneity of the population and counteract the selection pressures that reduce this variation).

Main Results: Two relatively stable strategies were shown to affect trust and cooperation between neighbors and between strangers. First, social proximity produced a pattern labeled "parochial solidarity" (i.e., cooperation with ingroups and defection with outgroups). Second, a player's intention to cooperate because of his or her own projection or detection of a partner's telltale behavioral signs produced a pattern of "universalistic solidarity" (i.e., openness to strangers). The success of the first strategy depended on the rate of adoption of neighborhood norms and was found to dominate populations where exits are impeded by the high cost of refusing to exchange. The success of the second strategy in affecting trust and cooperation between neighbors and between strangers depended on agreement with local norms but also on the probability of meeting like-minded strangers; moreover, it was found to dominate populations with a high capacity for "rugged self-reliance" and a high preference for mutual cooperation.

Conclusion: Social structures where there are a large number of small neighborhoods have advantages for both strategies. Small neighborhoods facilitate the emergence of trust conventions by reducing the coordination complexity in the standardization of signaling rules, and they facilitate the restoration of order after epidemics of distrust. On the other hand, occasional contact with strangers allows universal extension of trust conventions, and a greater number of neighborhoods improves the odds that a few neighborhoods will remain immune to epidemics of distrust until infection quells.

Commentary: By examining the coevolution of protocols for social exchange, this experiment identifies social structural factors that help breed trust and cooperation locally as well as facilitate the diffusion of these behaviors to others.

Correspondence: Michael W. Macy, Department of Sociology, Cornell University, NY; email: mwm14@cornell.edu.

 ⚗ Makaskill, A., Maltby, J., & Day, L. (2002). **Forgiveness of self and others and emotional empathy.** *Journal of Social Psychology, 142*(5), 663–665.

Objective: To explore the relationship between empathy and forgiveness of self and others.

Design: Nonexperimental questionnaire.

Setting: Sheffield Hallam University, England.

Participants: A total of 324 British undergraduate students (100 males, mean age 22.03) participated.

Assessment of Predictor Variables: Participants completed measures of forgiveness of self and forgiveness of others (Mauger et al., 1992). Both showed good reliability (Cronbach alphas = .73 and .75, respectively).

Assessment of Outcome Variables: Participants completed a measure of emotional empathy that encompasses a tendency to recognize others' feelings and an attempt to share the emotion (Mehrabian & Epstein, 1972). The measure showed good reliability (alpha = .81).

Main Results: Females scored higher on emotional empathy but equally on overall forgiveness, compared to males. There was a positive correlation between forgiveness of others and empathy for both males, $r(99)$ = .23, $p < .05$, and females, $r(223)$ = .33, $p < .01$. However, forgiveness of self was unrelated to empathy.

Conclusion: The ability to empathize is related to likelihood of forgiving others but not oneself. The results echo previous clinical findings that individuals tend to make harsher judgments of themselves than of others (Beck, 1989; Walen, DiGiuseppe, & Wessler, 1980).

Commentary: This research investigates a relationship that has received much attention in the literature, the empathy-forgiveness link, and reveals the limits of empathy on forgiveness—namely, that it can facilitate forgiveness of others but not of one's self.

Correspondence: Ann Makaskill, School of Social Science and Law, Sheffield Hallam University, Sheffield, England; email: a.macaskill@shu. ac.uk.

McCullough, M. E., & Hoyt, W. T. (2002). **Transgression-related motivational dispositions: Personality substrates of forgiveness and their links to the Big Five.** *Personality and Social Psychology Bulletin, 28*(11), 1556–1573.

Objective: To examine how the dispositional factors underlying forgiveness are related to the Big Five personality traits through the use of generalizability analyses of transgression-related motivational dispositions.

Design: Two experiments were conducted. The first measured responses to four scenarios in which participants reported their real or hypothetical responses to transgressions three separate times over a period of three months, which resulted in a 3 (relationship type) × 2 (transgression severity) × 2 (scenario type) within-subjects design. Using a similar design, the second included an additional method, measure, measurement occasion, and type of relationship (both parents, or male and female caregivers), which resulted in a 4 × 2 × 2 design.

Setting: Participants completed the experiments on computers in a large university setting.

Participants: A total of 137 undergraduate students participated for course credit in study 1. In study 2, ninety-five undergraduate students participated for course credit (and 145 peer raters were used as well).

Assessment of Predictor and Manipulated Variables: The Big Five traits were assessed three times in study 1, using the forty Big Five adjective markers

(John & Srivastava, 1999) the first time and the Big Five Inventory (BFI; John et al., 1991) the second and third times (alphas for subscales > .75 on each measurement occasion, except for Agreeableness and Openness, which were .73 and .68, respectively). In study 2, participants' Big Five traits were measured by self-reports of BFI three times and at least two peer-reports of the forty adjective markers (ratings showed adequate convergent and discriminant validity). Participants also completed the Transgression-Related Interpersonal Motivations inventory (TRIM; McCullough et al., 1998) in response to four scenarios about transgressions several times over a period of three months in study 1 and four months in study 2 (with three measurement occasions in the first and four in the second). The within-subjects variables in study 1 were relationship type (i.e., romantic partner, same-sex friend, and opposite-sex friend), transgression severity (moderate vs. severe), and scenario type (fictional vs. historical transgressions). The same within-subjects variables were used in study 2, except relationship type included same-sex and opposite-sex friend as well as mother and father or male and female caregiver.

Assessment of Outcome Variables: In both studies, participants completed the TRIM several times. In both studies the sources of the variance among the three transgression-related interpersonal motivations underlying forgiveness responses—avoidance, revenge, and benevolence—across the two types of transgression scenarios (fictional and historical) were estimated for each participant. Indices of transgression-related interpersonal dispositions toward avoidance, revenge, and benevolence made up the main dependent variables for both studies. Reliabilities for all three motivational disposition indices across the different transgression scenarios were sufficiently high for both studies (alphas ranging from .82 to .97). Also, perceptions of transgression severity were measured (on a ten-point scale) in study 2.

Main Results: The first study showed that people's avoidance, revenge, and benevolence motivations in response to transgressions (i.e., their TRIMs) were related to the Agreeableness and Neuroticism dimensions of the Big Five. Neuroticism positively predicted avoidance and negatively predicted Benevolence, and Agreeableness negatively predicted revenge. Revenge was the most cross-situationally consistent of the three. Also, the amount of variance due to individual differences in the TRIM responses to single transgressions was considerably less for the three motivational dispositions, compared to when the TRIM responses were aggregated across all six transgression scenarios. Using a broader range of relationships (i.e., with parents or caregivers), study 2 yielded similar findings; however, avoidance was predicted by Agreeableness in addition to Neuroticism, and revenge was predicted by Neuroticism in addition to Agreeableness. Moreover, perceived severity was associated with all three motivational dispositions and also partially mediated the link between Neuroticism and all three dispositions.

Conclusion: Both studies attest to the important role of Agreeableness and

Neuroticism in individuals' tendency to forgive. In particular, results indicate that these two dimensions of the Big Five are related to dispositions toward all three of the motivations that underlie forgiveness—avoidance, revenge, and benevolence. Moreover, aggregating forgiveness responses across time, relationships, and transgressions of different severity helps capture these relationships. Results suggest that the tendency to forgive can be explained in the following manner. Individuals who are more agreeable may have weaker or slower revenge responses, may be less likely to nurse a grudge or more likely to empathize with a relationship partner, and thus be more forgiving than less-agreeable individuals. Individuals who are more neurotic may ruminate more on an offense, may even incur more severe transgressions, may avoid their offenders more, and thus be less forgiving than less-neurotic individuals.

Commentary: This research articulates the particular relationships Agreeableness and Neuroticism have with dispositions toward forgiveness motivations. It also establishes a precedent for the methodology that can best capture individuals' motivational responses to interpersonal transgressions.

Correspondence: Michael E. McCullough, Department of Psychology, University of Miami, Miami, FL; email: mikem@miami.edu; or William T. Hoyt, Department of Counseling Psychology, University of Wisconsin, Madison, WI; email: wthoyt@education.wisc.edu.

᪂ Midlarsky, E., Kahana, E., Corley, R., Nemeroff, R., & Schonbar, R. A. (1999). Altruistic moral judgment among older adults. *International Journal of Aging and Human Development, 49*(1), 27–41.

Objective: To investigate altruistic moral judgment among older adults and examine its relationships to demographic and personality variables, self-reported helping, and subjective social integration (the perception that one is integrated into one's social milieu).

Design: Survey using a randomly selected sample.

Setting: Detroit metropolitan area.

Participants: The sample included 400 participants, which were 70.5 percent female and 82.5 percent white (thus the sample was not very representative in terms of gender and ethnicity). Among them, 21.7 percent had eight years of school or less, 53 percent had a high-school diploma, 19.5 percent had some college or a college degree, and 3.7 percent had done some graduate work.

Assessment of Predictor Variables: Individual interviews lasting approximately 1.5 hours were conducted in the respondent's own homes. The following measures were included in the interviews. Demographic items measured health, finances, occupation, and education. The Social Responsibility Scale (Berkowitz & Lutterman, 1968) and a locus of control scale (Rotter, 1966) modified for the elderly (Midlarsky & Kahana, 1994) measured the personality variables of social responsibility and locus of control. A situational variable of perceived opportunity to help (using five-point Likert scales) was also measured (e.g., "To what extent are there people in your environment who need your help?"). Self-reported helping behavior was measured (on five-point Likert scales) by asking respondents to indicate the amount of help they actually had given during perceived opportunities to help. Information was also elicited regarding the domains of helping (e.g., family, neighbors, and volunteering). Subjective social integration (Liang, Dvorkin, Kahana, & Mazian, 1980) included twenty closed-ended questions that measured the amount of contact and closeness with people in one's environment. Finally, a measure of altruistic moral judgment (Eisenberg, 1982, 1986), which was slightly modified for the elderly, included open-ended questions about what the respondent would or should do in response to three different dilemmas in which the needs of another person conflicted with the actor's own needs.

Assessment of Outcome Variables: The perceived opportunity to help measure showed adequate reliability (Cronbach's alpha = .79), as did the Subjective Social Integration Scale (Cronbach's alpha = .65). Altruistic moral judgment was scored according to several moral-reasoning tactics, which reflect ascending order of moral maturity (Eisenberg, 1986). Tactics included: 1) hedonistic reasoning, such as orientation to personal gain, to direct reciprocity, and to affectional relationships; 2) orientation to physical, material, or psychological needs of another; 3) orientation to stereotyped images of a good or bad person; 4) orientation to others' approval and acceptance in deciding what is the correct behavior; 5) self-reflective empathic orientation toward others; 6) orientation to feeling good, often of oneself, as a consequence of living up to internalized values; 7) orientation to an internalized responsibility, duty, or need to uphold the laws and accepted norms or values; and 8) other abstract and/or internalized types of reasoning such as concerns for generalized reciprocity, for the condition of society, for individual rights and justice, and for equality of people. Two independent observers achieved good interrater reliabilities for each of the tactics (Cronbach alphas ranging from .68 to .75), except for one tactic, which was dropped from analyses because of infrequent usage.

Main Results: The moral-reasoning tactics most used in judgments (in descending order of frequency) were: needs-oriented reasoning/nonhedonistic pragmatism (category 3), empathic orientation/internalized affect (category 5), abstract and/or firmly internalized reasons (category 6), and hedonistic concern (category 2). Only category 6 had significant positive correlations with overall self-reported helping. It also had significant positive correlations with social responsibility, internal locus of control, subjective social integration, perceived opportunity to help, and all domains of helping. Above and beyond the contribution of demographic variables in category 6 reasoning, social responsibility accounted for 12 percent of the variance and internal locus of control accounted for 7 percent. On the other hand, category 2 had significant negative correlations with social responsibility, internal locus of control, and overall helping (particularly for neighbor helping and volunteering).

Conclusion: This study showed that Eisenberg's moral-reasoning model could be successfully applied to older adults. Specifically, older adults who felt more in control of their lives and thought that they had responsibilities toward the community were more likely to have more internalized, abstract reasons for making judgments about whether or not to help another person at one's own expense, and this kind of reasoning tactic was positively related to social integration and self-reported helping with respect to family, neighbors, and volunteering.

Commentary: This study found relationships among personality, situational, and social-perceptual variables that are important for understanding altruistic behavior among elderly adults. The results neatly suggest that older adults who help others for morally mature reasons are more likely to feel well connected with their social milieu and able to make a difference in the environment, painting a picture of altruism that benefits both the giver and the receiver. Results also indicate that further research is needed to understand how these relationships hold up in other age groups.

Correspondence: Elizabeth Midlarsky, Teachers College, Columbia University, New York, NY 10027-6696.

Perrine, R. M., & Heather, S. (2000). Effects of a picture and even-a-penny-will-help appeals on anonymous donations to charity. *Psychological Reports, 86*(2), 551–559.

Objective: To explore the influences of a picture and the phrase "even a penny will help" on contributions to charity.

Design: Two experiments, one in the field and one in the laboratory.

Setting: Study 1: Veterinary offices, retail clothing or hardware stores, and a psychology department located throughout Madison County, KY (population approx. 60,000). Study 2: A mid-sized southeastern university.

Participants: Study 1: Charity givers to the "Madison County Humane Society." Study 2: 129 undergraduate students (110 women and 19 men, ages 18–47).

Assessment of Manipulated Variables: In the field experiment, the two independent variables, picture versus no picture and phrase versus no phrase, were fully crossed, so that four conditions (or types of charity boxes) were created. The picture (color picture of various puppies) and the phrase "even a penny will help" were added (or not) to standard charity boxes that had a brief description of the cause and the society's mission. To ensure equal attention for the boxes all four conditions were present at each location (so they could be compared to each other). In the lab experiment, picture and phrase were also fully crossed but within a between-subjects design, so that participants were exposed to both a control charity box (of a comparable organization) and an experimental charity box (one of the types of charity boxes described above). Participants were to allocate a nickel and a dime to the two boxes.

Assessment of Outcome Variables: Money collected from the donation boxes was the dependent variable for both studies. Study 2 had an additional questionnaire in response to the experience of donating to the two boxes.

Main Results: Both studies found a significant difference in donations as a function of the picture, and charity boxes with pictures yielded more money ($M = \$7.69$, $SD = \$4.84$ in experiment 1 and $M = \$10.08$, $SD = \$0.51$ in experiment 2) than boxes without pictures ($M = \$4.02$, $SD = \$4.15$ in experiment 1 and $M = \$8.33$, $SD = \$0.49$ in experiment 2). Phrase exhibited no such effect in either experiment. Moreover, participants in study 2 responded that the picture convinced them in their decision to donate.

Conclusion: It appears that charity campaigns using vivid pictures intended to evoke positive emotions can lead to more donations than campaigns with the phrase "even a penny will help."

Commentary: The use of vivid pictures that elicit positive feelings can be useful for charity organizations' campaigns. Such pictures may not only lead to more donations than phrases that ask for money, but they may be more effective than distressful pictures (e.g., handicapped children), which have been found to lead to reactance and fewer donations (Isen & Noonberg, 1979). The results of these studies suggest that lab studies can be useful for testing different social psychological principles in donating behavior.

Correspondence: Rose M. Perrine, Psychology Department, Eastern Kentucky University, Richmond, KY 40475.

⚶ **Perugini, M., & Gallucci, M. (2001). Individual differences and social norms: The distinction between reciprocators and prosocials.** *European Journal of Personality, 15*(1, SpecIssue), S19–S35.

Objective: To investigate the unique characteristics of reciprocity in the domain of individual differences, by differentiating reciprocity from prosociality both in terms of behavior and in terms of corresponding personality traits.

Design: Two studies were conducted, one that employs a trait-situational perspective (Ten Berge & De Raad, 1999, 2001) to investigate lay definitions of reciprocity, and one that employs an experiment involving hypothetical choices without material payoffs.

Setting: University of Rome, Italy (study 1) and University of Leicester, England (study 2).

Participants: In the first study, 166 people participated (109 females, 57 males; mean age = 28.3 years, $SD = 12.2$). Undergraduate students comprised two-thirds of the sample and students' friends, relatives, or parents the remaining third. In the second study, 134 students participated (111 females, 23 males, mean age = 21.3, $SD = 6.2$).

Assessment of Predictor and Manipulated Variables: In the first study, participants were asked to describe situations and behaviors that would demonstrate that somebody is a "reciprocator," "cooperator," or a "hostile" person. In the second, participants' social value orientation (SVO; Van Lange, Otten, De Bruin, & Joireman, 1997) was assessed through a series of nine decomposed games involving a choice between a prosocial, an individualistic, and a competitive option. They were classified as one of the three if they responded with that option at least six times, resulting in forty prosocials, sixty-seven individualists, and ten competitors. SVO served as a between-subjects factor. These participants also completed Perugini and colleagues' Personal Norm of Reciprocity questionnaire (PNR; unpublished manuscript), which measured positive and negative reciprocity (positive or negative reactions to positively or negatively valued behaviors) and beliefs about the effectiveness of both forms of reciprocity. Finally, they were engaged in six choice situations in which they were to decide on whether to give themselves six times more, just under two times more, or an equal amount compared to a partner. With each choice situation, the partner's previous behavior (positive vs. negative valence) and type of relationship (friendship vs. expectation of future relationship) were manipulated as within-subjects factors.

Assessment of Outcome Variables: Study 1 participants' sentences were coded by two independent raters according to valence (i.e., negative vs. neutral vs. positive) of the event and of the behavior and according to the congruence of the action with the event. The dependent variable in study 2 was the amount of average payoff across the six matrices.

Main Results: Study 1 showed that reciprocity has specific features as a personality disposition—it contains connotations of agents matching what has happened with what they are going to do as a result—while definitions of cooperativeness and hostility presented biases that were congruent with the personality dispositions they represent (regardless of other's previous behavior). Study 2 revealed that more was allocated when the partner behaved positively (rather than negatively) and when the partner was a friend (rather than a potential partner). It was also found that competitors, unlike prosocials and individualists, reacted by giving fewer payoffs to those who previously behaved rudely with them, regardless of the type of relationship.

Conclusion: These two studies provide a more precise understanding of the mechanism of reciprocity, and the kind of individual differences that modulate this mechanism and its effectiveness. It appears that reciprocators consider the valence of another's behavior in determining how much they should allocate to that person, irrespective of the type of relationship.

Commentary: A main weakness of the second study is that no incentives were used to motivate participants. Nonetheless, evidence was produced that complemented the first study's findings. Not only is a reciprocating person understood as distinct from a cooperative or a hostile person, but reciprocators also show a pattern of behavior that is distinct from prosocial behavior.

Correspondence: Marco Perugini, Department of Psychology, University of Essex, England; email: mperug@essex.ac.uk.

✍️ Rowatt, W. C., Ottenbreit, A., Nesselroade, K. P., & Cunningham, P. A. (2002). On being holier-than-thou or humbler-than-thee: A social-psychological perspective on religiousness and humility. *Journal for the Scientific Study of Religion, 41*(2), 227–237.

Objective: To investigate how religiousness is related to humility. In particular, to test if there are discrepancies in perceptions of one's own and perceptions of others' devotion or righteousness (with overvaluation of self presumed to reflect less humility and minimal discrepancy or undervaluation as evidence of more humility) and investigate how different components of religiousness relate to humility.

Design: Nonexperimental questionnaires were used in two studies.

Setting: Baylor University, Texas.

Participants: In study 1, 249 (176 females, 73 males, mean age = 19) undergraduate students participated for extra credit in a psychology course, and 191 (151 females, 40 males, mean age = 19.2) undergraduates participated in study 2. In study 1, 80 percent were regular attendees of church, and 89 percent were in study 2 (most students were Baptist, followed by Catholic, then Methodist, Presbyterian, Lutheran, Episcopalian, Church of Christ, and lastly Assembly of God).

Assessment of Predictor Variables: In study 1, participants completed Allport and Ross's (1967) intrinsic religious-orientation scale (Cronbach alpha = .82), an extrinsic religious-orientation scale (alpha = .74), Batson and Schoenrade's (1991) quest scale (i.e., degree to which one faces existential questions, sees religious doubts as positive, and remains open to change; alpha = .62), and Batson, Schoenrade, & Ventis's (1993) doctrinal orthodoxy scale (alpha = .93). All items on these measures were on nine-point Likert scales. They also completed a social-desirability scale (Paulhus, 1988; alpha = .83). In study 2, participants completed the same measures (revealing comparable alphas) as well as Altemeyer and Hunsberger's (1992) religious fundamentalism scale (alpha = .90) and DeNeve's (2000) general religiousness scale (alpha = .82).

Assessment of Outcome Variables: Participants in study 1 rated the degree to which they versus others followed twelve different biblical commandments, while in study 2 they rated themselves, other Baylor students, and the average person in terms of commandment adherence as well as in terms of nonreligious, positive traits (e.g., loyal, sincere, kind) and negative traits (e.g., inconsiderate, phony, insensitive). All items were measured on nine-point Likert scales.

Main Results: On average, participants in study 1 perceived the self to adhere more closely to biblical commandments than others (only 2% of the sample believed others adhere more than themselves). Contrary to hypotheses, individuals who were high in intrinsic religiousness, and not extrinsic religiousness, viewed themselves as adhering more to characteristics that are deemed righteous than other people. However, as hypothesized, those with higher quest motives were more likely to have lower self versus other discrepancies, even after controlling for social desirability and all components of religiousness. In study 2, people who were relatively high in intrinsic religiousness were more likely to overvalue their own commandment adherence as well as their ingroup's (other Baylor students). Moreover, highly religious people also evaluated themselves to be better than others on nonreligious attributes, compared to the not very religious.

Conclusion: These results show that intrinsic religiousness increases the holier-than-thou effect (and is related to less humility), that this bias is extended to ingroup members, that the bias generalizes to nonreligious traits, too, and that quest orientation decreases the holier-than-thou effect (and is related to more humility).

Commentary: This research found relationships between different components of religiousness and one conceptualization of humility. Humility in terms of adherence to biblical commandments was associated with embracing complex existential questions, viewing religious doubts as positive, and remaining open to religious change. The authors point out that future research should employ multiple methods and measures and use different samples (other than the unrepresentative one used in these studies) that include other religions and ages. Other research may also do well to investigate other conceptualizations of humility, perhaps ones that do not concern major, internalized principles such as the biblical commandments.

Correspondence: Wade C Rowatt, Department of Psychology and Neuroscience, Baylor University, Waco, TX; email: Wade_Rowatt@Baylor.edu.

&❧ **Sheldon, K. M., Sheldon, M. S., & Osbaldiston, R. (2000). Prosocial values and group assortation within an N-person prisoner's dilemma game.** *Human Nature,* 11(4), 387–404.

Objective: To examine natural interpersonal sorting processes and the effect of these processes on participants' ability to score points within a four-person's prisoner's dilemma.

Design: An N-person prisoner's dilemma game (PDG) methodology was used.

Setting: University of Missouri, Columbia.

Participants: A total of 274 freshmen (no demographics specified) participated in the study. An initial 95 freshmen who were in a year-long study of adjustment to college were asked to participate, and they were then asked to recruit three other peers from their existing networks of relationships.

Assessment of Predictor Variables: First, prosocial value orientation (PVO) was measured using the Aspirations Index (Kasser & Ryan, 1993, 1996), a measure that has participants rate (on five-point Likert scales) how important statements about the intrinsic values of emotional intimacy, self-acceptance, and community contribution are, as well as rating the extrinsic values of financial success, popularity/fame, and physical attractiveness. A single PVO score was computed for each participant by subtracting the sum of the extrinsic subscale from the sum of the intrinsic subscale. Participants were then engaged in a "group bidding game" with the peers they recruited. For an opportunity to receive movie tickets, they were instructed to get a high individual score or group score by choosing to cooperate or get ahead, and their choices were to be made alone and without communication with the rest of the group. They each made a series of five bids (i.e., five one-shot PDGs). Payoffs reflected a standard N-person PDG matrix where individuals could obtain more by defecting but groups obtain more when fewer defect.

Assessment of Outcome Variables: The dependent variable was amount of cooperation versus defection across the five bids.

Main Results: Asocial (or extrinsically motivated) individuals made more defection choices during the PDG, thus scoring more points than their group mates, but the overall character (i.e., values) of the group in which they were embedded (which also reflects the values of the primary participant who recruited the group) had an equally determinant effect on participants' scores. Thus, the extrinsic primary participants' points were diminished by the extrinsic group's high defection rate, and the opposite was true of intrinsic primary participants and their groups.

Conclusion: Results suggest that individuals with materialist values have no "suckers" to exploit when they choose their own kind as group mates; they cannot trust each other to cooperate, and this limits their ability to achieve both high individual and group scores in the PDG. In contrast, prosocial individuals who choose their own kind as group mates tend to mitigate their within-group disadvantage and create the potential to do very well in the group-level game.

Commentary: Use of an N-person PDG format is a major strength of this research. This technique creates a social dilemma that secures a group context that is a function of people's values as well as their choice of associates, and this is more ecologically valid than many of the scenarios typically employed in standard PDG research. This research provides convincing evidence that prosocials may very well be more harmonious and adaptive in "survival" situations. Furthermore, it implies that nice people may finish first in interdependent situations by bringing immediate cost to the individual but difficult-to-see group-level benefits.

Correspondence: Ken M. Sheldon, Department of Psychology, University of Missouri-Columbia, Columbia, MO; email: SheldonK@missouri. edu.

⁝ Silverstein, M., Conroy, S. J., Wang, H., Giarrusso, R., & Bengtson, V. L. (2002). Reciprocity in parent-child relations over the adult life course. *Journal of Gerontology, 57B*(1), S3–S13.

Objective: To investigate how parents' transfers of sentiment, time, and financial assets to their adolescent/young children affect the children's propensity in middle age to provide social support to their aging parents, and to test whether the mechanism is better modeled as a return on investment, an insurance policy triggered by the longevity or physical frailty of parents, or as altruism on the part of the adult children.

Design: Longitudinal and intergenerational survey using six waves of data.

Setting: Los Angeles, CA.

Participants: An analytic sample of 416 child-mother relationships and 317 child-father relationships was derived. Eligible sample members were generated from the families of grandparents randomly selected in 1971 from the membership of a large prepaid HMO in the Los Angeles area. Thus self-administered questionnaires were sent to the grandparents and their spouses (G1), their children (G2; mean age of parents was 43 years for mothers and 46 years for fathers in 1971, and 69 and 72 years respectively in 1997).

Assessment of Independent Variables: Independent variables included three types of self-reported transfers (Bengtson & Roberts, 1991) from mothers and fathers. Associational solidarity between generations was measured by amount of time spent (i.e., frequency on an eight-point scale) in shared activities (e.g., conversations, family gatherings, discussing important matters, dinner, gift exchanges). Emotional intimacy was measured by summing respondents' ratings (on a six-point scale) of perceived level of trust, fairness, respect, understanding, and affection in the relationship with each parent. Reliabilities for the two mother items were .90 and .93 and .88 and .91 for the two father items. Financial assistance was measured by respondents' rating of the amount of monetary support (on a four-point scale).

Assessment of Outcome Variables: The time-varying dependent variable in the analysis was amount of social support adult children gave to each parent at five time periods (1985, 1988, 1991, 1994, and 1997). Support provided in five areas (shopping/transportation, financial support, emotional support, discussing important life decisions, and information/advice) was assessed (reliabilities ranged from .62 to .70 across the five waves of measurement).

Main Results: Support to mothers was consistently greater than support to fathers. Mothers and fathers who shared activities with their children received higher levels of support (and in proportional amounts) from them later, and early financial transfers to children were reciprocated only over time, with greater baseline financial transfers being positively associated with average support provided to fathers and greater financial transfers from mothers being positively associated with rate of change in support provided to mothers. Frailty of mothers triggered greater support from children when there was emotional reserve in the relationship. The most consistent finding was that when early conditions were estranging (emotionally distant parent-child relationship, no time commitment, and no financial support), the amount of support children provided to their parents increased as they aged.

Conclusion: Partial support for each of the three models of intergenerational exchange (investment, insurance, altruism) was obtained. Early activity/time transfers led to reciprocation that was best explained in terms of investment. Early financial transfers led to reciprocation that was best explained in terms of insurance. There was also evidence that despite lack of all three transfers early in the relationship, children responded to the age-related needs of their parents later.

Commentary: It appears that early bonding with one's mother is most important for facilitating the child's willingness to support the mother later in life. This research sheds light on an important topic, intergenerational kinship helping. Results imply that motivation of adult children to provide social support to their older parents is rooted in early family experiences and guided by an implicit social contract that ensures long-term reciprocity.

Correspondence: Merril Silverstein, Andrus Gerontology Center, Los Angeles, CA; email: merrils@usc.edu.

Van Lange, P. A. M., Ouwerkerk, J. W., & Tazelaar, M. J. A. (2002). How to overcome the detrimental effects of noise in social interaction: The benefits of generosity. *Journal of Personality and Social Psychology, 82*(5), 768–780.

Objective: To demonstrate that the detrimental effect of noise (discrepancies between intended and actual outcomes for an interaction pattern due to unintended errors) can be overcome more effectively when one behaves a little more generously than one's partner does, rather than behaving reciprocally.

Design: Experiment using a social dilemma task in which participants are asked to choose how much money they should give to their opponent (e.g., ranging from one to ten coins)

Setting: University of Amsterdam, the Netherlands.

Participants: A total of 205 participants (65 men and 104 women, average age = 21 years).

Assessment of Manipulated Variables: Two variables were manipulated through the use of a series of computer interaction trials. Negative noise was induced by telling participants that the computer may in some of the trials change either their intended choice and that of their partner, just their intended choice, just their partner's intended choice, or they were told nothing at all in the no-noise condition. Rather than pit cooperation against competition as in the typical prisoner's dilemma game, participants interacted with a partner who used a tit-for-tat strategy (i.e., reciprocated same amount of coins back to the partici-pant) or with a partner who used a tit-for-tat + 1 strategy (i.e., reciprocated one more coin to the participant).

Assessment of Outcome Variables: Level of cooperation was measured by the amount of coins participants gave to their partner during the interaction trials. The amount of coins participants ended up with went toward a raffle for a book certificate. Also, their benign impressions of the partner were also meas-ured by a questionnaire after the interaction trials.

Main Results: Adding generosity to reciprocity helped overcome the detri-mental effect of negative noise on cooperation in social dilemmas. Noise led to reduced cooperation when the interaction partner used tit-for-tat, but not when the partner used tit-for-tat + 1. Moreover, there was evidence that the detrimental effect of noise was mediated by the creation of nonbenign impres-sions of the partner.

Conclusion: Two people who follow mere reciprocal strategies in dealing with social conflicts will pull each other toward less cooperation if negative noise is present. In contrast, when an interaction partner gives a person more in return, this prompts that person to return as much to keep balance in the ex-change. Thus, when negative noise challenges participants' beliefs of trust and benign intent with respect to an interaction partner, acts of generosity from that partner will help restore such beliefs.

Commentary: This experiment investigates an important factor in the quality and stability of relationships, coping with noise, and enhances our un-derstanding of why prorelationship behavior (e.g., self-sacrifice and communal orientation) rather than exchange behavior is associated with trust, benign in-tent, and healthy functioning in relationships.

Correspondence: Paul A. M. Van Lange, Department of Social Psychology, Free University, Amsterdam, the Netherlands; email: pam.van.lange@ psy.vu.nl.

📖 Walker, D. F., & Gorsuch, R. L. (2002). **Forgiveness within the Big Five personality model.** *Personality and Individual Differences, 32*(7), 1127–1138.

Objective: To examine the relationship between dimensions of disposition-al forgiveness and personality using both the Big Five and sixteen primary fac-tors.

Design: Nonexperimental questionnaire.

Setting: Religious and nonreligious universities in Southern California.

Participants: A total of 180 students participated in the study. They varied in age (18 to 55 years), sex (137 females, 43 males), ethnicity (117 white, 29 Asian, 16 Hispanic, 1 African American, and 13 multiracial participants), and religious denomination (113 Protestants, 27 Catholics, 9 Christian Scientists, 2 Mormons, 5 Buddhists, 2 Eastern Orthodox, 2 Jehovah's Witnesses, 3 Jewish, 2 Agnostic, 1 Atheist, 1 Bahai, 4 unstated, and 9 of no religious denomination).

Assessment of Predictor Variables: Participants completed Goldberg's (1990) International Personality Item Pool, which can be scored for both the Big Five items (Cronbach alphas ranging from .74 to .83) and Cattell, Saunders, & Stice's Sixteen Primary Personality Factors (1949) (alphas ranging from .69 to .87).

Assessment of Outcome Variables: Participants completed scales measuring four dimensions of dispositional forgiveness, which were adapted from McCullough, Worthington, & Rachal (1997)—forgiveness of others (FOO; alpha = .83) and receiving others' forgiveness (ROF; alpha = .86), forgiveness of self (FOS; alpha = .80), and receiving God's forgiveness (RGF; alpha = .69).

Main Results: All four dimensions of forgiveness were related to personality. Specifically, Neuroticism versus Emotional Stability showed a robust relationship, negatively predicting all but ROF. The primary Neuroticism factors of Anxiety and Emotional Stability contributed above and beyond the Big Five factors to the prediction of FOO and RGF and showed large correlations with FOS. Agreeableness overall as well as its two primary factors of Warmth and Sensitivity positively predicted ROF and RGF. Though overall Extraversion did not predict FOO as expected, the primary factors of Friendliness and Assertiveness were positively correlated with FOS and the primary factor of Reserve negatively predicted ROF and RGF. Overall Conscientiousness was not related to forgiveness, but the primary factor of Dutifulness positively correlated with FOO and RGF. Finally, overall Openness to Experience also did not correlate any of the forgiveness variables, but Imagination negatively correlated with FOO and Intellect positively correlated with FOS. Finally, older individuals were higher in FOO and Religiousness correlated negatively with FOS but positively with RGF.

Conclusion: The relationships between various elements of personality and forgiveness might reflect, in part, causal processes. Individuals who are high in Emotional Stability may avoid disagreements and later find the need to forgive themselves, while those who are high in Anxiety may be prone to guilt and constantly experience a need to forgive themselves. Both Warmth and Sensitivity are needed to receive forgiveness from others. Friendly individuals are not likely to negotiate forgiving themselves, as are those who make decisions for themselves. People who avoid appraising their emotions may be unwilling to make themselves available to be forgiven. The dutiful forgive others more and will receive it more from God, but they may miss the emotional benefits as a result. People high in Intellect may be more able to resolve issues of self-forgiveness, but those high in Imagination may ruminate more about the offense and offender and thus forgive others less.

Commentary: This research improves our understanding of the kinds of individuals who practice certain kinds of forgiveness. Use of more specific measures of personality factors underlying the Big Five helped explain the relationships between the types of forgiveness and personality more effectively.

Correspondence: D. F. Walker, 570 N. Los Robles, #11, Pasadena, CA; email: dfwalker@hotmail.com.

ぐ⊇ Witvliet, C. V., Ludwig, T. E., & Vander Laan, K. L. (2001). **Granting forgiveness or harboring grudges: Implications for emotion, physiology, and health.** *Psychological Science, 12*(2), 117–123.

Objective: To examine the immediate emotional and physiological effects of imagining hurtful memories and holding grudges versus imagining empathizing and granting forgiving to real-life offenders.

Design: Within-subjects experiment.

Setting: Hope College, Holland, MI.

Participants: Seventy-one introductory psychology students (36 females and 35 males).

Assessment of Manipulated Variables: All participants completed a two-part testing session. First they imagined a particular person they blamed for mistreating, offending, or hurting them and completed a questionnaire about the nature of the offense and their response to it. Then they actively imagined unforgiving and forgiving responses (the independent variable) toward the offender eight times by following a script that had them rehearse the hurt and harbor a grudge and a script that had them empathize with and grant forgiveness to the offender. Timing of experimental events and order of scripts (which was fully counterbalanced across participants) were delivered via computer.

Assessment of Outcome Variables: Dependent variables included self-reports of emotional valence and arousal, anger, sadness, and perceived control during the two types of imagery, and physiological measures of corrugator electromyograms (EMG), skin conductance level (SCL), heart rate, and mean arterial pressure. Both sets of dependent variables were measured on the computer, with physiological measures being constantly monitored.

Main Results: Participants felt significantly more negative, aroused, angry, and sad during unforgiving responses than during forgiving responses. They also felt less in control, which corresponded with greater brow tension (corrugator EMG). Other physiological outcomes included higher SCL, heart rate, and blood pressure during unforgiving responses than during forgiving responses, and elevated EMG, SCL, and heart-rate levels persisted into postimagery recovery periods.

Conclusion: Unforgiving responses yield more negative emotions and stronger emotional arousal, which affects sympathetic nervous system functioning (SCL) and cardiovascular functioning (heart rate, blood pressure) more than forgiving responses do. This suggests that the physiological effects of unforgiving responses are greatly influenced by the emotional quality of responses toward an offender and that real-life grudges may contribute to adverse health outcomes, particularly when they are intense and sustained.

Commentary: This study identifies key physiological mechanisms that may mediate the relationship between forgiveness and health. The immediate consequences found to result from simply imagining a hurtful event and holding a grudge seem to provide a window into the harmful immunological and cardiovascular effects of maintaining chronic patterns of unforgiveness. Implications are that forgiving responses may help reduce stress and improve cardiovascular health. These results have theoretical and practical significance because they begin to build on mental health research regarding forgiveness by highlighting the physiological harms of holding grudges and the physiological benefits of forgiving.

Correspondence: Charlotte vanOyen Witvliet, Psychology Dept., Hope College, Holland, MI 49422-9000; email witvliet@hope.edu.

References

Allport, G. W., & Ross, J. M. (1967). Personal religious orientation and prejudice. *Journal of Personality and Social Psychology, 5,* 432–443.

Altemeyer, B., & Hunsberger, B. (1992). Authoritarianism, religious fundamentalism, quest, and prejudice. *International Journal for the Psychology of Religion, 2,* 113–133.

Arriaga, X. B., & Agnew, C. R. (in press). Being committed: Affective, cognitive, and conative components of relationship commitment. *Personality and Social Psychology Bulletin, 27,* 1190–1203.

Axelrod, R. (1994). *The evolution of cooperation.* New York: Basic Books.

Batson, C. D., & Schoenrade, P. (1991). Measuring religion as quest: 2) reliability concerns. *Journal for the Scientific Study of Religion, 30,* 430–447.

Beck, A. T. (1989). Cognitive therapy and the emotional disorders. New York: Penguin Books.

Bengtson, V. L., & Roberts, R. E. L. (1991). Intergenerational solidarity in aging families: An example of formal theory construction. *Journal of Marriage and the Family, 53,* 856–870.

Berkowitz, L., & Lutterman, K. (1968). The traditionally socially-responsible personality. *Public Opinion Quarterly, 32,* 169–185.

Cattell, R. B., Saunders, D. R., & Stice, G. F. (1949). *The Sixteen Personality Factor Questionnaire.* Champaign, IL: Institute for Personality and Ability Testing.

Clark, J. P., & Tifft, L. L. (1966). Polygraph and interview validation of self-reported deviant behavior. *American Sociological Review, 31,* 516–523.

Costa, P. T., & McCrae, R. R. (1992). *NEO PI-R professional manual.* Odessa, FL: Psychological Assessment Resources.

Crown, D. P., & Marlowe, D. (1964). *The approval motive.* New York: Wiley.

Davis, M. H. (1983). Measuring individual differences in empathy: Evidence for a multidimensional approach. *Journal of Personality and Social Psychology, 44,* 113–126.

DeNeve, K. M. (2000). General religiousness scale development and validation. Manuscript in preparation.

Eisenberg, N. (1982). The development of reasoning regarding prosocial behavior. In N. Eisenberg (Ed.), *The development of prosocial behavior* (pp. 219–249). New York: Academic Press.

Eisenberg, N. (1986). *Altruistic emotion, cognition, and behavior.* Hillsdale, NJ: Lawrence-Erlbaum.

Ekman, P., & Friesen, W. V. (1978). *Facial action coding system: A technique for the measurement of facial movement.* Palo Alto, CA: Consulting Psychologists Press.

Frank, R. (1988). *Passions within reason: The strategic role of the emotions.* New York: Norton.

Gaertner, S. L., Dovidio, J. F., & Bachman, B. A. (1996). Revisiting the contact hypothesis: The induction of a common ingroup identity. *International Journal of Intercultural Relations, 20,* 271–290.

Gaertner, S. L., Mann, J. A., Dovidio, J. F., Murrell, A. J., & Pomare, M. (1990). How does cooperation reduce intergroup bias? *Journal of Personality and Social Psychology, 59,* 692–704.

Gaertner, S. L., Mann, J. A., Murrell, A. J., & Dovidio, J. F. (1989). Reduction of intergroup bias: The benefits of recategorization. *Journal of Personality and Social Psychology, 57,* 239–249.

Goldberg, L. R. (1990). An alternative description of personality: The Big Five structure. *Journal of Personality and Social Psychology, 59,* 1216–1229.

Hagen, P. J. (1993). Blood transfusion in Europe: A "White Paper." Strasbourg: Council of Europe.

Hamilton, W. D. (1964). The genetic evolution of social behavior: 1. *Journal of Theoretical Biology, 7,* 1–16.

Hendrick, S. S. (1988). A genetic measure of relationship satisfaction. *Journal of Marriage and the Family, 50,* 93–98.

Heyman, R. E., Weiss, R. L., & Eddy, J. M. (1995). Marital interaction coding system: Revision and empirical evaluation. *Behaviour Research and Therapy, 33,* 737–746.

Hindelang, M. J., Hirschi, T., & Weis, J. G. (1981). *Measuring delinquency.* Beverly Hills, CA: Sage.

Isen, A. M., & Noonberg, A. (1979). The effect of photographs of the handicapped on donation to charity: When a thousand words may be too much. *Journal of Applied Social Psychology, 9,* 426–431.

Jackson, D. N. (1994). *Jackson Personality Inventory—Revised Manual.* Port Huron, MI: Sigma Assessment Systems.

John, O. P., Donahue, E. M., & Kentle, R. P. (1991). *The "Big Five" inventory: Versions 4a and 54.* Berkeley: University of California, Institute of Personality and Social Research.

John, O. P., & Srivastava, S. (1999). The Big Five trait taxonomy: History, measurement, and theoretical perspectives. In L. A. Pervin & O. P. John (Eds.), *Handbook of personality: Theory and research* (2nd ed., pp. 102–138). New York: Guilford.

Johnson, D. W., & Johnson, F. P. (1975). *Joining together: Group theory and group skills.* Englewood Cliffs, NJ: Prentice-Hall.

Kasser, T., & Ryan, R. M. (1993). A dark side of the American Dream: Correlates of financial success as a central life aspiration. *Journal of Personality and Social Psychology, 65,* 410–422.

Kasser, T., & Ryan, R. M. (1996). Further examining the American Dream: Well-being correlates of intrinsic and extrinsic goals. *Personality and Social Psychology Bulletin, 22,* 281–288.

Keltner, D., Young, R. C., Heerey, E. A., Oemig, C., & Monarch, N. D. (1998). Teasing in hierarchical and intimate relations. *Journal of Personality and Social Psychology, 75,* 1231–1247.

Kilpatrick, S. D., & McCullough, M. E. (2002). Annotated bibliography of research on altruism. In S. G. Post (Ed.), *Altruistic love: Science, philosophy, and religion in dialogue* (pp. 387–490). New York: Oxford.

Kramer, R. M., McClintock, C. G., & Messick, D. M. (1986). Social values and cooperative response to a simulated resource conservation crisis. *Journal of Personality, 54,* 576–592.

Levenson, R., & Gottman, J. M. (1983). Marital interaction: Physiological linkage and affective exchange. *Journal of Personality and Social Psychology, 45,* 587–597.

Liang, J., Dvorkin, L., Kahana, E., & Mazian, F. (1980). Social integration and morale. *Journal of Gerontology, 35,* 746–757.

Mauger, P. A., Perry, J. E., Freeman, T., Grove, D. C., McBride, A. G., & McKinney, K. E. (1992). The measurement of forgiveness: Preliminary research. *Journal of Psychology and Christianity, 11,* 170–180.

McClintock, C. G. (1972). Social motivation: A set of propositions. *Behavioural Science, 17,* 438–454.

McCullough, M. E., Rachal, K. C., Sandage, S. J., Worthington, E. L., Jr., Brown, S. W., & Hight, T. L. (1998). Interpersonal forgiving in close relationships. II: Theoretical elaboration and measurement. *Journal of Personality and Social Psychology, 75,* 1586–1603.

McCullough, M. E., Worthington, E. L., & Rachal, K. C. (1997). Interpersonal forgiving in close relationships. *Journal of Personality and Social Psychology, 73,* 321–336.

Mehrabian, A., & Epstein, N. (1972). A measure of emotional empathy. *Journal of Personality, 40,* 525–543.

Midlarsky, E., & Kahana, E. (1994). *Altruism in later life.* Thousand Oaks, CA: Sage.

Orbell, J., & Dawes, R. (1991). A "cognitive miser" theory of cooperators' advantage. *American Political Science Review, 85,* 515–28.

Paulhus, D. L. (1988). Assessing self-deception and impression management in self-reports: The balanced inventory of desirable responding. Unpublished manual. Vancouver, Canada: University of British Columbia.

Perugini, M., & Gallucci, M. (1998). "Personal norm of reciprocity questionnaire." Unpublished manuscript.

Reif, K., & Marlier, E. (1996). Eurobarometer 41.0 (MRDF). Ann Arbor, MI: Inter-University Consortium for Political Research.

Reiss, S., & Havercamp, S. M. (1998). Toward a comprehensive assessment of fundamental motivation: Factor structure of the Reiss profiles. *Psychological Assessment, 10,* 97–106.

Rotter, J. B. (1966). Generalized expectancies for internal versus external locus of reinforcements. *Psychological Monographs, 80,* 1–28.

Rusbult, C. E. (1993). Understanding responses to dissatisfaction in close relationships: The exit, voice, loyalty, and neglect model. In S. Worchel & J. A. Simpson (Eds.) *Conflict between people and groups: Causes, processes, and resolutions* (pp. 30–59). Chicago: Nelson Hall.

Rusbult, C. E., Martz, J. M., & Agnew, C. R. (1998). The Investment Model Scale: Measuring commitment level, satisfaction level, quality of alternatives, and investment size. *Personal Relationships, 5,* 357–391.

Saucier, G. (1994). Mini-Markers: A brief version of Goldberg's unipolar Big-Five markers. *Journal of Personality Assessment, 63,* 506–516.

Sternberg, R. J. (1998). *Cupid's arrow: The course of love through time.* London: Cambridge University Press.

Stotland, E. (1969). Exploratory investigations of empathy. In L. Berkowitz (Ed.), *Advances in experimental social psychology* (Vol. 4, pp. 271–313). New York: Academic Press.

Tellegen, A. (2000). *Manual for the Multidimensional Personality Questionnaire.* Minneapolis: University of Minnesota Press.

Ten Berge, M. A., & De Raad, B. (1999). Taxonomies of situations from a trait psychological perspective: A review. *European Journal of Personality, 13,* 337–360.

Ten Berge, M. A., & De Raad, B. (2001). The construction of a joint taxonomy of traits and situations. *European Journal of Personality, 5,* 253–276.

Van Lange, P. A. M. (1999). The pursuit of joint outcomes and equality in outcomes. *Journal of Personality and Social Psychology, 77,* 337–349.

Van Lange, P. A. M., Otten, W., De Bruin, E. M. N., & Joireman, J. A. (1997). Development of prosocial, individualistic, and competitive orientations: Theory and preliminary evidence. *Journal of Personality and Social Psychology, 73,* 733–746.

Walen, S. R., DiGiuseppe, R. R., & Wessler, R. L. (1980). *A practitioner's guide to rational-emotive therapy.* London: Oxford University Press.

CHAPTER 2

Social Science Research on Altruism, Spirituality, and Unlimited Love

Byron Johnson, Lia Fantuzzo, and Marc Siegel

S ome would argue that the ills of contemporary life are largely traceable to a deficiency of altruistic behavior. Greed and the self-seeking nature of a consumer culture are considered responsible for the deterioration of social bonds that once kept life more humane. Americans from across the ideological spectrum have argued for the significance of civil society as an overlooked, yet integral, part of a functioning, healthy republic. As concerns about the level of civility and social capital in this country have grown, scholars have become increasingly interested in unraveling the very ingredients that define and produce civility and social capital.

Many with an interest in civil society have been particularly interested in the question of what role religious institutions and spiritually-motivated volunteers may play in countering the effects of self-serving and narcissistic behavior, thereby contributing to a more civil society in which altruistic behavior and other-directed love are more commonplace. So, does published research exist that documents the degree to which religious institutions or faith-based organizations may or may not be more effective than their secular or governmental counterparts in addressing various social problems?

Faith-based organizations such as the Salvation Army, Catholic Charities, Lutheran Social Services, Habitat for Humanity, Prison Fellowship, and Teen Challenge provide many altruistic and diverse social services such as counseling for depression, offender rehabilitation programs for youths and adults, drug treatment, shelter, housing rehab, childcare centers, afterschool programs, literacy, mentoring to at-risk youth, and welfare-to-work. A recent examination of faith-based childcare providers, for example, reveals that approximately one of every six childcare centers is housed in a religious facility (see "Unlevel Playing Field," a report prepared by the White House Office of Faith-Based and Community Initiatives, August 2001). Many of these social services are provided by volunteers to the most needy in society.

Faith-based organizations representing a variety of religious traditions provide a great deal of social services to many of the most disadvantaged in some otherwise mostly neglected communities. But from a social science perspective, we don't know much about the variables that influence a person's decision to become a volunteer in the first place, or the factors that help mobilize and sustain so many volunteers. What do we know about the altruistic work of religious or spiritually-motivated workers and volunteers to combat antisocial and egotistical behavior on the one hand, and to promote prosocial or conventional behavior on the other hand? What is the extent of other-directed love dispensed by faith-based organizations? Does the potential for altruism or unlimited love exist in all people?

What is the scope of the published research that examines the antecedents and consequences of possible linkages between altruistic behavior and other-directed or selfless acts? What factors motivate volunteers? Are other-directed virtues learned? Can we determine through research the factors that predispose individuals and groups to altruistic behavior? Perhaps more important, what factors strengthen or diminish individual and group commitments to volunteerism over time? What are the experiences of those who commonly provide self-sacrificial acts and what makes it possible to sustain such altruistic behavior? For example, is one's inclination or tendency toward altruistic behavior a function of maturation in a developmental sense during the life course? What drives the motivation toward gratitude, selfless, and empathic tendencies?

In order to answer these questions, we conducted a systematic search of the relevant research literature from a number of disciplinary perspectives. In short, the research reviewed below is woefully underdeveloped. We don't have empirically informed and thoughtful answers to many of these questions. As the annotated bibliography to follow will show, sociological studies of these issues are quite uncommon. There is, of course, no excuse for this oversight. The opportunity for conducting important social science research to address these questions is obvious. In addition to private funding, the federal government is now openly soliciting proposals for funded research that is theoretically and methodologically sophisticated. The work will certainly yield empirical insights to the long-neglected questions and issues raised earlier. The increased funding should create a wave of new and exciting research that should necessitate the need for completing a new annotated bibliography within the next five years.

Methodology for Completing the Annotated Bibliography

In order to annotate exhaustively published research relating both spirituality and unlimited love in the discipline of sociology and the social sciences, we first analyzed the databases of the University of Pennsylvania Library. The Penn library features numerous databases in seventy-six areas of interest. Of those, we deemed five relevant for our research: *philosophy, political science, religious studies, sociology,* and *urban studies.* Those five interest areas then contained a total of 300 databases. Upon thorough examination, we chose the best twenty-five databases to search all the probable synonyms of *spirituality* and *unlimited love* (see table 2.1). Within each database, all the permutations and combinations of the following two sets of synonyms were searched in order to determine every available journal article on the proposed research subject:

Religion	Altruism
Spirituality	Empathy
Faith	Compassion
Church	Volunteerism
Worship	Selflessness
Divinity	Generosity
Sacred	Benevolence
Theology	Charity
God	Humanitarianism
Creed	Philanthropy
Beliefs	Unselfishness
Dogma	Kindness
Mysticism	Civic Engagement

Each database contained unusually large amounts of hits. We then skimmed each of the results to determine which were primary research materials with at least a partial focus on unlimited love and other directed behavior. The journal articles were located, copied, read, and summarized according to the following guidelines. Each summary was to include the title and source, objective of the study, who or what were the subjects of the study, what research methods were utilized, the results, and, finally, what, if any, conclusions the author drew.

After concluding the summaries of the journal articles, we then examined the bibliographies of each of the articles to track down the remaining relevant research. Additional published research that was deemed an object of our focus was then summarized in the same method detailed above.

Bibliographical Items

✑ Annis, L. V. (1976). Emergency helping and religious behavior. *Psychological Reports, 39,* 151–158.

Objective: To determine if those with traditional religious views act as good Samaritans more often than who are less religiously committed.

Subjects: The subjects were college students in a general psychology class

Table 2.1. Interest areas and relevant databases

Subject Field	Database
Philosophy	Philosopher's Index POIESIS: Philosophy Online Serials JSTOR
Political Science	International Political Science Abstracts ICPSR Left Index Sage Urban Studies Abstracts
Religious Studies	ATLA Serials Collection ARDA—American Religion Data Archive Religious and Theological Abstracts
Sociology	Sociological Abstracts International Bibliography of the Social Sciences Social Services Abstracts Francis UNESBIB ARDA—American Religion Data Archive Periodicals Contents Index
Urban Studies	ISI citation Indexes PAIS International Academic Index Dissertation Abstracts ERIC LexisNexis Academic Social Science Research Network
Other	OneNet

(38 males, 35 females). The data indicate that the mean age of the subjects was 19.1 years for males and 19.0 for females. One-third claimed to be Baptists and three-fourths claimed to be of a major Protestant denomination.

Methods: In class, the subjects responded to a questionnaire that included a section to determine the activities most valuable to the subject, a section in which the subject agreed or disagreed with the authenticity of the Bible through a series of questions, and a section that asked questions to determine personal history and the frequency of church attendance and prayer both past and present.

Results: It appears that belief in the accuracy of the Bible is not a predictor of helping behavior. The analysis did not indicate any significant interaction between helping response and the size of the individual's community. 48 percent of the respondents helped according to the study protocol. Information of two aspects of religiosity, church attendance and prayer were analyzed. These seemed to have little effect on behavior as well. The results indicate that helping behavior is unrelated to scriptural belief, whether an individual accepts the Bible literally or figuratively. These results also seem to disprove the indication that the more religious an individual appears to be, the more likely he or she is to be altruistic. The results do support the suggestion that emergency helping behavior is unrelated to religious belief. The results also support the view that moral stages are developed independently from formal religion.

Conclusion: Religion does not necessarily translate into moral development for an individual. Moreover, morality indicates whether an individual has a strong sense of the division between good and evil, which may be developed outside of religion. This study says that it may be positive for future studies to delve further into the specific stages of moral development because the difference in stages may have an effect upon the level of altruism.

Bahr, H. M., & Martin, T. K. (1983). And thy neighbor as thyself: Self-esteem and faith in people as correlates of religiosity and family solidarity among Middletown high school students. *Journal for the Scientific Study of Religion, 22*(2), 132–144.

Objective: To examine the relationship between religiosity and one's self-esteem. Historically, as recently as 1979, the scientific studies of one's self-esteem were explored without considering any religious variables. The prevailing sentiment on religious effect on one's self-esteem is that it has a positive effect.

Subjects: For this study, 1,673 high-school students were surveyed. The subjects were randomly picked. However, the actual number tested was only 500 students.

Methods: The randomly chosen high-school students were surveyed in 1977. The survey was a replicate of the 1920s survey that Robert and Helen Lynd conducted in Middletown as a part of the Middletown III project. Each of the three types of survey was eight pages long. The bulk of the questions asked about family background, school life, and occupational aspirations. The students had fifty minutes to complete. For this study, 500 students who completed the same type of survey were used.

Independent variables consisted of parental status, education, and occupation; church attendance, religiosity preference, evangelism; and school achievement, leadership activity, and grades. Dependent variables, which were also composite, consisted of self-esteem and faith in people. The variables and sub-variables were sifted through in order to accurately group the variables into sets. The final variables were grouped into two categories: parental socioeconomic status and parent-child solidarity, and student leadership activity, high-school grades, church attendance, and evangelicalism.

Results: With all other variables held constant, the study found no relationship between church attendance and self-esteem. However, there is a substantial relationship between church attendance and faith in a person. Self-esteem is most positively related to high-school grades and leader activities. Overall, church attendance and parental socioeconomic status are found to affect one's perception of others, not one's self-esteem.

Conclusion: This study seems to deny the proposition that a positive relationship exists between religiosity and self-esteem. It seems that evangelicalism and church attendance are poor variables for predicting one's self-esteem. However, it may be that other variables, such as devotion or beliefs, may have stronger ties to self-esteem. Whether or not religion makes a difference is unclear from this study.

༄ Bassett, R. L., Baldwin, D., Tammaro, J., Mackmer, D., Mundig, C., Wareing, A., & Tschorke, D. (2002, Summer). Reconsidering intrinsic religion as a source of universal compassion. *Journal of Psychology and Theology,* 30(2), 131–143.

Objective: To examine whether Christians can accept homosexuals while simultaneously regarding the homosexual act as a sin. The question was referred to in this article, as "are Christians able to love the sinner but hate the sin?"

Subjects: Participants in this study were recruited out of psychology classes spanning two semesters from small Christian liberal arts colleges.

Methods: Participants were first given a questionnaire regarding Christian attitudes toward gays and lesbians. The first part of the survey was completed by participants outside of class and returned at a later class period. The questionnaire included typical demographics as well as data on the extent of their Christian affiliation. The survey attempted to discern how comfortable students were in everyday and religious situations with gay or lesbian persons. In the survey four types of homosexuals were placed in hypothetical situations: a non-Christian celibate homosexual, a Christian celibate homosexual, a non-Christian sexually practicing homosexual in a committed relationship, and a Christian sexually practicing homosexual in a committed relationship. A level of comfort was gauged on a five-point scale. Social desirability was also judged on a five-point scale. The study utilized a voluntary role-play situation where participants were placed in a hypothetical situation with another person portraying a fictional role. Situations dealt with having to decide whether to loan $30 to: (a) a sexually practicing gay/lesbian using the money to attend a gay pride rally; (b) a gay/lesbian person using the $30 to visit his or her grandparents; (c) a celibate homosexual using the $30 to visit his or her grandparents; or (d) a heterosexual using the money to visit his or her grandparents. All of this was to determine the social desirability and level of comfort that Christians had with homosexuals.

68   *Johnson, Fantuzzo, and Siegel*

Results: Participants who clearly affirmed their intrinsic faith accepted the homosexuals regardless of the homosexuals' actions. Participants who affirmed their extrinsic social faith rejected homosexuals. Participants decided to loan $30 to the following people with the indicated probabilities: (a) nongay person visiting grandparents, .54; (b) the gay/celibate person visiting grandparents, .42; (c) gay/practicing visiting grandparents, .40; and (d) gay/practicing attending a gay pride rally, .31.

Conclusion: The data shows that "high intrinsic Christians" do not distinguish between or accept gay behavior and gay persons. It was interesting to the authors that acceptance of homosexuals increased the second semester as opposed to the first. The authors concluded that students already attending the Christian liberal arts colleges that were studied had a more tolerant attitude toward homosexuals than did incoming Christian freshman. Overall, the study shows that many Christians were able to accept homosexuals and still believe homosexuality to be a sin.

Note: In the following six studies, using the term *religion as a quest,* C. Daniel Batson describes those persons who constantly question their religion and faith and the role it plays in their lives. They see the constant contradictions and hardships in their daily routines as opportunities to doubt and ask "why?" As previously determined by Allport, Batson also qualifies two other dimensions to religious involvement: extrinsic means orientation to religion and intrinsic means end religion. Intrinsic religion "is oriented toward a unification of being, takes seriously the commandment of brotherhood, and strives to transcend all self-centered needs" (Allport, 1966, p. 455). Those intrinsic believers see religion as an end in itself. On the other hand, extrinsic believers see religion as a means to an end. Extrinsic, means orientation to religion "is strictly utilitarian: useful for the self in granting safety, social standing, solace, and endorsement for one's chosen way of life" (455).

☙ Batson, C. D. (1976). Religion as pro-social: Agent or double agent? *Journal for the Scientific Study of Religion, 15*(1), 29–45.

Objective: To determine if three-dimensional models of religion are necessary in order to demonstrate once and for all if religion promotes prosocial behavior.

Subjects: In study 1, forty-two students at Princeton Theological Seminary originally completed a number of questionnaires for which they were paid $2 per questionnaire. In study 2 forty Princeton Theological Seminary students completed the six religious orientation scales. In study 3, the final study, the authors tried to replicate the second study with a different population in a different helping situation. In this one fifteen undergraduates either involved in the evangelicals' or the social-service group participated in a followup on how they help each other.

Methods: Study 1 subjects completed the six religious orientation scales. The five scales to measure prejudice were also used to develop a comparison study. Study 2 subjects completed the six religious orientation scales. They were then subjects of a study to measure their likelihood of offering help and what type of help they would offer in different situations. Study 3 subjects were given hypothetical situations in order to determine when they would indicate if they felt persons in each of six situations were to blame for the situation or if the circumstances were to blame.

Results: Study 1: The seminary students appeared completely free from prejudice. However, perhaps they simply knew what the socially acceptable answers would be. The results did not help in determining how the three religious orientations regard prejudice. Study 2: Forty percent of the students stopped to offer aid. However, none of the three religious orientations or six religiosity scales predicted whether or not one would stop. Coding of the data allowed the researchers to determine that those who normally stopped to help scored lower on the Interactional scale and the Religion as Quest measurement but more often than not scored big on the Doctrinal Orthodoxy scale than those who did not help very often. Study 3: As in study 2, those who felt the problem was the person's own fault scored higher on the Religion as Quest scale and higher on the Religion as End scale as those who felt the situation was out of the person's control.

Conclusion: Based on this research it appears that using religion as an end creates very different results than if religion is used as a quest. Thus, two-dimensional studies that have lumped these two together are inadequate and researchers in the future must take this claim into account in order to produce effective studies.

᪥ Batson, C. D., Eidelman, S., Higley, S., & Russell, S. (2001). "And who is my neighbor?" II: Quest religion as a source of universal compassion. *Journal for the Scientific Study of Religion, 40*(1), 39–50.

Objective: To examine whether those who see religion as a quest (open-ended, questioning approach to religion) are less likely to help a person if that person does not exhibit the values of open-mindedness and tolerance, and, if so, whether their helping is directed at the person or toward the behavior.

Subjects: Sixty undergraduate women enrolled in introductory psychology at the University of Kansas. All were of Christian background, and all responded with at least a 4 on a level of interest of religion ranging from 1 to 9. Ten additional students who reported little or no interest in religion were not included in the sample, and two more were excluded and replaced postdebriefing.

Methods: This procedure was closely modeled after the original "And Who Is My Neighbor . . ." study conducted by Batson in 1999. The subjects were given an opportunity to help another student's ("Amy") chances of winning a $30 gift certificate by performing simple digit-circling tasks. The subjects were divided evenly into three groups based on "Amy's" level of tolerance/intolerance, which was made clear by the letter from "Amy" asking the subjects to participate in the rally: (1) "Amy" was not intolerant of homosexuals and was planning to use the money for her grandparents, (2) "Amy" was intolerant of homosexuals and was planning to use the money for her grandparents, (3) "Amy" was intolerant of homosexuals and was planning to use the money for an antigay rally. Questions showing Allport and Ross's (1967) extrinsic and intrinsic scales and questions about reasons for helping the intolerant ones less were also included.

Results: The manipulations within the experiment were effective. The results suggested that the subjects exhibited more resistance in helping someone who was intolerant of gays, especially if the person was going to promote intolerance in an antigay rally. Those who scored low on the Quest scale were considerably less willing to help someone who was intolerant than those who scored above the median on the Quest scale. There were no significant differences between those who scored high on the extrinsic scale between helping those who were gay and helping those who were not; they were as likely to help when doing so promoted homosexuality as when it did not. They were, however, less willing to help someone who was intolerant and those who scored lower on the scale. Only one person, however, said that she helped "Amy" less because she disapproved of what "Amy" planned to do with the money.

Conclusion: Participants in this study who scored high on the Quest scale were much less likely to help someone who is intolerant if the person intended to use the money for a rally. This suggests that those who score high on the Quest scale disapprove of the action, not of the person's beliefs. For those who scored high on the Intrinsic scales, it was found that even their compassion was circumscribed. The source of tolerance by those with high scores on the Quest scale is yet unclear, but the authors suspect it is a matter of perception, not emotion. It is also unclear and unlikely that the tolerance is limitless among those of quest religion. It remains to be said what it means to be intolerant of intolerance.

    Batson, C. D., & Flory, J. (1990). Goal-relevant cognitions associated with helping by individuals high on intrinsic, end religion. *Journal for the Scientific Study of Religion, 29*(3), 346–360.

Objective: To determine whether intrinsic, end religion produces altruism for the sake of self-gratification or altruism due to the genuine desire to help those in need.

Subjects: Thirty-eight undergraduate women enrolled in introductory psychology at the University of Kansas who participated to fulfill part of a course requirement. All of them were of Christian background (26 Protestant, 11

Catholic, and 1 nondenominational), and all responded with at least a 4 on a level of interest of religion ranging from 1 to 9. Individual students who reported little or no interest in religion (approximately 15% of the sample) were not included in the sample, and two more were excluded preanalysis.

Methods: Subjects were first given a survey along with several hundred other introductory psychology students in order to measure their religiosity according to extrinsic and intrinsic scales (Allport & Ross, 1967) and External, Internal, Interaction, and Orthodoxy scales (Batson, 1976). Two to six weeks later, these women were called back to participate in a study in which they were unaware of anything to do with religion. They were then individually given one of four randomly chosen Stroop card sets containing victim-relevant words, reward-relevant words, punish-relevant words, and neutral words to test for latency in the cognition period of saliency of implied meanings for the words after learning of "Katie's" need for help.

Results: Scores on the six scales measuring religious orientation were interpreted to produce three components: religion as a means, religion as an end, and religion as a quest. Subjects perceived "Katie's" need as being significant ($M = 8.39$ on the nine-point scale). There were weak correlations between religious orientation and the amount of help subjects offered "Katie." After adjusting for individual variances in latency, the same procedure was applied as in Batson et al.'s 1988 study questioning whether intrinsic religion evokes altruistic motivation. Judging from the correlations for high scorers on the end component, it seemed that high scorers indeed were motivated by egoistic goals rather than selfless goals. For those high scorers on the End component who had intended not to help, there was a higher level of the saliency of guilt and shame.

Conclusion: This study supports the conclusions made in previous studies by Batson. An alternative explanation for the high correlation of high scorers on the End component and egoistic altruism may be that these subjects exhibited more latency because they took altruism more seriously and approached with greater thought, but two pieces of evidence make this explanation unlikely. Instead, it seems likely that those of intrinsic, end religious beliefs are altruistic because of social or self-rewards, not selflessness.

✪ Batson, C. D., Floyd, R. B., Meyer, J. M., & Winner, A. L. (1999). "And who is my neighbor?": Intrinsic religion as a source of universal compassion. *Journal for the Scientific Study of Religion, 38*(4), 445–457.

Objective: To determine if a person who is intrinsically religious is less likely to help a person whose actions violate his or her own values. Additionally, when there is an antipathy, this study attempts to demonstrate if it is directed at the actions or the person.

Subjects: Ninety undergraduate introductory psychology students at the University of Kansas participated in this study (30 men, 60 women). All were of a Christian background (38 Protestant, 36 Catholic, and 16 with no specific denomination). All claimed to have at least a moderate interest in religion and all received credit toward a course requirement.

Methods: Ten men and twenty women were randomly assigned to each of three experimental conditions. Each participant was first left alone to read a written introduction explaining that in this study they were the discloser recipient, and that their decisions would lead to a discloser having a chance to win a $30 gift certificate or another student having that chance. They were then given an initial note in which the discloser wrote something personal. For one group it said he or she was gay. For the other group it did not. They were then given a questionnaire to ask how similar they think that person is to them. Participants were then given a second note that stated what the discloser would do with the money if he or she won. For one group, that note said the discloser would use it to get to a gay pride rally in San Francisco. For the other group, it said the discloser would use it to visit his or her grandparents in Santa Fe. Respondents then had a choice of answering questions on task A or task B or both to determine who would get the opportunity to win a $30 gift certificate. Finally, participants were given a questionnaire that asked why they divided their time as they did and another questionnaire to determine their religious orientation. Upon completion, participants were carefully debriefed.

Results: Those in the not-gay/grandparents condition answered questions indicating that they thought the discloser was much more similar to them than did those in the gay/grandparents condition. Those who scored high on the Intrinsic scale were less willing to help the gay discloser simply because he or she was gay, not because they didn't want to promote homosexuality. Those who scored low on the Intrinsic scale were very willing to help the gay discloser so long as it did not promote homosexuality. Those scoring high on the Extrinsic scale tended to help the gay discloser less than they helped the not-gay discloser no matter how they were going to use the money. Those scoring low on the Extrinsic scale helped the gay/rally condition less than either the not-gay/grandparents or gay/grandparents conditions. Respondents chose to perform task A and B as they did for the following reasons: forty-nine claimed to know something about the discloser and need, thirty-one wanted to be fair, nine gave some other reason such as losing track of time, and one said he or she disapproved of homosexuality.

Conclusion: There are certain limitations to the study, and it is difficult to make generalizations. First, the recipient outgroup was constructed intentionally in opposition to traditional values. Additionally, even those with a high level of intrinsic religiosity showed a willingness to help the gay recipients. However, there is no evidence that intrinsic religion leads to a universal compassion for others. The opposite was in fact demonstrated in this study. Those devout, religious persons not only averted promoting homosexuality but also denied helping a homosexual in many instances even when the recipient was just trying to reach his or her grandparents.

  ℞   Batson, C. D., & Gray, R. A. (1981). **Religious orientation and helping behavior: Responding to one's own or to the victim's needs?** *Journal of Personality and Social Psychology, 40*(3), 511–520.

Objective: This study aims to examine the relationship between religious orientation and helping behavior. It was previously hypothesized that people with different religious orientations display distinct helping behavior. Those with an intrinsic end to religion respond to their own internalized needs to help victims, whereas those who are religious as an open-ended quest respond to the expressed needs of the victims.

Subjects: Sixty female undergraduate students from the University of Kansas who (1) were taking introductory psychology classes and (2) conveyed interest in religion took part in this study (34 Protestants, 20 Catholic, and 6 with no religious affiliation).

Methods: The participants were first asked to complete a questionnaire in order to determine their religious orientation. One to six weeks after completing the questionnaire, they were asked to participate in another study. In this experiment, each student communicated with another female student (who was actually a fictional confederate) through written notes. The confederate either indicated that she was seeking help or that she did not want to receive help because she wanted to resolve her problems by herself.

Results: The results of the study were, in general, consistent with the hypotheses. What drove individuals with an intrinsic end orientation to religion was their internalized need to be helpful. These individuals offered to help whether or not the victim explicitly requested help. Individuals with Quest orientation to religion were driven by their motivation to meet the expressed needs of the victims; help was offered to the victim when she asked for it, but was not offered when she did not explicitly express her needs.

Conclusion: It should be noted that this study did not actually evaluate the motivation of the participants' response to the fictional confederate. Therefore it cannot be concluded that the participants scoring higher on the end factor were motivated by their personal need to help others. This relationship is merely suggested through indirect evidence of a positive correlation between the score on the end orientation and self-evaluated helpfulness and concern. Furthermore, this study does not examine whether being religious influences one's responsiveness to the needs of others since it does not compare the results with a nonreligious group. This research merely determines how different ways being religious can affect responsiveness.

⚜ Batson, C. D., Naifeh, S. J., & Pate, S. (1978). Social desirability, religious orientation, and racial prejudice. *Journal for the Scientific Study of Religion, 17*(1), 31–41.

Objective: To evaluate the influence of social desirability on the relationship between religion and prejudice. More specifically, the research investigates the previously suggested proposition that the negative correlation between intrinsic religion and racial prejudice is the product of the positive relationship between intrinsic religion and social desirability.

Subject: Fifty-one white undergraduate students interested in religion took part in this research (20 male and 31 female).

Method: In order to measure the religious orientation of the participants, they were asked to fill out a questionnaire that consisted of six religious orientation scales. They were also asked to complete the Marlowe-Crowne Social Desirability scale and the Anti-Negro scale to measure social desirability and racial prejudice respectively. In addition to the standard questionnaire, racial prejudice was also measured under behavioral consequence conditions. Subjects were told that an in-depth interview would be conducted about their views on religion. They were given descriptions of a number of interviewers; attached to each information sheet was a photograph of the interviewer. From the photographs, the participants could see if the interviewer was white or black. The students indicated on a scale of 1 (not at all) to 9 (definitely) how much they would like to be interviewed by each interviewer. These numbers were analyzed and used for a racial prejudice index. In the final step of this study, a combined index of prejudice was constructed using psychometric and behavioral controls.

Results: When controlling for social desirability, the negative correlation diminishes between intrinsic religion and racial prejudice as measured by the survey. However, the results are different when the measure was behavioral, measured by the respondent selecting the interviewer. The Religion as End component correlated positively with prejudice. The Means and End components did not differ in their relationship to prejudice when using the behavioral measure. The Quest component however, did correlate negatively with prejudice measured both by survey and by behavior.

Conclusion: The results suggest that social desirability could be creating the previously reported relationship between intrinsic orientation to religion and prejudice. Where as before the relationship was explained that intrinsic religion lowers levels of enmity, contempt, and bigotry, this study concludes that it is equally plausible that intrinsic religion has a relationship with a desire to present oneself as righteous. However, there are possible alternative explanations. First, it is possible that the Social Desirability scale was not actually measuring social desirability, and thus the conclusions are based on the incorrect variables. Second, it could simply be that those who scale higher on the Social Desirability scale simply truly exhibit more socially desirable traits.

 Bernt, F. M. (1989). **Being religious and being altruistic: A study of college service volunteers.** *Personality and Individual Differences, 10*(6), 663–669.

Objective: To examine the difference between extrinsic, intrinsic, and quest-oriented religious orientation among college students who are volunteers in service work and those who are not.

Subjects: Of the 245 college students (age 22–25) surveyed, 90 percent were Catholic. 178 participants were juniors and seniors from four Catholic universities. Eighty-eight applicants to the Jesuit Volunteer Corps (JVC) were invited to participate in the study, with a yield of 73 percent. The sample represented a variety of socioeconomic backgrounds and college majors.

Methods: Participants were surveyed through a questionnaire containing items examining the Extrinsic and Intrinsic scales as performed by Allport and Ross (1967) and the quest scale performed by Batson (1967). The scales in the study were shorter than Allport and Ross's, but studies have shown that shorter scales are just as effective. The participants' age, gender, religious affiliation, major, and academic performance were also gathered through the questionnaire. The undergraduate sample completed the questionnaires in the classrooms during the spring semester, and surveys were mailed to the JVC applicants.

Results: The comparisons within the undergraduate sample regarding the three scales proved to be inconclusive. It was, however, found that those planning to join a service organization after college scored higher on the quest scale and lower on the extrinsic scale than those who had no such intentions.

Conclusion: It was shown that respondents scoring higher on the Intrinsic scales did not exhibit a higher willingness to participate in service work in JVC after college. On the other hand, although it may be true that the same acts of altruism can be done with very different motivations, this does not mean that those who scored higher on the extrinsic scales, for example, are not as genuinely helpful as the others. They may find different outlets of their altruistic expressions, and the lack of an established relationship between religion and altruism may be due to the failure of contemporary researchers to account for such a variance. The quest scale was found to exhibit the shortcomings mentioned in Spilka, Kojetin, and McIntosh's 1985 study. Perhaps a refinement of the scale should be considered. Because of the nature of the sample individuals (22–25 years of age) the results may have been somewhat skewed, as many may not exhibit the "mature religiousness" of intrinsic religiosity that they may eventually exhibit later in their lives.

᭥ Chaves, M., & Higgins, L. M. (1992). Comparing the community involvement of black and white congregations. *Journal for the Scientific Study of Religion, 31*(4), 425–440.

Objective: To explore the differences in nonreligious community activity by white and black congregations, specifically to investigate the changes in community involvement of black churches.

Subjects: This study used a data-set collected in 1988 by Gallup. Gallup's data used a sample of 1,862 religious congregations that answered an initial telephone survey followed by a more extensive mailed questionnaire. The sample made up a nationally representative group.

Methods: An initial telephone survey was used to gain basic information about the congregations, and a followup survey was then mailed. Race was the primary independent variable in the study. Black congregations were defined as those with over 80 percent black membership, and white congregations were those with over 80 percent white membership. More heavily mixed or predominantly Hispanic or Asian congregations were eliminated from the study. The survey also asked about a number of nonreligious activities. Another scale included four items focusing on nonreligious work, which involved helping underprivileged sectors of society and civil rights work.

Results: Overall, there was little difference in the nonreligious activities black and white churches engaged in. However, when looking more specifically at activities involving helping underprivileged sectors, black churches were significantly more active than white churches. The data also controls for other factors that theoretically could have impacted the results. The differences are not a result of size differences, urban versus rural locations, or southern versus northern locations. Even controlling for revenue does not eliminate the effect of race. Age is much less a factor for activity in white congregations than black congregations.

Conclusion: The data gathered in the study support earlier hypotheses that black congregations are more active in certain types of secular activities. However, the data reject the notion that black congregations are more active in general. Previously the idea that black churches were more active in the particular areas was merely anecdotal. More research can further refine the understanding of the differences in the types of secular activities black and white congregations engage in.

᭥ Christenson, J. A. (1976). Religious involvement, values, and social compassion. *Sociological Analysis, 37*(3), 218–227.

Objective: To determine if religious involvement creates distinctive values, specifically social compassion.

Subjects: In 1973, a statewide sample was created by randomly selecting names from telephone directories in North Carolina. Although 4,470 subjects

were sampled, only 3,115 members of the sample accurately completed questionnaires. Approximately 87 percent of the respondents reported themselves as
Protestants (40% Baptists, 18% Methodist, and the remaining various Protestant denominations). The sample was fairly representative of North Carolina's
population.

Methods: A statewide survey was sent through the mail to heads of house-
holds. Religious involvement was indicated using a Likert scale of importance
to determine the frequency with which they visited a place of worship. Respondents were asked to rank their three most important values and their three least
important values. Social compassion was measured in two ways. First, respondents were given a list of problems that could occur in their communities. They
were then asked how seriously they regarded each problem on a scale of 1 (not a
problem) to 4 (serious problem). Second, respondents were asked about government allocation of public funds and they had to indicate whether "no, less,
same, or more" money should be spent on different expenditure options. Independent variables such as age and family income were used to control for socioeconomic factors.

Results: The most important social value in the sample was moral integri-
ty/honesty and the most important personal value was individual freedom.
There was a positive correlation between the frequency of church attendance
and both honesty and humanitarianism. The respondents that attached greater
importance to helping others were more aware of situations facing the old,
poor, unemployed, retarded, and handicapped. These respondents were also
more willing to spend greater amounts of public funds to help the underprivileged. There was no correlation, positive or negative, between frequent church
attendance and social compassion issues. However, those who did place a higher importance to the value of helping people did appear to be more willing to
help others.

Conclusion: Adherence to the value of helping others related to a greater
sense of social compassion in the North Carolina sample. Church attendance
was not related to social awareness or to the willingness to help others. The authors suggested that further research might further elucidate this discrepancy.
Examining different factors, such as "types of commitment" and "types of de-
voutness," may prove to be important in influencing social compassion.

Clain, S. H., & Zech, C. E. (1999). A household production analysis of
religious and charitable activity. *American Journal of Economics and Sociology,*
58(4), 923–946.

Objective: To test the conventional theories regarding monetary contributions by churchgoers. First, are donations of time and money complementary?
Second, are churches in competition with other charitable organizations for
money?

Subjects: This study examined 1,509 respondents who answered to a lengthy set of questions administered by the Gallup Organization for the Independent Sector in 1994. However, only 1,145 persons were studied due to data collection issues.

Methods: A household model was used which views the household as a quasi-firm producing various household commodities. Religiosity is one such a commodity. This model of utility maximization was combined with the data collected.

Results: Members who contribute more money were found to contribute more time as well. Giving to religious organizations has a positive impact on church attendance. Church attendance has a positive impact on the giving of time and money to religious organizations. Further, there is no tradeoff between giving of time and money to religious organizations and giving that same time and money to other charitable organizations. If anything the relationship is mildly positive. Religious backgrounds demonstrate a role on giving. Catholics, Southern Baptists, and Missouri-Synod Lutheran attend church more but give less time and money. Whites attend church less than nonwhites but give more in terms of time and money. Married persons attend church more but give less. Older persons attend church less. And finally, women attend church more but also give less as compared to men.

Conclusion: The model for household giving suggests various policies by churches to increase contributions of both time and money, for example, requesting volunteers during evening hours in which time is more valuable. The data also suggest certain policies. Since most view contributions to secular and religious-based charities as complementary, churches should support secular charities because that will increase their own contributions in the long run.

❧ Cline, V. B., & Richards, J. M., Jr. (1965). A factor-analytic study of religious belief and behavior. *Journal of Personality and Social Psychology, 1*(6), 569–578.

Objective: To research the suggestively causal link between religion and social behavior empirically, scientifically, and rigorously.

Subjects: The greater metropolitan Salt Lake City directory was used to select 155 adult males and females. Every tenth name on the left-hand column on every tenth page was contacted. Of those chosen, 7 percent had moved, and 3 percent gave reasons for noncompliance, such as "I'm too busy."

Methods: A trained interviewer mailed a letter of intent letting the subjects know they were going to be surveyed for a research project without hinting at the nature of the research. A phone call or a visit was made to make an appointment for an interview. During the interview, three types of procedures were done: a modified TAT-type test (projective personality test), an in-depth interview, and a sixty-seven-item Religious Belief-Behavior Questionnaire. Fifty-eight variables—six from the TAT-type test, thirty-nine from the depth interview, and nine from the questionnaire were produced, in addition to four demographic variables. All were intercorrelated and factor-analyzed using a principal components solution (eigen value and eigen vector) with a varimax rotation.

Results: The intercorrelation between the projective tests, interview data, and questionnaire for the religious commitment index was .66, ranging from .50 to .84, which was much higher than expected. For women, the found factors of religiosity were religious belief and behavior, a spouse who had a good relationship with religious parents, altruism, projected guilt, having a good relationship with a religious father, projective test religiosity, tragedy and suffering, having a good relationship with a religious mother, religious hypocrisy, political preference, and dogmatic authoritarianism. For males, the found factors of religiosity were religious behavior, altruism, dogmatic authoritarianism, having a spouse who had a good relationship with his own religious parents, tragedy and suffering, loss of faith, religious belief, neuroticism, projective test religious conflict, and political preference.

Conclusion: The results indicate a far more complex picture of religiosity than other studies have previously indicated. This suggests that religious commitment and/or religiosity is not one-dimensional; there are many different ways to be religious and many more different ways of expressing these differences. There also was a marked difference between men and women, involving divergent correlations and factors in patterning. However, it is important to note that the sample is not representative of the U.S. population at large, especially in terms of religious preferences. The findings on non-Mormons, although the sample was decidedly smaller, were even clearer and more supportive of the results and conclusions.

⚐ Cnaan, R. A., Kasternakis, A., & Wineburg, R. (1993). Religious people, religious congregations, and volunteerism in human services: Is there a link? *Nonprofit & Voluntary Sector Quarterly, 22*(1), 33–51.

Objective: To examine the relationships between volunteerism and religious beliefs, intrinsic religious motivation and volunteerism, intrinsic religious motivation and volunteerism in the context of a local congregation, and the relationship between sociodemographics, volunteerism, and intrinsic religious motivation.

Subjects: This study selected 466 volunteers, not serving on boards or political organizations, who spend at least one hour every other week for six months helping those in need prior to the interview, and 405 nonvolunteers (friends of the volunteers) who corresponded in age and sex and did not differ too much in terms of sociodemographics from the volunteers except for religion, education, and work status. All were from the areas of Philadelphia, PA, Chapel Hill, NC, and Providence, RI.

Methods: Subjects were interviewed through a questionnaire with four sections: (1) background, (2) Motivation to Volunteer (MTV) scale, (3) assessment of volunteer experience, and (4) social-psychological scales. University of Pennsylvania School of Social Work students conducted the interviews in four cycles between 1989 and 1991.

Results: Using a t-test, it was found that volunteers scored slightly, yet insignificantly, higher than nonvolunteers for intrinsic religious motivation. A Pearson product-moment correlation coefficient was used to analyze the relationship between the amount of time spent volunteering and those with religious motivations, which proved low and insignificant. Then, a four-way analysis of variance was used to test for differences in education, sex, age, and religion. It was found that while gender was not associated with a newly created four-category variable, age, religion, and education were. Using a final t-test, it was found that it is likely that those with high intrinsic religious motivation found volunteerism in the context of congregations to be an outlet of altruism.

Conclusion: Although there were no significant differences between volunteers and nonvolunteers in terms of intrinsic religious motivation, it is questionable whether volunteerism is or is not motivated by religious beliefs. The sample of subjects, however, was not random, and the results of the study should be taken cautiously. Although there was no evidence that religious beliefs and volunteerism were linked, it was shown that volunteerism in the context of local congregations was linked with high levels of volunteering. More research on the motivating factors of members to volunteer within an active local congregation is necessary to further our knowledge of this issue. Further, more research should also be done on how congregations mobilize volunteers to help the community because it is clear that congregations are significant yet underappreciated contributors to volunteer work.

᪾ Crandall, V. C., & Gozali, J. (1969). The social desirability responses of children of four religious-cultural groups. *Child Development, 40,* 751–762.

Objective: To investigate if children from more religious communities have stronger social desirability than children from less religious environments. The study further examines if this pattern holds true within different countries.

Subjects: Three groups of children were examined in this study. The first group consisted of 426 American children from Catholic parochial schools; the second group was 154 Norwegian children from a village in which the residents attended regular State Lutheran Church; and the third group was children from Norway where most people belonged to a fundamentalist Lutheran sect.

Methods: Social desirability of the three groups of children was measured using the Children's Social Desirability (CSD) scale. For the Norwegian children, the CSD scale was first translated into Norwegian. Then, to ensure that the scale was culturally sensitive, five Norwegian judges completed the forty-eight items on the CSD scale the way it would be considered socially desirable for Norwegian children. The CSD data collected from these three groups of children were analyzed together with data from 735 American children from non-Catholic public schools which had been collected for a previous study.

Results: Children from more religious communities (i.e., Catholic parochial and fundamentalist Lutheran) scored significantly higher on the CSD scale than children from less religious communities (State Lutheran and non-Catholic). This pattern was also present between the two groups of varying religiosity in both Norway and the United States.

Conclusion: Possible reasons account for the higher level of social desirability among children of greater religiosity. The literature on this issue is extremely sparse and the researchers offer only tentative suggestions. One possible explanation could be that Catholic parents tend to use more severe and harsh child-rearing techniques than Protestant or Jewish parents (Lenski, 1961). Apart from this, other religious factors are suggested for the higher CSD scores of Catholic and fundamentalist children, including more rigorous and demanding religious training, and greater seclusion from other social groups. These factors could be correlated to more common use of denial or repression defense mechanisms, which further leads to tendencies of stronger social desirability.

⁂ Cohen, S. M., & Liebman, C. S. (1997). **American Jewish liberalism: Unraveling the strands.** *Public Opinion Quarterly, 61*(3), 405–430.

Objective: To examine Jews and Gentiles through six different frameworks that the authors designate to judge liberalism in a multidimensional attempt to explain the theory of Jewish liberalism.

Subjects: A total of 32,340 respondents took part in this study, of whom 758 were self-identified as Jewish. "Jews" were described as those who said they were currently Jewish (689) and those who were raised in a Jewish tradition and were presently not Protestant or Catholic; 31,582 were Gentiles (non-Jews). Numerous national surveys had to be pooled in order to draw a nationally representative sample of Jews, about 2 percent of the American population.

Methods: The data for this study derive from the National Opinion Research Center (NORC) and General Social Surveys (GSS) that were conducted annually from 1972 to 1994. Data sets were taken from each year, excluding the data taken in 1979, 1981, and 1992. The authors chose six areas with which to examine the variances in liberalism between Jews and Gentiles: political self-determination, church-state issues, civil liberties, permissive social and sexual codes, government spending, support for African Americans, and opposition to capital punishment.

Results: Jewish Americans are much more likely to identify themselves as liberal as compared with non-Jewish Americans (47% vs. 28%). Jews are much less likely to oppose prayer in schools than the average American (38% vs. 82%).

Jewish Americans are more committed than other Americans to civil liberties for minorities, that is, atheists, communists, homosexuals (81% vs. 60%). Jews are more open to permissive social and sexual codes than gentile Americans. They have more permissive perspectives on abortion (86% vs. 44%), pornography (71% vs. 45%), and women's rights (89% vs. 75%) than gentile Americans. Jewish Americans felt the government was spending enough as compared with their gentile counterparts (74% vs. 54%). Excluding black respondents, Jews were more liberal in their acceptance of blacks and support for policies on their behalf than their gentile counterparts (70% vs. 58%).

Conclusion: It is conclusive that Jewish liberalism is far from conclusive. After adjusting for sociodemographic patterns, Jews are not particularly liberal with regard to embracing the poor. However, on the issue of church-state separation, Jews are ultraliberal. And although historical circumstances and minority status may explain their liberal, Democratic affiliation, Jews show their conservative side on issues such as capital punishment. Thus, contrary to what others have argued, there is no standarized model of Jewish liberalism.

  ▄❦ **Darley, J. M., & Batson, C. D. (1973). From Jerusalem to Jericho: A study of situational and dispositional variables in helping behavior.** *Journal of Personality and Social Psychology,* 27(1), 100–108.

Objective: Based on previous research, there is evidence that general personality characteristics do not have a direct effect upon the behavior of an individual from situation to situation. The researchers turned to the parable of the good Samaritan because the parable implied that there was value of both personality and situation that were relevant to altruism. The researchers thus developed the hypotheses that religious and ethical thoughts will not make a person no more likely to offer aid to someone in a situation calling for a helping response. The second hypothesis was that persons encountering a possible helping situation are more likely to offer help based on their religious and ethical beliefs.

Subjects: Sixty-seven students at Princeton Theological Seminary. Forty-seven of these individuals were able to be reached by phone and were thus scheduled for an experiment.

Method: Participants were asked to be a part of a study on religious education and vocations. First, personality questionnaires were issued with emphasis placed upon religiosity. The individual was then asked to report on a certain subject (either jobs in which the seminary students would be most effective or the parable of the good Samaritan) in another building, with varying emphasis on how much pressure they were under to arrive. Along the way, the subject passes a "slumped victim" located in the alleyway. Observations are made on persons who stop to help the victim and those who do not.

Results: Subjects in a hurry were less likely to help than those who were not in a hurry. Of the forty subjects, sixteen (40%) offered some form of help to the victim, and twenty-four (60%) did not provide any aid. Of the subjects who offered aid, 60 percent of those in a low hurry, of those in a medium hurry 45 percent offered help, and for a high hurry 10 percent offered help. Religious personality variables did not indicate whether a person would help the victim or not.

Conclusion: The degree of hurry that an individual is in influences the chances that he will offer aid to another individual. The parable seemed to suggest that the pious would be more likely to help; the data presented with this study are congruent with this belief. Persons in a hurry may stop and offer help to someone in distress; however, they are much more likely to keep going. Ironically, they are more likely to keep going even if they are in a hurry to speak about the parable of the good Samaritan. The degree to which a person was in hurry definitely affected the likelihood of giving aid. Thinking about the good Samaritan did not increase helping behavior, but being in a hurry surely decreased it. In this study, personality factors are not useful in predicting behavior.

≪ Davidson, J. D., & Pyle, R. E. (1994). **Passing the plate in affluent churches: Why some members give more than others.** *Review of Religious Research, 36*(2), 181–196.

Objective: Why do some members of affluent churches give more money to their churches than others? What motivates members to give to their churches? How can exchange theory (benefit orientation), symbolic interactionism (belief orientation), and combining elements of both (intrinsic religiosity and participation) explain this phenomenon?

Subjects: This study used thirty of the thirty-one affluent Protestant and Catholic congregations in St. Joseph and Tippecanoe Counties in Indiana as identified by Davidson, Johnson, and Mock's study of affluent congregations in Indiana in 1984.

Methods: The contributions members of affluent churches gave to their churches and their average yearly incomes were indicated to be dependent variables. Twelve endogenous variables were subject to factor analysis: beliefs about the supernatural, certainty of one's faith, unquestioned beliefs, the effectiveness of pastoral leadership, the effectiveness of lay leadership, social cohesion in one's congregation, belief that one's congregation has a unique mission, extent to which religion is important in one's life, faith's challenge to serve others, beliefs about human interdependence, beliefs about doing good for others, and belief that one is God's instrument. Two measures of behavioral involvement (social participation and religious participation) were also analyzed. Finally, the effects of five exogenous variables (age, marriage, tenure, denominational distinctiveness, and church size) were analyzed as well.

Results: Income was far and away the strongest predictor of church contributions; however, it was not the sole predictor. The data showed that the greater the religious participation, the larger the contributions. Intrinsic religiosity affected giving greatly by means of increasing participation. Belief orientation and benefit orientation affect church giving as well, but have much smaller effects. Length of membership and affiliation with smaller and more demanding churches also has a slight effect on giving. Finally, it was indicated that church attendance and participation in religious education courses has a higher correlation with giving than does reading the Bible at home or praying outside of the church.

Conclusion: This study shows that church members do not only weigh their economic situation or their religious involvement when making decisions on how much to contribute. Instead, they take both into account through exchange theory and symbolic interactionism. Thus, future research should note this when attempting to explain why and how much members donate to their congregations. Failure to account for both factors would limit the study and lead to inaccurate results.

⬧ Donahue, M. J. (1994). **Correlates of religious giving in six Protestant denominations.** *Review of Religious Research, 36*(2), 149–157.

Objective: To investigate the relationship between certain religious, congregational, and sociodemographic factors and amounts of monetary giving to churches and other charities.

Subjects: A nationwide study was done on six Protestant denominations, the Christian Church, the Evangelical Lutheran Church in America, the Presbyterian Church, the Southern Baptist Convention, the United Church of Christ, and the United Methodist Church.

Methods: The national survey, entitled Effective Christian Education: A National Study of Protestant Congregations, was utilized. In 1988 and 1989 the surveys were given to a representative sample of each of the six Protestant denominations. In each denomination, 150 congregations were chosen. From each congregation, ten adults were chosen at random to take the survey. The survey asked questions pertaining to ninety-three factors, which were grouped in five large categories: perceived congregational emphasis and quality, religiousness measures, other denominational and congregational measures, sociodemographic variables, and religious socialization measures. The responses were compared to levels of giving, which were measured in two ways: first, the actual amount of money the respondent donated, and then the donation as a percentage of income.

Results: The strongest individual factor in determining donations to one's church was income. Education was also positively correlated. Religious variables had significant correlation. Church involvement, defined by attending services, attending programs or events, and volunteering, was positively correlated with giving. The level of religiosity or spirituality a respondent's spouse had was also correlated positively. When the study focuses instead on actual amounts given and analyzes giving as a percentage of income, very different trends appear. Income levels become negatively correlated with giving as a percentage of income. Age also becomes a much stronger predictor of giving. Throughout the study, no particular set of variables predicts levels of giving in absolute or relative terms, to other religious groups.

Conclusion: Some notable variables did not impact levels of giving. Congregational climate, quality, and loyalty all did not predict giving. Does this mean that congregations cannot do anything to increase levels of giving, and that people give a certain amount regardless of how much they like their congregation? A possible explanation of these survey results is that people do not reduce giving when they dislike their church, but rather they simply leave for another church. The analysis should be considered a suggestion for future research in the topic.

⁂ Ellison, C. G. (1992). **Are religious people nice people? Evidence from the National Survey of Black Americans.** *Social Forces, 71*(2), 411–430.

Objective: To examine the relationship between religiosity, interpersonal friendliness, and cooperation. What role does religion play in altruism and prosocial activities? "Are religious people really helpful, cooperative, friendly, and, in short, nice people?"

Subjects: This study used data from the National Survey of Black Americans. It contains a sample of 2,107 African Americans, including interviews on around 1,400 of them. The sample was intended to be nationally representative. However, the population is slightly older than the national average, black males and residents of western states are underrepresented, while residents of southern states are a little overrepresented. Additionally, the average income level of the sample is slightly higher than the national average.

Methods: Within the National Survey of Black Americans is an interviewer assessment of the respondent and aspects of the interview itself, which are completed following the interview. These questions include how much the interviewer liked the interview, and how would the interviewer rate the demeanor and personality of the respondent, and finally, how would the interviewer rate the respondent on a scale from "open" to "suspicious." Utilizing the responses to questions on the frequency of reading religious materials, of watching or listening to religious programs, of attendance at religious services, and of participation in other religious activities, as well as a few open-ended questions, the researcher was able to determine the religiosity of the respondents. Then after controlling for things such as age, education, gender, family income, physical attractiveness, and respondent's self-esteem the effects of religiosity upon interviewer assessment was determined using regression analysis.

Results: Those who are religiously inclined receive more favorable reviews by the interviewers. The data indicate that those respondents who engage in frequent prayer, Bible study, and/or watch and listen to religious programs often are more enjoyable to interview and more open. The devout are friendlier and less hostile. However, some of that could be conveyed through the fact that they have greater self-esteems. Respondents whose lives are driven by religion appear significantly less bored and more interested in the interview. Finally, those who focus on the morality of religion are deemed less suspicious than those who do not.

Conclusion: Positive interviewer ratings were only associated with some elements of religiosity, those being the frequency of private devotional activity, and the emphasis of religion as an ethical guide. The overall patterns do, however, suggest that religious norms have been socially internalized. However, it is also possible that some interviewers, being religious themselves, may have had some bias in their ratings.

Feather, N. T., Volkmer, R. E., & McKee, I. R. (1992). **A comparative study of the value priorities of Australians, Australian Bahais, and expatriate Iranian Bahais.** *Journal of Cross-Cultural Psychology, 23*(1), 95–106.

Objective: To examine comparative information about the value priorities of the Australians and expatriate Iranians and to inform about the values endorsed by adherents of a particular religion, the Bahais.

Subjects: Sixty-five expatriate Iranian Bahais (35 males, 30 females) resident in Australia, fifty-nine Australian Bahais (22 males, 37 females), and sixty-six unselected Australians (35 males, 31 females) were randomly selected from a larger sample of 205 subjects who had completed a lengthy survey as part of an unrelated study.

Methods: Subjects were presented with two lists of values that were described with short phrases identifying them. They were asked to use a rating scale numbered from 1 to 7 to rate how important that value was as a guiding principle in their life. Translations into Farsi were provided for the Iranian Bahais. In order to make comparisons, the values were classified according to the motivational domains described by two researchers, Schwartz and Bilsky (hedonism, achievement, power, self-direction, stimulation, maturity, benevolence, security, restrictive conformity, tradition, and spirituality). Expatriate Iranian Bahais were also asked to indicate the year they left Iran and the year they arrived in Australia.

Results: The Australian and Iranian Bahai groups had higher scores for values in the restrictive conformity, tradition, and spirituality domains when compared with the unselected Australians, but lower scores for values in the hedonism, self-direction, and stimulation domains. When compared with the Iranian Bahais, the Australian Bahais provided higher scores for values in the spirituality, maturity, and benevolence domains but lower scores for values in the power domain. As far as the unselected Australian group goes, the Australian Bahais had higher scores for values in the benevolence domain and lower scores for values in the achievement and power domains.

Conclusion: The results show strong effects of religious affiliation on value preferences. Many of the values considered important (or unimportant) by the Bahais are not singular to their religion; one would also expect to find them emphasized (deemphasized) in some other religions. Also, there was evidence of women providing significantly higher scores for values in benevolence and spirituality than men. Men's scores were significantly higher in the hedonism, achievement, power, and stimulation domains. The general conclusion is that women tend to emphasize communal and prosocial values and downplay agentic values, when compared to men. However, there was no evidence to suggest that the value priorities of the male Iranian Bahais were especially masculine, as thought previously to relate to the masculine-based Iranian culture. The Iranian sample in this study was a highly selected one, not representative of Iranian society as a whole.

⬧ Forbes, G. B., Te Vault, R. K., & Gromoll, H. F. (1971). **Willingness to help strangers as a function of liberal, conservative or Catholic church membership: A field study with the lost-letter technique.** *Psychological Reports, 28,* 947–949.

Objective: To discover if there are any differences among liberal Christians, conservative Christians, and Catholics in regard to their willingness to help people that they don't know.

Subjects: Random members of the ten most liberal and the ten most conservative churches in a mid-sized, midwestern city.

Methods: Study took place in a mid-sized midwestern city (population, 100,000) with 111 Christian churches. A theologian who was acquainted with the churches of the city picked the ten most liberal and the ten most conservative churches in the area. Those who were liberal scored low on an index (Stark and Glock, 1968) that measures the orthodoxy of religion, while those who were conservative scored high on this index. The churches were also chosen with the demographics of the city in mind, attempting to represent a cross-section of the entire population. Letters were dropped in the doorways and parking lots of the liberal and conservative churches during large morning services. Fifty-five letters were left at the liberal churches, and forty-eight letters were left at the conservative churches, while fifty letters were left at each of the Catholic churches. The letters were sealed but not stamped, and hand-addressed to Mr. and Mrs. Fred Guthrie at a local address. The letters did not have a return address.

Results: The return rates for conservative, liberal, and Catholic churches were 40 percent, 42 percent, and 36 percent respectively. Thus, there is no correlation between church membership and the rate of the return of the letters. Although researchers had anticipated that all returned letters would be mailed, some of the letters were brought directly to the address. The numbers of letters delivered was too small for statistical analysis; these were combined with the letters that had been stamped before mailing. Liberal and Catholic churches did not differ in the proportion of returns that were postage due. Many fewer conservative Christians actually stamped the letter and sent it back.

Conclusion: The findings imply that conservative Christians are much less willing than liberal Christians or Catholics to make even small economic sacrifices to help strangers. This is constant with other research stating that conservative Christians are much less intrinsically philanthropic.

    ✑ Forbes, K. F., & Zampelli, E. M. (1997). **Religious giving by individuals: A cross-denominational study.** *American Journal of Economics and Sociology, 56*(1), 17–30.

Objective: To examine religious giving on an individual basis as opposed to a congregational or denominational basis. This study attempted to reveal individual motivations for giving. It also intended to reexamine the religious giving patterns of Catholics and Protestants in an attempt to reevaluate notions that Protestants give more quantitatively and more frequently than Catholics. The authors hoped to research the strength of this hypothesis after exploring individuals within these denominations and their individual motivations for giving.

Subjects: A sample of 2,671 adult Americans, eighteen years of age or older, representative of the adult population of the United States in terms of age, education, marital status, occupation, size of household, region of the country, and household income.

Methods: The information was taken from the 1992 Survey on Giving and Volunteering conducted by the Gallup Organization through personal in-home interviews with the participants. Not all respondents were used because of missing data. Data was input into an algebraic formula that calculates religious giving. In this equation, religious contributors are a function of the contributor's individual socioeconomic class, demographics, religious behavior, and attitudes. Variables adding and subtracting to a respondent's overall score were, for example, charitable givers, the percentage of a household's income given to charity, number of members in the household, marriage status, confidence in religious organizations, and education. At the end, each respondent's total score calculated the household's total contributions to charity adjusted to include independent and dependent variables.

Results: The data suggest that the marginal propensity to contribute to religious organizations out of income is higher for Protestants than for Catholics and higher for those who tithe than for those who do not. Nevertheless, the data showed that as income rises for both Protestants and Catholics, the amount that each group contributes as a percent of their overall income decreases. Those respondents who are religiously committed tend to give more than those who lack religious commitment, regardless of the denomination. The marginal propensities to contribute are larger for those who say they try to give a certain percentage of their income. Further, the data indicate that marginal propensity to contribute and corresponding income elasticities are significantly larger for Catholics than for Protestants. However, these results lend no credence to the notion of "free riding" by either Catholics or Protestants.

Conclusion: This study reveals that the differences in religious giving by Protestants and Catholics cannot be explained by a higher marginal propensity to give out of income for Protestants. The authors believe that the differences would be more clearly understood with an examination of the denominational infrastructures for giving.

⚓ Friedrichs, R. W. (1960). Alter versus ego: An exploratory assessment of altruism. *American Sociological Review, 25*(4), 496–508.

Objective: To determine the extent to which altruism could be thought of as a measurable quality of social behavior.

Subjects: In all, 280 active members of five social fraternities at Columbia University took part in this study, which made up 95 percent of the entire active membership. The average respondent was a white male between nineteen and twenty in an exclusively Jewish or predominantly Protestant fraternity from an urban family with an annual income of $9,000 or more.

Methods: The subjects were first told what should and should not be defined as altruism. Sixteen hypothetical situations were presented with three possible responses deemed the "egoistic" response, the "altruistic" response, or the "utilitarian" response by a team of independent reviewers. The questionnaire included thirty-five quantifiable items to determine the demographic, social, and social-psychological natures of the respondents.

Results: There is a high correlation between reluctance of change and altruism; the opposite holds for values emphasizing change. Religiosity is relevant to altruism. When urbanization is controlled for, differences in altruism between faith groups disappear. Neurotic behavior often leads to either very high or low levels of altruism. Greater socioeconomic status is correlated with egoistic rather than altruistic behavior. Additionally, involvement in the aspects of economics corresponds with little altruism. Further, altruism is in fact related to tolerance of egoism. If asked to do so, one can give a fairly true estimate of one's own altruism, but it can only be projected by the insightful. Finally, altruism is related to how much one values his or her social relationships. However this study does not show as hypothesized that those who attend houses of worship are more likely to be altruistic, that altruism is conducive to neurotic behavior, that those whose interests lie in the social sciences are more likely to be altruistic than those who are interested in law, business, or engineering, that those whose ideology lies to the liberal left are more apt to be altruistic than those on the conservative right, that altruism is highly correlated with professed ease in social relationships, and that children are significantly more altruistic than the average person.

Conclusion: This study demonstrates that the construct sacred is not only objectively possible, but in fact objectively probable. Thus, since the sacred actually shows to be a good indicator of many facets of life to the sociologist and social psychologist, we ought to look at it often and quantitatively in-depth.

⚓ Hodgkinson, V. A., Weitzman, M. S., & Kirsch, A. D. (1990). From commitment to action: How religious involvement affects giving and volunteering. In *Faith and Philanthropy in America* (pp. 93–114). San Francisco: Jossey-Bass.

Objective: To explore what relationships exist between religious involvement and charitable giving and volunteering of all kind. Also, to explore any connection between activities of religious institutions and charitable contributions made by members of that institution.

Subjects: The group consisted of 2,775 individuals eighteen years or older, chosen to determine the level and extent of giving and volunteering in the "Giving and Volunteering in the United States" survey. African Americans, Hispanics, and affluent Americans were oversampled.

Methods: Weighting procedures were used to create a nationally representative sample. The survey entitled "From Belief to Commitment: The Activities and Finances of Religious Congregations in the United States," which provides data on 1,862 congregations that completed questionnaires to determine their activities, giving, volunteering, and allocation of time and resources, was also utilized. Through detailed institutional responses, it was determined that the 1,862 congregations were nationally representative.

This study analyzed the first survey comparing giving and volunteer behavior among religious congregation members and nonmembers. The second survey was added into the picture to determine similarities between members' giving and volunteer behavior and the activities of the congregations.

Results: Congregations are actively involved in their communities. Members of religious congregations give and volunteer in their communities in greater proportions than nonmembers. In fact, members of religious congregations are half again as likely as nonmembers both to give and to volunteer.

Conclusion: Based on the characteristics of members of religious organizations and the activities of religious congregations, it is deemed likely that what is learned in religious arenas seems to have an influence on giving and volunteering. It has been accepted that religious organizations give Americans opportunities to do good and remind them of their surroundings. Thus, we should not neglect but, in fact, emphasize the role of religion in stimulating giving and volunteering, for it will be extremely valuable toward increasing the social capital in our society.

⌘ Hoge, D. R., & Yang, F. (1994). **Determinants of religious giving in American denominations: Data from two nationwide surveys.** *Review of Religious Research, 36*(2), 123–148.

Objective: To determine how giving varies across denominations, individuals and personal factors.

Subjects: Two highly respected, nationwide surveys were utilized. Approximately 1,500 people eighteen years of age and older who had been interviewed for the General Social Survey in 1987 and again in 1988 and 1989 were used in the study. Additionally, this study utilized the 2,556 personal interviews of persons eighteen years and older commissioned by the Gallup Organization for the Independent Sector and the Catholic Committee on Evangelization.

Methods: Those questions used to measure family income, religious preference, contributions to religious organizations, age, ethnic group, marital status, personal faith, church involvement, background characteristics, and family characteristics were examined and subjected to regression analysis to determine which ones have a significant effect upon giving.

Results: Conservative Protestants give the most, followed by mainline Protestants and then Catholics. The largest denominational discrepancy occurs among the highly educated and high-income persons. As far as individual giving is concerned, about one-fifth of the population gives 75 percent of the total contributions. The highest giving occurs by those with the strongest faith, greatest church involvement, most conservative theology, and most conservative views on moral issues. There was a lack of measures on things like church size, rules of church membership, and satisfaction with church leaders. Finally, conservative Protestantism, that which is most associated with giving, is also positively correlated with greater church attendance.

Conclusion: The denominations vary widely on several topics. Additionally, categorizing Protestants into one category as many previous studies have can, in fact, be misleading. Thus, future studies should make this distinction. Further the Gallup survey showed that levels of giving among denominations are similar, although religious giving does vary significantly. Those who plan on giving ahead of time give more. Finally, as far as volunteering goes, church attendance and activity in the community do the most to predict that variable. Income does not factor into it and, as with giving, Catholics are at the bottom of the hierarchy.

⟡ Hoge, D. R., Zech, C., McNamara, P., & Donahue, M. J. (1998). The value of volunteers as resources for congregations. *Journal for the Scientific Study of Religion* 37(3), 470–480.

Objective: To examine which church members volunteer to help their churches' programs and why. This study also enters into whether church members substitute time for money, or vice versa, when members contribute to their churches and what the members' volunteer work is worth to the churches.

Subjects: Thirty members were picked randomly from churches across the United States. The churches were also picked randomly in each of nine clusters, with one in each region, adjusted to correctly represent the denominations correctly in each region.

Methods: The authors analyzed data from the American Congregational Giving Study, which involved 625 congregations in the United States to produce lists of churches that were representative of the demographics of each region and denomination. Of all the churches asked to participate, 84.8 percent agreed. A four-page questionnaire was mailed to thirty members of each church, of whom 61.2 percent responded, producing $N = 10{,}902$. Adjustments were made to account for variations of church size and to eliminate an "activity bias" according to church attendance rates reported in the General Social Survey, 1991–94.

Results: Among volunteer work directly for a church, the Assemblies of God and Baptists had the highest rates of attending programs and volunteering, and the Catholics had the lowest. Approximately 50 percent of church members did not participate in volunteer activities. Higher education and higher family income were associated with more volunteering, along with higher levels of church attendance. The number of hours volunteered to one's church had high correlations with the amount of money given to the church. Age, education, theological orientation, and attitudes toward the congregation had little correlation with volunteerism. Church attendance was clearly the strongest predictor of volunteer work within the church. There were weak positive correlations between volunteering and monetary contribution, which show that time and money are not substitutable resources in the minds of church members. After analyzing the opportunity cost of volunteering for the individual and the cost of paid workers for the church, it was found that the value of volunteers vary according to denominations, ranging from very valuable to not very valuable.

Conclusion: There is a close association between church attendance and volunteering within the church. The reasons for this may be because members see volunteering as a more rewarding form of personal participation and because parishioners are more likely to ask regular attendees for help. It is clear that participation in the form of attendance does not differ from participation in the form of volunteer work.

꽃 Kniss, F., & Campbell, D. T. (1997). The effect of religious orientation on international relief and development organizations. *Journal for the Scientific Study of Religion, 36*(1), 93–103.

Objective: To find out if differences in religious orientation affect the structures and policies of emergency relief programs and long-term development organizations. This study examines how the substantive content of religious ideas makes for social change.

Subjects: Sixty-three American faith-based organizations and agencies that provide emergency relief and long-term economic development services to communities in Third World countries. The study consists of mostly Protestant or Christian ecumenical organizations with only a few Catholic or Jewish organizations.

Methods: The authors first identified a list of American organizations that were faith-based and had some kind of formal program in international relief and development. The list was comprised by an organization called Interaction. Surveys were then sent to the organizations. The survey asked each organization for their mission statement, their most recent annual report and budget, and their most recent IRS Form 990. Examining these documents from each organization, the authors estimated the degree of religious influence on relief and development. They provided useful information about the how differences in religious tradition affect program policy and about how resources are allocated to various program areas. This study also includes a statistical analysis examining the financial aspects of program policy along with qualitative analyses of each organization's mission statement, religious roots, history, size, location, narrative, a description of program activities, and other independent variables.

Results: Agencies of evangelical and mainline denominations are more likely to give greater importance to relief than to long-term development. The surveys found that 60 percent of the evangelical organizations focus primarily on relief, while fewer than 20 percent focus on development. This leaves the more challenging long-term development programs to ecumenical Para churches (organizations that have volunteers from all sorts of denominations, such as Prison Fellowship or Campus Crusade) and transdenominational agencies. For these liberal Protestant or ecumenical organizations, 50 percent focused primarily on development, while about 30 percent focused on relief.

Conclusion: Differences in religious traditions have a very small effect on the program's size or in the ratio of program costs to overhead costs. Religious traditions have a slightly larger effect on the actual program activities and they have a significant influence on the way organizations justify their activities to their constituents.

Krohn, G. A. (1995). The receipts and benevolences of Presbyterian congregations, 1973–1988. *Journal for the Scientific Study of Religion,* 34(1), 17–34.

Objective: To investigate why benevolences have been falling as a percentage of receipts over the past three decades. An economic model was used to explain these changes examining factors such as membership size, economic forces, and many other variables.

Subjects: A national sample of forty Presbyterian congregations was chosen randomly from 100 congregations across the nation from 1973 to 1988. The sample congregations varied greatly by location and size, residing in eighteen different states and ranging from under 100 members to over 1,000 members.

Methods: A model of religious congregations was used, based on the theory of household production. The congregations produce goods and services such as religious services, religious education, and other services. Congregations are, however, constrained by their given financial limitations. The model was combined with data on the receipts, expenditures, and membership levels of Presbyterian congregations gathered from the Minutes of the General Assembly of the Presbyterian Church. Data on per capita receipts and per capita benevolences were compiled and compared across congregations of various sizes.

Results: There is a trend of increasing per capita receipts. However, except for the two extra large congregations, there was very little increase in per capita benevolences. Per capita country income, number of members, capital expenditures per member, and the poverty rate had effects on both per capita receipts and per capita benevolences. The amount of impact varied across different sizes of congregations. Income tax rates and government transfer payments were unrelated to receipts and benevolences in the study.

Conclusion: While changes have been observed in the Presbyterian congregations, it is still not entirely clear what causes them. For example, poverty rates and government transfer payments do not appear to be a factor in per capita benevolences, which would suggest that national social policy and conditions are not factors. However, poverty rates and transfer payments are only rough measurements of social factors, so more research may be warranted on that front. Moreover, while the household model is useful for analyzing congregational behaviors, future studies may benefit from using other types of models.

Lunn, J., Klay, R., & Douglass, A. (2001). Relationships among giving, church attendance, and religious belief: The case of the Presbyterian Church (USA). *Journal for the Scientific Study of Religion,* 40(4), 765–775.

Objective: To study the relationships between giving, religious belief, and church attendance.

Subjects: Data collected by the Presbyterian Church USA in November 1997 were used. A questionnaire was sent to 6,283 members, elders, and ministers. The return rate of response was 64 percent for members and 77 percent for elders.

Methods: The questionnaire sent to Presbyterian respondents, who were asked to identify themselves as theologically very conservative, moderately conservative, liberal, or very liberal. They had to indicate the frequency of church attendance on a scale that ranged from never to every week. Respondents were then asked to report how much they gave to each of the following: local congregations, special campaigns at local congregations, denominational appeal, religious groups outside the Presbyterian Church, and nonreligious charities.

Results: In general, the more conservative a person was, the more frequently that person attended church. Those who identified themselves as very liberal gave less importance to church attendance than all the other members. A respondent's theological belief was also closely related to giving. Conservative members, despite their lower family income, gave more to local church and other religious organizations. Those who attended church with a greater frequency also gave more, other variables being equal. Other variables affected theological views, such as one's age and family income (the younger the respondent, the higher the family income, the more liberal one's views were).

Conclusion: In general, conservative Presbyterians had a higher per capita giving than the liberal members. The conservative Presbyterians gave more to mostly the local church and non-Presbyterian religious organizations, while their liberal counterparts tended to give more to secular organizations. Presbyterians give their money where they invest their time. Their theological beliefs have an effect on both.

🦋 Lwin, M. O., Williams, J. D., & Lan, L. L. (2002). Social marketing initiatives: National Kidney Foundation's organ donation programs in Singapore. *Journal of Public Policy and Marketing, 21*(1), 66–82.

Objective: To explore the influence spiritual beliefs may have on one's willingness to donate an organ.

Subject: A sample of 368 multiracial Singapore residents who fully completed a survey was chosen. The sample comprised 177 men and 191 women and was nationally representative of Singapore's high literacy rate of 93 percent.

Methods: Adaptation of the basic method used in a previous study based in the United States by Horton and Horton (1991) which constructs a model of a person's willingness to donate an organ. A survey of eighty questions was given. The values data was compiled using a Rokeach's value survey (1973). Twenty-one true false questions regarding organ donation were asked to ascertain the respondent's level of knowledge. Finally, in order to measure spiritual beliefs, an adapted scale of Tobacyk and Milford's was used.

Results: Some trends appeared in the results of the surveys. The more altru-

istic a person's values, the more positive his or her attitude toward organ donation. Such positive relationships were also found with greater levels of factual
knowledge about organ donation. However, the stronger a person's spiritual beliefs, the more negative his or her attitude was toward organ donation.

Conclusion: The relationship between higher levels of spirituality and negative feelings toward organ donation suggests that people with strong spiritual
beliefs may fear that signing an organ donor card will interfere with the afterlife. Further research may be able to shed light onto what causes this correlation. Other demographic or personality variables may not have been taken into
account for this study. Future studies may be able to include more factors to get
a more complete picture of what influences a person's attitude toward organ
donation.

⚖ Monroe, K. R. (1991). John Donne's people: Explaining differences
between rational actors and altruists through cognitive frameworks. *Journal of
Politics, 53*(2), 394–433.

Objective: To determine whether there are any sociocultural predictors of
altruism and selfless behavior. Additionally, this study attempted to find out if
there are similarities in cognitive schema in altruistic beings in respect to their
perception of self and identity. Finally, it aimed to explain the existing differences in altruistic and self-interested beings using economics and rational
choice theory.

Subjects: Typical rational actors (e.g., entrepreneurs), philanthropists, he-
roes, and rescuers of Jews in Nazi-occupied Europe were interviewed.

Methods: The first part of the interview consisted of an hour-long discussion about the subject's life in order to grasp one's conception of self. The second
part was a fourteen-page questionnaire that was used to interview the subjects,
who were divided into four groups. The duration of the interviews ranged from
two to eight hours. The questionnaire was designed to address the hypotheses
from Social Learning Theory, Developmental, Psychological, Social Cognition,
and Economic. The questions were grouped into ten categories: family background, political views, group ties, situational factors, views on human nature,
life's emphasis on duty, view of self, expectations, costs, and empathy.

Results: The study suggests that sociocultural predictors, such as age, gender, education, religion, or socioeconomic background, do not explain altruistic
behavior. Social psychology, evolutionary biology, resource hypothesis from
economics, and anthropological explanations do not explain altruistic behavior.
However, one consistent link among altruistic beings is that they all perceive
themselves as having commonality in humanity with other people.

Conclusion: There are no systematic sociocultural predictors of altruism.
There are similar cognitive frameworks among altruistic beings with respect to
their identity. The altruists' cognitive framework, particularly their view of one's

self in relation to others, differs systematically from that of traditional rational actors. Existing differences in cognitive frameworks do not differentiate between altruists and traditional rational actors. The cognitive framework differences do not reflect prior cultural variations. Existing economical or psychological theories do not explain the pattern of altruistic behavior. However, self-perception among altruists differs significantly from typical rational actors in that they see themselves as sharing strong humanity with others.

☪ Morgan, M. M., Goddard, H. W., & Givens, S. N. (1997). **Factors that influence willingness to help the homeless.** *Journal of Social Distress and the Homeless* 6(1), 45–56.

Objective: To determine which variables relate to people's expressed willingness to assist the homeless. How do individual levels of empathy, measures of religiosity, a liberal political orientation, and socioeconomic status relate to the willingness to help the homeless?

Subjects: Two hundred and four undergraduates (69 males, 135 females) from a major four-year university in the Southeast participated in the present study. Single respondents accounted for 94 percent; white respondents accounted for 89 percent.

Methods: Individual variables measured were empathy, religiosity, household income, political orientation, gender, and race. Dependent variables consisted of questions that unveiled participant willingness to help (giving time or money to a homeless shelter or soup kitchen), reactions to situations involving the homeless, and whether they had ever volunteered/ given money directly to the homeless or a homeless organization.

Results: The majority of participants indicated that they would be willing to help the homeless, and 36 percent indicated a strong interest to help. After examining the independent variables, that which was most clearly associated with intentions to help the homeless was high levels of empathy. Highly expressed religiosity followed levels of empathy. Nonwhites indicated a greater willingness to help the homeless than whites. However, readers should interpret this finding with caution because of the underrepresentation of minorities in the sample. Gender was not significantly associated with an overall willingness to help. However, females were more willing to help than men in specific situations involving the homeless.

Conclusion: Service programs, volunteer organizations, and public service announcements should emphasize the positives of empathy and individual identification in order to increase appeal and to increase assistance. Also, schools, parents, churches, and other social institutions should foster more empathetic attitudes to promote helping behaviors. The authors suggest a mandatory community service requirement in order to remedy social ills and form empathetic attitudes in young adults. Willingness to help homeless people appears strongly related to empathy while moderately related to an individual's level of religiosity, and perhaps to race.

&c? **Morgan, S. P. (1983). A research note on religion and morality: Are religious people nice people?** *Social Forces, 61*(3), 683–692.

Objective: To determine if and how religion relates to morality. Are religious people more friendly and cooperative than less religious ones? How do respondents with a devotional or intrinsic religious orientation appear to other respondents?

Subjects: The National Opinion Research Center interviewed 1,467 respondents to comprise a sample of the noninstitutionalized adult population of the United States.

Methods: This national sample was asked a series of questions to determine whether respondents display good, friendly or cooperative behavior. Those questions include asking whether they have ever intensely disliked someone, whether they usually stop to comfort a crying child, whether they sometimes feel resentful when they don't get their way, whether they like to gossip at times, whether they are always a good listener no matter whom they are talking to, whether they find it particularly difficult to get along with loud-mouthed obnoxious people, and whether there have been occasions when they felt like smashing things. Finally, certain controls were put in place to separate out factors. Further, questions were asked as to their thoughts on other people. Interviewers were asked a series of follow up questions upon completion of the interview to determine the interviewer's opinions of the respondents.

Results: Those heavily involved in prayer do not intensely dislike anyone as often as those who do not engage in prayer frequently. They don't feel resentful as often when they don't get their way. They don't like to gossip as often. They are less often angry or upset. They are more likely to stop and comfort a child, be a good listener, and get along with loud, obnoxious people. They are more likely to trust others and consider others fair and friendly. Additionally, interviewers judged them more cooperative and friendly than the less religious.

Conclusion: Religious people do appear friendlier and more cooperative when it comes to interpersonal relations. However, results could change with questions referring to subjects such as the activities of the government. Therefore, this notion of religious people being friendlier should be accepted in this instance, but more research is needed on the matter when it comes to other opinionated aspects of their lives.

✎ Musick, M. A., Wilson, J., & Bynum, W. B., Jr. (2000). Race and formal volunteering: The differential effects of class and religion. *Social Forces,* 78(4), 1539–1571.

Objective: To determine whether or not racial differences in volunteering, as indicated in a survey suggesting that whites volunteer more than blacks, are attributable to race or to other independent variables. The main focus of this study was to examine the separate impact that race and class have on volunteering. What ulterior reasons do people have for volunteering? Are these ulterior motives more prevalent in the lives of whites or blacks?

Subjects: The data was taken from a panel survey that used a multistage stratified area probability sample of persons twenty-five years of age or older and living in the contiguous United States. A total of 3,617 respondents were the primary study subjects first surveyed in 1986.

Methods: Respondents were interviewed on the categories of volunteering, personal resources, social resources, and cultural resources. There was also a variable that was controlled (e.g., gender, marriage status, the number of children). All were interviewed in wave 1 in 1986; 2,867 persons were reinterviewed in 1989. Of the individuals not surveyed in the second wave, 584 were living but did not respond and 166 had died. Those that neither identified their race as white or black were omitted from the study. Both blacks and persons older than sixty were sampled at twice the rate of others.

Results: Whites volunteer at a rate 50 percent higher than blacks. The number of hours volunteered by whites is 40 percent higher than blacks. Independent variables such as education, income, functional health, informational social interaction, and religious service attendance are positively correlated to volunteerism. Fewer of the independent resources translate into fewer opportunities to volunteer. Whites are asked to volunteer more often than blacks and single parents are least likely to volunteer.

Conclusion: This study proves that ulterior factors contribute to volunteering rates besides the "race effect." Social resources (social interaction with friends, neighbors and relatives) encourage volunteering. Furthermore, since the study demonstrates that blacks have less education, lower incomes, poorer functional health, are more likely to be single parents, less likely to be married with no children, interact less frequently with friends and neighbors, and are less likely to have been asked to volunteer, it is of little surprise that they volunteer at lesser rates than whites. But the study also indicates that those blacks do attend church at greater rates and feel religion plays a greater role in their lives than whites.

❦ Nelson, L. D., & Dynes, R. R. (1976). The impact of devotionalism and attendance on ordinary and emergency helping behavior. *Journal for the Scientific Study of Religion, 15*(1), 47–59.

Objective: To test the hypothesis that there is a positive correlation between devotionalism ("a measure of the intensity of religious organizational participation") and helping behavior. The two functions of religion, which promote this relationship between the two variables, are reinforcement and mobilization.

Subjects: In 1971 a questionnaire was mailed to a sample of male residents of a medium-size city (with approximately 150,000 residents) in the Southwest. The sample was randomly taken from the city telephone directory. The return rate was 70 percent. About eight months prior to the survey, the city had been hit by a tornado that resulted in various helping activities.

Methods: The participants were asked three questions to determine their level of devotionalism: how often table prayers were said in the homes, how often they prayed privately or with their spouse, and how much importance they gave to praying in their lives. Church attendance rates were categorized according to their frequency. The questionnaire also investigated their ordinary and emergency helping behavior. Control variables, such as income, level of education, and age, were examined. The sample used in this study overrepresented individuals with high levels of both education and income.

Results: Religion is a predictor of both ordinary and emergency situations, but there are marked differences in the nature of the religious influence on the different types of situation. Each type of helping has a positive correlation with religiosity. Church attendance has a stronger correlation than devotionalism when it comes to emergency helping. Those two are, in fact, on equal playing fields when it comes to affecting the providing of ordinary goods and funds. However, devotionalism has a greater predictor value than church attendance on informal and formal services. Finally, the donation of emergency funds is predicted by both congregational friendship and church attendance.

Conclusion: Devotionalism predicts ordinary, but not emergency helping behavior, suggesting that nontranscendental reinforcement is either more available or less crucial following emergencies than in other situations. Religion's impact on helping behavior in emergency situations can be explained by the way churches hold organizational participation in a high regard. Results indicate that a comprehensive theory of exchange needs to consider symbolic reinforcement stemming from constructions of transcendentalism as well as social reality.

✑ Olsen, D. V. A., & Caddell, D. (1994). Generous congregations, generous givers: Congregational contexts that stimulate individual giving. *Review of Religious Research, 36*(2), 168–180.

Objective: To analyze why some churchgoers give more money to their congregations than others.

Subjects: The 1,199 United Church of Christ (UCC) congregations that participated in the Church Membership Inventory Study in 1975 and 1978, minus the congregations that had only eleven or fewer respondents. In addition to the congregation subjects, individual subjects were used. The 92,818 people who completed the forty-three-item questionnaire for the Church Membership Inventory Study were included as well.

Methods: The data were used to examine both individual traits and congregation traits, as well as the influence on per capita of congregations and the influence on individual giving. The analysis of entire congregations enabled the researchers to determine what qualities are a part of the most generous congregations. The individual data allowed the researchers to study what makes individuals give more. A comparison of congregation giving and individual giving was used to see which has a greater effect on giving.

Results: There is a large correlation between the amount of money church attendees give and their income level, level of church participation, and desire for the meaning of life. Certain types of UCC churches lead to greater giving. In fact, in these instances, those attendees give more than one would otherwise assume. Attendees give more to more financially stricken congregations than wealthier congregations. However, when membership declines, giving does not become more generous.

Conclusions: Based on the results indicated above, there is little churches can do to increase giving. However, focusing aspects of the UCC church on finding meaning in the members' lives might allow for such an increase. It is questionable, based on one's interpretation of the data, whether or not increased participation may also increase giving. Further research is needed to help in ways that churches could increase their resources through greater charitable giving.

✑ Park, J. Z., & Smith, C. (2000). "To whom much has been given . . .": Religious capital and community volunteerism among churchgoing Protestants. *Journal for the Scientific Study of Religion, 39*(3), 272–286.

Objective: To find if faith factors, specifically religiosity, religious identity, religious socialization, and involvement in religious networks, influence the rate of volunteering.

Subjects: A sample of churchgoing Protestants (*N* = 1,738) from the Pew-funded 1996 Religious Identity and Influence Survey was utilized. This cross-sectional, nationally representative survey probes religious beliefs, identities, and behaviors of Americans over the age of seventeen. Only those Protestants who listed church attendance as two to three times a month or more were selected.

Methods: Utilizing the Religious Identity and Influence Survey, all the questions were answered to gain data on the dependent and independent variables. Thus, respondents answered questions to determine how often they volunteer, the importance of faith, church activity participation, church attendance, religious identity, parents' religious identity, family's importance of faith, attendance at a religious school, children in religious schools, and the number of Christian family and friends.

Results: The greatest predictor of increased involvement in church-related volunteering is church activity participation. Identifying oneself as "evangelical" increases the probability of church-related volunteering. The opposite is true for identifying oneself as "other Protestant." Those who identify their parents with the "mainline identity" have an increased likelihood of church-related volunteering. Larger numbers of Christian family and friends as well as residential stability and greater amounts of education and income also increase volunteering. For volunteering through a non-church program, church activity participation is the most highly correlated with volunteer activities. However, church attendance and nonchurch volunteering have a negative relationship. The other factors that increase the odds of participation are adherence to a major religious tradition, a "charismatic" label, greater levels of "family's importance of faith," education, and income. The only factors that increase the likelihood of general volunteering are increased church activity participation, identifying as evangelical or charismatic, having theologically liberal parents, and having greater levels of education and income.

Conclusion: This study shows that the religious subculture may actually invoke a greater sense of civic responsibility upon its participants. However, while it does show that certain religious qualities increase the likelihood of volunteering, it also indicates that certain religious factors actually decrease volunteering. More research is needed on the influence religion has on volunteering. Only with this will we gain a true measure of the role religion could play on what Robert Putnam (1995) considers the current decline in civic engagement.

Pickering, J. F. (1985). Giving in the Church of England: An econometric analysis. *Applied Economics 17,* 619–632.

Objective: To analyze and explain the variations in levels of financial giving among the forty-two dioceses in the Church of England.

Subjects: The Church of England is composed of over 13,000 parishes, which are grouped into deaneries and then into dioceses, of which there are forty-two in England, excluding one on the Isle of Man. It is estimated that there are approximately 1.8 million active members.

Methods: Due to the fact that all of the abundant statistical information on financial and other matters of the Church is available at the diocesan level, the level of analysis stops there, although this is not ideal due to its relatively high degree of aggregation.

Three different measures of giving were used, two reflecting the per capita giving, and one the absolute levels of giving by dioceses. Not every variable related to the same year, but it is unlikely that this would be a significant problem. Multiple regression analysis was used. The results are based on stepwise analyses with a cutoff after significant variables were included or when the value of coefficient of determination adjusted for variations in the degrees of freedom was maximized.

Results: Employment rates have a significant and sizable influence on giving, perhaps due to a higher projected income. The amount of giving proportionally to one's income is higher with those with a lower income than those with a high income, although high income leads to higher absolute giving. This may be due to the lack of tax relief from these charitable donations in the United Kingdom compared to the United States. There is a negative relationship between giving and church income, suggesting that church members see their giving as a substitute for church income. Higher levels of manpower are associated with higher levels of giving, but it is suggested that higher levels of manpower, that is, an extra clergyman, does not raise the amount of giving from existing church members but merely attracts new members to the church. Because of the negative relationship between the giving per member or as a proportion of income and the percentage of members who are regular Sunday attendees, it is suggested that there is a core of committed members who give proportionally much more than the other members of a church.

Conclusion: It is concluded that, like other studies, this analysis shows that the income elasticity of giving in a church is low. Giving in proportion to income decreases as the level of income increases. This is consistent with the behavioral model of consumer discretionary behavior. Some findings—that of core members who donate more and that of members perceiving their giving as substitutes of church income—are interesting and call for further research.

⟐ Pyle, R. E. (1993). **Faith and commitment to the poor: Theological orientation and support for government assistance measures.** *Sociology of Religion, 54*(3), 385–401.

Objective: To examine the relationship between religious orientation and support for government-assistance spending, in particular, whether there is a relationship between theological conservatism and economic conservatism. Previous studies have found that class, race, and political-party preference have a significant effect on whether one supports government-assistance spending. In this study, Pyle attempts to determine whether theological conservatism has an effect on whether an individual supports government-assistance spending.

Subjects: The respondents from this study are derived from the combined 1983–1989 General Social Surveys conducted by the National Opinion Research Center. The total number of respondents for the study was 10,913. The respondents were classified into twenty-five denominational groupings.

Methods: The GSS survey measured the responses of the respondents to six items used to assess religious group support for government-assistance efforts. Questions were asked measuring support for government action to reduce income differences, measuring support for government efforts to improve the standard of living, asking respondents to characterize current spending levels on the poor, and asking if government should spend less on the poor, meet people's needs, and insure jobs and stable prices. In the regression analysis, class, race, and political-party indicators were also included.

Results: Using regression analysis, the study shows that liberal and moderate Protestants, Jews, Unitarians, and Mormons show less support than the nation as a whole for government-assistance spending. Conservative Protestants, Catholics, and nonaffiliates score near the mean in support for government-assistance spending. Jehovah's Witnesses and black Protestants show strong support for government-assistance efforts. Using multivariate analysis, indicators of race and party affiliation showed the strongest correlations with support to government-assistance spending.

Conclusion: This study found no support for a correlation between fundamentalist views of the Bible and conservative economic restructuring policies. Conservative Protestants were found to be no more likely than liberal or moderate Protestants to adopt conservative economic views on the subject of government-assistance spending. This study calls for more research in order to examine the political and religious differences among the different branches of conservative Protestants in order to determine if there is a relationship to conservative economic principles.

꙰ **Regnerus, M. D., Smith, C., & Sikkink, D. (1998). Who gives to the poor? The influence of religious tradition and political location on the personal generosity of Americans toward the poor.** *Journal for the Scientific Study of Religion, 37*(3), 481–493.

Objective: To determine the effect religion, religiosity, and religious and political viewpoints have when it comes to giving money to organizations that help the poor.

Subjects: Data from the 1996 Pew-funded Religious Identity and Influence Survey is analyzed. This survey is a cross-sectional, nationally representative survey probing religious beliefs, identities, and behaviors of Americans over the age of seventeen. This includes a total of 2,591 completed surveys (2,087 being churchgoing Protestants). Thus weighting procedures were applied to correct for the oversampling of Protestants.

Methods: Questions were asked on the Religious Identity and Influence Survey to determine respondents' religious location by asking about their religious identity and religiosity (determined through church attendance and importance of faith). In order to determine their political location, they were asked if they usually vote Republican and if they have relied on conservative Christian leaders or political organizations, such as the Christian Coalition, to help them decide how to vote in an election. Further, many factors were controlled for, such as race, gender, education, age, income, number of children under eighteen, county population size, southern residence, marital status, and ten-year financial situation before using an ordered logic regression.

Results: The data shows that religion is a factor in giving to organizations that help the poor. In fact, a nonreligious person is only .7 times as likely to give as a religious person is. Within Christianity, evangelical Protestants are most likely to give "a lot," followed by liberal Protestants, then mainline Protestants, and practicing Catholics. However, those that indicated "other religious" give far and away the most. It was also indicated that religiosity is a factor. The more frequent the church attendance and the greater the importance of faith in the person's life, the more he or she gives. Liberal Protestants and devout Catholics are not less likely to give to the poor than others as hypothesized. Additionally, those who label themselves often voting Democratic, Independent, or Republican are insignificantly different. Finally, those who rely on the Christian Coalition do not give less to the poor; they give more.

Conclusion: While some of the results are counterintuitive to previous reports and research, one should realize that only aspects of giving to the poor has been studied. Attitudes toward the poor, support for government aid, and nonfinancial giving have not been analyzed. However, the indications of this study should demonstrate that it would be dangerous to make broad conclusions on this issue as many before have.

✎ Rokeach, M. (1970). **Religious values and social compassion.** *Review of Religious Research* 11, 24–39.

Objective: To determine to what extent religious values are related to a compassionate outlook. It intends to examine the relation between the following of Christianity and views on contemporary (in 1968) social and political issues.

Subjects: In April 1968 1,400 adult Americans took the Value Survey proctored by the National Opinion Research Center. The members of the sample were asked their opinions on numerous issues of the day.

Methods: The Value Survey asked its respondents to give their opinions about issues such as reactions to the assassination of Dr. Martin Luther King, equal rights for blacks in housing, education, and employment, race differences in intelligence, providing the poor with a college education, medical and dental care, a guaranteed income, the student protest movement, and finally the role that churches in general and the National Council of Churches in particular should play in political and social affairs.

Results: Every significant difference and even every difference deemed insignificant pointed to the fact that those who attend church demonstrate themselves to be less compassionate than those who do not attend church. These results stay the same if those who do not go to church are compared with frequent attendees of church or infrequent attendees. The data also indicate no curvilinear relationship between frequency of attending church and social compassion. In fact, those who attended church more often were found to be a bit less compassionate. Thus there is no evidence in this study to support Allport and Ross's (1967) claims.

Conclusion: The findings suggest that religion may be having the opposite effect of its teachings. They demonstrate that religious values may lead to hatred and judgment rather than caring and compassion. The data define the hypocrisy of the church and the researcher calls for someone with an in-depth knowledge of Christianity to explain this result.

⌁ Rushby, W. F., & Thrush, J. C. (1973). Mennonites and social compassion: The Rokeach hypothesis reconsidered. *Review of Religious Research, 15*(1), 16–28.

Objective: To highlight the limitations of Rokeach's 1970 study of "Religious Values and Social Compassion," which indicates that orthodox Christianity promotes uncompassionate social behavior such as dogmatism, bigotry, and authoritarianism.

Subjects: Ninety-one students from Goshen College, Indiana, were randomly selected. Out of this original sample, eighty-one completed the questionnaire (58 were members of Mennonite church, 3 were Mennonite adherents, and 20 were non-Mennonites).

Methods: A sample of Goshen students completed a standard questionnaire concerning their personal backgrounds. They also completed the Rokeach values scale. The Goshen students were then asked to respond to attitude questions. Data examining the results of Goshen students were compared to similar data collected by an introductory psychology class at Michigan State University (1971). Students at Goshen were finally compared with students at Central Michigan University (1968) for a study focused on attitudes toward political and economic issues

Results: The majority of Mennonite students (40 out of 61) gave "salvation" a rank 1 on the Rokeach Terminal Value Scale with a median score of 1.26. Conversely, the data collected at Michigan State University showed that collectively, students ranked "salvation" last with a median score of 16.58. The sample of Mennonite students gave more importance to "salvation" when compared to other groups. The Mennonite students were less establishment-minded than other groups. They only responded in a more establishment-minded on the issue of "inequality." Mennonite students also gave compassionate answers to questions concerning economic social compassion. In this section, the number of compassionate answers increased for Mennonite students of welfare policies were removed from the equation. On questions concerning civil rights, Mennonites more frequently gave compassionate answers than did their non-Mennonite counterparts.

Conclusion: The Mennonites were highly orthodox in their religious beliefs and held fairly compassionate social attitudes. They are therefore an exception to Rokeach's theory that orthodox Christianity promotes uncompassionate social behavior. Furthermore, the authors reject the idea of a causal relationship between religion and social compassion. Instead, conventionality of attitudes seems to be the cause of the relationship between these two variables.

Schwartz, S. H., & Huismans, S. (1995). **Value priorities and religion in four western religions.** *Social Psychology Quarterly, 58*(2), 88–107.

Objective: To study the relation between value priorities and the degree of commitment to religion, which we call religiosity. What are the empirical relations between value priorities and religiosity? Is there a pattern of relations that holds regardless of the specific religion?

Subjects: Data from a cross-cultural project in thirty-eight nations was used to gain respondents in Greece ($N = 400$ Greek Orthodox), the Netherlands ($N = 218$ Protestants), Israel ($N = 635$ Jews), and Spain ($N = 478$ Roman Catholics). These samples were comprised of 48 percent public elementary and high-school teachers, about 22 percent other adults, and around 30 percent university students. All had at least twelve years of formal education.

Methods: To address these questions the research focuses on the values of four religions, Protestantism, Roman Catholicism, Greek Orthodoxy, and Judaism, to which these values were given indexes. The indexes empirically represented a comprehensive set of ten distinct value types. They focus on these religious types in four countries. The four countries are fairly advanced and modernized. Respondents first completed a value survey. After completing this survey, the respondents answered sets of demographic questions, including their religiosity.

Results: The values of the religion seemed to have an effect on the values of the individual. Religion is most often related negatively to attributing importance to values classified in the Benevolence, Tradition, Conformity, and Security types. Associations for values in Achievement and Universalism were less consistent. They found no examples where powers were valuable. Differences existed between the values of the highly religious and the not so highly religious.

Conclusion: The researcher's entire hypothesis was confirmed by the research. There was a very close match between the observed pattern of correlations and the part predicted from the structure of dynamic relations of conflict and compatibility among value types. This finding demonstrates the validity of relating value priorities as an integrated system rather than as an aggregation of loosely related value preferences.

❦ Simmons, R. G., Schimmel, M., & Butterworth, V. A. (1993). The self-image of unrelated bone marrow donors. *Journal of Health and Social Behavior, 34*(3), 285–301.

Objective: To investigate the self-image of bone-marrow donors

Subjects: Individuals who donated bone marrow through the National Marrow Donor Program. Surveys were administered to bone-marrow donors before donating ($N = 849$), one week after donating ($N = 754$), and one year after donating ($N = 370$).

Methods: Bone-marrow donors completed quantitative surveys at three different periods: before donating, one week after donating, and one year after donating. Also, in-depth interviews were conducted on the phone with fifty-two donors at the same three stages. These interviews questioned several social psychological issues. The donors were asked to evaluate the "content" of their self-image such as "If someone asked you, what would you say was your motive for donating?"

Results: Most data for this study came from the in-depth interviews and only a small proportion came from the large-scale quantitative questionnaire. Most donors believed that their traits differed from those of ordinary people and therefore saw their traits as special. In general, they also viewed themselves as altruistic, giving, risk-taking, and adventurous, and saw their donation as a way to actualize these special traits. Out of the fifty-two interviewed, forty-seven saw bone-marrow donation as typical of them, given their distinctive personality traits. The results of this qualitative survey were then compared to the results of a prior study on kidney donors. Kidney donors were different than bone-marrow donors in that the former emphasized their concerns for the relative who needed a kidney while the latter stressed their personality traits. Also, the bone-marrow donors said that their involvement in social groups influenced their decision to donate. An important social identity for donors was their religion. Many also identified themselves helping as professionals and role models. The data show that the health of the recipient one year after donation affected the self-evaluation of the donors as it affected their self-esteem.

Conclusion: Personality traits and social identities influenced the decisions to donate bone marrow. Many donors believed that donation of bone marrow was an actualization of their special and distinct personality traits. An important common trait among the donors was their helpfulness and generosity. The donors also considered social identities important. For some donors, donation boosted their self-evaluation and self-esteem. However, this self-esteem is donation-specific and not global. Unlike kidney donors, there wasn't an overall enhancement of global self-esteem among the donors.

◈ Smidt, C. (1999). **Religion and civic engagement: A comparative analysis.** *Annals of American Academy of Political and Social Science,* 176–192.

Objective: To examine the relationship between religious involvement and civic engagement in a comparative, cross-cultural perspective.

Subjects: The Angus Reid Corporation surveyed 3,000 Canadians and 3,000 Americans via telephone in the fall of 1996.

Methods: Survey data was adjusted via statistical weighting according to each country's gender and age composition in order to create a nationally representative sample. The U.S. sample included a sample booster of 200 Hispanic Americans. Two items within the survey measured social trust within responses given in the Likert scale format. Respondents were also asked whether they were a member of any associations or voluntary organizations and if they were, whether they were actively engaged in the group via volunteer work.

Results: Americans were much more likely than Canadians to report church attendance at a high level. Americans were also more likely to answer positively to questions with religious undertones. Most Americans and Canadians felt they could trust their neighbors, but Americans showed slightly lower levels of social trust despite the fact that they exhibited higher levels of civic engagement. Levels of trust, however, were curvilinearly related to a person's level of church attendance.

Conclusion: Different levels of social trust and civic engagement are associated with many different sociodemographic and religious variables. National differences persisted in all of these analyses. However, church attendance and religious tradition have a positive impact on civic engagement independent of education, level of social trust, race, age, gender, and national residence. More important, levels of social trust and civic engagement differ by specific religious traditions. It suggests that future analyses on social trust and civic engagement should focus on the influence of particular religious traditions on this issue.

◈ Smith, H. L., Fabricatore, A., & Peyrot, M. (1999). **Religiosity and altruism among African American males: The Catholic experience.** *Journal of Black Studies, 29*(4), 579–597.

Objective: To study the religiosity of African American males in comparison to other race/gender groups, and if religious involvement for African American men increases positive attitudes and attitudes toward others. This study also aims to uncover racial and gender differences among those of similar religious groups.

Subjects: Respondents in a parishioner study totaled 20,143 adults (excluding those people who were neither African American nor white). Of these, 5 percent were African American males, 12.9 percent were African American females, 32.1 percent were white males, and 49.9 percent were white females.

Methods: Surveys were distributed to half of the parishes in the metropolitan regions of Baltimore in 1987. The other half of the parishes received the same survey in 1990. Questionnaires were given to those whom attended Mass, including teenagers and nonmembers. The questionnaire consisted of twenty-one statements relating to the parishioners' perception of the impact of their religious experience, their feelings of belonging in the parish, volunteering, and attendance.

Results: The data showed that white Catholics in Baltimore attend Mass significantly more often than African American Catholics. While white Catholics reported attending church once per week, African Americans reported attending several times per month. The data also shows that African Americans rate the impact of their spiritual experience significantly higher than whites. African American males score highest on all measures of altruism. The results show that mass attendance has the highest correlation with hours volunteered. The correlation was much greater than that of feelings of community with hours volunteered, and evidence of impact with hours volunteered. Those African Americans in predominantly black parishes reported much greater personal impact from the whole worship experience, a stronger sense of community, and a greater level of volunteering than those in parishes with only a small number of African Americans.

Conclusion: Results indicate that, while white Catholics attend church more often, African American males report a greater impact of worship experience than white males on all but one item and on most items when compared to white females. African American males also report higher feelings of community and links to their parish. This fact may be due to the notion that African Americans, more so than whites, seek the church as a haven for cultural support.

    ✺ Smith, R. E., Wheeler, G., & Diener, E. (1975). Faith without works: Jesus people, resistance to temptation, and altruism. *Journal of Applied Social Psychology* 5(4), 320–330.

Objective: This study was designed to examine the extent to which involvement in the Jesus movement (a Christian movement on college campuses emphasizing strong religious morals) was directly correlated to an increased tendency to translate moral beliefs into behavior. Utilizing two different phases, the study sought to compare a sample of college-age Jesus people with three other groups (religious, nonreligious, atheists) in order to determine the frequency of both doing good and avoiding evil, and the frequency of performing an altruistic act.

Subjects: The subjects for the study consisted of 402 University of Washington undergraduates enrolled in an introductory psychology course (165 males, 237 females) and included only those students who remained in the course for the entire time and participated in both the resistance-to-temptation and altruism phases of the study.

Methods: The level of religiosity among the respondents was defined through a questionnaire entitled "Survey of Attitudes and Behaviors" that was administered during their first class. It consisted of twenty-seven Likert-type attitude items and another two items about specific behaviors, which sought to determine each student's religiosity. After determining which of the four groups (Jesus people, religious, nonreligious, atheists) each respondent fit in, the first phase of the study consisted of the assessment of resistance to temptation, which was measured by the distribution of a multiple-choice test completed in class. Each student was then given the opportunity to correct the tests at home, using the answer key under the supervision of the honor system. The second phase of the study consisted of the assessment of altruism, in which each student on the final exam of the course was given the opportunity to perform an altruistic act—stating whether or not he or she was interested in volunteering to help mentally challenged children.

Results: Analysis of the frequency of cheating in the eight cells formed by sex of the subject and group membership showed no significant difference in honesty. The Jesus people did not end up having a lower frequency of cheating than did the other three groups. Examination of the frequency of performing an altruistic act showed no significant difference in relation to religion, but there was a significant difference when controlling for sex. Females indicated far more willingness to help. A final analysis assessing the concurrence between cheating and altruism using correlation coefficients indicated that the two classes of moral behavior (cheating and performing an altruistic act) are independent of each other and not affected by religious tendencies.

Conclusion: Neither cheating nor altruistic behavior was significantly affected by level of religious belief. These results indicate that involvement in the Jesus movement does not necessarily result in a greater tendency to do good or avoid evil.

᪥ Testa, M. F., & Slack, K. S. (2002). The gift of kinship foster care. *Children and Youth Services Review, 24*(1&2), 79–108.

Objective: To further define the roles and responsibilities of the family and state in kinship foster-care placements. Kinship foster care is effective and sustainable because of altruistic and reciprocally beneficent acts. This study examines kinship foster care with regards to altruism and reciprocal giving. The authors use the altruistic and reciprocal gift-giving components of kinship care.

Subjects: In 1994 data was collected from 983 relative foster caregivers in the

Chicago and suburban Cook County, Illinois, who are caring for related foster children. Surveys were conducted by individual agencies.

Methods: The survey data from 1994 was linked to a database from the Illinois Department for Children and Family Services in an attempt to create a five-year longitudinal study. The study then examined the placement history of these 983 children from June 1994 to June 1999. Multiple processes were evaluated, such as the rate at which children were removed from kinship foster care and returned to their biological parents and the rate at which children were removed from kinship foster homes and placed in nonrelated foster homes. In examining these processes, the study utilized four explanatory variables: reciprocity, payment incentives, empathy, and duty. Also included in the survey were additional variables the authors referred to as covariates. The several covariates were the size of the kinship network, the income of the caregiver's household, the age of the caregivers, the number of people in the caregiver's household, the behavioral problems of the child, and the caregiver's burden.

Results: The data show that a positive perception of the caregiver toward the birth parents relates to 407 percent higher rates of reunification and a 64 percent lower rate of foster-care replacement. Also, the study suggests that kinship foster caregivers are 74 percent less likely to abandon or harm their foster relationship than nonkinship caregivers. Data show that it was 150 percent more likely for the child to be returned to foster care when payments to the kin caregivers were terminated as opposed to merely reducing payments. Caregiver-child relationships that were characterized as fair to poor were 283 percent more likely to terminate in replacement than those rating the caregiver-child relationship as good to excellent. Children living in homes with infrequent churchgoers were 141 percent more likely to be replaced.

Conclusions: The study reveals that the stability of kinship care is dependent on variables such as reciprocity, payment, empathy, and duty. When examining the duty element in kinship foster-care relationships, religious activity and cultural learning can mitigate selfish or spiteful impulses in the relationship. The authors conclude that policymakers cannot ignore the benefits of kinship foster care and the intrinsic values it provide to the caregiver-child relationship.

Watson, P. J., Hood, R. W., Jr., Morris, R. J., & Hall, J. R. (1984). Empathy, religious orientation, and social desirability. *Journal of Psychology 117,* 211–216.

Objective: To study how religious orientation and social desirability affect empathy.

Subjects: A total of 180 undergraduates (84 males and 96 females) from the University of Tennessee at Chattanooga who were taking introductory psychology classes participated. All students took part in this study voluntarily.

Methods: The students were asked to complete three empathy questionnaires: The Mehrabian and Epstein Empathy Scale, the Hogan Empathy Scale, and the Smith Empathic Personal Questionnaire. Each questionnaire was based on a different definition of empathy and therefore a complex and diverse dimension of the empathy phenomenon could be studied. The Allport and Ross Religious Orientation Scales were administered to distinguish between intrinsic and extrinsic religiosity. The Marlowe-Crowne Social Desirability Scale was used to assess the need for approval. The different variables measured in these questionnaires and scales were analyzed.

Results: There is direct relationship between intrinsic religiosity and empathy, while there is an inverse relationship between extrinsic religiosity and empathy. There was no such correlation between social desirability and empathy.

Conclusion: The data in the study confirm the recent theories that empathy is a component of religiosity. Intrinsic was generally associated with unselfishness while extrinstic became linked with selfish religiousity. Furthermore, the data from this investigation suggest empathetic motivation may have mediated religiosity-helping behavior relationships.

⌘ Will, J. A., & Cochran, J. K. (1995). **God helps those who help themselves?: The effects of religious affiliation, religiosity, and deservedness on generosity toward the poor.** *Sociology of Religion 56,* 327–338.

Objective: To examine the role of religious affiliation and religiosity affecting the levels of generosity to the poor, specifically relating to the issue of deservedness. Current literature offers little insight concerning the influence of religion on the amount of compassion and charity felt for the poor.

Subjects: The respondents of both the General Social Survey and the Factorial Survey Component for 1986 were used.

Methods: The researchers utilized the General Social Survey and its accompanying Factorial Survey Component from 1986. Respondents to this survey were asked to tell the level of economic support (measured in dollars per week) they would award to hypothetical families portrayed in several vignettes. The researchers defined generosity as the level of economic support respondents award the hypothetical welfare families displayed in the situations. They then distinguished among the religious affiliations of the respondents to understand differences in conservative, moderate, and liberal faith groups. There were also measures of actual religiosity: attendance at church and religious identity salience.

Results: Generosity was measured as the dollar amount that people thought these families deserved. The amount of money awarded by the participants depended greatly on the status of the father. If the father wasn't looking for work, his family received less; if he was disabled, they received more; if he was in prison, his family received slightly more. The number of children and the family's cash flow also had a strong effect. However, the marital status of the parents had little effect on the money that was awarded. Compared to liberal Protestants, other Protestant denominations showed significantly reduced levels of generosity. Catholics and nondenominational Christians showed a higher level of generosity than the liberal Protestants. Jews displayed similar levels of generosity as compared to the liberal Protestants. There were also differences in the rate of generosity when it factored in the socioeconomic status of the respondents.

Conclusion: The support for government-assistance programs is more complex than had been previously indicated by previous research. Furthermore, the attitudes of different denominations were illustrated by the respondent's thoughts on the vignettes. No link was found between religious conservatism and economic conservatism. The main focus for the respondents was not exactly their faith groups, but it was more based on who they felt was at fault for the family's situation. There were deep differences in the responses of conservatives and nonconservatives.

Wilson, J., & Janoski, T. (1995). The contribution of religion to volunteer work. *Sociology of Religion, 56*(2), 137–152.

Objective: To find the connection between church membership, church activism, and volunteering. Are those persons raised by religious parents more likely to volunteer than those not brought up by religious parents? Are certain denominations more likely to have volunteers than others? Do churches with greater memberships offer greater rates of volunteering?

Subjects: Those respondents to the Youth-Parent Socialization Panel Study who were interviewed in all three waves and had at least one parent interviewed in each of the first two waves were selected ($N = 924$).

Methods: First differences in volunteering are studied across the four denominational categories and at the two separate ages of twenty-six and thirty-five. Changes in volunteering between the two ages are noted. Then, controlling for age, it is determined if education, occupation, and parental status make a difference in volunteerism. Studies are performed on each separate denomination to see if this is a factor. Further, based on the Youth-Parent Socialization Panel Study that provides the researchers with a group mostly at age eighteen years old in the first wave, twenty-six in the second, and thirty-five in the third, the researchers are able to determine the effect of parental religiosity upon respondents' initiation into volunteering through questions given to both the respondent and the parent on religious affiliation, church attendance, and participation in church-related activities.

Results: Those who are church members are more likely to volunteer than those who are not, especially when the persons are highly involved in the church. As far as Catholics go, the connection between church and volunteering occurs early and stays with the respondents into middle age. Liberal Protestants do not have that cohesive force until middle age. There is almost no connection between church and volunteering among moderate and conservative Protestants. In fact, conservative Protestants likely involve themselves in church-related volunteering rather than secular volunteering.

Conclusion: The relationship between religion and volunteering is actually quite complex. Very little generalization can occur as everything changes based upon denomination and other surrounding circumstances.

⚓ Zokaei, S., & Phillips, D. (2000). Altruism and intergenerational relations among Muslims in Britain. *Current Sociology, 48*(4), 45–58.

Objective: To examine intergenerational altruism and community relations among Muslims in Britain. The study attempts to explore how these values vary within the spheres of family and community, among different ethnic groups, and across different generations.

Subjects: In all, 123 respondents were interviewed. Sixty-five individual interviews were conducted (22 Sheffield, 22 Bradford, 21 London; 50 male, 15 female). Seven group interviews were conducted with thirty retired men (Bradford and Sheffield), six older women (Sheffield), sixteen boys in their early teens (Bradford, London, and Sheffield) and seven young men in their late teens and early twenties (Sheffield). Last, three family interviews (Sheffield; 4 males, 5 females,) were also conducted.

Methods: For this qualitative study, seventy-five in-depth interviews were carried out. Careful sampling was administered in an attempt to accurately reflect the range of national and ethnic diversity among Muslims in Britain. Questions were asked regarding altruism, family background, and their relationships within the local Muslim and non-Muslim communities.

Results: The results found that Islamic family values are still very strong and offer social and personal guidance for many Muslims. The experience of modernity, especially social and geographical mobility, has influenced younger Muslim generations by allowing them to rearrange their identity, usually toward greater individualism. However, they still strongly associate themselves with their Islamic identity. In general, there is a strong sense of altruism within Muslim families. Outside the family, altruism is characterized as particularistic and directed toward kinship groups and other smaller groups. However, the main source of universalistic altruism is from the belief that individuals identify themselves as universal members of the Islamic faith (*ummah*). Data showed that Muslims' extended sense of inclusion is more likely to result in a collective sentiment prevailing over personal sentiment.

Conclusion: Young Muslims, living in a modern welfare state, face uncertainty that often causes confusion, arbitrariness, and temporary diversion from their Islamic values. *Ummah* embodies the desired combination of particularistic and universalistic identities, which could ultimately create a caring society for Muslims and non-Muslims.

References

Allport, G. W. (1966). The religious context of prejudice. *Journal for the Scientific Study of Religion, 5*(3), 447–457.

Allport, G. W., & Ross, J. M. (1967). Personal religious orientation and prejudice. *Journal of Personality and Social Psychology, 5,* 432–443.

Batson, C. D., Dyck, J., Batson, J., Powell, A., McMaster, M., & Griffitt, C. (1988). Five studies testing two new egoistic alternatives to the empathy-altruism hypothesis. *Journal of Personality and Social Psychology, 55,* 52–77.

Horton, R. L., & Horton, P. J. (1991). A model of willingness to become a potential organ donor. *Social Science and Medicine, 33,* 1037–1051.

Lenski, R. C. H. (1961). *The Interpretation of St. Matthew's Gospel.* Minneapolis: Augsburg.

Putnam, R. (1995). Bowling alone: America's declining social capital. *Journal of Democracy, 6*(1), 65–78.

Pyle, R. E. (1993). Faith and commitment to the poor: Theological orientation and support for government assistance measures. *Sociology of Religion, 54*(3), 385–401.

Rokeach, M. (1973). *The nature of human value.* New York: Free Press.

Schwartz, S. H., & Bilsky, W. (1987). Toward a universal psychological structure of human values. *Journal of Personality and Social Psychology, 53,* 550–562.

Spilka, B., Kojetin, B., & McIntosh, D. (1985). Forms and measures of personal faith: Questions, correlates and distinctions. *Journal for the Scientific Study of Religion, 24,* 437–442.

Stark, R., & Glock, C. Y. (1968). *Patterns of religious commitment.* Berkeley: University of California Press.

Tobacyk, J., & Milford, G. (1983). Belief in paranormal phenomena: Assessment instrument development and implications for personality functioning. *Journal of Personality and Social Psychology, 44,* 1029–1037.

CHAPTER 3

Altruism from an Evolutionary Perspective

David Sloan Wilson and Kevin M. Kniffin

W e have assembled a bibliographic database on altruism from an evolutionary perspective that consists of over 1,000 articles and books drawn from the fields of biology, anthropology, and psychology. While not exhaustive, it provides a comprehensive and relatively unbiased sample of the scientific literature. The database consists of citations and abstracts for the entries plus a number of categorizations, all of which can be searched and sorted by categories, authors, key words, and so on. This introduction to the study of altruism from an evolutionary perspective will be followed by an appendix describing the details of the database. We will provide our own analysis of the database in the following chapter, but the database's main virtue is that it can be made available to anyone for his/her own analysis of altruism from an evolutionary perspective.

A Primer on Altruism from an Evolutionary Perspective

Altruism can be defined both psychologically and behaviorally. An act counts as psychologically altruistic when the actor has the goal of helping others as an end in itself rather than as a means to personal ends. An act counts as behaviorally altruistic when it increases the welfare of others at a cost to the actor, regardless of how the actor thinks or feels about the act. Both kinds of altruism can be studied from an evolutionary perspective (Sober & Wilson, 1998), but the evolutionary literature concentrates almost entirely on behavioral altruism. By defining welfare as fitness, the evolution of behaviors that benefit others at the expense of the self can be studied in all organisms, including bacteria and plants that do not have nervous systems and presumably do not think or feel at all. Nevertheless, this panoramic view of behavioral altruism, which encompasses the entire diversity of life, is highly relevant to the evolution of behavioral altruism in humans and forms the background for the evolution of psychological altruism.

Altruism has been studied in a diversity of organisms and from a diversity of theoretical perspectives within evolutionary biology. Indeed, these perspectives are superficially so different that they seem to alter the very character of altruism. In some cases, behavioral altruism appears "genuine" while in other cases it appears only "apparently" self-sacrificial while "really" increasing the fitness of the individual actor. Newcomers to the subject have every reason to be confused when they read that altruism is a form of gene selfishness, that helping kin is really a case of individuals increasing "their" inclusive fitness, or that group selection, the one process that can evolve "genuine" behavioral altruism, is an insignificant evolutionary force.

Before we describe these perspectives and their relationships to each other, it is worth asking why there should be multiple perspectives in the first place. Why can't there be a single theory of altruism from an evolutionary perspective? To appreciate the benefits of multiple perspectives, imagine a group of people standing together trying to map the contours of a mountain at a distance. If they separate to view the mountain from different angles, they will be able to discern the contours more clearly than if they remain together. However, the benefits of separating can only be achieved if they continue talking to each other. Otherwise, they might confuse the same features of the mountain viewed from different angles as different features. In short, multiple perspectives are advantageous, but only if they are clearly related to each other.

The same principle applies to science. One theoretical perspective can "see" a result that was "hidden" from another perspective, but once the result is pointed out, the second perspective can also "see" it. On another occasion, the second perspective might "see" a result that is "hidden" from the first. The different perspectives are entirely consistent with each other and deserve to coexist as long as they pay their way with valid insights not forthcoming from the other perspectives. Notice that the relationship between coexisting perspectives is different than the relationship between competing theories that provides the foundation for the scientific method. Competing theories make different predictions about measurable aspects of the world, and then one is permanently rejected on the basis of the evidence. There is such a thing as being "just plain wrong"! In contrast, coexisting perspectives can only appear to make different predictions, which must be resolvable to maintain their consistency with each other.

Returning to the subject of altruism, "theories" such as "multilevel selection theory," "selfish gene theory," "inclusive fitness theory," and "evolutionary game theory" need to be seen as coexisting perspectives that are mutually consistent with each other rather than as competing theories in which some can be permanently rejected in favor of the others. Much of the confusion in the literature can be traced to a failure to make this distinction, as we will see.

Multilevel Selection Theory

Altruism poses a problem for evolutionary theory because it seems to be disfavored by natural selection. If "survival of the fittest" means surviving and reproducing better than others, how can behavioral altruism possibly evolve? Darwin was the first person to perceive this problem and propose a theoretical solution. Very simply, he pointed out that groups of altruists are more fit than groups of selfish individuals, even though selfish individuals are more fit than altruistic individuals within groups.

To make this idea less abstract, imagine two groups of people. One group is so altruistic that its members cannot even conceive of what it is like to be selfish. It is their instinct to follow the Golden Rule and Ten Commandments. The other group is so selfish that its members cannot conceive of what it is like to be altruistic. Their instinct is purely to gain an advantage over other members of their group, no matter what the cost, like the man in a folktale who was granted a single wish by a genie as long as his neighbor gets double. "Put out one of my eyes!," the man replied.

It is obvious that the first group will function better as a society than the second group, even in purely biological terms. Now imagine that a small amount of migration takes place between the two groups. Altruists that migrate into the selfish group will perish almost immediately, but selfish individuals that migrate into the altruistic group will prosper, gaining from the selflessness of their neighbors while giving nothing in return. In short, the altruistic group is more fit than the selfish group, but selfish individuals are more fit than altruistic individuals within each group.

Darwin's insight was that natural selection is a multilevel process that can take place between groups in a total population in addition to between individuals within groups. Altruism is selectively disadvantageous within groups but can be highly advantageous at the group level. Altruism can be explained as a product of evolution as long as group-level selection is stronger than individual-level selection. Here is Darwin's insight in his own words, with respect to human morality:

It must not be forgotten that although a high standard of morality gives but a slight or no advantage to each individual man and his children over the other men of the same tribe, yet than an increase in the number of well-endowed men and advancement to one tribe over another. There can be no doubt that a tribe including many members who, from possessing in a high degree the spirit of patriotism, fidelity, obedience, courage, and sympathy, were always ready to aid one another, and to sacrifice themselves for the common good, would be victorious over most other tribes; and this would be natural selection. At all times throughout the world tribes have supplanted other tribes, and as morality is one important element in their success, the standard of morality and the number of well-endowed men will thus everywhere tend to rise and increase. (Darwin, 1871, p. 166; cited in Sober & Wilson, 1998, p. 4)

Modern multilevel selection theory can be complicated in its details, but conceptually it is a direct outgrowth of Darwin's original insight. Populations are envisioned as a nested hierarchy of units; genes exist within individuals, individuals exist within social groups, social groups exist within demes (the population within which gene flow occurs), and so on. Fitness differences, and therefore evolutionary change, can occur at all levels of the hierarchy. Genes can evolve by outcompeting other genes in the same individual (between gene/ within individual selection), by causing individuals to outcompete other individuals in the same social group (between individual/within group selection), by causing their social group to outcompete other groups (between group/ within deme selection), and so on. The term *outcompete* can refer to direct interactions, as in Darwin's scenario of the warring tribes, but it also can refer to differences in efficiency that cause some groups to contribute more to the gene pool than others without any direct interactions. Just as a drought tolerant plant can "outcompete" a susceptible plant in the desert without direct interactions, a group of altruists can "outcompete" a group of selfish individuals simply by virtue of its functionality. In any case, this nested series of relative fitness comparisons is the hallmark of multilevel selection theory, within which the question of altruism can be framed as follows: When can a trait evolve by benefiting whole groups, despite being selectively disadvantageous within groups?

Some quick observations will help establish an intuition about multilevel selection and facilitate comparison with other perspectives. First, Darwin envisioned altruism as a trait that is inherited just like any other trait. What makes altruism different is that it is selectively disadvantageous within groups and therefore requires group-level selection to evolve. Similarly, modern multilevel selection models assume that altruism has a genetic basis just like any other trait; the trick, once again, is to explain how altruism evolves despite its selective disadvantage within groups. The point is that multilevel selection models are as gene-centered as any other evolutionary model in terms of focusing on the evolution of a genetically-inherited trait.

Second, multilevel selection theory requires a clear definition of groups. If groups are defined arbitrarily, then the nested series of relative fitness comparisons also becomes arbitrary. Fortunately, there is nothing arbitrary about the way that groups are defined in multilevel selection theory or any other evolutionary model of social behavior. The purpose of an evolutionary model is to predict when a given trait evolves, which requires measuring fitness. When the trait is a social behavior, fitness depends on: a) how a given individual behaves, and b) the behaviors of the other individuals with whom the focal individual interacts. These other individuals constitute the focal individual's group and must be determined accurately to correctly measure fitness. If we exclude individuals who are in fact influencing the focal individual's fitness, we will simply arrive at the wrong answer. If we include individuals who have no effect on the individual's fitness, we will again arrive at the wrong answer. It follows that different traits require different definitions of groups. If we are interested in alarm calls in birds that altruistically warn others at the expense of the caller, all the birds within earshot are the appropriate group because the fitness of an individual depends upon whether it is a caller and the proportion of other callers among the birds within earshot. If we are interested in "prudent predators" that altruistically conserve their resources, all the animals that share the same resources are the appropriate group. If we are interested in gentle "doves" that altruistically share food but lose in competition to belligerent "hawks," the number of individuals that interact at food resources are the appropriate groups. These criteria for defining groups are seldom discussed in general terms, but in practice they are followed for specific traits so naturally that it seems as if discussion is not required. For example, the way that we defined the two human groups in our earlier example seemed natural because interactions were taking place within groups but not between groups.

Third, some readers might object to the simplicity of our examples, which only include two types of organisms, and especially the depiction of altruists as defenseless dupes. What would happen if we included more sophisticated altruists with the ability to avoid selfish individuals, punish selfish individuals, reward each other for good behavior, and so on? Is group selection required to explain these forms of altruism? The only way to answer this question is to build multilevel selection models that include these more sophisticated types. For example, imagine a mutant altruist who expends energy to keep selfish individuals out of its group. Now we have three types of individuals instead of two, but our basic task of determining relative fitness within and among groups has not changed. Many of the papers in our database are devoted to exploring these more complex social games. The general conclusion is that even sophisticated prosocial strategies are vulnerable to subversion from within, if only by other strategies that do not break the rules but also do not share in the punishment of those who do (e.g., Bowles & Gintis, 2002; Boyd & Richerson, 1992; Fehr & Gachter, 2002). Darwin's basic insight that adaptation at the level of groups requires a process of group-level selection has proven remarkably robust—at least according to multilevel selection theory.

Naïve Group Selection and the Rejection of Group Selection in the 1960s

Many of the biologists who followed Darwin did not share his clarity with respect to multilevel selection. Phrases such as "for the good of the individual," "for the good of the group," and "for the good of the species" were used interchangeably as if there was no need to distinguish among them. Higher-level units such as social groups and ecosystems were assumed to function adaptively. Higher-level selection was either ignored entirely or assumed to be strong enough to counteract lower-level selection. As two examples of what has been called "naïve group selection," Emerson (1960) was a termite biologist who envisioned all of nature as like a termite colony, and Wynne-Edwards (1962) interpreted many forms of social behavior as adaptations for preventing populations from overexploiting their resources. The Gaia hypothesis (Lovelock, 1979) is a third and more recent example of naïve group selection, in which the entire earth is envisioned as an organism that regulates its atmosphere without careful discussion of the selection processes that would be required to evolve adaptations at such a large scale.

Naïve group selection came under critical scrutiny in the 1960s, most notably by G. C. Williams (1966) in a book titled *Adaptation and Natural Selection*. Williams forcefully reminded his readers that higher-level adaptations should never be assumed to exist without demonstrating a process of natural selection at the same level. Then he argued that even though altruism and other group-level adaptations could evolve by group selection in principle, group selection in practice was almost invariably too weak to counteract within-group selection. Here is a key passage in which Williams first acknowledged the theoretical soundness of Darwin's original insight, but then cast group selection into oblivion on empirical grounds.

It is universally conceded by those who have seriously concerned themselves with this problem that . . . group-related adaptations must be attributed to the natural selection of alternative groups of individuals and that the natural selection of alternative alleles within in populations will be opposed to this development. I am in entire agreement with the reasoning behind this conclusion. Only by a theory of between-group selection could we achieve a scientific explanation of group-related adaptations. However, I would question one of the premises on which the reasoning is based. Chapters 5 to 8 will be primarily a defense of the thesis that group-related adaptations do not, in fact, exist. (Williams, 1966, pp. 92–93)

The arguments of Williams and others were so successful that it became a heresy to invoke group selection in any form, leading to what Wilson (2002) has called an "age of individualism" in evolutionary biology. A number of theoretical frameworks arose to explain the evolution of "apparently" altruistic behavior in more individualistic terms. The history of this period is recounted in more detail elsewhere (Sober & Wilson, 1998; Wilson, 1983), but for the purposes of this essay two points need to be stressed. First, Williams's empirical claim is a straightforward example of the scientific method that has nothing to do with differences in perspective. For any given trait that seems altruistic, we merely need to: a) identify the relevant groups; b) examine the relative fitness of the trait within groups; and c) examine the relative fitness of the trait between groups. If all traits evolve by within-group selection, no matter how altruistic in appearance, then Williams is right and group selection deserves to be rejected. If some traits are indeed selectively disadvantageous within groups and evolve on the strength of group selection, then Williams is wrong and the importance of group selection needs to be evaluated on a trait-by-trait basis. No one at the time talked about multiple perspectives or claimed that what counts as group selection depends on how you look at it. As Williams himself states in the passage quoted above, there was near-universal consensus on what counts as group selection and the need for group selection to explain higher-level adaptations. It was the universal consensus that made Williams's verdict seen so decisive.

Second, the theories that were proposed as alternatives to group selection proved to be nothing of the sort. They, too, assume the existence of groups and the "apparently" altruistic traits are selectively disadvantageous within these groups, exactly as Darwin proposed. Of course, the fact that group selection had been rejected in name only was discovered in retrospect, since the "theories" were self-consciously developed as alternatives to group selection. In hindsight, these "theories" were merely different perspectives that viewed the process of multilevel selection from different angles. In no case was an alternative perspective developed in full knowledge that it was merely an alternative perspective.

For the rest of this essay we will describe the theoretical frameworks that claimed to explain the evolution of altruism without invoking group selection. Then we will show how they contain group selection within their own structure. It is not our purpose to diminish the importance of these theories by calling them special cases of multilevel selection theory. In each case they have revealed critical factors in the evolution of altruism, such as genetic relatedness and repeated interactions among nonrelatives, which remain important no matter what the perspective. In addition to appreciating the separate insights, it is also important to achieve a unified evolutionary theory of altruism and understand that the individualistic appearance of some perspectives does not alter the fundamental fact that behaviors can evolve "for the good of the group," despite being selectively disadvantageous within groups.

Selfish Genes and Extended Phenotypes

In addition to his claim that genes almost never evolve by between-group selection, Williams also developed the concept of genes as replicators, or the "fundamental unit of selection." Williams said that, in a sexually reproducing population, individuals cannot be units of selection because each individual is unique. The combination of genes that made up Socrates will never come again, no matter how reproductively successful he was. For something to be a unit of selection, it must persist for multiple generations. Sexually reproducing individuals do not have this property, but genes do. Therefore, genes have a special status as a "unit of selection" not shared by sexually-reproducing individuals, much less groups. Richard Dawkins (1976) developed this idea in his famous book *The Selfish Gene*. Williams and Dawkins both regarded this gene-centered view as a powerful argument against group selection, and even today it is common to read that group selection doesn't work because the gene is the fundamental unit of selection.

The gene's-eye view is a useful perspective as a bookkeeping device for recording evolutionary change. A given gene can exist in association with many other genes within individuals, which in turn can exist in association with many other individuals within social groups, but it is the net effect of all these contexts that determines whether the gene will increase or decrease in frequency in the total population. It is easy to portray this accounting method metaphorically as like a selfish agent who cares only about increasing copies of itself. However, in retrospect, it has become obvious that the gene-centered view, whatever its other merits, says nothing whatsoever about multilevel selection, as both Williams (1992) and Dawkins (1982) eventually acknowledged. The criterion for being a replicator is based on *permanence,* whereas the criterion for being a level of selection is based on *where fitness differences reside in the biological hierarchy.* Comparing the two is like comparing apples and oranges. Put another way, even after we decide that genes are the replicators, we still need to decide whether they evolve by between-gene/within-individual selection, between-individual/within-group selection, between-group/within-deme selection, or another combination.

It is puzzling that the concept of genes as replicators could ever have been taken as an argument against group selection. In many respects, Williams (1966) was interpreting basic concepts in population genetics theory for a wider biological audience. Natural selection has always been defined within population genetics theory as a change in gene frequency, so the focus on genes is not new. Individuals have always been regarded as units that differ in fitness but that dissociate into genes during sexual reproduction. Group selection models have always been as gene-centered as other evolutionary models, in the sense of asking how a genetically inherited trait evolves, as we described earlier. So why should the basic fact that traits are coded by genes ever be used as an argument against group selection? Perhaps the phrase "unit of selection" to describe replicators has something to do with it, since the same phrase is used to describe the units that differ in fitness in multilevel selection theory. In any case, even Williams and Dawkins shrugged their shoulders when asked this question by one of us (David Sloan Wilson), replying that the 1960s were a long time ago (personal communication).

Once we realize that selfish gene theory in its entirety does not constitute an argument against group selection, how do we go about evaluating group selection within the framework of selfish gene theory? A hint is provided by the fact that sexually reproducing individuals do not qualify as replicators but remain highly functional units. The replicator concept must be supplemented by a second concept—vehicles—to explain the obvious functionality of individual organisms. Individuals are vehicles of selection because the genes in an individual are "in the same boat" and can benefit themselves only by working together. In other words, genes evolve by causing individuals to outcompete other individuals rather than by outcompeting other genes within the same individual. The vehicle concept begins to provide the nested comparison of relative fitnesses that is the hallmark of multilevel selection theory. To evaluate altruism and group selection within the framework of selfish gene theory, we must evaluate groups as vehicles of selection rather than as replicators. Whenever a trait evolves by between-group/within-deme selection in a multilevel selection model, the group will be a vehicle of selection in a selfish gene model. The two theoretical frameworks must converge in this way because they differ only in perspective, like two people viewing a mountain from different angles.

Dawkins (1982) also developed the concept of genes having extended phenotypes that reach outside the body of the individuals containing the genes. Once again, whatever the merits of this idea, in its totality it does not constitute an argument against altruism or group selection. As one example of an extended phenotype, consider a gene in a male mouse that produces a pheromone that alters the hormones of a female in a way that causes her to mate with the male. This is an extended phenotype that evolves by between-individual/within-group selection. It doesn't evolve by between-gene/within-individual selection because the gene benefits all the genes in the individual male. Neither does it evolve by between-group/within-deme selection because groups containing the male do not contribute more to the gene pool than other groups. As a second example of an extended phenotype, consider a gene in a beaver that causes it to work hard to build a dam. This gene does not evolve by between-gene/within-individual selection or between-individual/within-group selection. On the contrary, beavers who work hard to build a dam are providing a public good at their own expense that can be enjoyed by freeloading beavers who do not build dams. The gene for dam building evolves by between-group/within-deme selection and qualifies as altruistic as the word has always been defined within multilevel selection theory. To summarize, saying that a gene has an extended phenotype says nothing about how it evolves in a nested hierarchy of units and therefore says nothing about its status as altruistic.

Inclusive Fitness Theory

Hamilton's theory of inclusive fitness (1964; relabeled "kin selection" by Maynard Smith, 1964) was widely acclaimed as a way to explain apparent altruism without invoking group selection. To follow Hamilton's logic and why it makes altruism appear only apparent, consider a dominant mutation (*A*) that turns a single individual into an altruist (*Aa*), in an otherwise selfish (*aa*) population. Suppose that the altruism is expressed only during the juvenile stage of the life cycle and that the mutant survives to mate and have a clutch of offspring. It will mate with an *aa* individual and their clutch will consist on average of 50 percent altruists (*Aa*) and 50 percent selfish individuals (*aa*). Now imagine that these siblings remain together as a group and interact only with each other. The altruistic behavior decreases the fitness of the actor by an amount *c* and increases the fitness of a single recipient by an amount *b*. What values of *b* and *c* will cause a net increase in the number of altruistic genes? The answer is any combination that satisfies the inequality $b/2 - c > 0$. The cost always decreases the number of *A* genes because only altruists behave altruistically. The benefit must be discounted by one half because the recipient of the altruism is an altruist only 50 percent of the time on average. Thus, the altruistic behavior will increase the number of altruistic genes if the benefit to the recipient is greater than twice the cost to the actor. This is one example of what became known as Hamilton's rule, whose general formulation is $br - c > 0$, where *r* is a coefficient of relatedness that ranges from 1 (for identical twins) to 0 (for nonrelatives).

Hamilton defined an individual's inclusive fitness as the effect of an individual on its genes identical by descent, regardless of whether the genes reside in the body of the individual or in the bodies of relatives. Thus, when Hamilton's rule is satisfied, the altruists in Hamilton's model do not increase their classical fitness $(- c)$ but they do increase their inclusive fitness $(br - c)$. Of course, once we think of altruism as a way for an individual to maximize its "own" inclusive fitness, it ceases to appear altruistic; hence the tendency for some (but not all) authors to add the qualifier "apparent" to altruism among relatives.

So far, so good, but how can we relate Hamilton's inclusive fitness theory to multilevel selection theory? The calculation that we performed tells us when there will be a net increase in the number of altruistic genes, but it does not perform the nested series of relative fitness comparisons that multilevel selection theory requires. Returning to our single of group of siblings with 50 percent altruists, the nonaltruists are more fit than the altruists because they are equally likely to serve as recipients and never pay the cost. The altruists may have benefited each other, but they benefited their selfish siblings even more, reducing the *proportion* of altruistic genes in the group to below 50 percent. On the other hand, the group with 50 percent altruists contributes more to the total gene pool than the other groups with 0 percent altruists. Hamilton's model includes the information that we need to make the nested series of relative fitness comparisons, and when we do we discover that altruism is selectively disadvantageous within groups and evolves only by between-group selection, exactly as

Darwin proposed. Hamilton was right that altruism can evolve among genetic relatives, but wrong to regard his theory as an alternative to group selection. In fact, genetic relatedness facilitates the evolution of altruism by increasing the strength of between-group selection (by increasing variation among groups) compared to within-group selection.

Hamilton himself realized his mistake when he encountered the work of George Price (1970, 1972), which explicitly partitions total gene frequency change into within- and between-group components. He described his revised interpretation of kin selection as a form of group selection in a 1975 paper, in private correspondence (Schwartz 2000), and in his autobiographical essays (Hamilton 1996). Nearly all theoretical biologists are in agreement on this issue, but many other biologists continue to portray group selection as a failed theory and kin selection as a triumphant alternative.

When the relationship between inclusive fitness theory and multilevel selection theory is clearly understood, genealogical relatedness emerges as only one of numerous important factors in the evolution of altruism. Sober and Wilson put it this way:

For all its insights, kin selection theory has played the role of a powerful spotlight that rivets our attention on genetic relatedness. In the center of the spotlight stand identical twins, who are expected to be totally altruistic toward each other. The light fades as genetic relatedness declines, with unrelated individuals standing in the darkness. How can a group of unrelated individuals behave as an adaptive unit when the members have no genetic interest in one another?

Replacing kin selection theory with multilevel selection theory is like shutting off the spotlight and illuminating the entire stage. Genealogical relatedness is suddenly seen as only one of many factors that can influence the fundamental ingredients of natural selection—phenotypic variation, heritability, and fitness consequences. The random assortment of genes into individuals provides all the raw material that is needed to evolve individual-level adaptations; the random assortment of individuals into groups provides similar raw material for group-level adaptations. Mechanisms of nonrandom assortment exist that can allow strong altruism to evolve among nonrelatives. Nothing could be clearer from the standpoint of multilevel selection theory, and nothing could be more obscure from the standpoint of kin selection theory. The implications of seeing the full stage extend to virtually every topic studied in the evolution of social behavior and of multispecies interactions. (1998, p. 332)

Reciprocal Altruism and Evolutionary Game Theory

A third effort to explain altruism without invoking group selection was called reciprocal altruism by Trivers (1971) and developed into a theoretical framework called N-person evolutionary game theory, where N is the number of individuals that socially interact with each other (Axelrod, 1984; Maynard Smith, 1982). As an example, consider a population in which fraction p of the population is altruistic and the rest $(1 - p)$ are selfish. Social interactions take place in groups of size $N = 2$ (two-person game theory) and altruists benefit their partner (b) at a cost to themselves (c), just as in Hamilton's model. In a pair of altruists, each member gets $(b - c)$, which is their own cost plus the benefit from their partner. In a mixed pair the altruist gets c and the selfish partner gets b. In a pair of selfish individuals, neither member gets anything. If the pairs form at random, then the average altruist and selfish individual in the global population will have the following fitnesses:

Fitness of average altruist

$$W_A = p\,(b - c) + (1 - p)(-c)$$

Fitness of average selfish individual

$$W_S = p(b) + (1 - p)(0)$$

The "payoffs" for interacting with altruists and selfish individuals are multiplied by the probability of interacting with these two types respectively. W_S is greater than W_A in this model for all values of p, so selfishness evolves and altruism goes extinct. Before continuing, however, let's look at this model from within the framework of multilevel selection theory. If groups are the sets of individuals that interact with each other, they are clearly defined by N in N-person game theory and as pairs in this particular model. Selfish individuals are more fit than altruists within groups and are therefore favored by between-individual/within-group selection. However, altruists are favored by between-group/within-deme selection because groups of altruists contribute more to the gene pool ($2b - 2c$) than mixed groups ($b - c$), which in turn contribute more than selfish individuals (0). Thus, altruism is selectively disadvantageous within groups and favored by group selection in this model, as Darwin envisioned and as in all the other models we have reviewed so far; in this case, within-group selection outweighs between-group selection and selfishness prevails.

This model can be elaborated in many ways, and in some cases the balance between levels of selection favors the altruists. For example, in groups that persist for a number of social interactions, the famous tit-for-tat strategy starts altruistically but copies the previous behavior of its partner on subsequent interactions (Axelrod and Hamilton, 1981). In a population in which a fraction p are tit-for-tats and the rest $(1 - p)$ are selfish, and in which the pairs last for an average of I interactions, the average fitness of the two types in the total population looks like this:

Fitness of average tit-for-tat

$$W_T = pI(b - c) + (1 - p)(- c)$$

Fitness of average selfish individual

$$W_S = p(b) + (1 - p)0$$

Pairs of tit-for-tat trade benefits for all *I* interactions. In mixed groups, the tit-for-tat gets burned during the first interaction but then reverts to selfishness for the rest of the relationship. The selfish individual in a mixed group gets a free *b* only during the first interaction and pairs of selfish individuals get nothing throughout their relationship. If we perform our nested series of relative fitness comparisons, we see that conditionally altruistic tit-for-tat strategy is selectively disadvantageous within groups but advantageous at the group level, just like the unconditional altruist in the first model. However, the fitness differences between groups are much greater due to the fact that pairs of altruists are so much more productive than the other groups. This difference shifts the balance between levels of selection in favor of group selection and tit-for-tat evolves; that is, the average tit-for-tat is more fit than the average selfish individual in the total population ($W_T > W_S$), even though tit-for-tat is less fit than the selfish individual within each and every mixed group. So, tit-for-tat evolves by between-group selection, right? That's not how the first evolutionary game theorists saw it. They defined individual selection as fitness averaged across the groups (the Ws), not fitnesses within groups. Based on this definition, selfishness evolves by individual selection in the first model ($W_S > W_A$) and tit-for-tat evolves by individual selection in the second model ($W_T > W_S$). Since tit-for-tat evolves by individual selection, it is only "apparently" altruistic.

It is interesting that Anatol Rapoport, the person who submitted the tit-for-tat strategy in two famous computer simulation tournaments sponsored by Robert Axelrod (1980a,b), did not think of the strategy of selfishness. Although Rapoport was not familiar with multilevel selection theory, the following passage beautifully illustrates multilevel thinking and how altruism must be defined on the basis of *local* social interactions to be seen clearly.

The most interesting and instructive result of those contests was the initial misconception about the reason for the success of Tit-for-tat. This author, who submitted the program, was invited to give talks about the contest. In the discussions that followed, it became clear that many people had believed this program was "unbeatable." . . . The effects of ideological commitments on interpretations of evolution were never more conspicuous. To me, the most welcome result of Axelrod's experiments was the opportunity they provided for pointing out that "nice guys sometimes come in first" and for putting this homily into a scientific perspective. . . .

Altruism is naturally defined as a predisposition to act so as to benefit others at a cost to oneself. But this definition applies only to interactions between a pair of individuals. In a population, altruistic behavior by many may result in benefits to many, including the altruists.

Returning to the Prisoner's Dilemma contests, it is easy to see that Tit-for-tat is anything but "unbeatable." In fact, it is eminently beatable. The only way a player of iterated Prisoner's Dilemma can get a higher score than the coplayer is by playing more D's [the selfish behavioral option] than the other, for only when one plays D while the other plays C [the altruistic behavioral option] does one get a larger payoff. But Tit-for-tat can never get more D's than its partner in a sequential play contest, because the only time it can play D is after the coplayer has played D. Therefore, in every paired encounter, Tit-for-tat must either lose or draw. It can never win a paired encounter.

The reason Tit-for-tat won both contests is because the "more aggressive" or "smarter" strategies beat each other. . . . In fact, the one unbeatable program is the one that prescribes unconditional D, since no other program can possibly play more D's than it. But in Axelrod's contests, two All-D programs playing each other would secure 1 point per play, whereas two Tit-for-tat . . . would get 3 points per play. (Rapoport, 1991, pp. 92–93)

As with inclusive fitness theory, a number of important ideas have developed under the names of game theory and reciprocal altruism that remain important from all perspectives. Among these important ideas are indirect reciprocity (Alexander, 1987), which extend beyond pairwise interactions, and mechanisms such as commitment (Frank, 1988) and moralistic punishment for preventing cheating in reciprocal interactions (Boyd & Richerson, 1992). From a multilevel evolutionary perspective, these mechanisms often emerge as forms of low-cost altruism that promote behaviors that would qualify as highly altruistic if performed voluntarily (Sober & Wilson, 1998, chap. 4).

The Importance of Culture in the Evolution of Altruism

In many respects, the models that explain the evolution of altruism in non-human species are equally relevant to humans. In addition, cultural processes are vastly more elaborated in our species than in any other species, which may help explain our own brand of ultrasociality. A number of authors have speculated along these lines, including Boyd and Richerson (1985), Campbell (1975), Dawkins (1976; see also Blackmore, 1999), and Wilson (2002). As with strictly genetic theories of altruism, cultural theories are diverse and poorly integrated with each other. As Wilson put it:

Although culture has for many decades been envisioned as an evolutionary process, there is little agreement about its precise nature, importance, or relationship to genetic evolution. The most severe critics of sociobiology rely upon culture as an alternative, which they think can be studied without reference to biology (e.g., Sahlins 1976). Some biologists regard culture as a handmaiden of genetic evolution that evolves the same phenotypic adaptations, only faster (e.g., Alexander 1979, 1987). Other biologists try to decompose culture into gene-like units that do not necessarily benefit their human hosts (e.g., Dawkins 1976; Blackmore 1999). Instead, they can act more like disease organisms as they spread from head to head. (2002, p. 28)

Perhaps the most important point to emphasize in the context of this essay is that cultural evolution is a multilevel process no less than genetic evolution. A cultural trait can spread at the expense of other traits within the same group by causing the entire group to prevail against other groups, and so on. Some forms of cultural transmission can vastly facilitate group selection and, therefore, the evolution of altruism, as emphasized by Boyd and Richerson (1985) and Boehm (1999). However, there is nothing intrinsic about cultural evolution that makes it favorable for the evolution of altruism. The cultural transmission rule, "copy the most successful individual in your group," would be disastrous for the evolution of altruism because it would cause everyone to emulate selfishness. If cultural processes promote the evolution of altruism in human societies, it is because a long period of gene-culture coevolution has produced this effect, compared to many other effects that could be imagined.

Conclusion

The puzzle of behavioral altruism begins with the fact that by providing benefits to their social partners at their own expense, altruists place themselves at a selective disadvantage within their own groups. The solution to the puzzle is that groups with more altruists do better as collectives than groups with fewer altruists. It is impossible to see either the puzzle or its solution without looking at fitness differences within and between groups. Of course, after we see the levels of selection separately we must put them together to calculate their combined effect on evolutionary change in the total population. Whichever type evolves—altruistic or selfish—will be more fit by definition, than the type that doesn't evolve in the total population.

All of the theories that were developed as alternatives to group selection share some things in common. They all assume the existence of groups and define groups as they are defined in multilevel selection theory. They all contain the information required to do the nested series of relative fitness comparisons, but they do not define altruism and selfishness on the basis of relative fitness within and between groups. Instead, the type that is most fit in the total population is labeled "selfish" and said to evolve by "individual selection," which makes selfishness a vacuous term for "anything that evolves" and defines both altruism and group selection out of existence.

In the introduction we said that multiple theoretical perspectives can be useful but only if they are clearly related to each other. It should be obvious from our essay that this was initially not the case for the perspectives outlined above. They were initially imagined as competing theories and their status as coexisting perspectives only emerged over the course of years and decades. This makes the evolutionary literature on altruism confusing because the task of relating the perspectives to each other is left to the reader rather than the authors. Although a new "universal consensus" is emerging, the process has been slow, in part because science is a sociological process in addition to an intellectual process and former heresies are not revived easily, even when their revival is richly deserved. Textbooks are seriously out of date and even some of the most recent articles in our database portray group selection as a failed theory replaced by triumphant individualistic alternatives. This essay will hopefully equip the reader with the intellectual tools to relate the various theoretical frameworks to each other.

When the dust settles, we are left with a picture of altruism remarkably close to Darwin's original vision and some pleasing generalities. Altruism and other prosocial traits can evolve, but only by a process of group selection. Williams was wrong when he claimed that between-group selection is invariably weak compared to within-group selection. Between-group selection is often a force to be reckoned with, and its importance for any particular trait must be determined on a case-by-case basis. Fortunately, the question of whether a trait evolves by within- or between-group selection can be straightforward. The appropriate groupings can be identified and fitness differences within and between groups can be measured. The universal consensus that Williams referred to in the passage quoted above can be regained and the answer can be equally decisive, even if it is a different answer than what he had in mind. The advantages of multiple perspectives can be realized without confusion by clearly relating the perspectives to each other.

Our database on altruism from an evolutionary perspective includes many fascinating empirical observations, experiments, and theoretical results that are not included in this essay, but which, we hope, can be better appreciated with this essay in mind. We will provide our own more advanced and detailed review in a second paper, but the reader need not wait for our review to enjoy the database on his or her own.

Appendix

The bibliography in the following chapter is the product of systematic searches conducted October 15–26, 2001. We chose Biological Abstracts, Sociological Abstracts, and Anthropological Literature as the source databases for our searches. We selected these sources because they represent different disciplinary foci, and they have superior reach when compared with other available options. Biological Abstracts and Sociological Abstracts are both Silverplatter-brand databases, while Anthropological Literature is organized and administered by Harvard University's Tozzer Library.

We initially searched the Biological Abstracts database for altruism and found 212 references. We also searched BasicBIOSIS for altruism, finding 88 references. Cross-checking the two reference-sets, we found that 66 of the 88 BasicBIOSIS references were already found through the Biological Abstracts search. Most of the articles found only in BasicBIOSIS were published in popular, nonpeer-review media, including *Newsweek* and the *New Yorker*. For this reason, we felt comfortable not including BasicBIOSIS in our review.

We selected a set of search terms with the intention of finding research reports that relate to "evolution and altruism" even if the word "altruism" is not explicitly mentioned. Therefore, we searched for reports containing the phrases "altruism," "cooperation and evolution," "kin selection," "group selection," "multilevel selection," "multi-level selection," and "reciprocity and evolution."

For the anthropological and sociological databases, we delimited the "altruism" search term by adding "evolution" in order to maintain a focus on research with direct biological relations. This was the only difference in our application of search terms across databases. We should note as background, however, that Biological Abstracts and Sociological Abstracts each allow searches to check for terms in the title or abstract of an article while a simple keyword search is the most powerful option available through Anthropological Literature. This is consistent with the fact that Anthropological Literature does not store abstracts of the articles.

After saving the results of each search term within each database into separate text files, we eventually created EndNote Libraries reflecting the yield from each set of searches. While there were variable numbers of articles retrieved by more than one search term, we cleaned the EndNote Libraries so that no duplicates (or triplicates) were saved. This process left us with 93 references (without abstracts) from the Anthropological Literature, 317 references from Sociological Abstracts, and 1,018 references from Biological Abstracts. A combined EndNote Library incorporating the three database-specific libraries yielded a collection of 1,373 nonduplicated references (most with abstracts).

References were then imported into FileMakerPro version 5.5, which is more general and comprehensive as searchable database software than End-Note. We classified citations according to whether they were empirically and/or theoretically focused; we identified whether each item did or did not concern humans, in general, and religion, in particular. We also discarded references whose abstracts clearly indicated that they lacked relevance to our subject. For example, many discarded articles concerned issues such as the "evolution" of social constructs like poverty. After discarding such articles, we were left with more than 900 articles. Many of the references included complete abstracts, but several hundred abstracts had to be scanned from hard copies. For those articles lacking abstracts, we scanned the first paragraph as a substitute.

The searchable nature of our database permits query-driven reviews. Two preliminary sets of questions we have chosen to answer through the database are:

•What is the taxonomic distribution of subjects considered by researchers?
•How do the researchers consider the evolution of altruism?

We present answers to these and related questions below.

Predictably, much of the research that has considered the evolution of altruism focuses on social insect communities. In addition, however, we found articles considering altruism within plant and bacteria communities as well as bird and human groups.

In order to test our subjective impressions against quantitative measures of the database's content, we used the "find" function within FileMakerPro to search for "bacteria," "plant," "insect," "bird," "reptile," "mammal," and "human" in the article abstracts. We also searched for "bee," "ant," and "termite" within the category of insects. Table 3.1 shows the total number of entries per search term and the percentage of all abstracts including the search term.

The pattern of table 3.1's data is consistent with our subjective impressions of the database, but readers should be careful about making claims based on abstract-word searches. For example, while abstract-word searching yielded 107 articles about "human," we coded 222 articles as related to the evolution of altruism within human communities. This discrepancy reflects the "added-value" of our time-intensive coding system. The fact that "insect" is not included in most of the abstracts including "bee" demonstrates another reason why keyword-counts need to be scrutinized.

Within the set of studies about human evolution, we took special note of four articles that we coded for their focus on the subject of religion.

With regard to the second general question of how researchers approach the evolution of altruism, we categorized articles according to whether they pursued theoretical and/or empirical studies of altruism. We found a theoretical focus in 559 articles and an empirical focus in 356 entries. We defined "empirical" to include controlled experiments and naturalistic observations.

Throughout the database, we found that a large number of articles focused heavily upon questions related to kin selection. To help the reader quantify this impression, table 3.2 reports the results of word searches through the database's abstracts. We can see that "gene selection," "kin selection," and "individual selection" are frequently used by researchers. "Group selection" is used in a significant number of abstracts as well, but our experience is that this label in particular is used to describe a wide range of phenomena including species-, ecosystem-, and planetary-level selection. In contrast, articles mentioning the concept "multilevel

Table 3.1. Number and percentage of abstracts containing names of each kingdom

Bacteria	16	(1.8%)	Termite	8	(0.9)
Plant	32	(3.5)	Bird	58	(6.4)
Insect	59	(6.5)	Reptile	0	(0.0)
Ant	88	(9.7)	Mammal	30	(3.3)
Bee	234	(25.9)	Human	107	(11.8)

Table 3.2. Number and percentage
of abstracts containing names of
each conceptual label

Gene selection	247	(27.3%)
Kin selection	263	(29.1)
Individual selection	191	(21.1)
Group selection	197	(21.8)
Multilevel selection	8	(0.01)

selection" are more likely to demonstrate a coherent perspective with regard to the levels-of-selection debate.

With respect to the articles with an empirical research focus, we found a relatively small percentage of cases in which hypotheses were identified and tested. This impression is reflected by the fact that a search for the root "hypothes" in the database's abstract-field yields 119 articles (out of 904). Both of these observations are consistent with the refrain that is very common to the levels-of-selection debate that "more studies testing hypotheses are necessary."

In addition to the 904 citations described above, we added additional important works that were not detected by the database-searching. Most of these contributions were books or book-chapters that were likely not available in the databases we searched. Other citations that we added likely outdated the timespans covered by the databases.

References

Alexander, R. D. (1979). *Darwinism and human affairs.* Seattle: University of Washington Press.

Alexander, R. D. (1987). *The biology of moral systems.* New York: Aldine de Gruyter.

Axelrod, R. (1980a). Effective choices in the prisoner's dilemma. *Journal of Conflict Resolution, 24,* 3–25.

Axelrod, R. (1980b). More effective choices in the Prisoner's Dilemma. *Journal of Conflict Resolution, 24,* 379–403.

Axelrod, R. (1984). *The evolution of cooperation.* New York: Basic Books.

Axelrod, R., & Hamilton, W. D. (1981). The evolution of cooperation. *Science, 211,* 1390–1396.

Blackmore, S. (1999). *The meme machine.* Oxford: Oxford University Press.

Boehm, C. (1999). *Hierarchy in the forest: Egalitarianism and the evolution of human altruism.* Cambridge: Harvard University Press.

Bowles, S., & Gintis, H. (2002). Homo reciprocans. *Nature, 415,* 125–128.

Boyd, R., & Richerson, P. J. (1985). *Culture and the Evolutionary Process.* Chicago: University of Chicago Press.

Boyd, R., & Richerson, P. J. (1992). Punishment allows the evolution of cooperation (or anything else) in sizable groups. *Ethology and Sociobiology, 13,* 171–195.

Campbell, D. T. (1975). On the conflicts between biological and social evolution and between psychology and moral tradition. *American Psychologist, 30,* 1103–1126.

Dawkins, R. (1976). *The selfish gene* (1st ed.). Oxford: Oxford University Press.

Dawkins, R. (1982). *The extended phenotype.* Oxford: Oxford University Press.

Darwin, C. (1871). *The descent of man and selection in relation to sex.* New York: Appleton.

Emerson, A. E. (1960). The evolution of adaptation in population systems. In S. Tax (Ed.), *Evolution after Darwin* (pp. 307–348). Chicago: University of Chicago Press.

Fehr, E., & Gachter, S. (2002). Altruistic punishment in humans. *Nature, 415,* 137–140.

Frank, R. H. (1988). *Passions within reason.* New York: W. W. Norton.

Hamilton, W. D. (1964). The genetical evolution of social behavior: I and II. *Journal of Theoretical Biology, 7,* 1–52.

Hamilton, W. D. (1975). Innate social aptitudes in man, an approach from evolutionary genetics. In R. Fox (Ed.), *Biosocial anthropology.* London: Malaby Press.

Hamilton, W. D. (1996). *The narrow roads of gene land.* Oxford: W. H. Freeman/Spektrum.

Lovelock, J. E. (1979). *Gaia: A new look at life on earth.* Oxford: Oxford University Press.

Maynard Smith, J. (1964). Group selection and kin selection. *Nature, 1145*–1146.

Maynard Smith, J. (1982). *Evolution and the theory of games.* Cambridge: Cambridge University Press.

Price, G. R. (1970). Selection and covariance. *Nature, 277,* 520–521.

Price, G. R. (1972). Extension of covariance selection mathematics. *Annals of Human Genetics, 35,* 485–490.

Rapoport, A. (1991). Ideological commitments and evolutionary theory. *Journal of Social Issues, 47,* 83–100.

Sahlins, M. D. (1976). *The use and abuse of biology: An anthropological critique of sociobiology.* Ann Arbor: University of Michigan Press.

Schwartz, J. (2000). Death of an altruist. *Lingua franca, 10*(5), 51–61.

Sober, E., & Wilson, D. S. (1998). *Unto others: The evolution and psychology of unselfish behavior.* Cambridge: Harvard University Press.

Trivers, R. L. (1971). The evolution of reciprocal altruism. *Quarterly Review of Biology, 46,* 35–57.

Williams, G. C. (1966). *Adaptation and natural selection: A critique of some current evolutionary thought.* Princeton, NJ: Princeton University Press.

Williams, G. C. (1992). *Natural selection: Domains, levels and challenges.* Oxford: Oxford University Press.

Wilson, D. S. (1983). The group selection controversy: History and current status. *Annual Review of Ecology and Systematics, 14,* 159–187.

Wilson, D. S. (2002). *Darwin's cathedral: Evolution, religion, and the nature of society.* Chicago: University of Chicago Press.

Wynne-Edwards, V. C. (1962). *Animal disperson in relation to social behavior.* Edinburgh: Oliver & Boyd.

CHAPTER 4

Research on Evolutionary Biology

Kevin M. Kniffin, David Sloan Wilson, and Jeffrey P. Schloss

*T*his section of the chapter contains a selection of books and articles concerning altruism from an evolutionary perspective, taken from a larger searchable database on evolution and altruism, described in Wilson and Kniffin (2002), and a larger annotated bibliography on evolution and human nature (Schloss, 2001, unpublished). This abridged version contains some of the most influential classic works and instructive recent works.

Where available, abstracts for each of the records follow the citations. In other cases, efforts were made to reproduce excerpts that approximate abstracts. In such cases, we cite the page number(s) from which we drew excepts. In a minority of cases, we excerpted one or two main sentences from a series of introductory paragraphs and/or we inserted a description when references to preceding text required it (e.g., references to "these ideas"). In the cases where we have written our own summary, we precede our description with an asterisk (*).

Alexander, R. D. (1979). *Darwinism and human affairs.* Seattle: University of Washington Press.

*Alexander's monograph was a seminal and groundbreaking application of general sociobiological theory to human behavior and culture, and helped launch the field of human sociobiology. While taking a reductive, gene-centric approach, Alexander does not merely extrapolate sociobiological theory to humans, but posits developmental and cultural mechanisms unique to human beings. Although highly deterministic and speculative, Alexander was one of the few sociobiologists who from the start acknowledged the crucial developmental factors we didn't understand about the mediation of genes to behavioral phenotypes.

◁🖉 Alexander, R. D. (1987). *Biology of moral systems.* Hawthorne, NY: Aldine de Gruyter.

*As his 1979 *Darwinism and Human Affairs* helped launch human sociobiology, Alexander's theory of moral evolution both stimulated the "second generation" of interdisciplinary sociobiological theorizing and posited one of the first comprehensive evolutionary proposals for human morality that went beyond kin selection or reciprocal altruism, without invoking hierarchical processes. Alexander elaborates a robust notion of indirect reciprocity (conscience is a "reputational bank account" and guilt is "the alarm that goes off when we are cheating in a way likely to be detected"). He maintains the evolutionary significance of competition between groups, though with selection at the individual and not group levels. The present work contains an unusually comprehensive and nuanced analysis of human morality in the context not only of evolutionary origins, but of larger biological concepts of both organismal development and life history. This is still the most expansive location of human morality within biological theory to date. From the author's note:

> When a biologist publishes a treatise with a title like *The Biology of the Amphibia, The Biology of the Mountain Bluebird,* or *The Biology of the Gene,* he means "everything about the life and natural history" of the group or unit in question, as seen through the eyes of a biologist. That is precisely how the title of this book should be translated. I have tried to discuss everything about the life and natural history of moral systems, as seen through the eyes of a biologist.

In many respects, Robert Wright's (1995) widely read popularization of evolutionary psychology a decade later is popularized Alexander. See Wilson (1999) for a critique of Alexander's views from a multilevel evolutionary perspective.

◁🖉 Alexander, R. D., & Borgia, G. (1978). **Group selection, altruism, and the levels of organization in life.** *Annual Review of Ecology and Systematics, 9,* 449–474.

As the early papers of [William] Hamilton attracted increasing attention, a trend began in identification of the unit of natural selection that paralleled the "atomistic" approach to population genetics. The gene began to be treated as the sole unit of selection, with arguments at genotypic or higher levels seen as imperfect, holistic, or unnecessarily complicated. On the other hand, unsupportable holism also persisted. Thus, in a book concerned with sex and evolution, Ghiselin scarcely mentioned subgenotypic units of any kind. (p. 4149). [The authors conclude that]

> Humanity is unlikely to understand itself adequately except through knowing exactly what its genes have evolved to accomplish in particular environments, especially in social environments. As a result there may be few problems in biology more basic or vital than

understanding the background and the potency of selection at different levels in the hierarchies of organization of living matter. The approaches currently being used by evolutionary ecologists and behaviorists in assessing the likelihood of effective selection at the level of groups or populations of individuals may also be used to advantage by those concerned with function at intragenomic levels. (p. 471)

Aunger, R. (2000). *Darwinizing culture: The status of memetics as a science.* New York: Oxford University Press.

*This is the definitive—indeed the only serious—assessment of the scientific merits of memetics. It is both scientifically rigorous and perspectivally balanced. There are excellent chapters by advocates, agnostics, and critics of memetics from evolutionary, neuroscientific, sociological, and philosophical perspectives.

Axelrod, R. (1980). Effective choice in the prisoner's dilemma. *Journal of Conflict Resolution, 24,* 3–25.

This is a "primer" on how to play the iterated Prisoner's Dilemma game effectively. Existing research approaches offer the participant limited help in understanding how to cope effectively with such interactions. To gain a deeper understanding of how to be effective in such a partially competitive and partially cooperative environment, a computer tournament was conducted for the iterated Prisoner's Dilemma. Decision rules were submitted by entrants who were recruited primarily from experts in game theory from a variety of disciplines: psychology, political science, economics, sociology, and mathematics. The results of the tournament demonstrate that there are subtle reasons for an individualistic pragmatist to cooperate as long as the other side does, to be somewhat forgiving, and to be optimistic about the other side's responsiveness.

Axelrod, R. (1980). More effective choice in the Prisoner's Dilemma. *Journal of Conflict Resolution, 24,* 379–403.

This study reports and analyzes the results of the second round of the computer tournament for the iterated Prisoner's Dilemma. The object is to gain a deeper understanding of how to perform well in such a setting. The sixty-two entrants were able to draw lessons from the results of the first round and were able to design their entries to take these lessons into account. The results of the second round demonstrate a number of subtle pitfalls which specific types of decision rules can encounter. The winning rule was once again tit-for-tat, the rule which cooperates on the first move and then does what the other player did on the previous move. The analysis of the results shows the value of not being the first to defect, of being somewhat forgiving, but also the importance of being provocable. An analysis of hypothetical alternative tournaments demonstrates the robustness of the results.

Axelrod, R. (1984). *The evolution of cooperation.* New York: Basic Books.

*This book builds upon Axelrod's earlier seminal work and reviews insights about the existence and evolution of cooperation drawn upon simulations driven by game theory. Axelrod complements these findings with case studies from diverse human settings, such as World War II bunker warfare and international diamond traders.

Axelrod, R., & Hamilton, W. D. (1981). The evolution of cooperation. *Science, 211*(4489), 1390–1396.

Cooperation in organisms, whether bacteria or primates, has been a difficulty for evolutionary theory since Darwin. On the assumption that interactions between pairs of individuals occur on a probabilistic basis, a model is developed based on the concept of an evolutionarily stable strategy in the context of the Prisoner's Dilemma game. Deductions from the model, and the results of a computer tournament, show how cooperation based on reciprocity can start in an asocial world, can thrive while interacting with a wide range of other strategies, and can resist invasion once fully established. Potential applications include specific aspects of territoriality, mating, and disease.

Badcock, C. R. (1986). *The problem of altruism: Freudian-Darwinian solutions.* Oxford: Basil Blackwell Ltd.

*Badcock was the first person to attempt an integration of evolutionary and Freudian perspectives on human altruism and, in so doing, suggested connections between Darwinian fitness and libido, parental investment and Oedipal conflict, sibling rivalry and kin selection. This work anticipates what has become the emerging field of evolutionary psychiatry.

Barkow, J. H. (1989). *Darwin, sex, and status: Biological approaches to mind and culture.* Toronto: University of Toronto Press.

*Barkow integrates anthropology, psychology, and evolutionary biology into a comprehensive statement of human sociobiology. His approach is highly adaptationist, though he is wary of the assumption that all behaviors (or other characteristics) must be adaptive. The primary adaptationist tools of analysis he uses are the attainment of social status and the attraction of mates; it is not until his subsequent coedited volume on evolutionary psychology (1992) that reciprocal cooperation receives more attention. An especially significant aspect of this volume is the substantial attention given to maladaptive characteristics at both the individual and cultural levels; Barkow provides one of the most extensive treatments of maladaptation available.

◄◙ Barkow, J. H., Cosmides, L., & Tooby, J. (Eds.). (1992). *The adapted mind: Evolutionary psychology and the generation of culture.* New York: Oxford University Press.

This edited volume is widely regarded as both launching and defining the field of evolutionary psychology. There is a significant introductory section on the psychological foundations of culture and the use and misuse of Darwinism in studying human behavior. The volume clarifies how the field goes beyond sociobiological determinism by taking human psychology seriously, as a mediation of selected genetic endowments. There are sections on cooperation, mating and sexual systems, parental care, language, and gossip and social stratification. The chapter by Cosmides and Tooby on cognitive adaptations for social exchange is seminal, and important reading for any student of biopsychological perspectives on cooperation and human nature.

◄◙ Boehm, C. (1999). *Hierarchy in the forest: The evolution of egalitarian behavior.* Cambridge: Harvard University Press.

*A comprehensive look at human evolution from a multilevel evolutionary perspective, in which a form of guarded egalitarianism is the key to explaining the ultrasocial nature of our species. In many respects, Boehm's book is a compliment to the group selectionist argument made by Sober and Wilson (1998). Boehm recognizes that human beings have a unique capacity for altruism and locates the origin of this in the unique role group selection played in our evolutionary origin. He maintains that the influence of group selection became more pronounced with the origin of egalitarian morality or social systems, by reducing the costs for being a cooperator in groups with such values. One of the most interesting and theologically significant implications of his account is that human nature thus entails a deep ambiguity about cooperation. The cognitive underlayment that developed early on entails affective dispositions that reflect hierarchy and status conflicts of most primate societies. An accretion "onto" this foundation over the course of social evolution was egalitarian or cooperative dispositions. Boehm argues that this deeply embedded ambiguity in human nature is part of what accounts for the significantly discrepant optimistic and pessimistic accounts of human nature in both evolutionary theory and theology. He is one of the few scholars who is not crusading for a monolithic construction of human nature, but portrays humans as torn or divided between conflicting native dispositions. From the book jacket:

Are humans by nature hierarchical or egalitarian? Hierarchy in the forest addresses this question by examining the evolutionary origins of social and political behavior. Christopher Boehm, an anthropologist whose field work has focused on the political arrangements of human and nonhuman primate groups, postulates that egalitarianism is in effect a hierarchy in which the weak combine forces to dominate the strong. Hierarchy in the forest claims new territory for biological anthropology and evolutionary biology by extending the domain of these sciences into a crucial aspect of human political and social behavior. This book will be a key document in the study of the evolutionary basis of genuine altruism.

⁂ Bowles, S., & Gintis, H. (2002). Homo reciprocans. *Nature, 415,* 125–128.

Humans are often generous, but cooperation unravels when others take advantage of them. Many people punish such "free riders," even if they do not benefit personally, and this "altruistic punishment" sustains cooperation.

⁂ Boyd, R., & Richerson, P. J. (1985). *Culture and the evolutionary process.* Chicago: University of Chicago Press.

This book outlines a Darwinian theory of the evolution of cultural organisms. By "culture" we mean the transmission from one generation to the next, via teaching and imitation, of knowledge, values, and other factors that influence behavior. Cultural transmission may have a variety of structures. By "structures" we mean the patterns of socialization by which a given trait or set of traits are transmitted in a given society. For example, parents may enculturate each other. A Darwinian theory ultimately should be capable of answering two closely related questions about the evolutionary properties of cultural transmission. First, the theory should predict the effect of different structures of cultural transmission on the evolutionary process. For example, do particular kinds of behaviors become common when individuals imitate their peers? Second, the theory should allow us to understand the conditions under which different structures of cultural transmission might evolve. For example, when should natural selection favor the mutual enculturation of individuals by their peers? Clearly, we must be able to answer the first kind of question before we can address the second (p. 2).

⁂ Boyd, R., & Richerson, P. J. (1992). Punishment allows the evolution of cooperation (or anything else). *Ethology and Sociobiology, 13*(3), 171–195.

Existing models suggest that reciprocity is unlikely to evolve in large groups as a result of natural selection. In these models, reciprocators punish noncooperation by withholding future cooperation, and thus also penalize other cooperators in the group. Here, we analyze a model in which the response is some form of punishment that is directed solely at noncooperators. We refer to such alternative forms of punishment as *retribution.* We show that cooperation enforced by retribution can lead to the evolution of cooperation in two qualitatively different ways. (1) If benefits of cooperation to an individual are greater than the costs to a single individual of coercing the other $n-1$ individuals to cooperate, then strategies which cooperate and punish noncooperators, strategies which cooperate only if punished, and, sometimes, strategies which cooperate but do not punish will coexist in the long run. (2) If the costs of being punished are large enough, *moralistic* strategies which cooperate, punish noncooperators, and punish those who do not punish noncooperators can be evolutionarily stable. We also show, however, that moralistic strategies can cause any individually costly behavior to be evolutionarily stable, whether or not it creates a group benefit.

⬧ Campbell, D. T. (1975). On the conflicts between biological and social evolution and between psychology and moral tradition. *American Psychologist, 30*(12), 1103–1126.

Reports the APA presidential address delivered at the Chicago convention, August 1975. Urban humanity is considered as a product of both biological and social evolution. Evolutionary genetics shows that when there is genetic competition among the cooperators (as for humans but not for the social insects), great limitations are placed upon the degree of socially useful, individually self-sacrificial altruism that biological evolution can produce. Human urban social complexity is a product of social evolution and has had to counter with inhibitory moral norms the biological selfishness which genetic competition has continually selected. Because the issues are so complex and the available data are so uncompelling, all of this should be interpreted more as a challenge to an important new area for psychological research than as established conclusions. It is emphasized, however, that these are important issues to which psychology should give much greater attention, and that scientific reasons exist for believing that there can be profound system wisdom in the belief systems our social tradition has provided us with.

⬧ Campbell, D. T. (1994). How individual and face-to-face-group selection undermine firm selection in organizational evolution. In J. A. C. Baum and J. V. Singh (Eds.), *Evolutionary dynamics of organizations* (pp. 23–38). New York: Oxford University Press.

*This book chapter is an important, early attempt to integrate evolutionary theories and the study of business organizations. Campbell outlines a set of ways in which an understanding of the multiple levels of selection and organization can be profitably applied in future work.

⬧ Chisholm, J. S. (1999). *Death, hope and sex: Steps to an evolutionary ecology of mind and morality.* New York: Cambridge University Press.

*One of the few attempts to integrate notions of biological development (ecologically informed life-history theory) with psychosocial development (informed especially by attachment theory). The review of several vast literatures is extensive. Chisholm's general thesis suggests that genuine other-regard (or attachment) is central to human nature, but the way we attach and, in particular, the family and mating systems we converge upon reflect biologically underdetermined openness that is itself a biologically useful adaptation to uncertain environmental challenges. Values are in part a reflection of an anticipated future. Especially helpful is ecological-developmental reflection on a review of the relationship between behavioral syndromes and attachment (e.g., the "absent father syndrome" and male violence and promiscuity). Open for debate is the assumption that this framework is an adequate general foundation for behavioral analysis.

&❦❧ Crawford, C., & Krebs, D. L. (Eds.). (1998). *Handbook of evolutionary psychology: Ideas, issues, and applications.* London: Lawrence Erlbaum Associates.

*This anthology is in many respects a follow-up to the groundbreaking, seminal volume edited by Barkow, Cosmides, and Tooby (1992) in the beginning of the decade. Many of the same contributors present updated reviews of progress on moral behaviors, mate choice, aggression, sex differences, altruism, and a variety of more specific topics. Geoffrey Miller has a chapter-length description of his sexual-selection hypothesis, which argues that extravagant and ostensibly counterreproductive behaviors such as altruism or excessive cognitive resources function as costly displays for mate recruitment. Harmon Holcomb has a chapter on testing evolutionary hypotheses that is neither polemical nor accomodationist, and notes both progress and cautions since his earlier philosophical monograph on sociobiology.

&❦❧ Cronin, H. (1991). *The ant and the peacock: Altruism and sexual selection from Darwin to today.* New York: Cambridge University Press.

*A scientifically accurate and nuanced, yet broadly accessible exposition of sociobiological theory. Each section has a helpful survey of both contemporary and historical thinking. The main focus of the book is how evolutionary theory accommodates ostensibly counterreproductive anomalies through sexual selection and selfish-gene theory. The section on altruism is a clear articulation of and apology for the selfish-gene proposal to solve the altruism quandary.

&❦❧ Cronk, L. (1999). *That complex whole: Culture and the evolution of human behavior.* Boulder, CO: Westview Press.

*Cronk's treatment is one of the first attempts to map a detailed middle road between essentially reducing culture to genetic inclinations (à la traditional sociobiology) and largely uncoupling it from natural selection (à la dual inheritance models). In dual inheritance memetic models, cultural units of information become the replicators that, like genes, manipulate organisms for their own reproductive ends. Cronk turns that idea on its head and argues that culture is what individual organisms use to manipulate others. Rather than memes being viruses that infect unwitting human agents, they are weapons that humans use to do reproductive battle with each other. Thus Cronk very much preserves and extends the individual self-interest perspective of sociobiology, while rejecting the deconstructive approach of memetics and attempting to affirm the importance of both cultural anthropology and human agency.

✍ Cronk, L., Chagnon, N., & W. Irons (Eds.). (2000). *Adaptation and human behavior: An anthropological perspective.* Hawthorne, NY: Aldine de Gruyter.

*This volume is edited by two architects of contemporary Darwinian anthropology. Chagnon was one of the first cultural anthropologists to attempt to apply sociobiological reasoning to his observations, in his influential and controversial studies of the Yanomamo. This volume takes stock of the discipline twenty years after the seminal 1979 volume edited by Chagnon from the meetings of the American Anthropological Association on sociobiology (*Evolutionary Biology and Human Social Behavior: An Anthropological Perspective*). It contains evolutionary interpretations of anthropological field studies organized in sections on mating, parenting, demographic transition (an ostensible anomaly to fitness optimization), and sociality. There are excellent chapters on adoption, reciprocal altruism in food sharing, and the grandmother hypothesis (a proposed solution to why humans live so long beyond reproductive senescence). The volume's conclusion suggests the term *sociobiology* be replaced with *selectionist social science* and maintains that the sophistication of current studies both points the direction for cultural anthropology and—admittedly controversial—holds promise for informing social policy.

✍ Darwin, C. (1871). *The descent of man and selection in relation to sex.* New York: Appleton.

*This is Darwin's major attempt to relate evolution to the human condition, including the evolution of human altruism and morality, and it is highly relevant to the modern study of altruism from an evolutionary perspective. Darwin integrates approaches from animal behavior, comparative anthropology, individual selection, and group selection at biological and cultural levels.

✍ Dawkins, R. (1989). *The selfish gene* (Rev. ed.). New York: Oxford University Press.

*While E. O. Wilson may have launched the sociobiological revolution by integrating the ideas of William Hamilton (kin selection) and Robert Trivers (reciprocal altruism), Richard Dawkins both brought it into the public eye and rhetorically capitalized on the notion of reproductive self-interest. This book makes the argument that organisms, including humans, are robot vehicles enslaved to the reproductive agenda of their masters, genes. Behaviors are deterministically conformed to the reductive telos of replication. In many respects, the proposal is not just extensions of sociobiology, but of the more fundamental gene-centrism advanced by George Williams a decade earlier. In response to criticisms of the metaphorical hyperbole of the "selfish gene," Dawkins maintains in this 1989 revision that his is not a mere metaphor. From the original, "We are survival machines—robot vehicles blindly programmed to preserve the selfish molecules known as genes. This is a truth which still fills me with astonishment. Though I have known it for years, I never seem to get fully used to it. One of my hopes is that I may have some success in astonishing others" (p. ix). "This book is not intended as a general advocacy of Darwinism. Instead, it will explore the consequences of the evolution theory for a particular issue. My purpose is to examine the biology of selfishness and altruism" (p. 1).

Dawkins, R. (1982). *The extended phenotype.* New York: Oxford University Press.

*This follow-up to his influential *The Selfish Gene* entails an elaboration genetic replicators as the atom or fundamental unit of natural selection, and advances this proposal to solve the altruism problem, an ostensible challenge to Darwinian evolution. Dawkins's solution is to reconceptualize the organism: not only is it a robot vehicle that exists to transmit genes, but the boundaries of its identity are not absolutely demarcated. Because genes have influence outside traditional organismal boundaries (e.g., beaver dams) and because the genes of one organism obviously influence the behavior of another organism (e.g., the appearance or behavioral displays of babies that invoke maternal care), Dawkins argues that the boundaries of organisms are relative. He posits the existence of a skinless organism or extended phenotype, which solves by rhetorical innovation Darwin's problem of a "characteristic in one organism that exists for the benefit of another" because characteristics are defined as belonging to the organism whose genes they benefit. There has been ongoing debate over the biological and philosophical implications of these notions.

Parts of some early chapters are frankly retrospective and even defensive. Reaction to a previous work (Dawkins 1976) suggests that this book is likely to raise needless fears that it promulgates two unpopular "-isms"—"genetic determinism" and "adaptationism." I myself admit to being irritated by a book that provokes me into muttering "Yes but . . ." on every page, when the author could easily have forestalled my worry by a little considerate explanation early on. Chapters 2 and 3 try to remove at least two major sources of "yes-buttery" at the outset. Chapter 4 opens the case for the prosecution against the selfish organism, and begins to hint at the second aspect of the Necker cube. Chapter 5 opens the case for the "replicator" as the fundamental unit of natural selection. Chapter

6 returns to the individual organism and shows how neither it, nor any other major candidate except the small genetic fragment, qualifies as a true replicator. Rather, the individual organism should be thought of as a "vehicle" for replicators. Chapter 7 is a digression on research methodology. Chapter 8 raises some awkward anomalies for the selfish organism, and Chapter 9 continues the theme. Chapter 10 discusses various notions of "individual fitness," and concludes that they are confusing, and probably dispensable. Chapters 11, 12, and 13 are the heart of the book. They develop by gradual degrees, the idea of the extended phenotype itself, the second face of the Necker Cube. Finally, in Chapter 14, we turn back with refreshed curiosity to the individual organism and ask why, after all, it is such a salient level in the hierarchy of life. (p. 8)

Dawkins, R. (1987). *The blind watchmaker.* New York: W. W. Norton.

Natural selection is the blind watchmaker, blind because it does not see ahead, does not plan consequences, has no purpose in view. Yet the living results of natural selection overwhelmingly impress us with the appearance of design as if by a master watchmaker, impress us with the illusion of design and planning. The purpose of this book is to resolve this paradox (p. 21).

Dawkins, R. (1995). *River out of Eden.* New York: Basic Books.

Piet Hein captures the classically pristine world of physics. But when the ricochets of atomic billiards chance to put together an object that has a certain, seemingly innocent property, something momentous happens in the universe. That property is an ability to self-replicate; that is, the object is able to use the surrounding materials to make exact copies of itself, including replicas of such minor flaws in copying as may occasionally arise. What will follow from this singular occurrence, anywhere in the universe, is the Darwinian selection and hence the baroque extravaganza that, on this planet, we call life. Never were so many facts explained by so few assumptions. Not only does the Darwinian theory command superabundant power to explain. Its economy in doing so has a sinewy elegance, a poetic beauty that outclasses even the most haunting of the world's origin myths. One of my purposes in writing this book has been to accord due recognition to the inspirational quality of our modern understanding of Darwinian life. There is more poetry in Mitochondrial Eve than in her mythological namesake. The feature of life that, in David Hume's words, most "ravishes into admiration all men who have ever contemplated it" is the complex detail with which its mechanisms—the mechanisms that Charles Darwin called "organs of extreme perfection and complication"—fulfill an apparent purpose. The other feature of earthly life that impresses us is its luxuriant diversity: as measured by estimates of species numbers, there are some tens of millions of different ways of making a living. Another of my purposes is to convince my readers that "ways of making a living" is synonymous with "ways of passing DNA-coded texts on to the future." My "river" is a river of DNA, flowing and branching through geological time, and the metaphor of steep banks confining each species' genetic games turns out to be a surprisingly powerful and helpful explanatory device. In one way or another, all my books have been devoted to expounding and exploring the almost limitless power of the Darwinian principle—power unleashed whenever and wherever there is enough time for the consequences of primordial self-replication to unfold. *River Out of Eden* continues this mission and brings to an extraterrestrial climax the story of the repercussions that can ensue when the phenomenon of replicators is injected into the hitherto humble game of atomic billiards (pp. xi–xii).

&⊙ Dennett, D. C. (1995). *Darwin's dangerous idea: Evolution and the meanings of life.* New York: Simon & Schuster.

*Dennett combines his earlier arguments for consciousness as a noncausal, epiphenomenal byproduct with a gene-centric, adaptationist version of evolutionary theory to argue against teleology, and ultimately genuine agency in nature. Nature is to be viewed reductively and disteleologically, moving by "cranes rather than skyhooks," i.e., processes grounded in blind, naturalistic causes, not goals or transcendent realities. He suggests this truth—the ultimate contribution of Darwinism—was anticipated by both Nietzsche and Hume (precursors to Darwin and essentially Darwinists themselves), and is a universal acid that eats away religious or metaphysical commitments to the causal efficacy of design or ideas. In a provocative passage, Dennett suggests that those who persist in believing antievolutionary fictions may be relegated to cultural zoos, and their children may need to be taken away. The book was highly praised by selfish gene theorists (Dawkins, Pinker, Wilson) and criticized by other evolutionary biologists (Gould, Orr). A vitriolic and widely cited exchange between Dennett and Gould appeared in the *New York Review of Books.* One critic of Dennett's gene-centrism commented, "if Huxley was Darwin's bulldog, Dennett is Dawkins' lapdog."

Part I of the book locates the Darwinian Revolution in the larger scheme of things, showing how it can transform the world-view of those who know its details. This first chapter sets out the background of philosophical ideas that dominated our thought before Darwin. Chapter 2 introduces Darwin's central idea in a somewhat new guise, as the idea of evolution as an algorithmic process, and clears up some common misunderstandings of it. Chapter 3 shows how this idea overturns the tradition encountered in chapter 1. Chapters 4 and 5 explore some of the striking—and unsettling—perspectives that the Darwinian way of thinking opens up. Part II examines the challenges to Darwin's idea—to neo-Darwinism or the Modern Synthesis—that have arisen within biology itself, showing that contrary to what some of its opponents have declared, Darwin's idea survives these controversies not just intact but strengthened. Part III then shows what happens when the same thinking is extended to the species we care about most: *Homo sapiens.* Darwin himself fully recognized that this was going to be the sticking point for many people, and he did what he could to break the news gently. More than a century later, there are still those who want to dig a moat separating us from most if not all of the dreadful implications they think they see in Darwinism. Part III shows that this is an error of both fact and strategy; not only does Darwin's dangerous idea apply to us directly and at many levels, but the proper application of Darwinian thinking to human issues of mind, language, and ethics, for instance illuminates them in ways that have always eluded the traditional approaches, recasting ancient problems and pointing to their solution. Finally, we can assess the bargain we get when we trade in pre-Darwinian for Darwinian thinking, identifying both its uses and abuses, and showing what really matters to us and ought to matter to us shines through, transformed but enhanced by its passage through the Darwinian Revolution. (pp. 22–23)

    de Waal, F. (1996). *Good natured: The origins of right and wrong in humans and other animals.* Cambridge: Harvard University Press.

*Explicitly articulated goals of this book are, first, to confront the picture of human nature painted by selfish-gene theoreticians and, second, to argue against the dualistic bifurcation of human nature into biological and transbiological domains, with "goodness" being restricted only to the latter domain. With theoretical argumentation and citation of pertinent primate studies, de Waal attempts to root empathetic concern for others in human biological nature and to provide an alternative to the most extreme versions of sociobiological selfishness and memetic dualism. The book does not attempt an exploration of how the most dramatic aspects of radical self-relinquishment ostensibly unique to human beings arise from analogues in nonhuman animals.

    Degler, C. (1992). *In search of human nature: The decline and revival of Darwinism in American social thought.* New York: Oxford University Press.

*An intellectual history of the ambivalence toward Darwinian interpretations of human nature. A historian at Stanford, Degler started to write a history of the ideologically motivated rise of ethically pernicious biological determinism and consequent rejection by cultural sciences in the earlier part of the last century, and the more recent rise of the same ideas in sociobiology. What he found surprised him: that the rejection of Darwinian theories of human nature (many of which were indeed racist and/or eugenic) by Boas, Montagu, and Mead appears to have been largely ideologically motivated and scientifically questionable. Moreover, Degler became convinced that later ethological and recent sociobiological theories were scientifically credible and also helpful for social science. He has written a social and intellectual history of the transition from early theories of social Darwinism, through cultural relativism, back to biological theories of Nobel laureates in ethology (Lorenz, Tinbergen) and E. O. Wilson, and finally, the recent ideological critiques of these theories.

◎ Diamond, J. (1992). *The third chimpanzee.* New York: Harper Perennial.

*This is essentially a popular treatise on human sociobiology with an emphasis on life history and sexual selection. Diamond argues that many features of human behavior can be understood in light of our life cycle (long lives, high infant dependency, intense socialization) and challenges of mate recruitment and retention. He also argues that many ostensibly nonadaptive behaviors from gang violence, to acquisition of art, to drug experimentation and wild risk-taking are related to extravagant displays for attracting mates.

The story of our rise and fall divides itself into five natural parts. In the first part, I'll follow us from several million years ago until just before agriculture's appearance ten thousand years ago. The second part deals with changes in the human life cycle, which were as essential to the development of language and art as were the skeletal changes discussed in Part One. With Parts One and Two thus having surveyed the biological underpinnings of our cultural flowering, Part Three proceeds to consider the cultural traits that we consider as distinguishing us from animals. Besides chemical abuse, our black traits include two so serious that they may lead to our fall. Part Four considers the first of these: our propensity for xenophobic killing of other human groups. The other black trait that now threatens our survival is our accelerating assault on our environment. Part Five seeks to dismantle the Rousseauian fantasy that this behavior did not appear in us until the Industrial Revolution by facing up to our long history of environmental mismanagement. (pp. 7–9)

◎ Diamond, J. (1997). *Guns, germs, and steel.* New York: W. W. Norton.

Authors are regularly asked by journalists to summarize a long book in one sentence. For this book, here is such a sentence: "History followed different courses for different peoples because of differences among peoples' environments, not because of biological differences among people themselves" (p. 25). [This book won the Pulitzer Prize.]

◎ Dugatkin, L. A. (1997). *Cooperation among animals: An evolutionary perspective.* New York: Oxford University Press.

*Dugatkin provides a comprehensive theoretical and empirical review of cooperation in the animal kingdom, surveying historical and contemporary theoretical approaches, and then providing state-of-the-art descriptions of what we know of cooperation in fish, birds, mammals (nonprimate), primates (nonhuman), and insects. This is an extensive review and contains a new proposal for an integrative taxonomy of cooperation.

 Dugatkin, L. A. (1999). *Cheating monkeys and citizen bees: The nature of cooperation in animals and humans.* Cambridge: Harvard University Press.

Dugatkin wrote this book with the very explicit intention of making the implications of his earlier scholarly treatment of cooperation (1997) accessible to a popular audience, and extending it to human beings, in an effort to blunt the interpretations of humanity proffered by some accounts of sociobiological of self-interest, while still affirming the animal character of the human organism. He only partially succeeds. The book develops a rationale for the biological receptiveness of human nature to cooperation. It does not provide a basis upon which to understand not just cooperation, but radical altruism, as an outgrowth of an evolved disposition.

 Dugatkin, L. A. (2000). *The imitation factor: Evolution beyond the gene.* New York: Free Press.

One of the important controversies in cultural evolution theory in general, and memetics in particular, is over how memes are transmitted. We know how genes are transmitted, but replication and transmission of their ideational counterparts is debated. Memeticist Susan Blackmore argues it is primarily imitation (Dawkins derived the word *memetics,* or mimetics from "mime" or "imitation"). Other options are coercion or independent logical discovery (in which case memes would not, technically, be transmitted at all). Dugatkin has done the most extensive empirical study of imitation in animals, and develops a theoretical model for social evolution based on adaptationist reasoning.

 Emerson, A. E. (1960). The evolution of adaptation in population systems. In S. Tax (Ed.), *Evolution after Darwin* (pp. 307–348). Chicago: University of Chicago Press.

*Emerson represents the kind of thinking that has been called "naïve group-selectionism" by modern evolutionary biologists, in which higher-level units such as social groups, multispecies communities, and ecosystems are portrayed as like single organisms without careful attention to the evolutionary processes required for such higher-level adaptations to evolve. Although the early naïve group selectionists need to be read with caution, they still can be a source of good ideas that can be justified from a modern evolutionary perspective.

 Eldredge, N., & Greene, M. (1992). *Interactions: The biological context of social systems.* New York: Columbia University Press.

*This book critiques sociobiology and explores a reformulation of evolutionary theory on three counts. First, it revisits questions of biological ontology and argues that the prevailing depiction of the gene as the fundamental unit of biology is inadequate and unjustifiably dismissive of hierarchy. Second, it critiques hyperadaptationism, not only on the basis that not all characteristics can be expected to be optimal or even adaptive, but also because adaptation is not what drives natural selection, but what derives from it and to assert otherwise is teleological. Traits do not exist *for* reproductive success, but instead are sustained through it. Third, the book argues for two different hierarchies in biological systems: genealogical (genome-organism-species) and ecological (organisms–local ecosystems–regional ecosystems). The former mediates the flow of genetic information, the latter the exchange of material and energetic resources. The first is reproductive, the second is economic, and while related, they are not to be conflated. In humans, social systems mediate interactions between the two, and because human social systems change via the stochastic uncertainties of historical contingency and not the regularities of natural selection, sociobiology cannot be used to "predict" the features of human social systems. In short, this is a coevolutionary account that does not reduce human society to reproductive self-interest or apply hyperselectionist reasoning to cultural transmission.

᷇ Fehr, E., & Gachter, S. (2002). Altruistic punishment in humans. *Nature, 415,* 137–140.

Human cooperation is an evolutionary puzzle. Unlike other creatures, people frequently cooperate with genetically unrelated strangers, often in large groups, with people they will never meet again, and when reputation gains are small or absent. These patterns of cooperation cannot be explained by the nepotistic motives associated with the evolutionary theory of kin selection and the selfish motives associated with signaling theory or the theory of reciprocal altruism. Here we show experimentally that the altruistic punishment of defectors is a key motive for the explanation of cooperation. Altruistic punishment means that individuals punish, although the punishment is costly for them and yields no material gain. We show that cooperation flourishes if altruistic punishment is possible, and breaks down if it is ruled out. The evidence indicates that negative emotions toward defectors are the proximate mechanism behind altruistic punishment. These results suggest that future study of the evolution of human cooperation should include a strong focus on explaining altruistic punishment.

᷇ Fox, R. (1989). *The search for society: Quest for a biosocial science and morality.* New Brunswick, NJ: Rutgers University Press.

*This book attempts to do several things, each of them done rarely, and none of them attempted together. First, it endeavors to unify the social sciences with a biosocial rubric, not reducing, much less dismissing traditional sociological accounts of Durkheim, but relating them to evolutionary theory. Second, it attempts to give a biosocial account of the nature and function of human morality. Third, it attempts to develop a scientifically informed ethical system, without committing the naturalistic fallacy. One of the most helpful and theologically pregnant treatments in the book is the chapter on kinship categories as natural categories.

   🕮 Frank, R. H. (1988). *Passions within reason: The strategic role of the emotions.* New York: W. W. Norton.

   *A groundbreaking attempt to explain emotions as a set of adaptations for regulating social behavior, based upon both economic and evolutionary concepts. Included in the book is the notion of commitment devices, such as the incapacity to lie, which superficially appear disadvantageous but nevertheless evolve because of their effects on the behavior of others. Frank is one of several economists (e.g., Herbert Simon, Marvin Becker) who have made important contributions to the evolutionary literature. This book presents an evolutionary interpretation of human emotions as an adaptation to social exchange. But it does more than that. While Frank accepts the necessity of fundamental human dispositions contributing to reproductive "profit," he soundly rejects the sociobiological (and economic) notion that human behavior is restricted to that which is consistent with rational self-interest. Rather, he recognizes that humans do things both altruistically and maliciously that can be reasonably expected to have no net payoff and even have negative consequences. He posits irrational emotions driving such behaviors, which ironically do end up paying off in the context of social exchange. If someone demonstrates levels of beneficence or loyalty that are not constrained by the logic of compensation, Frank suggests others will trust them more easily (overcoming "commitment barriers") and enter more freely into cooperative alliances. On the other hand, if someone is known to pursue revenge at self-injurious personal cost, others will not tangle with that person. Thus there is an adaptive logic to human emotion, but its functionality entails the paradox that the behaviors it motivates cannot be pursued because they have payoffs, but precisely because reason suggests they don't.

   🕮 Frank, R. H. (1996). What price the moral high ground? *Southern Economic Journal, 63,* 1–17.

   The labor market is examined for evidence relevant to the claim that the economic choices of many people are significantly guided by unselfish motives. A variety of evidence of a strong negative correlation between annual earnings is seen, on the one hand, and the degree to which an employee's employer and occupation are viewed as being socially responsible, on the other. The most systematic of this evidence came from a survey of graduates of Cornell University's College of Arts and Sciences. The same pattern was observed in comparison of the fees paid to expert witnesses who testify on behalf of the tobacco industry and their counterparts who testify for the American Heart Association and their public interest groups. Dramatic pay differences are seen between public interest lawyers and those employed in the segments of the legal profession. Survey evidence is seen from a sample of graduating seniors who reported that they would require large premiums before being willing to switch to a less socially responsible employer.

✒ Frank, R. H., Gilovich, T., & Regan, D. T. (1993). Does studying economics inhibit cooperation? *Journal of Economic Perspectives, 7*(2), 159–171.

In this paper, we investigate whether exposure to the self-interest model commonly used in economics alters the extent to which people behave in self-interested ways. The paper is organized into two parts. In the first, we report the results of several empirical studies—some our own, some by others—that suggest economists behave in more self-interested ways. By itself, this evidence does not demonstrate that exposure to the self-interest model causes more self-interested behavior, since it may be that economists were simply more self-interested to begin with, and this difference was one reason they chose to study economics. In the second part of the paper, we present preliminary evidence that exposure to the self-interest model does in fact encourage self-interested behavior.

✒ Frank, S. A. (1995). George Price's contributions to evolutionary genetics. *Journal of Theoretical Biology, 175*(3), 373–388.

George Price studied evolutionary genetics for approximately seven years between 1967 and 1974. During that brief period Price made three lasting contributions to evolutionary theory; these were: (i) the Price Equation, a profound insight into the nature of selection and the basis for the modern theories of kin and group selection; (ii) the theory of games and animal behavior, based on the concept of the evolutionarily stable strategy; and (iii) the modern interpretation of Fisher's fundamental theorem of natural selection, Fisher's theorem being perhaps the most cited and least understood idea in the history of evolutionary genetics. This paper summarizes Price's contributions and briefly outlines why, toward the end of his painful intellectual journey, he chose to focus his deep humanistic feelings and sharp, analytical mind on abstract problems in evolutionary theory.

⟨Ǫ Frank, S. A. (1997). The price equation, Fisher's fundamental theorem, kin selection, and causal analysis. *Evolution, 51*(6), 1712–1729.

A general framework is presented to unify diverse models of natural selection. This framework is based on the Price Equation, with two additional steps. First, characters are described by their multiple regression on a set of predictor variables. The most common predictors in genetics are alleles and their interactions, but any predictor may be used. The second step is to describe fitness by multiple regression on characters. Once again, characters may be chosen arbitrarily. This expanded Price Equation provides an exact description of total evolutionary change under all conditions, and for all systems of inheritance and selection. The model is first used for a new proof of Fisher's fundamental theorem of natural selection. The relations are then made clear among Fisher's theorem, Robertson's covariance theorem for quantitative genetics, the Lande-Arnold model for the causal analysis of natural selection, and Hamilton's rule for kin selection. Each of these models is a partial analysis of total evolutionary change. The Price Equation extends each model to an exact, total analysis of evolutionary change for any system of inheritance and selection. This exact analysis is used to develop an expanded Hamilton's rule for total change. The expanded rule clarifies the distinction between two types of kin selection coefficients. The first measures components of selection caused by correlated phenotypes of social partners. The second measures components of heritability via transmission by direct and indirect components of fitness.

⟨Ǫ Gintis, H. (2000). Beyond *Homo Economicus. Ecological Economics,* 35(3), 311–322.

Environmental policies are generally based on a model of the human actor taken from neoclassical economic theory. This paper reports on laboratory experiments suggesting weaknesses in this model and describes alternative models correcting these weaknesses. One finding is that economic actors tend to be *hyperbolic* as opposed to *exponential* discounters who discount the immediate future at a higher rate than the more distant future. Another finding is that economic actors are not self-regarding, but rather in many circumstances are *strong reciprocators* who come to strategic interactions with a propensity to cooperate, respond to cooperative behavior by maintaining or increasing cooperation, and respond to free-riders by retaliating against the "offenders," even at a personal cost, and even when there is no reasonable expectation that future personal gains will flow from such retaliation. We discuss some implications for policy analysis.

Goodnight, C. J., & Stevens, L. (1997). Experimental studies of group selection: What do they tell us about group selection in nature? *American Naturalist, 150S,* 59–79.

The study of group selection has developed along two autonomous lines. One approach, which we refer to as the adaptationist school, seeks to understand the evolution of existing traits by examining plausible mechanisms for their evolution and persistence. The other approach, which we refer to as the genetic school, seeks to examine how currently acting artificial or natural selection changes traits within populations and focuses on current evolutionary change. The levels of selection debate lies mainly within the adaptationist school, whereas the experimental studies of group selection lie within the genetic school. Because of the very different traditions and goals of these two schools, the experimental studies of group selection have not had a major impact on the group selection debate. We review the experimental results of the genetic school in the context of the group selection controversy and address the following questions: Under what conditions is group selection effective? What is the genetic basis of a response to group selection? How common is group selection in nature?

Goodwin, B. (1994). *How the leopard changed its spots: The evolution of complexity.* New York: Scribner's.

In this book, I explore the consequences of the sciences of complexity as they apply to our understanding of the emergence of biological forms in evolution, particularly the origin and nature of the morphological characteristics that distinguish different types of organisms. These questions overlap those addressed by Darwin, but they focus on the large-scale, or global, aspects of biological form rather than on small-scale, local adaptations. As a result, there is no necessary conflict between the approaches, nor with insights of modern biology into the genetic and molecular levels of organisms. These contribute to the construction of dynamical theories from which emerge higher-level properties of biological form and the integrated behavior of organisms. Conflict arises only when there is confusion about what constitutes biological reality. I take the position that organisms are as real, as fundamental, and as irreducible as the molecules out of which they are made. They are a distinct level of emergent biological order, and the one to which we most immediately relate (p. x).

Gould, S. J. (1981). *The mismeasure of man.* New York: W. W. Norton.

This book seeks to demonstrate both the scientific weaknesses and political contexts of determinist arguments. Even so, I do not intend to contrast evil determinists who stray from the path of scientific objectivity with enlightened antideterminists who approach data with an open mind and therefore see truth.

Rather, I criticize the myth that science itself is an objective enterprise, done properly only when scientists can shuck the constraints of their culture and view the world as it really is (p. 21). A note on title: I hope that an apparently sexist title will be taken in the intended spirit—not only as a play on Protagoras' famous aphorism, but also as a commentary on the procedures of biological determinists discussed in the book. They did, indeed, study "man" (that is, white European males), regarding this group as a standard and everybody else as something to be measured unfavorably against it. That they mismeasured "man" underscores the double fallacy (p. 16).

&❧ Gould, S. J., & Lewontin, R. C. (1979). The spandrels of San Marco and the Panglossian paradigm: A critique of the adaptationist programme. *Proceedings of the Royal Society of London, B205,* 581–598.

An adaptationist program has dominated evolutionary thought in England and the United States during the past forty years. It is based on faith in the power of natural selection as an optimizing agent. It proceeds by breaking an organism into unitary "traits" and proposing an adaptive story for each considered separately. Trade-offs among competing selective demands exert the only brake upon perfection; nonoptimality is thereby rendered as a result of adaptation as well. We criticize this approach and attempt to reassert a competing notion (long popular in continental Europe) that organisms must be analyzed as integrated wholes, with Bauplane so constrained by phenotypic heritage, pathways of development, and general architecture that the constraints themselves become more interesting and more important in delimiting pathways of change than the selective force that may mediate change when it occurs. We fault the adaptationist program for its failure to distinguish current utility from reasons for origin (male tyrannosaurs may have used their diminutive front legs to titillate female partners, but this will not explain why they got so small); for its unwillingness to consider alternatives to adaptive stories; for its reliance upon plausibility alone as a criterion for accepting speculative tales; and for its failure to consider adequately such competing themes as random fixation of alleles, production of nonadaptive structures by developmental correlation with selected features (allometry, pleiotropy, material compensation, mechanically forced correlation), the separability of adaptation and selection, multiple adaptive peaks, and current utility as an epiphenomenon of nonadaptive structures. We support Darwin's own pluralistic approach to identifying the agents of evolutionary change.

❧ Greenwood, D. L. (1984). *The taming of evolution: The persistence of nonevolutionary views in the study of humans.* Ithaca, NY: Cornell University Press.

*Greenwood presents a critique not of creationist or expressly antievolutionary accounts of human nature, but of historical and contemporary scientific accounts that purport to be based upon or amenable to evolution but turn out in his analysis to be both ideological and nonevolutionary. In this regard, he mounts vigorous critique of anthropologist Marvin Harris's cultural materialism. He also critiques sociobiology for its internal inconsistencies and non-Darwinian essentialism.

❧ Hahlweg, K., & Hooker, C. A. (Eds.). (1989). *Issues in evolutionary epistemology.* Albany: State University of New York Press.

The first section of this book is devoted to papers within which new approaches to evolutionary epistemology are proposed. Aside from proposing new approaches to evolutionary epistemology it is important to clarify and expand models which are already well known and find new areas of application for them. By exploring new "niches" the approach shows its potential. Several of the papers in this volume are directed toward this task: we have collected them in the second section of this volume. The third section of this book contains material which was written in a critical mood. In the fourth section of this book we present a group of papers that deal with the relationship of evolutionary epistemology to the nature of the mind. That this issue is an important one hardly needs emphasizing; it is the nature of our mental powers that is the ultimate reference point for all philosophical objections to evolutionary epistemology (pp. 1–2).

❧ Hamilton, W. D. (1964). The genetical evolution of social behavior: I and II. *Journal of Theoretical Biology, 7,* 1–52.

A genetical mathematical model is described which allows for interactions between relatives on one another's fitness / making use of Wright's Coefficient of Relationship as the measure of the proportion of replica genes in a relative, a quantity is found which incorporates the maximizing property of Darwinian fitness / this quantity is named "inclusive fitness" / species following the model should tend to evolve behaviour such that each organism appears to be attempting to maximize its inclusive fitness / this implies a limited restraint on selfish competitive behaviour and possibility of limited self-sacrifices /// special cases of the model are used to show (a) that selection in the social situations newly covered tends to be slower than classical selection, (b) how in populations of rather nondispersive organisms the model may apply to genes affecting dispersion, and (c) how it may apply approximately to competition between relatives, for example, within sibships / some artificialities of the model are discussed.

⨭ Hamilton, W. D. (1975). **Innate social aptitudes in man, an approach from evolutionary genetics.** In R. Fox (Ed.), *Biosocial anthropology.* London: Malaby Press.

*In this important but rarely cited paper, Hamilton revised his theory of inclusive fitness based on the covariance approach of George Price. This is important because the new formulation showed the evolution of altruism among genetic relatives to be a kind of group selection rather than an alternative mechanism for the evolution of altruism, as Hamilton originally thought. In addition, Hamilton used the article to speculated on human evolution from a multilevel evolutionary perspective.

⨭ Hamilton, W. D. (1996). *The narrow roads of gene land.* Oxford: W. H. Freeman/Spektrum.

*This anthology reprints Hamilton's classic papers on the evolution of altruism along with accompanying sketches that provide a whimsical autobiography and the background for the writing of each paper.

⨭ Heinrich, J., Boyd, R., Bowles, S., Camerer, C., Fehr, E., Gintis, H., & McElreath, R. (2001). **Cooperation, reciprocity, and punishment in fifteen small-scale societies.** *American Economic Review, 91,* 73–78.

Recent investigations have uncovered large, consistent deviations from the predictions of the textbook representation of *Homo Economicus:* in addition to their own material payoffs, many experimental subjects appear to care about fairness and reciprocity and reward those who act in a cooperative manner while punishing those who do not even when these actions are costly to the individual. These deviations from what we will term the canonical Economic Man model have important consequences for a wide range of economic phenomena, including the optimal design of institutions and contracts, the allocation of property rights, the conditions for successful collective action, the analysis of incomplete contracts, and the persistence of noncompetitive wage premia. However, existing research is limited because virtually all subjects have been university students: we would like to know how universal these behaviors are and whether they vary with local cultural or economic environments. To address these questions we and our collaborators (11 anthropologists and 1 economist) conducted ultimatum, public good, and dictator game experiments with subjects from fifteen hunter gatherer, nomadic herding and other small-scale societies exhibiting a wide variety of economic and cultural conditions. We can summarize our results as follows. First, the Economic Man model is not supported in any society studied. Second, there is considerably more behavioral variability across groups than had been found in previous cross-cultural research and the canonical model fails in a wider variety of ways than in previous experiments. Third, group-level differences in the structure of everyday social interactions explain a substantial portion of the behavioral variation across societies: the higher the degree of market integration and the payoffs to cooperation in the production of their livelihood, the greater the level of cooperation in experimental games. Fourth, individual-level economic and demographic variables do not explain behavior either within or across groups. Fifth, behavior in the experiments is generally consistent with economic patterns of everyday life in these societies.

🕮 Hodgson, G. M. (1993). *Economics and evolution: Bringing life back into economics.* Ann Arbor: University of Michigan Press.

This book is about the application to economics of evolutionary ideas from biology. It is not, however, about selfish genes, or the alleged determination of our behaviour by the genetic code. It does not establish the superiority by breeding of the English aristocracy, or any other favored race, gender, or social class. The idea of economic evolution endorsed here has much more to do with social culture and has little, if anything, to do with genes. Further, the conception of evolution as progress toward greater and greater perfection, along with the competitive individualism sometimes inferred from the notion of "survival of the fittest," are found to be problematic (p. vii).

🕮 Holcomb, H. R., III (1993). *Sociobiology, sex, and science.* Albany: State University of New York Press.

*Sensationalistic title notwithstanding, this monograph undertakes a comprehensive analysis of sociobiology from the perspective of philosophy of science. E. O. Wilson (who comes under fire from Holcomb) describes him as the "leading authority on sociobiology" among philosophers. Holcomb argues that sociobiology constitutes a scientific revolution, with theoretical reconceptualization just as significant as the original Darwinian and subsequent synthetic revolutions. While he is supportive of and hopeful for this revolution, he argues it is presently incomplete. Holcomb's analysis is unique in that, while emphatically positive about sociobiology, it strongly criticizes the rhetorical excesses of sociobiological extremism and the popularizers thereof. Especially relevant to the issue of altruism, it explicitly points out the current explanatory inadequacies and theoretical incompleteness of evolutionary theory, arguing that it has developed revolutionary advances in explaining animal behavior, but human altruism still poses an unexplained challenge to the expectations of evolutionary theory. Holcomb eschews what he regards to be present compromises in selection theory to make peace with empirical anomalies; instead, he recognizes tension between prediction and observation, and hopes for resolution if the revolutionary "new synthesis" in evolutionary theory is to be complete.

《》 Hull, D. L. (1989). *The metaphysics of evolution.* Albany: State University of New York Press.

*This is not a systematic exposition of the metaphysical implications of evolution or an examination of the metaphysical presuppositions of evolution. It has several sections that focus primarily on the ethics (altruism, sociobiology) and ontology (species as evolutionary units, levels of selection, classification theory) of evolution, with a few chapters on evolutionary methodology and philosophy of science. There is an excellent chapter on human nature and altruism, and a historical-philosophical analysis of sociobiological methodology compares the new discipline to the early stages of Darwinian evolution and phrenology, noting similarities in all three.

《》 Hull, D. L. (2000). Activism, scientists, and sociobiology. *Nature, 407,* 673–674.

*In this report, Hull comments upon the political background to debates concerning sociobiology. Most notably, however, he recounts his memory of an (in)famous episode in 1978 when E. O. Wilson was part of a panel on sociobiology at the 1978 meetings of the American Association for the Advancement of Science. Hull writes:

As [Wilson] began his presentation, a dozen or so members of the International Committee Against Racism marched up onto the stage, chanting: "Racist Wilson you can't hide, we charge you with genocide!" A woman then poured water over Wilson's head. How much water is a matter of conjecture. Usually we are told it was a pitcher of water. Segerstråle remembers a jug. I am sure that it was a small paper cup. One bit of evidence that supports my memory of the incident is that Wilson was able to mop up the water with a single handkerchief. Such are the problems of eye-witness reports.

《》 Katz, L., Ed. (2000). *Evolutionary origins of morality: Cross-disciplinary perspectives.* Bowling Green, Ohio: Imprint Academic.

*This volume is put together in four sections, each representing a major contemporary controversy, and each entailing a substantial principal paper by an architect of the field, followed by responses from ten or so leading scholars from a variety of disciplines, concluded with response by the primary author. The sections represent major evolutionary approaches to understanding morality, and also altruism. The first section is on human uniqueness versus continuities between humans and primates by primatologist Frans de Waal (author of *Good Natured: The Origins of Right and Wrong in Humans and Other Animals*).

The second starts with an ascription of uniqueness in human altruism, positing a biologically mediated theory of social evolution for its origin. It is written by Christopher Boehm (*Hierarchy in the Forest*). The third section is by Elliott Sober and David Wilson, and is essentially a chapter-length summary of their argument in the seminal book, *Unto Others*. This is an excellent review of the group selection hypothesis and the social-psychological data underlying it. The responses by a wide variety of leading scholars both supporters and critics is outstanding. Finally, Brian Skyrms contributes a description of the application of game theory to evolution and rational self-interest, with scientific and ethical critiques following.

⬥ Kauffman, S. (1995). *At home in the universe: The search for the laws of self-organization and complexity.* New York: Oxford University Press.

This book describes my own search for laws of complexity that govern how life arose naturally from a soup of molecules, evolving into the biosphere we see today. Whether we are talking about molecules cooperating to form cells or organisms cooperating to form ecosystems or buyers and sellers cooperating to form markets and economies, we will find grounds to believe that Darwinism is not enough, that natural selection cannot be the sole source of the order we see in the world. In crafting the living world, selection has always acted on systems that exhibit spontaneous order. If I am right, this underlying order, further honed by selection, augurs a new place for us expected, rather than vastly improbable, at home in the universe in a newly understood way (p. viii).

⬥ Keller, L. (1997). Indiscriminate altruism: Unduly nice parents and siblings. *Trends in Ecology and Evolution, 12*(3), 99–103.

Many animals can identify their relatives and bias altruistic behavior in their favor. However, recent studies have also uncovered cases where nepotism might be expected but is weak or absent within social groups. For instance, in some bird and mammal species, males apparently feed offspring that have been sired by other means at the same rate as their own offspring. Similarly, social insect workers fail to favor more closely related individuals within their colony. Why is this so?

⬥ Konner, M. (2002). *The tangled wing: Biological constraints on the human spirit.* New York: W. H. Freeman.

*In this revised edition of his widely acclaimed 1982 book, Konner provides a series of essays that reflect on the nature of life in the spirit of Lewis Thomas's *Lives of the Cell* (1974), but that also consider the ambivalent interaction between human freedom and biological disposition. While he is on the biologically deterministic end of the continuum, he makes the case for ambiguities within human nature and considers the relationship between evolutionary biology and the human life experience. This book contains accessible, humane reflections on the biological embeddedness of selfishness and altruism.

 Lewin, R. (1996). Evolution's new heretics. *Natural History, 105*(5), 12–16.

Many evolutionary biologists have been led to believe that natural selection grins inexorably at the level of individual interests. David Sloan Wilson argues that groups of organisms have evolutionary interests too. Other biologists, such as George C. Williams, criticize Wilson's ideas.

 Lewontin, R. C. (1970). The units of selection. *Annual Review of Ecology and Systematics, 1,* 1–18.

*One of the first rigorous treatments of natural selection as a process that acts on a nested hierarchy of units. In addition to his rigorous conceptual analysis, Lewontin was among the first to appreciate that disease organisms provide an excellent model system for studying multilevel selection and discussed the evolution of reduced virulence in the myxoma virus introduced to Australia to control the rabbit population as an example of group selection (and altruism) in action.

 Lopreato, J. (1984). *Human nature and biocultural evolution.* Boston: Allen & Unwin.

*In this monograph Lopreato develops one of the first integrated theories of cultural evolution from a biological perspective. His organizing framework is distinctly sociobiological. Especially significant is his exploration of the evolutionary significance of the human propensity for self-deception, and his conclusion that human beings are capable—unique among animals—of reproductively subversive behavior that opposes the self-serving thrusts of genes. He calls this ascetic altruism and argues that the cause of this behavior is human belief in the fiction of a soul.

 Lovelock, J. E. (1979). *Gaia: A new look at life on earth.* Oxford: Oxford University Press.

*In this influential book, Lovelock compares the entire earth as like a single organism that adaptively regulates its atmosphere. From a multilevel evolutionary perspective, this would be regarded as a modern example of naïve group selectionism, similar to the early example of Emerson provided above, because adaptation at the level of the planet would require an unlikely process of interplanetary selection.

🕮 Maynard Smith, J. (1964). Group selection and kin selection. *Nature,* 1145–1146.

*This is part of an exchange of letters between Maynard Smith and V. C. Wynne-Edwards, in which Maynard Smith coined the term "kin selection" to describe W. D. Hamilton's inclusive fitness theory and constructed a brief model of group selection to demonstrate its implausibility. Despite its brevity, it was influential in the rejection of group selection in the 1960s.

🕮 Maynard Smith, J. (1982). *Evolution and the theory of games.* Cambridge: Cambridge University Press.

*An early summary of evolutionary game theory, which Maynard Smith was influential in developing during the late 1970s and early 1980s. Most of the models are devoted to understanding the evolution of cooperation.

🕮 Midgley, M. (1995). *Beast and man: The roots of human nature.* London: Routledge.

*A revised edition of her 1979 critique of sociobiology, itself an elaboration of her famous *Philosophy* paper, entailing a vigorous criticism of Richard Dawkins. Midgley rejects both evolutionary determinism and reductionism, and argues it proceeds from (bad) metaphysics rather than from either legitimate science or compelling philosophy. At the same time, she does not wish to reject either appropriately understood biological constraints on human freedom or legitimate causal explanations of human behavior. Although not theological, Midgley advocates a vision of human nature that is somewhat Pascalian. She locates her discussion of human nature within chapters that provide clear reflections on natural evil, natural purpose and teleology, problems with reductionism (evolutionary and neurological), the relationship of facts and values, and human uniqueness and the role of culture.

🕮 Midgley, M. (1995). The ethical primate: Humans, freedom and morality. London: Routledge.

*Although published the same year as the above, this is in many respects an extension of one particular issue, that of human freedom and moral responsibility. Midgley's goal is to find a middle ground between sociobiological reductionism that deconstructs human nature to fit animal models of behavior, and idealism that locates human nature altogether outside of or imposed upon our character as organic beings. Moreover, she is concerned to demonstrate that our moral qualities are a fulfillment of, not in opposition to, our organic nature, which is not, she argues, purely vile and self-centered as many ethologists and sociobiologists have contended. The book is shorter, less analytically nuanced, and more proscriptive than the above.

◈ Muir, W. M. (1996). Group selection for adaptation to multiple-hen cages: Selection program and direct responses. *Poultry Science, 75,* 447–458.

A selection experiment was initiated with a synthetic line of White Leghorns in 1982 to improve adaptability and well-being of layers in large multiple-bird cages by use of a selection procedure termed "group selection." With this procedure, each sire family was housed as a group in a multiple-bird cage and selected or rejected as a group. An unselected control, with approximately the same number of breeders as the selected line, was maintained for comparison and housed in one-bird cages. Annual percentage mortality of the selected line in multiple-bird cages decreased from 68 percent in Generation (G)2 to 8.8 percent in G6. Percentage mortality in G6 of the selected line in multiple-bird cages was similar to that of the unselected control in one-bird cages (9.1%). Annual days survival improved from 169 to 348 days, eggs per hen per day (EHD) from 52 to 68 percent, eggs per hen houses from 91 to 237 eggs, and egg mass (EM) from 5.1 to 13.4 kg, whereas egg weight remained unchanged. The dramatic improvement in livability demonstrates that adaptability and well-being of these birds were improved by group selection. The similar survival of the selected line would not further reduce mortalities, which implies that group selection may have eliminated the need to beak-trim. Corresponding improvements in EHD and EM demonstrate that such changes can also be profitable. The most surprising finding was the rate at which such improvement took place, with the majority of change in survival occurring by the third generation. However, EHD continued to improve at the rate of 4 percent per generation.

◈ Ostrom, E. (2000). Collective action and the evolution of social norms. *Journal of Economic Perspectives, 14*(3), 137–158.

I assume multiple types of players—"rational egoists," as well as "conditional cooperators" and "willing punishers"—in models of nonmarket behavior. I use an indirect evolutionary approach to explain how multiple types of players could survive and flourish in social dilemma situations. Contextual variables that enhance knowledge about past behavior assist in explaining the origin of collective action. Among the important contextual variables are types of goods, types of groups, and rules that groups use to provide and allocate goods. Finally, I reexamine a series of design principles that were derived earlier from an examination of extensive case materials.

◈ Oyama, S. (2000). Evolution's eye: A systems view of the biology-culture divide. Durham, NC: Duke University Press.

*Oyama is one of a small but growing number of critics of sociobiological gene centrism, of the standard social science model of cultural autonomy, and even of the integrative attempts of dual-inheritance theory to bring the latter two together through hierarchy. She maintains that all of these positions are dualistic in their view of the relationship between genes and environment or nature and nurture. She advocates developmental systems theory (DST), which posits not just interaction between genes and environment, but codetermination in a way that makes their very delimitation illegitimate. She takes issue with the biological ontogeny assumed by mainstream evolutionary theory and proposes a new, more holistic account of development.

&♒ Pinker, S. (1997). *How the mind works.* New York: W. W. Norton.

*Pinker integrates a Darwinian interpretation of human behavior with a computational theory of mind to provide a reductionistic, highly adaptationist account of human cognition and behavior. Along with other evolutionary psychologists, Pinker does not believe the mind is organized by general-purpose rationality, but by discrete cognitive modules designed to solve specific social or environmental problems, and that both what we learn and what we do are innately biased by selection. He also invokes exploitation of neural processes by memes as an explanation for some modes of behavior that appear counteradaptive. Pinker argues the mind is more epiphenomenal than some other evolutionary psychologists posit, who give greater weight to the causal efficacy of reasoning.

&♒ Plotkin, H. (1993). *Darwin machines and the nature of knowledge.* Cambridge: Harvard University Press.

*An attempt to integrate evolutionary epistemology with cultural evolution, this volume's significance to altruism is the case it makes for human freedom to pursue counterreproductive, sacrificial behavior. It contains a survey of the variation in evolutionary models of selectional change. It then acknowledges the difficulty biologists have had in defining adaptation and posits a nested, hierarchical account of adaptation involving genetic change, mental change (individual learning), and cultural change (group transmission). Plotkin argues that the latter has become "uncoupled" from the former, and this generates the unique human capacity for both radical beneficence and pathological self-destructive behaviors.

&♒ Plotkin, H. (1998). *Evolution in mind: An introduction to evolutionary psychology.* Cambridge: Harvard University Press.

*This monograph is not a survey, but an exploration of the significance that humans are not constrained by a sociobiological "genetic leash," and that cultural processes constitute an important, higher (tertiary) level of human behavior, on top of both individual psychology and genetics. The book includes a comprehensive single-chapter description of the sociobiological revolution and its importance for biological explanations of behavior, along with an assessment of the various forms of reductionism found in sociobiology. What it proposes is a similarly Darwinian but nongenetic explanation of cultural evolution, which opens up possibilities for altruism.

✒ Post, S. G., Underwood, L. G., Schloss, J. P., & Hurlbut, W. B. (Eds.). (2002). *Altruism and altruistic love: Science, philosophy, and religion in dialogue.* New York: Oxford University Press.

*This edited volume is an interdisciplinary synopsis of what is currently known about altruism and what the significant research questions are in a variety of scientific fields, with contributions by leaders in each field. Sections assess altruism from the perspectives of religion/philosophy (Elliot Sober, Stephen Pope, Steven Post), social and developmental psychology (Samuel Oliner, Daniel Batson, Jerome Kagan, Kristen Monroe), neurobiology (Antonio Damasio, Thomas Insel, William Hurlbut), and evolutionary biology (David Sloan Wilson, Melvin Konner, Michael Ruse, Frans de Waal, Jeffrey Schloss). The section on the evolution of altruism contains a balanced array of proposals representing individual selection (reciprocity), multilevel selection (group function), and pleiotropy (internal benefit) interpretations of altruism.

✒ Price, G. R. (1970). Selection and covariance. *Nature, 277,* 520–521.

*This and the following paper presented a new method for breaking evolutionary change in a large population into additive components based on variance and covariance coefficients. The Price equation, as it has come to be called, has become increasingly influential among theoretical biologists starting with Hamilton (1975) and has played a large role in the revival of multilevel selection thinking in evolutionary biology.

✒ Price, G. R. (1972). Extension of covariance selection mathematics. *Annals of Human Genetics, 35,* 485–490.

This paper gives some extensions of the selection mathematics based on the covariance function published in Price (1970). Application of the mathematics to "group selection" is briefly illustrated. . . . The mathematics given here applies not only to genetical selection but to selection in general. It is intended mainly for use in deriving general relations and constructing theories, and to clarify understanding of selection phenomena, rather than for numerical calculation (p. 485).

✒ Price, G. R. (1995). The nature of selection. *Journal of Theoretical Biology, 175,* 389–396.

A model that unifies all types of selection (chemical, sociological, genetical, and every other kind of selection) may open the way to develop a general "Mathematical Theory of Selection" analogous to communication theory. [*Note added by S. A. Frank:* "This previously unpublished manuscript was found among Dr. Price's papers when he died in 1975. In this paper Dr. Price did not provide a complete, general theory of selection. Rather, he argued why such a theory is needed and what some of its properties might be. The accompanying article provides commentary on this paper and describes Dr. Price's significant contributions to evolutionary genetics" (373–388).]

➷ Rapoport, A. (1991). Ideological commitments and evolutionary theory. *Journal of Social Issues, 47,* 83–100.

*This paper is important for showing how a single behavior can be portrayed as selfish or altruistic, in the scientific literature no less than in everyday life. Rapoport submitted the "tit-for-tat" strategy which won Axelrod's (1980a,b) famous game-theory computer tournaments. Tit-for-tat was widely regarded as a selfish ("unbeatable") strategy but in this paper Rapoport points out that it is anything but unbeatable. In fact, the "tit-for-tat" strategy is incapable of beating its social partner—it can only lose or draw—and wins the tournament only because it causes it and its partner to succeed as a collective. According to Rapoport, "the effects of ideological commitments on interpretations of evolutionary theories were never more conspicuous" (p. 92).

➷ Richards, R. J. (1987). Darwin and the emergence of evolutionary theories of mind and behavior. Chicago: University of Chicago Press.

*Richards provides an extensive historical survey of evolutionary notions of mind and behavior from precursors in the seventeenth century, to Lamarck, Darwin, Spencer, James, Baldwin, and sociobiological reformulations. He has substantive chapters on the interaction between Darwin's theory and natural theology, a review of Darwin's theory of moral faculty, and a chapter on science, metaphysics, and religion. Richards also has an interesting consideration of the unsolved problem of altruism in social insects as a cause of Darwin's delay in publishing. Finally, he concludes with an exploration of group selection, a critique of the fallacious status of the naturalistic fallacy, and an attempt to derive an evolutionary-based ethics.

➷ Ridley, M. (2001). The cooperative gene: How Mendel's demon explains the evolution of complex beings. New York: Free Press.

*Ridley maintains that it is the cooperative gene and not the selfish gene that constitutes a driving force for the evolution of complexity from cellular to organismal to social integration. Yet how do such structures emerge from a reproductively self-interested process? The answer is while selection is reproductively conservative, mutation is not and random variations can generate interactive alliances with benefits attending complexity. Ridley ends up positing a directionality to evolution.

⟨⟩ Ridley, M. (1993). *The red queen: Sex and the evolution of human nature.* New York: Penguin Books.

*In this volume, Ridley provides an accessible though accurate interpretation of human nature in light of sexual selection: particularly the differential assurance of paternity and maternity, the asymmetric investment by males and females, different mate choice criteria, and so on.

This book is an inquiry into the nature of human nature (i.e., bedrock of similarity that underlies the human race). Its theme is that it is impossible to understand human nature without understanding how it evolved, and it is impossible to understand how it evolved without understanding how human sexuality evolved. For the central theme of our evolution has been sexual. (p. 4)

⟨⟩ Ridley, M. (1997). Origins of virtue: Human instincts and the evolution of cooperation. New York: Viking.

*Richard Dawkins claims this book is an extrapolation of selfish-gene theory to focus on human nature; yet, interestingly, Frans de Waal, staunch critic of Dawkinsian reductionism, also praises Ridley's perspective. Ridley walks a middle ground here by arguing that biological explanations are basically adequate to explain human behavior without recourse to hierarchy or genetically transcendent memes, but that the picture of human nature in general and morality in particular that emerges therefrom, while reproductively self-interested, is motivationally cooperative and not devoid of what most would call genuine goodness. The book contains a very helpful survey of theories of moral sentiments. From the book jacket:

If evolution by natural selection relentlessly favors self-interest, why do human beings live in complex societies and show so much cooperative spirit? In *The Origins of Virtue,* Matt Ridley, a zoologist and former American editor of the *Economist,* shows that recent research in a number of fields has suggested a resolution of the apparent contradiction between self-interest and mutual aid. Brilliantly orchestrating the new findings of geneticists, psychologists, and anthropologists, *The Origins of Virtue* re-examines the everyday assumptions upon which we base our interactions toward others, whether we are nurturing parents, siblings, or trade partners.

⟨⟩ Rose, H., & Rose, S. (2000). *Alas, poor Darwin: Arguments against evolutionary psychology.* New York: Harmony Books.

*One of the fascinating things about the history of sociobiological theories over the last twenty-five years is that after a spate of fierce condemnations in the 1970s, and a modest flowering of more reasoned critiques in the early 1980s, there has been little criticism in either the popular or scholarly press, even though the discipline itself has continued to develop under new labels, such as evolutionary psychology and Darwinian anthropology. Indeed, many of the early critics (e.g., Philip Kitcher, Peter Singer) have become cautious advocates. This is the first major criticism of second-generation sociobiology to emerge, and the only concerted scholarly counterattack in over a decade. There are excellent chapters critiquing the adequacy of evolutionary psychology's account of religion (Dorothy Nelkin), memes (Mary Midgley), Dawkinsian gene-centrism (Gabriel Dover), Darwinian fundamentalism à la Dennett (Stephen Gould), the reduction of mind to cognitive modules, reducing the human behavioral to biological sciences, and a feminist critique of individual self-interest. While the most extensive single critique of evolutionary psychology, it is not wholly commensurate with the substantive and manifold articulations of the discipline itself. Written in essay format reminiscent of the exchanges on these issues that have appeared in the *New York Review of Books,* the chapters are sparsely documented and do not engage the scientific issues at a level of detail or nuance comparable to the proponents they critique.

    ℚ Sahlins, M. (1976). *The use and abuse of biology: An anthropological critique of sociobiology.* Ann Arbor: University of Michigan Press.

    *This was one of the first and most substantial critiques of sociobiology. Its analysis of the inadequacies of adaptationism in general, and in particular when applied to cultures, is still viable today. However, Sahlins betrays a number of misunderstandings of biological theory, and the anthropological data he cites against sociobiology can actually be effectively used to support it.

The publication of Edward O. Wilson's *Sociobiology: The New Synthesis* in the fall of 1975 was greeted both within and beyond the academy, with a response of historic proportions. At least the reaction was all out of proportions usually accorded a scholarly work issued by a scholarly press. Actually the storm had been building for years: Mr. Wilson, as he would readily acknowledge, is not the first sociobiologist, although he is clearly the most effective and comprehensive. The book in any case became a "media event," subject to feature stories and even front-page headlines in the *New York Times,* the *Chicago Tribune,* and other leading American dailies. It set off a running debate, as yet without resolution, in the pages of the *New York Review of Books* and in *Science,* the journal of the American Association for the Advancement of Science. By the spring of 1976, lectures and entire courses, pro and con, were being offered on the new discipline of sociobiology at Harvard, the University of Chicago, the University of Michigan, and other distinguished places of higher learning. A critical attack, issued by the Boston-based collective "Science for the People," was being vended at advanced intellectual kiosks across the country. The American Anthropological Association reserved two days of symposia on the subject at its annual meetings in November, 1976, at which Wilson as well as other biologists and sympathetic anthropologists would argue the case for a major redirection in social-science thinking. In brief, *Sociobiology* has occasioned a crisis of connaissance and conscience, with overtones as much political or ideological as they have been academic. Willy-nilly, the present essay becomes part of the controversy. It addresses the general intellectual and ideological issues raised by *Sociobiology* and related writings from the particular vantage of a practicing anthropologist, which is to say, from a traditional vantage of what *culture* is. The tenor will be critical but I hope not hysterical. (pp. ix–x)

✦ Schwartz, J. (2000). Death of an altruist. *Lingua franca, 10*(5), 51–61.

*This article reviews the life of George Price, whose papers are recorded in this bibliography and described by contributions from Steven Frank that are also recorded in this bibliography. Schwartz's article is based on interviews and direct observation of materials related to Price's quite unique life and death.

✦ Schwartz, B. (1987). The battle for human nature: Science, morality, and modern life. New York: Norton.

*This book develops a critique of scientism and the deconstruction of human nature to fit what the author argues are ideologically biased materialist accounts. Schwartz has chapters describing economic, evolutionary, and behaviorist determinisms. He then has three chapters critiquing them on the basis of both their scientific inadequacies and social-ethical impacts. He has an opening chapter on is-ought relations in human nature, and concluding chapters on the limits of science. His chapter on the limits of evolutionary biology is not antievolutionary but is strongly antiscientistic. He argues throughout that we must not interpret human nature to fit a particular evolutionary scenario, but must attempt to develop an account of human origins that comports with what we know about humanity from all the learned disciplines.

✦ Segerstråle, U. (2000). *Defenders of the truth: The battle for science in the sociobiology debate and beyond.* New York: Oxford University Press.

*This is an extensive historical and sociological assessment of the debate over sociobiology, with virtually every major and minor skirmish chronicled through exhaustive reviews of the scholarly and popular literatures. The book is scientifically accurate but assesses the controversy or, better, controversies inherent in sociobiological debates from the sociology and philosophy of science (more the former). It contains a comprehensive historical assessment of the initial debates over sociobiology; less emphasis is placed on the recent explosion of manifold critiques and modifications. What it does not offer is an assessment, or even thorough representation, of the evidential basis for the scientific debates. Instead, the author maintains the debates may be more over worldview than naked evidence.

     ⳿⳿ Singer, M. (1996). Farewell to adaptationism: Unnatural selection and the politics of biology. *Medical Anthropology Quarterly, 10,* 496–515.

*This article presents the position held by "critical medical anthropologists" that evolutionary explanations for health conditions distract attention from environmental conditions, which are presumed to be more flexible, in principle at least. Singer's essay offers a more contemporary and specific example of the general argument advanced by Sahlins (1976), also referenced in this bibliography.

     ⳿⳿ Sober, E., & Wilson, D. S. (1998). *Unto others: The evolution and psychology of unselfish behavior.* Cambridge: Harvard University Press.

*This book examines the evolution of biological (based on fitness effects) and psychological (based on intentions) altruism from a multilevel evolutionary perspective. It is divided into two sections on the evolution and psychology of altruism. The evolutionary section provides a historical survey of the altruism issue and the longstanding debates over the nature and levels of selection. It argues very compellingly for a rehabilitation of "group-selection" theory and, moreover, demonstrates that when appropriately mathematically understood, group selection does not even conflict with—in fact, is contained within—sociobiological models of selection. Then the book surveys and critiques the literature on psychological egoism and altruism, concluding it is much more ambiguous than proponents of either pole acknowledge. From the book jacket:

No matter what we do, however kind or generous our deeds may seem, a hidden motive of selfishness lurks—or so science has claimed for years. This book, whose publication promises to be a major scientific event, tells us differently. In *Unto Others* philosopher Elliott Sober and biologist David Sloan Wilson demonstrate once and for all that unselfish behavior is in fact an important feature of both biological and human nature. Their book provides a panoramic view of altruism throughout the animal kingdom—from self-sacrificing parasites to insects that subsume themselves in the superorganism of a colony to the human capacity for selflessness—even as it explains the evolutionary sense of such behavior.

     ⳿⳿ Stanley, S. M. (1975). A theory of evolution above the species level. *Proceedings of the National Academy of Sciences, 72*(2), 646–650.

Gradual evolutionary change by natural selection operates so slowly within established species that it cannot account for the major features of evolution. Evolutionary change tends to be concentrated within speciation events. The direction of transpecific evolution is determined by the process of species selection, which is analogous to natural selection but acts upon species within higher taxa rather than upon individuals within populations. Species selection operates on variation provided by the largely random process of speciation and favors species that speciate at high rates or survive for long periods and therefore tend to leave many daughter species. Rates of speciation can be estimated for living taxa by means of the equation for exponential increase and are clearly higher for mammals than for bivalve mollusks.

✍️ Stone, V. E., Cosmides, L., Tooby, J., Kroll, N., & Knight, R. T. (2002). Selective impairment of reasoning about social exchange in a patient with bilateral limbic system damage. *Proceedings of the National Academy of Sciences of the USA, 99*(17), 11531–11536.

Social exchange is a pervasive feature of human social life. Models in evolutionary biology predict that for social exchange to evolve in a species, individuals must be able to detect cheaters (nonreciprocators). Previous research suggests that humans have a cognitive mechanism specialized for detecting cheaters. Here we provide neurological evidence indicating that social exchange reasoning can be selectively impaired while reasoning about other domains is left intact. The patient, R.M., had extensive bilateral limbic system damage, affecting orbitofrontal cortex, temporal pole, and amygdala. We compared his performance on two types of reasoning problem that were closely matched in form and equally difficult for control subjects: social contract rules (of the form, "If you take the benefit, then you must satisfy the requirement") and precaution rules (of the form, "If you engage in hazardous activity X, then you must take precaution Y"). R.M. performed significantly worse in social contract reasoning than in precaution reasoning, when compared both with normal controls and with other brain-damaged subjects. This dissociation in reasoning performance provides evidence that reasoning about social exchange is a specialized and separable component of human social intelligence, and is consistent with other research indicating that the brain processes information about the social world differently from other types of information.

✍️ Strohman, R. (1997). Epigenesis and complexity: The coming Kuhnian revolution in biology. *Nature Biotechnology, 15,* 194–200.

The paradigm of the gene stands as a model that has presided over the development of an extremely successful molecular biology that continues to reveal the enormous complexity of living things. As a paradigm of life genetic determinism it is an illegitimate offspring of the former, showing all real signs of a Kuhnian revolution. In promising to penetrate and reveal the secrets of life, it has extended itself to a level of complexity where, as a paradigm, it has little power and must eventually fail. The failure is located in the mistaken idea that complex behavior may be traced solely to genetic agents and their surrogate proteins without recourse to the properties originating from the complex and nonlinear interactions of these agents.

☙ Swenson, W., Wilson, D. S., & Elias, R. (2000). Artificial ecosystem selection. *Proceedings of the National Academy of Science USA, 97*(16), 9110–9114.

Artificial selection has been practiced for centuries to shape the properties
of individual organisms, providing Darwin with a powerful argument for his
theory of natural selection. We show that the properties of whole ecosystems
can also be shaped by artificial selection procedures. Ecosystems initiated in the
laboratory vary phenotypically and a proportion of the variation is heritable,
despite the fact that the ecosystems initially are composed of thousands of
species and millions of individuals. Artificial ecosystem selection can be used
for practical purposes, illustrates an important role for complex interactions in
evolution, and challenges a widespread belief that selection is most effective at
lower levels of the biological hierarchy.

☙ Swenson, W., Arendt, J., & Wilson, D. S. (2000). Artificial selection of
microbial ecosystems for 3-chloroaniline biodegradation. *Environmental Mi-
crobiology, 2*(5), 564–571.

We present a method for selecting entire microbial ecosystems for biore-
mediation and other practical purposes. A population of ecosystems is established in the laboratory, each ecosystem is measured for a desired property (in
our case, degradation of the environmental pollutant 3-chloroaniline), and the
best ecosystems are used as "parents" to inoculate a new generation of "offspring" ecosystems. Over many generations of variation and selection, the ecosystems become increasingly well adapted to produce the desired property. The
procedure is similar to standard artificial selection experiments except that
whole ecosystems, rather than single individuals, are the units of selection. The
procedure can also be understood in terms of complex system theory as a way
of searching a vast combinatorial space (many thousands of microbial species
and many thousands of genes within species) for combinations that are especially good at producing the desired property. Ecosystem-level selection can be
performed without any specific knowledge of the species that comprises the
ecosystems and can select ensembles of species that would be difficult to discover with more reductionistic methods. Once a "designer ecosystem" has been created by ecosystem-level selection, reductionistic methods can be used to identify the component species and to discover how they interact to produce the
desired effect.

☙ Taylor, M. (1987). *The possibility of cooperation.* Cambridge: Cambridge University Press.

*This book is a good complement to Axelrod's *The Evolution of Coopera-
tion* (1984).

⚜ Thomas, L. (1974). *The lives of a cell: Notes of a biology watcher.* New York: Viking Press.

*This collection of short essays includes Lewis Thomas's observations on a range of questions considered by biological scientists. Entries that are most relevant include "On Societies as Organisms" and "On Various Words," where he reviews the origin of the terms *superorganism* and *holism.*

⚜ Tooby, J., & Cosmides, L. (1997). Friendship and the banker's paradox: Other pathways to the evolution of adaptations for altruism. In W. G. Runciman, J. Maynard Smith, and R. I. Dunbar (Eds.), *Evolution of social behavior patterns in primates and man* (pp. 119–143). Proceedings of the British Academy 88. Oxford: Oxford University Press.

*Tooby and Cosmides develop a hypothesis for the evolution of friendship, which they recognize is characterized by commitment to going beyond strict reciprocity. They argue that relationships that do not keep strict accounts of repayment can be considered adaptive solutions to the "banker's paradox," which involves the fact that we are most in need of a loan when we are least able to demonstrate the ability to repay. The kind of intersubjective commitment that values others independent of resources may have been internalized a human need for intimate relationship.

The classical definition of altruism in evolutionary biology requires that an organism incur a fitness cost in the course of providing others with a fitness benefit. New insights are gained, however, by exploring the implications of an adaptationist version of the "problem of altruism," as the existence of machinery designed to deliver benefits to others. Alternative pathways for the evolution of altruism are discussed, which avoid barriers thought to limit the emergence of reciprocation across species. We define the Banker's Paradox, and show how its solution can select for cognitive machinery designed to deliver benefits to others, even in the absence of traditional reciprocation. These models allow one to understand aspects of the design and social dynamics of human friendship that are otherwise mysterious.

⚜ Trivers, R. L. (1971). The evolution of reciprocal altruism. *Quarterly Review of Biology, 46,* 35–57.

A model is presented to account for the natural selection of what is termed reciprocally altruistic behavior. The model shows how selection can operate against the cheater (nonreciprocator) in the system. Three instances of altruistic behavior are discussed, the evolution of which the model can explain: (1) behavior involved in cleaning symbioses; (2) warning cries in birds; and (3) human reciprocal altruism. Regarding human reciprocal altruism, it is shown that the details of the psychological system that regulates this altruism can be explained by the model. Specifically, friendship, dislike, moralistic aggression, gratitude, sympathy, trust, suspicion, trustworthiness, aspects of guilt, and some forms of dishonesty and hypocrisy can be explained as important adaptations to regulate the altruistic system. Each individual human is seen as possessing altruistic and cheating tendencies, the expression of which is sensitive to developmental variables that were selected to set the tendencies at a balance appropriate to the local social and ecological environment.

⚡ Wade, M. J. (1976). **Group selection among laboratory populations of** *Tribolium*. *Proceedings of the National Academy of Sciences, 73*(12), 4604–4607.

Selection at the population level or group selection is defined as genetic change that is brought about or maintained by the differential extinction and/or proliferation of populations. Group selection for both increased and decreased adult population size was carried out among laboratory populations of *Tribolium castaneum* at thirty-seven-day intervals. The effect of individual selection within populations on adult population size was evaluated in an additional control series of populations. The response in the group selection treatments occurred rapidly, within three or four generations, and was large in magnitude, at times differing from the controls by over 200 percent. This response to selection at the populational level occurred despite strong individual selection which caused a decline in the mean size of the control populations from over 200 adults to near fifty adults in nine thirty-seven-day intervals. "Assay" experiments indicated that selective changes in fecundity, developmental time, body weight, and cannibalism rates were responsible in part for the observed treatment differences in adult population size. These findings have implications in terms of speciation in organisms whose range is composed of many partially isolated local populations.

⚡ Wilkinson, R. (2000). *Mind the gap: Hierarchies, health, and human society.* London: Weidenfeld and Nicolson.

This book is about health and evolution. But it is not about the most obvious links such as the evolution of antibiotic resistance in bacteria or genetic susceptibility to disease in humans. Rather, it is about the socioeconomic factors that make some societies, and some groups within societies, healthier and longer-lived than others. The causes of changes in health over time, of differences in health between countries, or between social classes are to be found not in genetic changes and differences, but in environmental change and environmental differences. This book is, in short, about environmental influences on health. Why, then, is it published in a series on modern evolutionary thinking? The answer is that it is difficult to make sense of what appear to be environmental causes of population health without evolutionary theory (p. 1).

❧ Williams, G. C. (1966). *Adaptation and natural selection: A critique of some current evolutionary thought.* Princeton, NJ: Princeton University Press.

*Williams's seminal critique of group selection and argument for the primacy of individual selection laid the foundation for selfish-gene theory and for the sociobiological revolution, and was determinative in defining evolutionary orthodoxy for four decades.

I hope this book will help purge biology of what I regard as unnecessary distractions that impede the progress of evolutionary theory and the development of a disciplined sciences for analyzing adaptation. It opposes certain of the recently advocated qualifications and additions to the theory of natural selection, such as genetic assimilation, group selection, and cumulative progress in adaptive evolution. It advocates a ground rule that should reduce future distractions and at the same time facilitate the recognition of really justified modifications of the theory. The ground rule or perhaps doctrine would be a better term is that adaptation is a special and onerous concept that should be used only when it is really necessary. When it must be recognized, it should be attributed to no higher a level of organization than is demanded by the evidence. In explaining adaptation, one should assume the adequacy of the simplest form of natural selection, that of alternative alleles in Mendelian populations, unless the evidence clearly shows that this theory does not suffice. (pp. 4–5)

❧ Williams, G. C. (1992). *Natural selection: Domains, levels and challenges.* Oxford: Oxford University Press.

*An update on the paradigm that Williams established in 1966. From the book jacket:

In this work, George C. Williams—one of evolutionary biology's most distinguished scholars—examines the mechanism and meaning of natural selection in evolution. Williams offers his own perspective on modern evolutionary theory, including discussions of the gene as the unit of selection, clade selection and macroevolution, diversity within and among populations, stasis, and other timely and provocative topics. In dealing with the levels-of-selection controversy, he urges a pervasive form of the replicator-vehicle distinction. Natural selection, he argues, takes place in the separate domains of information and matter. Levels-of-selection questions, consequently, require different theoretical devices depending on the domain being discussed. In addressing these topics, Williams presents his synthesis of three decades of research and creative thought which have contributed greatly to evolutionary biology in this century.

❧ Wilson, D. S. (1983). The group selection controversy: History and current status. *Annual Review of Ecology and Systematics, 14,* 159–187.

This review attempts to place the modern concept of group selection within its historical context. A historical perspective is important for several reasons. First, group selection is a fascinating example of how scientific questions arise from unscientific attitudes, and how their development is often haphazard and unsystematic. Second, much of the recent debate over group selection centers around the semantic question of whether these new models should, in fact, be called group selection. This question cannot be answered without an appreciation of history. Third, even though the modern concept of group selection lies squarely within the older tradition, fundamental differences do exist that must be emphasized. Finally, one of the most striking features of the "new" group selection is its relation to other major concepts, such as inclusive fitness, game theory, and reciprocity. In the past these have been treated as rival theories, with every effort being devoted to accentuating their differences. Now it is apparent that they can be united within a single framework and that far more is to be gained by emphasizing their similarities. This change in itself is a development whose history is worth tracing.

Wilson, D. S. (1997). Altruism and organism: Disentangling the themes of multilevel selection theory. *American Naturalist, 150S,* 122–134.

The evolution of groups into adaptive units, similar to single organisms in the coordination of their parts, is one major theme of multilevel selection theory. Another major theme is the evolution of altruistic behaviors that benefit others at the expense of self. These themes are often assumed to be strongly linked, such that altruism is required for group-level adaptation. Multilevel selection theory reveals a more complex relationship between the themes of altruism and organism. Adaptation at every level of the biological hierarchy requires a corresponding process of natural selection, which includes the fundamental ingredients of phenotypic variation, heritability, and fitness consequences. These ingredients can exist for many kinds of groups and do not require the extreme genetic variation among groups that is usually associated with the evaluation of altruism. Thus, it is reasonable to expect higher-level units to evolve into adaptive units with respect to specific traits, even when their members are not genealogically related and do not behave in ways that are obviously altruistic. As one example, the concept of a group mind, which has been well documented in the social insects, may be applicable to other species.

Wilson, D. S. (1999). A critique of R. D. Alexander's views on group selection. *Biology and Philosophy, 14*(3), 431–450.

Group selection is increasingly being viewed as an important force in human evolution. This paper examines the views of R. D. Alexander, one of the most influential thinkers about human behavior from an evolutionary perspective, on the subject of group selection. Alexander's general conception of evolution is based on the gene-centered approach of G. C. Williams, but he has also emphasized a potential role for group selection in the evolution of individual genomes and in human evolution. Alexander's views are internally inconsistent and underestimate the importance of group selection. Specific themes that Alexander has developed in his account of human evolution are important but are best understood within the framework of multilevel selection theory. From this perspective, Alexander's views on moral systems are not the radical departure from conventional views that he claims, but remain radical in another way more compatible with conventional views.

&Ⓒ Wilson, D. S. (2002). *Darwin's cathedral: Evolution, religion, and the nature of society.* Chicago: University of Chicago Press.

*Society is often metaphorically compared to a single organism. This book asks if the organismic concept of groups can be treated as a serious scientific hypothesis, using human religious groups as a case study. Chapter 1 reviews the relevant evolutionary concepts, concluding that groups can evolve the properties inherent in the word *organism*, but only if special conditions are met. Chapter 2 reviews the relevant concepts in the social sciences, arguing that the largely rejected tradition of functionalism needs to be revived and placed upon a multilevel evolutionary foundation. Chapters 3 and 4 examine four religious systems in detail from a multilevel evolutionary perspective (Calvinism, the water temple system of Bali, Judaism as a broad religious tradition, and early Christianity), concluding that they are largely adaptive at the group level. Chapter 5 evaluates the modern social science literature on religion, concluding that it broadly supports the organismic concept but that the study of religion can profit from an explicitly evolutionary perspective. Chapter 6 shows how evolution can be used to understand the Christian concept of forgiveness as a complex adaptation. Chapter 7 goes beyond religion to sketch a general theory of unifying systems and summarizes other themes of the book, including the importance of cultural and psychological in addition to genetic evolutionary processes and the need to understand both rational thought and the seemingly irrational elements of religious thought in terms of adaptation and natural selection.

&Ⓒ Wilson, D. S., & Sober, E. (1994). Reintroducing group selection to the human behavioral sciences. *Behavioral and Brain Sciences, 17*(4), 585–654.

In both biology and the human sciences, social groups are sometimes treated as adaptive units whose organization cannot be reduced to individual interactions. This group-level view is opposed by a more individualistic one that treats social organization as a byproduct of self-interest. According to biologists, group-level adaptations can evolve only by a process of natural selection at the group level. Most biologists rejected group selection as an important evolutionary force during the 1960s and 1970s, but a positive literature began to grow during the 1970s and is rapidly expanding today. We review this recent literature and its implications for human evolutionary biology. We show that the rejection of group selection was based on a misplaced emphasis on genes as "replicators," which is in fact irrelevant to the question of whether groups can be like individuals in their functional organization. The fundamental question is whether social groups and other higher-level entities can be "vehicles" of selection. When this elementary fact is recognized, group selection emerges as an important force in nature and what seems to be competing theories, such as kin selection and reciprocity, reappear as special cases of group selection. The result is a unified theory of natural selection that operates on a nested hierarchy of units.

The vehicle-based theory makes it clear that group selection is an important force to consider in human evolution. Humans can facultatively span the full range from self-interested individuals to "organs" of group-level "organisms." Human behavior not only reflects the balance between levels of selection but it can also alter the balance through the construction of social structures that have the effect of reducing fitness differences within groups, concentrating natural selection (and functional organization) at the group level. These social structures and the cognitive abilities that produce them allow group selection to be important even among large groups of related individuals.

🕮 Wilson, E. O. (1975). *Sociobiology: The new synthesis.* Cambridge: Harvard University Press.

*An encyclopedic review and synthesis of social behavior from an evolutionary perspective, which became controversial by attempting to include humans within the same theoretical framework, along with the rest of life on earth. Wilson combined kin selection and reciprocal altruism theory to attempt "a biological explanation of all social behavior." Although the expansive volume only included one chapter on humans, debate arose over the deterministic and reductionistic implications of asserting the goal of biologizing the social sciences and replacing epistemologists with endocrinologists.

🕮 Wilson, E. O. (1978). *On human nature.* Cambridge: Harvard University Press.

*A book-length and popularized extension of sociobiological principles to human beings. It is an overt apologetic not only for what he terms *scientific materialism,* viewed through a Darwinian lens, but also for the replacement of traditional religion by this worldview. Two chapters are seminal. His treatment of altruism provides one of the clearest sociobiological interpretations of human love available (religious orders and the gangs differ in form, are identical in function or substance). And his chapter on religion attempts not only the first functionalist account of religion from the perspective of sociobiology, but argues on this basis for the necessity of religion to human flourishing. He suggests that the history of engagement between religion and scientific materialism is a history of retreat and defeat for religion, and all that currently remains is an anemic deism or process theology. Wilson argues that once an entirely adequate materialistic account of not only the function, but the mechanism of religious belief is provided, theology will disappear.

෴ Wynne-Edwards, V. C. (1965). *Animal dispersion in relation to social behavior.* Edinburgh: Oliver and Boyd.

*This book is regarded as the paradigmatic example of "naïve group selection," which interpreted many forms of social behavior as adaptations that prevent populations from overexploiting their resources. Wynne-Edwards thought that he had discovered a major principle of evolution but his book provided the basis for the widespread rejection of group selection. Curiously, Wynne-Edward's basic thesis, that populations can evolve to avoid overexploiting their resources, has been confirmed for disease organisms that evolve reduced virulence and remains plausible for at least some nondisease organisms, although not in the grandiose form envisioned by Wynne-Edwards.

෴ Zahavi, A., & Zahavi, A. (1997). *The handicap principle: A missing piece of Darwin's puzzle.* Oxford: Oxford University Press.

*One of the upshots of reciprocal altruism theory is that the most effective reproductive strategy would involve cheating or nonreciprocation in a group of cooperators. To solve this problem, cooperators demand displays of group membership, much as mate choice demands displays of viability. In response, deceptive displays develop to attract both mates and reciprocators. This volume develops an extensive theory of how organisms handicap themselves by costly displays that are hard to fake, because of the compensatory gain by mate attraction or inclusion in the reciprocating alliance. This constitutes an important (though difficult to falsify) attempt to explain ostensibly maladaptive behaviors or anatomical features.

෴ Zahn-Wexler, C., Cummings, E. M., & Iannotti, R. J. (Eds.). (1986). *Altruism and aggression: Biological and social origins.* London: Cambridge University Press.

*This collection of papers constitutes one of the few attempts to explore biological and anthropological approaches to human behavior that does not attempt either to enfold one into another or syncretistically integrate the two. For this reason, it is a helpful and unique treatment, and the more so because it rightly perceived development as the bridge between biological and social influences. There are possible two shortcomings with the volume. First, an outgrowth of the attempt to avoid syncretism is the fact that there is little integration. Genetic, evolutionary, developmental, personality, and sociological approaches are portrayed. Second, "altruism" is frequently conflated with "prosocial behavior," and thus the difficult challenges to and from evolutionary theory are not squarely engaged.

CHAPTER 5

Profiles in Unlimited Love
Lives Ennobled by Purpose

Emma Y. Post

*U*p to this point, this book provides a wonderful introduction to love and altruism scientifically considered. But another source of data is the narrative of countless lives dedicated to love for humanity. A simple act of kindness can make a world of difference to someone. People who live their lives every day more for the sake of others than for themselves are models for us all. These stories tell of the acts of kindness themselves; more importantly, they indicate why and how people have such wholesome and compassionate intentions. If every person in the world could tap into the kindness that lies within him- or herself, it would be a much better life for everyone.

In this day and age, it's easy to forget what altruism is, or that it even exists. My generation is so distracted by pop culture, materialism, sex, and drugs that the lines between what's wrong and what's right are often blurred. While reading about the lives described in this chapter, I was reminded of what true unselfishness and compassion are. Figures like Gandhi, Millard Fuller, and the rest of the people I read about are an example to everyone. I only wish that such a way of life could become more prevalent among my peers. I hope that by my summarizing their lives, a few more people my age can discover that there is more to life than what we often think or are exposed to.

As for the rest of the world, I think we all need a little extra love and compassion. You do not have to be a confused teenager to know that there is meaning in kindness. Some of the people in these stories started off in difficult circumstances or experienced the hardest of times. However, the harder they fell, the higher they rose in love. Look upon these people as a representation of the hope and love everyone can attain, no matter how broken they might be at some point in life's journey. We all have the potential to shine.

Millard Fuller

By the age of thirty, Millard Fuller had it all. He was a millionaire with a beautiful wife and all of the material possessions he could desire. Despite those riches, however, Fuller's marriage to his wife, Linda, was not working out. When they separated, Linda left their home in Montgomery, Alabama, and went to New York City to rethink their marriage. Fuller followed his wife to New York, where they went through a period of soul-searching and prayer. Once they realized that their lives had been led astray, they reconciled and felt a "strong desire to come back to the Lord and to find His plan for us" (Fuller, 1986, p. 26). They sold Fuller's business and gave their money away. The Fullers arrived at Koinonia Farm in Americus, Georgia, in December 1965 to begin a personal healing process. Koinonia was a Christian fellowship, established by Clarence Jordan, in which the members taught improved agricultural methods to poor local tenant farmers.

In the summer of 1968 Fuller and Jordan met with friends. Out of this meeting arose the idea for "Partnership Housing." Jordan dedicated forty-two half-acre home sites of his property for rural families without homes. A park and recreational area were included as well. The money for this community would come from a "Fund for Humanity." Unfortunately, Jordan died just one year after the idea was born. But his death only strengthened the Fullers' passion for the project. In 1976, Habitat for Humanity was born to provide all people on the earth with homes.

Ten years later, twenty-five Habitat projects were underway in locations such as Zaire, Gulu, Uganda, India, and Peru. But these were just the beginnings of an attempt to solve a much larger problem. That same year, 1986, the United Nations Center for Human Settlements estimated that 1–1.5 billion people did not have adequate living conditions. Habitat for Humanity was originally intended to "enlarge . . . [the] attack on the problem of poverty housing" (33). Obviously, this was a massive undertaking.

When asked in a 1981 radio interview about the goal of Habitat for Humanity, Fuller answered without hesitation, "To eliminate poverty housing from the face of the earth" (20). In 1984, Habitat board member Jimmy Carter elaborated on Habitat's mission:

This is what Habitat wants to do. Plant projects all over the world; sow seeds of hope, encouraging the poor to do all they can to help themselves; and cultivate consciences among the affluent, urging them, privately or corporately, to join less fortunate folks in a spirit of partnership, to solve the problem together.

For years, Millard Fuller preached to "get rid of shacks!," even writing a book titled *No More Shacks* in 1986. In order to succeed, however, the "partnership" to which Carter referred was vital. First and foremost, Fuller put his faith in his partnership with God. He believed that Habitat was "God's movement, and there's nothing that can stop it" (22). Second, people were in partnership with each other. The beauty of Habitat was that all peoples, regardless of race, gender, or ethnicity, could work together building houses. Fuller said, "We might disagree on how to preach or how to dress or how to baptize or how to take communion or even what communion is for. But we can all pick up a hammer and, sharing the love of Christ, we can begin to drive nails. Thank God we can agree on a nail!" (22)

Fuller had lots of ideas for raising money. In 1983 a celebration was scheduled in Indianapolis for Habitat's seventh anniversary. "For several weeks I had been thinking about walking from Americus to Indianapolis, a distance of seven hundred miles" (47). As preposterous as the idea seemed, planning began. The idea caught on and people gradually began signing up to walk all or part of the distance or give pledges to people who were walking. The experience was very rewarding and the walk raised thousands of dollars. Through this event Habitat volunteers were able to "deliver the Habitat message in person to several thousand people along the way and expose thousands more to the work through extensive publicity. At least one new Habitat project would start as a direct result of the walk" (70).

Over the years, Habitat for Humanity grew in size and support, gaining international recognition. In 1982 Jimmy Carter spoke at an annual gathering of Habitat directors and representatives. From this came a lasting partnership in which Carter gave his time and energy to Habitat for Humanity. Projects were not only expanding across the nation, but across the world, from India to Nicaragua to Uganda.

The gratitude and happiness that families feel after receiving their houses is inspiring. "Families have such strong feelings about their new houses not only because of the overcrowded or sub-standard situations they are leaving. They are also touched by the love and concern they experience form the Habitat people" (176). After being asked how she felt about acquiring the house, one new homeowner said, "The most wonderful part of it all was the realization that there were people who cared enough to make it possible" (176).

In 1985 Fuller was asked about what Habitat was becoming. He replied, "I envision Habitat for Humanity becoming the conscience of the world concerning shelter" (189). Fuller realized that "we must educate consciences. We must publicize the need, promote the goal, and provide the opportunity for change in so many ways that poor housing will become unacceptable, and good housing will become a matter of conscience" (189). This "conscience" is universal, and not limited to matters concerning Habitat for Humanity. Fuller wants this conscience to spread in every way possible. "Wherever you go, there are opportunities. I ride in thousands of airplanes every year. I never know who will be sitting beside me, but I do know this: by the time our wheels touch down at the next airport, my seatmate will have heard about Habitat for Humanity" (190). For

Fuller, any goal is attainable. Nothing is impossible. When he said, "No more shacks!" he meant it. And with God's help, he began to make it happen.

Patty Anglin

In the 1960s missionaries Dr. and Mrs. Richard Pelham took their family, including daughter Patty, to Africa, where he worked as a surgeon for the American Baptist mission hospital. Patty's mother was a devoted Christian and a loving mother. "Mother was the most unselfish person I have ever known and she greatly influenced my own values and beliefs" (Anglin, 1999, p. 16). At an early age Patty wondered about her mission in life. When she was only nine, she prayed that God would show her how she could serve Him.

When Patty was sent to a boarding school for missionary kids, she struggled. "In addition to my loneliness and homesickness, I had great difficulty learning" (18). Reading and writing even simple words was difficult, leading to the discovery that she had dyslexia. Later on in life, this would help her understand her own children's disabilities. Patty also had a difficult relationship with her dorm parents, whom she knew as Uncle Joe and Aunt Min. One night, after dinner, Patty was overwhelmed with homesickness. Instead of doing her homework, she went to a window to get some fresh air and began thinking about her parents. In the midst of her thoughts, the voice of Uncle Joe scolded, "Why aren't you doing your homework?" (20). Patty tried to explain that she was only thinking of her parents, whom she missed so much. Uncle Joe berated her and made her write a five-hundred-word essay on why she should not wish to go home. Patty had a horrible time completing this task, and it affected her greatly. After she handed the essay to Uncle Joe, she began crying uncontrollably and was unable to breathe. Patty had an emotional breakdown, and her parents were called in to rescue her. She went home for a few weeks but returned to school in complete fear of Uncle Joe.

In 1969 Dr. Pelham decided to bring the family back to the United States. Once again, Patty felt lost because her "heart and roots were in Africa and the only culture that I knew was in Africa" (29). She grew homesick and dreamt of being back in Africa, holding African babies in her father's maternity ward. She envisioned herself running an orphanage there. "Although I did not realize it, God had been preparing me for my mission in life through these painful experiences. He knew that I would need to understand the feelings of abandonment, loneliness, fear, and the sense of not belonging—the same feelings that children from abusive, dysfunctional, and broken homes feel" (29). Patty's past was the foundation for her future.

After suffering through her own divorce and her parents' separation, Patty met and married Harold Anglin. Their child, Thomas James, or "T.J.," joined Patty's two children from her previous marriage and Harold's four children.

The Anglins were instantly a large family. One day, while T.J. was still a toddler, a social worker came to their family church and spoke about the growing need for foster parents. Harold and Patty were deeply moved by the social worker's message about children needed a loving environment to help them avoid emotional problems, as well as social or learning disorders. "We felt God telling us that there was room for other kids and we should help them by providing a loving Christian foster-care environment for them" (48). Harold and Patty decided to care for special-needs infants during the first months of their lives after parental rights had been terminated by the court. The Anglins' biological children were all involved in the infants' lives; "They all took it in stride and in the process each of them developed a sensitivity of their own for special-needs children" (50).

Eventually, the Anglins were ready to open their home in Michigan to foster children. The first child they took in was a three-year-old Hispanic boy. Although Patty and Harold were not aware of Pedro's exact family background, they agreed to give him a home. The Anglins were quite surprised when they were confronted with a crazy little kid who tried to hit and kick everyone in sight. Harold finally grabbed Pedro and held him down for hours, while Pedro struggled to get away. The next day, the social worker called to tell them that Pedro had been one of eleven children who had been physically abused and tortured by their father. "The months that followed were very trying. I had to constantly call upon God for His help. We had to deal with all kinds of physical and emotional problems that Pedro acquired in his brief little life in that dysfunctional family" (59).

Pedro was the first of many children whom the Anglins would come to love. Luckily for them, Pedro's biological father relinquished custody, and Pedro was theirs. The adoption process took three years, but it was worth it. He grew into a "creative, intelligent, sensitive, personable, and wonderful human being. It was all there inside him when he came to us that day. We only had to peel back the layers of hurt and resentment that he had built as a defense mechanism" (65).

Other foster children followed, each with specific problems and histories. Many of them had traumatic experiences growing up, a teenage mother who could not support them, or some form of disability. Letting them go became traumatic for the Anglins. Patty said, "The anguish of giving up these children that we had come to love was awful" (60). After Pedro, the Anglins adopted Cierra, who had a thirteen-year-old mother, and her little sister Serina. Before the Anglins could continue their mission, though, they needed a new home. They were already running out of room and wanted a bigger yard where the children could play. "Harold and I had talked and dreamed about the possibility of moving to the West, maybe Montana, and finding an old small ranch and living off the land. . . . However, a dream was all it was. I could never see a way for us to act on it" (155). Before they knew it, though, the Anglins had an opportunity to make their dream come true.

Harold was offered an early retirement package from the high school where he taught, which would give the Anglins the opportunity to earn more money to buy a new home. They didn't decide to take the offer until Patty went to visit her sister in Wisconsin and noticed a farm across from a school building. She immediately fell in love with it. Even though Patty's sister told her that the farmer who lived there was *not* willing to sell, Patty persisted and drove down the long driveway to the house. The farmer who owned it offered to take her on a tour of the two-hundred-acre farm. She told him her story and explained that her family would love his property. She tentatively asked if he would sell, and after just a moment's pause, he agreed—and for a very low price! After Patty talked with Harold back in Michigan, the Anglins acquired the two hundred acres, a farmhouse, barn, buildings, timber, grassland, cropland, and a beaver pond. "I recall praying as we drove down the lane with our family for the first time. *Lord, this farm is going to be for our children. This place is a vision I have as a safe haven for children, a place of hope. Acres and acres of hope. Yes, that's it! That'll be the name of our farm, Acres of Hope*" (164). And just like that, the Anglins' dream came true.

Harold and Patty acquired some animals, and Harold learned how to farm. Everyone had different chores to do, but there was plenty of playing to be done in the hills or in the woods. After the Anglins bought Acres of Hope, they adopted more children, an Indian boy named Ari, and two brothers, Tirzah and Tyler, who had lived in six different foster homes in just eighteen months. Soon afterwards, Patty and Harold also took in Levi, a boy who had been placed in a dumpster by his drunken mother in Cincinnati. Finally, the Anglins saved the life of little Zachary, who was born to Nigerian parents vacationing in America. The parents wished to kill the child, as was their custom when a baby was retarded. In fact, Zachary had severe limb impairments. After social workers told Patty that the parents wished to kill their child, she immediately agreed to take care of him and make him her own.

Patty and Harold ended up with a total of fifteen children. They were also kept busy advocating for special-needs children in many ways. "The overwhelming majority of foster parents are not in it for the money. Most could do better financially at other jobs, even flipping hamburgers at the local fast food chain at minimum wage" (272). It was, in fact, her love of children and belief that it was her mission in life to help them that drove her desire to take care of so many, especially ones with disabilities.

Patty Anglin is now the chairman of Children's Health Alliance of Wisconsin. She works with families and agencies in Wisconsin to solve child health issues and lobby for better state involvement in providing health care for children. She is also regional coordinator for Adopt America Network, helping hundreds of families find children like her own to adopt. Finally, Patty speaks at churches and addresses her concerns about adopting special-needs kids. After all, she believes that "Jesus told us to look after the children, widows, and orphans. We *all* need to take responsibility for the problem and be part of its solution" (281). Patty invites us to "reach out in love to a needy child and give that little boy or girl something valuable—*love* and *hope*" (282).

The Anglins still live on their farm, functioning as a large, loving family while advocating the need to adopt special-needs children. In the future, Patty hopes to set up a home on their property for lost teenage mothers, like the one who gave them two of their own children, Cierra and Serina. Patty's dream is to "help them, one at a time, if that's all I can do . . . maybe one day we will find a way" (287). Acres of Hope is the name of the Anglins' farm and their nonprofit organization, which is dedicated to helping children and giving emotional support and financial assistance to families dealing with children who have emotional or physical challenges. "In addition, our mission is to promote greater community understanding, acceptance, and support for families involved in adopting special-needs children cross-racially and cross-culturally" (288).

Christina Noble

The eldest of eight children and the daughter of an alcoholic, Christina Noble was born in the Liberties in 1944, a "God-struck, beer-soaked slum in south-west Dublin" (Noble, 1994, p. 25). Christina had such a painful childhood that even forty years later her voice becomes "high and tight and there is a hint of fear" (25) when she speaks of it. She grew up in a dingy flat with one bedroom, a living room, and a tiny scullery. The living room served as a bedroom for all of the children, who had only one blanket. "The institutional memory of many Dublin people is one of failure, deprivation, ceaseless toil, and monumental hardship. And nowhere in Dublin is that more true than in the Liberties" (34).

Apart from her already miserable existence as a child living in utter poverty, Christina experienced many other awful things. She struggled against her alcoholic father, who was always promising to stay off the drink in order to help support their family and was always breaking that promise. When her father was sober, it was a dream come true. "With daddy at home we were a family" (59).

One Saturday night after Christina's father had stayed sober for months, her worst fears came true. Mrs. Noble had made a beautiful dinner of fish, mashed potatoes, and peas, a tasty treat to celebrate her husband's sobriety, but her husband had not yet arrived home. She sent Christina to find him, and a neighbor said that he was at the pub. However, Christina "couldn't go into the pub. I did not want to see my father drunk. It would have destroyed the world in which I had been living and brought me back to all the horror of my life. So I walked around for a while and then I went home and told mam I couldn't find daddy" (62). With tears streaming down her face, her mother responded that he was probably drunk.

When her father did finally stagger home that night, his wife made the sign of the cross and braced herself for his homecoming. She tried to bring her children into the bedroom, but her husband caught her and threw her across the room, where she hit her head on the iron frame of the bed. Christina was terrified. "'You're killing my mam,' I screamed. 'God will never forgive you.' He stopped and lurched across the room towards me. 'Please don't hurt mammy,' I said. I was very frightened. I wanted to hit my father, I wanted to smash him so hard he would never wake up" (65). The abuse did not end there. It only ended when Christina's father drove his wife to her death because of the emotional and physical abuse he had inflicted upon her.

After her mother died, Christina had to take care of the rest of her siblings, emulating the loving, caring figure that their mother had been. Because her father was spending his wages drinking, the children had no food. Christina collected scraps from people's plates all around Dublin, a miserable and embarrassing experience for a little girl. Often she would wake up as early as 4 A.M. to go to the markets and pick up food that had fallen onto the street. The children were dirty and unkempt, and developed scabies, scurvy, and fleas. Christina's only outlet was singing. "Singing was my island of sanity," she said, her escape from suffering, something that she had loved to do ever since she could remember (89). So Christina sang and put on concerts, providing entertainment for herself, her siblings, and other neighborhood children.

That life didn't last long either. Soon after her mother's death, Christina and her siblings were sent to live with her father's family because her father was sick and in the hospital. This, too, was traumatizing. Her own relative, whom she calls the "man," emotionally, physically, and sexually abused her at the age of twelve. Fortunately, a man from the Society for the Prevention of Cruelty for Children came to the house one day and explained that the doctor who treated the children for lice had reported them. A few days later, a hearing was held at Dublin Castle that would change the children's lives forever.

After the hearing Christina and her siblings were sent to different institutional homes for children all around Ireland. "We were children whose only crime was that our mother had died, our father was an alcoholic, and our relatives beat us and abused us, but we were being treated like criminals" (106). The children were put into a van, and each one was dropped off with a teary goodbye at a different home. Christina promised to come back and find each of her siblings as they parted that day, but it would be many years before they would all be reunited.

Christina escaped and became a child of the streets at the age of twelve.

"During the winter, I slept in public toilets and coal sheds; in the summer and on balmy days, I slept under the bushes in Phoenix Park" (114). She would play with the children in the park each day and retreat to a little cove in the bushes each night. She could never find food. When it was too cold outside, she walked to stay warm. She sometimes saw her father, but he was no help. Christina's life as a street child ended briefly when she was caught by the police and sent to St. Joseph's Industrial School. This was "the worse place in all of Ireland for a girl . . . where Ireland hid its illegitimate daughters and its orphans, as well as young girls who were sent there by the courts" (121).

After a traumatic experience at St. Joseph's, Christina once again escaped and was homeless. She was now sixteen and more scared of living on the streets than ever. A priest once caught her eating candle wax and threw her out of the church. "I've never forgotten that. He wore warm clothes, lived in a nice house, and worked in a church where there was gold everywhere. And there I was with nothing but candle wax to eat and he saw fit to throw me out" (142). Incidents like these led to Christina's loss of faith in the Catholic Church.

One night Christina was afraid to sleep because of nightmares, and walked the streets instead. Around 1 A.M., a car began driving alongside of her. Two men got out of the car and shoved her into it. There were four men in all. Petrified, Christina began screaming for her dead mother. Eventually, the car stopped. She was forced to walk into an unknown room and onto a bed. She laid down while they tore off her clothes and beat her until she was half-conscious. "And then, one by one, they raped me" (143). After this continued for awhile, they dropped her back off on the streets. "I walked slowly through the breaking dawn until I came back to the park. I wanted to scream but my mouth was swollen and torn and my face was contorted and locked in a rictus of horror. My thighs ached. My lower spine ached. I was bleeding badly from my vagina and knew that the men had done me serious harm" (144).

"The thing I remember most vividly about the aftermath of that experience was the horrible realization that there was nobody for me to go to. I needed just one person who would not see me as dust, or barely more than an animal" (145). To add to her suffering, she became pregnant from the rape. Having an illegitimate child was considered a horrible crime in Ireland. Christina was again placed in a home and her child was taken away from her. This time, she ran away for good. "When a person is almost destroyed on the inside, you can't see it. But that person must live with the loss, and get on with life" (151). She decided to go to England.

Christina hid on a boat and arrived in England the next morning. She had heard that her brother Andy lived in Birmingham, and she intended to find him. Eventually, she did, and she stayed with him for a short period. While there, she held a steady job and found some nice girls her own age to befriend. She also met a Greek man, Mario, and began seeing him regularly. Christina's brother did not approve of Mario, so Christina moved in with her friend Joan. At age eighteen, Christina moved in with Mario and became pregnant a few months later. Their relationship was not a healthy one. He abused her and cheated on her countless times. Their relationship resulted in three children, to whom she would always remain close.

"It was during this time in my life, at a time of great misery and pain, that I had the dream about Vietnam" (178). This dream would shape Christina's future forever. She still doesn't know why she dreamed of Vietnam, but the dream shook her. "In my dream, naked Vietnamese children were running down a dirt road fleeing from a napalm bombing . . . one of the girls had a look in her eyes that implored me to pick her up and protect her and take her to safety. Above the escaping children was a brilliant white light that contained the word, 'Vietnam'" (179). At that time, Christina had no idea what to make of the dream. She was very confused, but knew that it was her destiny to go to Vietnam and work with children.

Christina's life finally took a turn for the better when she left Mario, gained custody of her three children, and met Simon, a man who treated her well. While she was with him, he supported her and helped her. Christina ran a successful catering business, hosting parties for different clubs around the area. For once, she had a good life.

In 1989 when she was forty, Christina would finally answer her dream. She and Simon separated, and she began seeing another man, whom she told about her destiny to go to Vietnam. One day he told her that he had been offered a job in Vietnam. Several weeks later, he called her from Ho Chi Minh City and told her that there was plenty of opportunity there because the streets were overrun with poor children. "The time had come" (206). With only a few hundred pounds in her pocket, Christina left her children to go to Vietnam. "This was no summer holiday. I was going half-way around the world. Although I had dreamed of this moment for almost twenty years, I was frightened . . . one way or another my destiny was about to be filled" (206).

When Christina arrived in Vietnam, it seemed like a movie set. She was full of questions and had nowhere to go. She caught a cab to Ho Chi Minh City, already wondering if this was what she was supposed to be doing. The city was chaotic. Cars, bikes, and people flooded the filthy streets. Christina arrived at the Rex Hotel, where she would be staying longer than she thought. For the next few weeks, she wandered through the city, venturing further and further on foot each day from the hotel. She met My Loc, a nice woman who sold children's clothes from a little stall. Everywhere she went, she saw ragged children. "They are called *bui doi*, a harsh, dismissing term meaning 'the dust of life.' They are terribly poor . . . no one will touch the bui doi. No one wants to be close to them. They are treated like vermin" (17).

One day, while standing outside of her hotel talking to the doorman, she saw two little girls playing in the dirt across the street. Christina stared at them and one of the girls caught her eye and smiled, holding out her hand. Suddenly, Christina was filled with painful memories from Ireland. "I did not want that pain again" (19). She tried to ignore the children and began walking away. However, she soon paused and turned around impulsively, looking back at the children again. "I stared at the two girls. Even with her gap-toothed smile, the one who had reached towards me was a child of uncommon beauty. . . . I wanted to turn to the right and go round the corner and walk down Le Loi and look at the shops, but I simply could not walk away. I slowly crossed the street towards the two girls" (19). Christina studied the girls a little longer, contrasting the little Vietnamese girls to herself, a successful European woman. Yet, she realized that "there's no difference between an Irish gutter and a Vietnamese gutter. At the end of the day they are the same" (21).

At that moment, Christina knew that she was facing a major turning point in her life. The girl reached for her hand again, but Christina panicked and backed away. Then she froze, as she realized that the girl's hands and expression were those of the girl in her dream. A slight breeze sprang up, and the smoke-filled air seemed to swirl about. Across from her was a billboard advertising a product, and the word "Vietnam" was written on it. "I sobbed. I reached for the girl but I could not see through my tears. She found my hand. And then I was sitting in the dirt holding the children in my lap. I pulled them to me and I rocked back and forth and I cried for a long time and promised that I would take care of them" (22). With this encounter, Christina's destiny was fulfilled. "Here the pain and sorrow and the anger of my childhood in Ireland would be resolved. I would work with the street children of Ho Chi Minh City. Here I would stay. Here I would find happiness. . . . Vietnam would be the bridge across my sorrows" (22).

And so began Christina Noble's crusade for the street children of Vietnam. All of the pain and suffering that she had gone through in Ireland led to a much higher cause. These experiences helped to strengthen her and give hope to destitute children in Vietnam. She began on a small scale by sneaking the two little girls into her hotel, which did not allow street children. The Rex was only for wealthy foreigners. She bathed, clothed, and fed the two little girls and let them stay with her. She began taking a group of children to an ice-cream parlor every Saturday morning. She sat with a dozen children and bought them ice cream, all the while talking about life on the street. One morning Christina was walking with all of her children when the police came. The authorities would not let her spend time with the children. When they took the children away at the police station, the children sobbed and begged for Christina, whom they called "Mama Tina." Afterwards, Christina cried for those children and for all of the suffering children in the world, determined to make a change.

Each day, Christina found more and more children. She brought them into the hotel and fed them. That December she decided to have a Christmas party. She made the appropriate arrangements and bought and wrapped presents for days. The Rex could only accommodate 150 children, although there were many more that she would have liked to invite. By this time, Christina were a celebrity to the children. They looked up to her and knew that she would help them. At the party Christina taught the children to sing. They cried, "We are the world, we are the children." When the party ended, many children were still outside the hotel who had not been allowed inside. Christina gathered these children up and took them to the ice-cream shop. The children who had been at the party began following her as well, and kept singing, "We are the world, we are the children." "The people on the street were perplexed . . . some smiled . . . our voices were raised in a song that could be heard for blocks" (236). While sitting at the ice-cream shop, Christina noticed some of the children huddled in a corner. One little boy who sold maps on the street came forward and handed her a map. At that moment, all the children said in English, "Happy Birthday, Mama Tina." Christina was speechless. "I clasped the map to my bosom and tried to control my voice as I talked to the children. 'Thank you. Thank you. Thank you. This is the most beautiful thing I've ever been given in my life. Nothing has ever been given to me in so much love'" (237). That was the best Christmas of her life.

Soon after the Christmas party, Christina realized that she had to get organized, even though she had no money, no office, and could barely speak Vietnamese. "How was I to realize my dream of helping street children on a large-scale permanent basis?" (242). At this point, Christina decided to go on a long walk in order to think. She stopped by a church and prayed to God for help, even though she had little faith in Him. She walked past the church for hours, to no avail. Finally, she saw an orphanage and knew that this was her answer.

Christina approached the orphanage and asked the security guards for permission to enter. She met the owner and visited with the children. She explained her situation and what she wanted to do. After looking around, she left and promised she'd be back the next day. Christina knew that she could fulfill her destiny with that orphanage, but she also knew that she needed official government permission and money to start her work. She wrote down her goals and began fundraising around the city. To her surprise, she kept getting turned down. Finally, she met a businessman who was willing to listen. When he and his associates questioned her about why she wanted to do this, she told them of her vision. The business donated $10,000, the beginning of her dream. With that money they built the Children's Medical and Social Centre, a brand-new building next to the orphanage. But there was no money for equipment. The needs were endless. Yet again, Christina began making rounds to different business people in Ho Chi Minh City, but she knew that she needed more. She could not do this on her own. It was time to get official help and approval from the government.

Christina flew to Hanoi for an appointment with the Ministry of Labour. The officials questioned why a Westerner would want to help these children. After hearing about Christina's dream and how she herself had been a street child, they were still hesitant. "We talked more. I put the Irish on them. I cried. I waved my arms. I talked incessantly. This was my one chance and I had to make it work. I even got down on my knees" (263). After two hours of carrying on like this, Mr. Tue smiled and told her that they trusted her. They gave her official permission to work with the children of Ho Chi Minh City, and Christina was ecstatic.

Soon afterwards, Christina left for the United Kingdom to raise money for the children. While there, she raised thousands and thousands of dollars and established the Christina Noble Foundation in London. Upon her return to Vietnam, Christina brought incubators, cots, machines, sterilizers, and all sorts of medicines for the children. In July of 1991, only two years after she had first arrived in Vietnam, the Children's Medical and Social Centre in Ho Chi Minh City officially opened.

"Sometimes it seems only yesterday that I was so dependent on Mario . . . now many people are dependent on me . . . the children depend on me to be strong enough to protect them from the world" (280). The Centre was up and running, and Christina was fulfilled. "I am first, last, and always, a mum. I am a mum to every street child in Vietnam" (280).

Instead of calling the children "bui doi," Christina calls them her sunshine children. However, the children and society still consider them "bui doi," so she has taught them to be proud of their name. "When I walk around the streets of Ho Chi Minh City, children will give me a thumbs-up and say, 'Hey, Mama Tina. Bui doi Number One'" (281). She continues her mission, walking around the streets of the city and helping whomever she can. Many times, Christina has heard of suspicious foreign men sexually abusing children; she confronts them. Case by case, she has made a difference to each of those little children, preventing them from going through the pain and suffering that she once experienced.

One of Christina's goals is to set up havens for girls who have been abused by foreigners. She came a long way after arriving in Vietnam and is proud of that fact. The Centre is well known. "If you come here, wave down a taxi, and give the driver the address of the Centre, chances are the driver will turn around, smile in approval, and say, 'Ah, you go see Mama Tina. She good to children'" (292).

People everywhere began giving money to the Foundation. The British ambassador has given her supplies. There are now foundations in France, the United States, and Australia. "We have come a long way in a short time. I'm talking less of the building and the equipment and the staff at the Centre than the attitude. To me the attitude we have towards children is far more important than buildings and equipment" (299).

The Centre has an intensive care unit, which receives acutely ill children. At any given time, the Centre has about seventy-five children as patients, and it treats a thousand children each month on an out-patient basis. Christina also opened the Sunshine School next to the Centre with about eighty students. A Centre was also established in Hanoi, and Christina is determined to open still more.

Although Christina misses England and her children very much, she knows that her place is in Vietnam, helping the children. "When I began here in Vietnam, people said what I wanted to do was impossible. 'You are only one person,' they said. But when I was a child, I needed only one person to understand my suffering and pain, one person to love me. One is very important" (307). The difference that she has made is incredible.

Christina has revolutionized the way the Vietnamese think about their own street children. The long-established policy of rounding up street children and taking them to homes is not as common. Authorities are caught between this tradition and the increasing public desire to help the children.

Her story is one of a homeless child who grew up with nothing. All she had was a dream. One little dream and an ordinary woman was all it took. "When reporters come here they see my work and invariably refer to me as a Mother Teresa. I don't know why they do that, it only proves that they don't really know me. I do all the things a saint wouldn't do. I belt out songs in clubs. . . . I enjoy a double whisky now and then. I love dancing. I like to ride fast on the back of a Honda. Although I detest violence if I have to protect a child by giving someone a wallop, I'll do it. I'm more than a bit wild. I'm Irish. Mother Teresa I am not" (306). Pretty close though.

Mitch Albom

In *Tuesdays with Morrie,* Mitch Albom writes about his encounters with Morrie Schwartz, his old college professor from Brandeis University. When Albom graduated in 1970, he knew he had a special connection to his professor. When they said goodbye, Morrie told him, "Mitch, you are one of the good ones" (Albom, 1997, p. 4), and made him promise to keep in touch. In 1994, the death sentence came. Morrie, now in his sixties, developed asthma and had trouble breathing. A few years later, he began to have trouble walking. After seeing many doctors, Morrie was diagnosed in 1994 with ALS, Lou Gehrig's disease, which damages the neurological system. There is no cure.

After college Albom did not keep in touch with Morrie or with his old college friends. He moved to New York, where he performed at empty nightclubs and played the piano with bands that kept breaking up. Albom's dream of being a famous musician was not working out. He realized that "the world . . . was not all that interested" (14).

Around the same time, his favorite uncle died. After the funeral, Albom changed direction. He stopped performing and returned to school. He earned a master's degree in journalism and took the first job he was offered, as a sports writer. Eventually, he took a job at the *Detroit Free Press,* wrote sports books, did radio shows, and appeared on TV. He bought a large house, cars, and stocks. He married Janine and continued living his busy life. Morrie Schwartz rarely crossed his mind. That all changed when something on TV caught Albom's attention. It was March of 1995 and *Nightline*'s Ted Koppel was interviewing Morrie Schwartz about life, death, and Morrie's sickness.

After seeing that episode of *Nightline,* Albom decided to visit Morrie. "I had not seen him in sixteen years. His hair was thinner, nearly white, and his face was gaunt. I suddenly felt unprepared for this reunion" (27). Upon seeing Albom, Morrie gave him a kiss. "I was surprised at such affection after all these years, but then, in the stone walls I had built between my present and past, I had forgotten how close we once were" (28). Morrie asked Albom if he wanted to know what it was like to die. And so began Albom's last lessons from Morrie. During the first visit, Albom realized that he had been lost in the hustle and bustle of his life, too busy with work, and only concerned about getting a bigger paycheck. Morrie asked Albom, "Are you giving to your community? Are you at peace with yourself? Are you trying to be as human as you can be?" (34). Albom, of course, had not been doing these things.

The two decided to meet every Tuesday. Each week that they met, Morrie had something inspirational to share with Albom. On their second Tuesday, they talked about feeling sorry for yourself. Morrie explained how some mornings he would wake up and feel his body, whatever he could still move, and mourn. Sometimes, he'd even give have a good cry. Then, however, he would stop, and give himself the opportunity to concentrate on all the good things he still had in his life. In fact, Morrie considered himself lucky to have all the time he had to say goodbye. "I studied him in his chair, unable to stand, to wash, to pull on his pants. Lucky? Did he really say lucky?" (57).

The next week, Albom arrived at Morrie's with bags of food that they would share over some good conversation and a tape recorder, so that he could remember what they talked about. "Now, the truth is, that tape recorder was more than nostalgia. I was losing Morrie, we were all losing Morrie. . . . And I suppose tapes, like photographs and videos, are a desperate attempt to steal something from death's suitcase. . . . But it was also becoming clear to me—through his courage, his humor, his patience, his openness—that Morrie was looking at life from some very different place than anyone else I knew. A healthier place. A more sensible place. *And he was about to die*" (64). They spoke about regrets, Albom's life, and how culture wraps people up in egotistical things instead of looking at the deeper meaning.

Albom wrote out a list of things that he wanted to talk about with Morrie, including death, fear, aging, greed, marriage, family, society, forgiveness, and a meaningful life. One Tuesday Albom and Morrie spoke about family. Morrie shared with Albom that family is the foundation for everything; without family support and love, there is nothing. Morrie said, "Love is so supremely important. As our great poet Auden said, 'Love each other or perish'" (91). Morrie shared that his disease would be so much harder to deal with if he didn't have his family, and that family is about letting others know there's someone who is watching out for them.

The next week, Albom arrived with more food. Morrie's wife informed him that Morrie could no longer eat most of the food Albom was bringing because it was too hard for him to swallow. That day the subject of emotions came up. Morrie told Albom how it is important to learn to detach because everything is impermanent. Albom was confused. "Aren't you always talking about experiencing life? All the good emotions, all the bad ones? How can you do that if you're detached?" (103). Morrie responded with a wise answer. "Detachment doesn't mean you don't let the experience penetrate you. On the contrary, you let it penetrate you fully. That's how you are able to leave it" (103).

By their ninth Tuesday together, Morrie was visibly worse. That afternoon, they spoke of love and how it never ends. Albom asked Morrie if he was afraid of being forgotten after he died, and Morrie was not. "I've got so many people who have been involved with me in close, intimate ways. And love is how you stay alive, even after you are gone" (133). The next week, Morrie gave Albom some of his secrets about marriage. Albom was not very successful at it and had taken seven years to propose to his wife. Morrie recognized the problems in today's society—how young people rush into marriage and then get divorced, or how people just do not know what to look for in the right partner. Morrie knew that there were a few essential components to any marriage. "If you don't respect the other person, you're gonna have a lot of trouble. If you don't know how to compromise, you're gonna have a lot of trouble. If you can't talk openly about what goes on between you, you're gonna have a lot of trouble. And if you don't have a common set of values in life, you're gonna have a lot of trouble. Your values must be alike" (149).

On their twelfth Tuesday, toward the end of Morrie's life, they discussed forgiveness. Morrie could not even wiggle his toes at this point, but still felt pain. Morrie liked it when people gave him massages to relieve the pain, so Albom did. He would do anything to make Morrie happy at this point. Forgiveness, Morrie said, was one of life's most important lessons. Vengeance and stubbornness were two things that he regretted feeling in his life. Although such feelings are inherent in human nature, there are ways to move beyond it. "You need to make peace with yourself and everyone around you. Forgive yourself. Forgive others. Don't wait, Mitch. Not everyone gets the time I'm getting. Not everyone is as lucky" (167).

On the thirteenth Tuesday, Morrie described his perfect day to Albom. To

Albom's surprise, Morrie's description was of a completely average day. Morrie said that he would wake up in the morning, have a good breakfast, go for a swim, and then have friends over for a nice lunch. Then he would go for a walk in a garden, taking in nature and the beauty around him. Finally, he would go to a restaurant with all his friends and dance all night. "It was so simple. So average. After all these months, lying there, unable to move a leg or a foot—how could he find perfection in such an average day? Then I realized this was the whole point" (176).

The next week, it was time to say goodbye. Morrie had withered away into a small huddle on his bed, barely able to speak. He softly grunted to Albom. Slowly, obviously struggling, Morrie told Albom that he loved him. And Albom told Morrie he loved him, too. "I leaned in and kissed him closely, my face against his, whiskers on whiskers, skin on skin, holding it there, longer than normal, in case it gave him even a split second of pleasure. I blinked back the tears, and he smacked his lips together and raised his eyebrows at the sight of my face. I like to think it was a fleeting moment of satisfaction for my dear old professor: he had finally made me cry" (186).

That Saturday, November 4, Morrie died peacefully in his bed. His funeral site was beautiful, with trees and grass and a sloping hill. Albom tried speaking to Morrie, and to his happiness found that his imagined conversation with Morrie felt almost completely natural. "I looked down at my hands, saw my watch and realized why. It was Tuesday" (188). Morrie had taught Albom more than he could have learned in an entire lifetime, and his lessons will continue to be learned.

Gandhi

Mahatma Gandhi, the son of Kaba Gandhi, prime minister in Porbandar, India, and Putlibai, was born on October 2, 1869, in Porbandar, also known as Sudamapuri. Gandhi attended elementary school but struggled in his studies. Throughout his years of school, Gandhi was very shy and avoided people, especially large groups. He was afraid that people would make fun of him. When Gandhi was thirteen, he was married. At such a young age, the marriage did not mean much. It was not "anything more than the prospect of good clothes to wear, drum beating, marriage processions, rich dinners and a strange girl to play with" (9). His bride was Kasturbai, and the marriage would last sixty-two years. Gandhi grew very fond of Kasturbai.

Gandhi's first experience with *Ahimsa*, or "love and nonviolence," came at a young age. When he was about fifteen, a friend of his convinced him to try meat, which was against his Hindu religion. Gandhi was persuaded, but he could barely eat it and got sick after one bite. That night, he had a horrible nightmare. His friend persisted, though, and started making delicious meats to tempt him. Gandhi took a liking to meat and ate it secretly for about a year. But his guilt was overwhelming because "I knew that if my mother and father came to know of my having become a meat-eater they would be deeply shocked. This knowledge was gnawing at my heart" (14). Finally, Gandhi decided it was time for a confession. He wrote it out, asking for his father's forgiveness. In the note, Gandhi confessed his guilt, requested a proper punishment, and asked his father not to punish himself over this. Gandhi's father read it and cried. "For a moment he closed his eyes in thought and then tore up the note. . . . He again laid down. I also cried. I could see my father's agony. . . . Those pearl-drops of love cleansed my heart and washed my sin away. Only he who has experienced such love can know what it is" (15). Gandhi thought that his father would be angry with him, but he was instead peaceful because "a clean confession, combined with a promise never to commit the sin again, when offered before one who has the right to receive it, is the purest type of repentance" (15).

Soon after this incident, Gandhi was exposed to the *Laws of Manu,* Hindu religious laws. From these, he learned that morality was the basis of things and that truth was the substance of all morality. "Truth became my sole objective and my definition of it also has been ever widening" (16). Gandhi's experiences, combined with such strong convictions at a young age, would prepare him for his life's mission and teachings.

After graduating from high school at nineteen, Gandhi went to England to further his studies. After three years in England, he became a lawyer and traveled to South Africa to take a lawsuit in Pretoria, the capital of Transvaal. First-class train accommodations were purchased, but while Gandhi was on the train, a white man entered the compartment and looked him up and down. "He saw that I was a 'colored' man. This disturbed him" (35). Afterwards, an official approached Gandhi and asked him to move to the third-class area. Gandhi protested in vain. Because he objected to being moved, he was kicked off the train with his luggage. He went and sat in the waiting room. "Should I fight for my rights or should I go on to Pretoria without minding the insults and return to India after finishing the case? Thus, I obtained full experience of the conditions of Indians in South Africa" (37). Gandhi was now fully aware of the societal prejudices.

Within a week of arriving in Pretoria, Gandhi summoned all the Indians of the city to a meeting. Only twenty-four years old, he gave his first public speech to "present to them a picture of their condition" (37). He also decided to teach merchants and other Indians around Pretoria how to speak English. Eventually, it was decided that such meetings would be held on a regular basis. "The result was that there was now in Pretoria no Indian I did not know or whose condition I was not acquainted with" (38). Because of what was happening to the Indians there, Gandhi decided to establish a permanent organization to safeguard Indian interests. Three hundred members enrolled in the Natal Indian Congress within a month. At monthly meetings members asked questions and discussed relevant issues. The community was deeply interested. The Congress also used propaganda to acquaint the English in South Africa and England and the people in India with the Indians' living conditions in South Africa.

Gandhi could not figure out why Indians were persecuted in South Africa when whites were a minority. He continued his campaign. In just three short years, Gandhi had become a prosperous lawyer and was widely known as the champion of indentured laborers who worked for the white South Africans. He addressed conferences, drafted memoranda to government ministers, wrote letters to newspapers, circulated petitions, and published two pamphlets: "An Appeal to Every Briton in South Africa" and "The Indian Franchise, An Appeal." "Appeal" was essential to Gandhi's politics. He appealed to the common sense and morality of his adversary.

In 1896 Gandhi returned to India to fetch his family. He also distributed his pamphlets to the leaders of every party in India. When he returned to South Africa, he brought eight hundred free Indians in an attempt to arouse Indian public opinion on the South African issue. The South African press exaggerated the situation and when the ships arrived from India, protesters began pelting Gandhi with stones and rotten eggs. Others battered and kicked him. Fortunately, the wife of the police superintendent, whom Gandhi knew, happened to pass by and opened her parasol between the crowd and Gandhi. The mob grew calm, since they could not attack Gandhi without hurting the police superintendent's wife. Finally, police were sent and Gandhi was escorted to safety. He had the opportunity to prosecute the assailants but didn't. This refusal made a profound impression on the Europeans and those who were in the mob were ashamed of their conduct. "The press declared me to be innocent and condemned the mob. Thus the lynching ultimately proved to be a blessing for me, that is, for the cause. It enhanced the prestige of the Indian community in South Africa and made my work easier" (52). Through such nonviolent, peaceful methods, Gandhi would break down racial barriers and continue to succeed in his crusade.

Because Gandhi felt that he should be of service more in India and friends were pressuring him to return, he decided to take a one-year leave from South Africa and return to India with his family. Upon his arrival home, he received gifts of gold, silver, and diamonds. "What right had I to accept all these gifts? Accepting them, how could I persuade myself that I was serving the community without remuneration?" (57). He returned the gifts and they were deposited in a bank to be used for the service of the community. Gandhi believed that this rejection of gifts saved him from many temptations.

Eventually, Gandhi came to the belief that not only was it wrong to accept gifts, it was wrong to have any material possessions. This came slowly and painfully in the beginning. Material goods began to slip away from Gandhi, and "a great burden fell off my shoulders, and I felt I could now walk with ease and do my work also in the service of my fellow men with great comfort and still greater joy. The possession of anything then became a troublesome thing and a burden" (62). Gandhi viewed possession as a crime because not all people could possess the same things; therefore, the only thing that every person could possess was nonpossession.

In 1903 Gandhi began publishing the *Indian Opinion,* which struggled in its early months. Gandhi took a trip to Durban, where the journal was published. An Englishman named Henry S. L. Polak gave him a copy of John Ruskin's *Unto This Last,* which would change Gandhi's life forever. "That book marked the turning point in my life" (68). Gandhi discovered that some of his deepest thoughts and convictions were expressed in this book. He realized that "the good of the individual is contained in the good of all," and that "a lawyer's work has the same value as the barber's, in as much as all have the same right of earning their livelihoods from their work." Last, he learned that "a life of labor—the life of the tiller of the soil and the handicraftsman—is the life worth living" (68). Gandhi talked about all this with the editor of the newsletter and they decided that the *Indian Opinion* should be removed to a farm where everyone could labor.

In 1906 Gandhi took a vow of celibacy to help him in his path of self-purification. He realized that one has to become passion-free in thought, deed, and action in order to purify oneself. One must "rise above the opposing currents of love and hatred, attachment and repulsion ... to conquer the subtle passions seems to me to be harder far than the physical conquest of the world by the force of arms" (70). He had no relish for sensual pleasures, he saw no room for self-indulgence in life. Gandhi strove to "be jealous of no one, a fount of mercy, without egotism, selfless ... treat alike cold and heat, happiness and misery ... ever forgiving, always contented, with firm resolutions ... dedicated mind and soul to god ... causes no dread ... not afraid of others ... free from exultation, sorrow and fear ... pure ... untouched by respect or disrespect ... not puffed up by praise and love silence and solitude" (71).

Throughout his life, Gandhi continued to fight for his people against oppression and for Indian independence in Britain. He spent many days in jail, but this only strengthened his cause. The concept of *ahimsa,* or civil disobedience and nonviolence, was critical to his fight. Toward the end of his life, Gandhi claimed that he had ceased to hate anybody. He hated the systems that were unfair to Indians, such as the system of government the British people set up in India or the caste system of untouchability for the Hindus. However, he could not hate the people who were a part of such things. Gandhi only had love for everyone. "Mine is not an exclusive love. I cannot love Moslems or Hindus and hate Englishmen. For if I love merely Hindus and Moslems because their ways are on the whole pleasing to me, I shall soon begin to hate them when their ways displease me, as they may well do any moment. A love that is based on the goodness of those whom you love is a mercenary affair" (193).

On January 25, 1948, a man named Nathuram Godse assassinated Gandhi at a prayer meeting. Godse was bitter that Gandhi made no demands on the Moslems, but he did not hate Gandhi. With a simple gunshot, Gandhi fell and died with a murmur. Prime Minister Nehru conveyed the news to India by radio. He told the people of India,

The light has gone out, I said, and yet I was wrong. For the light that shone in this country was no ordinary light. The light that has illumined this country for these many years will illumine this country for many more years, and a thousand years later that light will still be seen in this country, and the world will see it and it will give solace to innumerable hearts. (369)

Gandhi's light continues to shine and his influence is everlasting. He was a nonviolent revolutionary, changing politics and the world. As Albert Einstein stated, "Generations to come, it may be, will scarce believe that such a one as this ever in flesh and blood walked upon this earth" (369). Indeed, it is so.

Bhave

Vinova Bhave was born in Maharashtra, India, in 1894. For nine years, Bhave lived in a large house in the village because his father was a landlord. In 1905 the family moved to Baroda for his father's job. Bhave's family would play a significant role in his life, especially his grandfather, mother, and father.

Bhave's grandfather was very religious and spent hours in the ritual of worship. One morning his grandfather was seated and going about his usual process of worship when a scorpion settled on a sacred image. Some villagers had gathered around as well, and everyone began to panic. They wanted to kill the scorpion. Bhave's grandfather solemnly declared, "The scorpion has taken refuge with the Lord. He is in sanctuary, let no one touch him" (29). He continued with the service while the scorpion remained motionless. When the service was over, the scorpion walked away. For Bhave, the incident "made a deep impression on me: one who takes sanctuary with the Lord is to be treated with respect, no matter who he may be" (29). Bhave felt that he owed his purity of spirit to his grandfather.

Bhave's mother was also very religious and placed the Lord before everything. She would cry every day while begging for the Lord's forgiveness. "Mother was an ordinary housewife, busy all day long with her work, but her mind dwelt continually on the Lord" (33). She insisted that he water the *tulsi*, a sacred Hindu plant, every day. If Bhave didn't water it, she would not give him his dinner. "This was her lasting gift to me. She gave me so much else, milk to drink, food to eat, and stayed up night after night to care for me when I was sick; but this training in right human conduct was the greatest gift of all" (35).

Finally, Bhave's father influenced him. In fact, Bhave compared his father to Gandhi in the way that "he was flexible in many things . . . [and] firm on points of principle" (43). Bhave's father strove not to cause pain to others, respect elders, and be helpful to one's neighbors. Bhave realized the importance of these things at a very early age.

Bhave's father sent him to many different schools, including a technical school that taught the art of dyeing. Bhave always struggled in school. Instead of going to school or studying, he would wander the streets and pick up friends. One of his childhood friends said Bhave had "wheels on his feet" (49). He also enjoyed running. He knew the streets very well since he had roamed them so many times. Eventually Bhave decided it was time to leave home. In 1916 he set off for Benares because it was a "storehouse of knowledge . . . of Sanskrit and the Scriptures" (57). He also wanted to go to Benares because it was on the way to the Himalayas and Bengal, both places he wished to visit. "Love and attachment for my parents could not stop me from leaving home. Everything else paled before the force of the spiritual quest" (58).

Still searching for his spirituality, Bhave arrived at Kashi. While there, he followed the ways of *Bapu*, or Gandhi. Bhave found him to be "both the peace of the Himalayas and the revolutionary spirit of Bengal" (64). After reading a copy of one of his speeches addressed to the local Hindu University, Bhave agreed with Gandhi's ideas on nonviolence. He began sending Gandhi letters, inquiring more about the subject. One day, Bhave received a postcard that said, "Questions about non-violence cannot be settled by letters; the touch of life is needed. Come and stay with me for a few days in the Ashram, so that we can meet now and again" (64). And so began a dynamic relationship.

Bhave stayed at the Ashram and was invited to live there in a life of service. He eagerly accepted. At twenty-one, Bhave was engrossed in meditation and reflection. In 1917 he took a one-year leave in order to restore his health and to study. While on leave, he started a students' club and walked four hundred miles on foot. He visited four or five districts of Maharashtra to expand his knowledge. At each village, Bhave gave talks. He returned to the Ashram exactly one year later.

From 1921 to 1951, Bhave spent his life in educational and constructive work. He studied, taught, and reflected. "These thirty years of my life were shaped by faith in the power of meditation" (76). Bhave felt the strong conviction to help even the lowliest peoples. He believed in the principle of *Sarvodaya*, which meant that "all should rise, should grow, and all includes the lowliest and the last" (107).

In 1945 Gandhiji was shot and killed, leading to a breakdown for Bhave. He came to realize, however, that Gandhi's death made him immortal. "When Bapu was in the body, it took time to go and meet him; now it takes no time at all. All I have to do is close my eyes and I am with him" (73).

In 1946 Bhave decided to help the villagers with their work in the village of Surgaon, near where he lived in Paunar. In 1948, after Indian independence, Bhave felt a new calling. He took a six-month leave in service to those made homeless by the partition of the country. Bhave was working for the resettlement of refugees. Many had asked for land but did not receive any.

Bhave decided to travel throughout the country, on foot, to spread the ideas of Gandhi and peace. "Going on foot brings one closer, both to the country and to the people, than any other form of travel; that was why I did it" (126). Bhave went to countless villages, spreading peace. He would preach about unity and God. In 1951 Bhave set out for Delhi, in North India. His one purpose was to get land for the poor. Riots between landless peasants and the mighty landlords in south India had been breaking out over land ownership. "Mother Earth must no longer be separated from her sons, she and they must be brought together again. The winds of generosity, of giving, must be set blowing across the whole nation" (133). This was the beginning of the Bhoodan, Bhave's movement for land. Bhave felt that if people knew the basic idea of his movement, they would give land out of pure good will.

In 1952 Bhave entered Bihar and began asking for land—which he often received. He later began accepting gifts of money as well. When landlords made gifts of land that could not be cultivated, Bhave requested that they make it workable and the landlords agreed. Bhave walked through Bihar from September 1952 to the end of December 1954 and received twenty-three acres of land. "But more important than that, I can say that as I went about Bihar I had visible tokens of the love of God" (139). Bhave preached everywhere he went. He said to the landlords, "If you have five sons consider me the sixth son, the representative of the poor, and give me one sixth of your land to share with the landless" (15).

Bhave entered Bengal next. While walking from village to village, he recited prayers to the Lord. He received acres and acres of land. After five years of this pilgrimage, Bhave decided he needed to cover more ground. So he began walking double the distance. "I do not feel elated when I get large gifts of land, nor discouraged when they are small" (144). Soon people began to give whole villages to the cause. Since so much land had been donated, Bhave set up a *Shanti Sena*, a Peace Army, to safeguard the freedom that had been won. He figured that one "peace soldier" would be needed for every 5,000 people. Therefore, 70,000 peace soldiers would be needed for India, which had 350 million people. "Let India raise such an army of devotees of peace. The task of the Peace Army was to prevent any outbreak of violence by being always alert for signs of tension" (149). Bhave appointed a commander of the Peace Army, Sri Kelappan, who had been active in party politics. He was greatly respected in his area, Kerala, and fifty young men volunteered to join the army right away. Bhave continued to recruit people for his Peace Army.

Bhave continued to travel, on foot, all throughout India until the age of seventy-five. By the end of his journeys, he had acquired over four million acres of land for the poor. He then stopped his travels and spent time in meditation and prayer. When Bhave was eighty-seven, he became weak and died in complete peace after an eight-day fast. Throughout his life, Bhave claimed that he was "moved by love." He said, "There is nothing so powerful as love and thought—no institution, no government, no 'ism,' no scripture, no weapon. I hold that these, love and thought, are the only sources of power. . . . All are my kinsfolk and I theirs. It is not in my heart to love some more and others less" (18). Because of this philosophy, Bhave was able to accomplish what he wanted, and he helped thousands in the process. Bhave was a true spiritual leader whose work moved everyone from wealthy landlords in India to Gandhi.

Martin Luther King Jr.

Martin Luther King Jr. is widely known for leading the struggle for African American civil rights in the 1950s and 1960s. Less recognized are the sermons that he preached to the parishioners in his churches in Montgomery, Alabama, and Atlanta, Georgia. These sermons, collected in *The Strength to Love*, were essentially lessons, expressing his feelings on subjects such as love, fear, death, and God. They were made during or after the infamous bus protest in Montgomery, Alabama, and are truly inspiring.

In his first set of sermons, King wrote about "a tough mind and a tender heart." He said that a strong man is a living blend of strong opposites. "Life at its best is a creative synthesis of opposites in fruitful harmony" (13). King believed that a person needed a tough mind in order to be realistic and decisive. Yet he realized that most people have a tendency toward softmindedness. These soft-minded citizens are the ones who are easily influenced or persuaded by others. "The softminded man always fears change. He feels security in the status quo, and he has an almost morbid fear of the new. For him, the greatest pain is the pain of a new idea" (15). These were the types of people that King had to fight for equality, because softmindedness is a main cause of racial prejudice. A person who is strong of mind will examine the situation and not judge until after he knows the facts; a softminded person will prejudge. Therefore, King knew, "The shape of the world today does not permit us the luxury of softmindedness. A nation or a civilization that continues to produce the softminded men purchases its own spiritual death on an installment plan" (17).

In addition to a tough mind, King recognized that the gospel also demanded a tender heart. "Tough-mindedness without tenderheartedness is cold and detached, leaving one's life in a perpetual winter devoid of the warmth of spring and gentle heat of summer" (17). A hardhearted person lacks the capacity to love and feel compassion, two very important elements. "Jesus reminds us that the good life combines the toughness of the serpent and the tenderness of the dove" (18). King felt that this duality of character was essential for African Americans to move toward their goals of freedom and justice.

Being a good neighbor is also key in King's beliefs and teachings. Good Samaritans will "always be an inspiring paragon of neighborly virtue" (31). King thought that man's goodness could be described in one word, *altruism*. "What is altruism? The dictionary defines altruism as 'regard for, and devotion to, the interest of others.'" The Samaritan was good because "he made concern for others the first law of his life" (31). The true altruist will be altruistic to everyone, and not be limited by characteristics such as race, class, or gender. During the civil rights movement, most whites were not altruistic. They were not concerned with people outside of their own group. "The good neighbor looks beyond the external accidents and discerns those inner qualities that make all men human and, therefore, brothers" (33). Altruism, though, is not meant only in terms of kindness and compassion toward others. King believed that the Samaritan possessed the capacity for a "dangerous altruism," in which he would risk his life to save a brother. "The ultimate measure of a man is not where he stands in moments of comfort and convenience, but where he stands at times of challenge and controversy. The true neighbor will risk his position, his prestige, and even his life for the welfare of others. In dangerous valleys and hazardous pathways, he will lift some bruised and beaten brother to a higher and more noble life" (35).

The fourth chapter discusses love, perhaps the most important and inspiring subject. King cites the Bible, "Father, forgive them, for they know not what they do." King observes a great tragedy in life—that very rarely do people actually live life by how they say or know it should be lived. "On the one hand, we proudly profess certain sublime and noble principles, but on the other hand, we sadly practice the very antithesis of those principles." Jesus, however, bridged this gap in deed and speech. He really did love his enemies instead of just saying he did. Even when being put to death on the cross, the ultimate test in love and compassion, Jesus was able to forgive the people who were murdering him. "This was Jesus' finest hour; this was his heavenly response to his earthly rendezvous with destiny." Instead of overcoming evil with evil, Jesus was able to overcome evil with good. "Only goodness can drive out evil and only love can conquer hate" (40–42).

King knew that loving one's enemies was very hard. However, he looked upon the notion as a challenge from Jesus. In a world full of hatred and evil, "the command to love one's enemy is an absolute necessity for our survival. Love even for enemies is the key to the solution of the problems of our world" (50). In order to love our enemies, King said that we have to have the capacity to forgive our enemies. "It is impossible even to begin the act of loving one's enemies without the prior acceptance of the necessity, over and over again, of forgiving those who inflict evil and injury upon us" (50). Forgiveness means that the evil or injury does not remain a barrier to the relationship. It is important in creating a new beginning in the relationship. King also believed that some goodness can be found in any person, even our enemy, despite their wrongdoing. Therefore, there is some good in the worst of us and some evil in the best of us. "We must not seek to defeat or humiliate the enemy but to win his friendship and understanding . . . every word and deed must contribute to an understanding with the enemy and release those vast reservoirs of goodwill which have been blocked by impenetrable walls of hate" (52). Forgiveness and love are important, too, because hating someone has just as negative an effect on the person who hates. "Like an unchecked cancer, hate corrodes the personality and eats away its vital unity" (53).

Another topic that King discusses is how to live in a world full of shattered dreams. This is a part of life that cannot be helped, and people have to do their best to cope. When a person loses hope, he or she may tend to withdraw completely and become an introvert. "Such persons give up the struggle of life, lose their zest for living, and attempt to escape by lifting their minds to a transcendent realm of cold indifference" (89). King said that one must face difficulties by accepting unwanted and unfortunate circumstances but still clinging to hope. "You must honestly confront your shattered dream" (91). In order to deal with shattered dreams, people must have a faith in God, and hope. "Genuine faith imbues us with the conviction that beyond time is a divine Spirit and beyond life is Life. However dismal and catastrophic may be the present circumstances, we know we are not alone, for God dwells with us in life's most confining and oppressive cells" (96).

Finally, King gives antidotes for fear. Fear appears everywhere in the world, in different forms for different people. We may fear water, darkness, loneliness, or not being financially successful in life. In order to face these fears, we must ask why we are afraid. "This confrontation will, to some measure, grant us power. We shall never be cured of fear by escapism or repression, for the more we attempt to ignore and repress our fears, the more we multiply our inner conflicts" (117). To master fear, a person must possess or attain courage. Courage is the power of the mind to overcome fear. "Courage takes the fear produced by a definite object into itself and thereby conquers the fear involved" (118). Fear can be mastered through love. This is why Christ was not scared when he laid on the cross. "Hatred and bitterness can never cure the disease of fear; only love can do that. Hatred paralyzes life; love releases it. Hatred confuses life; love harmonizes it. Hatred darkens life; love illumines it" (122). Recognizing these steps and being able to live one's life possessing these virtues can lead to a much more peaceful, content life.

Although Martin Luther King Jr. was assassinated in 1968, his words still live on and speak to us through time. He is still the leader that he once was.

King's beliefs and principles are both inspiring and thoughtful. Many more of these important lessons are touched on in his book, *Strength to Love,* and through these lessons we are truly given that strength.

Albert Schweitzer

Born in Switzerland on January 14, 1875, Albert Schweitzer had a very happy childhood and loved spending time with his parents and siblings. At the age of five, he began music lessons taught by his father. By the time he was seven, he could play hymns on the piano. A year later, with his feet barely able to touch the pedals, young Albert learned how to play the organ. This was only the beginning of the emergence of his genius. He went on to become a brilliant theologian, philosopher, and medical missionary in Africa.

From as far back as he could remember, Schweitzer was saddened by the amount of misery in the world around him. In particular, he was moved by the pain and suffering that humans inflicted on animals. "The sight of an old limping horse, tugged forward by one man while another kept beating it with a stick to get it to the knacker's yard at Colmar, haunted me for weeks" (Schweitzer, 1965, p. 1). Therefore, Schweitzer prayed every evening not only for humans, but also for all living creatures. When he was only seven or eight, Albert and a friend made rubber catapults out of which stones could be shot. His friend wanted to shoot at birds, and he was too scared to refuse. However, right before the two were poised and ready to aim at the birds, the church bells began to ring. "And for me it was a voice from heaven" (2). When he heard the music, Schweitzer shooed the birds away, and they fled home. Since then, he reflects "with a rush of grateful emotion how on that day their music [the church bells] drove deep into my heart the commandment: 'Thou shalt not kill'" (2). This was quite a noble realization for an eight-year-old. Because of such experiences at a young age, Albert Schweitzer felt the conviction that humans had no right to inflict suffering and death on any other living creature unless it was completely necessary.

In July 1899, after many years of school, Schweitzer completed his degree in philosophy. He believed that the purpose of all philosophy was to "make us aware as thinking beings of the intelligent and intimate relationship with the universe in which we have to stand, and of the way in which we must behave in the presence of stimuli that come from it" (10). Schweitzer was compelled to leave nature at peace and assert himself in it both spiritually and creatively.

In 1905 Schweitzer decided to become a medical student in order to go to Africa as a doctor. Because he had been thriving as a theologian and philosopher, he felt that it was unfair that he was allowed to lead such a happy life while so many others around him were suffering. "While at the university and enjoying the happiness of being able to study and even to produce some results in science and art, I could not help thinking continually of others who were denied that happiness by their material circumstances or their health" (Schweitzer, 1953, p. 70).

Schweitzer wanted to commit his life to direct human service in Africa. His friends and family were upset, believing that Schweitzer should use his gifts in music and science. However, Schweitzer was not going to be stopped. He recognized that he would have to work very hard for a few years in order to become a doctor in Africa. From 1905 to 1912, he studied medicine. "Now began the years of continuous struggle with fatigue" (1953, p. 80). He had a difficult time with exams in anatomy, physiology, and the natural sciences. But in 1911 he passed the state medical examination. He still had to complete a year of work as a volunteer in the hospitals and write his thesis for the doctorate. Once he completed all of this, he made preparations for Africa.

To obtain the funds for this quest, Schweitzer had to go around begging for money from his acquaintants. He also received money from his university and his congregation. Eventually, Schweitzer collected all the money he needed to start a small hospital in Gaboon, Africa, where he intended to work. In 1913 Schweitzer and his wife arrived in Africa. As soon as he arrived, he was flooded with sick people. He chose Lambarene as the site for his hospital because the sick could be brought to him in canoes along the Ogowe River. Schweitzer dealt with malaria, leprosy, sleeping sickness, dysentery, frambesia, and ulcers. His wife helped as a nurse. Schweitzer worked because he recognized the grace in the fact that "we are allowed to be active in the service of the mercy of Jesus among the poorest of the poor. . . . In this we feel ourselves lifted above the not always small difficulties which work among primitives who cannot be accustomed to any discipline brings with it" (1965, p. 21).

After the Schweitzers had completed two seasons in Africa, they started making plans to go home for a respite. On August 5, 1914, he learned that war had broken out in Europe and they were informed that they were now considered prisoners of war. They were to obey unconditionally the regulations of the soldiers who were assigned to them as guards. Schweitzer was also commanded to stop work at the hospital. During his internment, Schweitzer began writing his *Philosophy of Civilization*. He determined that "the only possible way out of chaos is for us to come once more under the control of the ideas of true civilization through the adoption of an attitude toward life that contains those ideals. But what is the nature of the attitude toward life in which the will to general progress and to ethical progress are alike founded and in which they are bound together? It consists in an ethical affirmation of the world and life" (1965, p. 65).

In 1917 the Schweitzers were ordered onto a ship in a camp as prisoners of war. Just before they were taken on board, the father of the Catholic mission of Lambarene shook hands with Schweitzer and his wife and thanked them for all the good that they had done during their stay. The couple was taken to an internment camp in the Pyrenees. Schweitzer was the only doctor in the camp and was soon allowed to utilize his talents. He was even given a room to work in. "I was able to give especially effective help to those who had been brought there from the colonies, as well as to the many sailors who were suffering from tropical diseases. Thus I was once more a doctor" (Schweitzer, 1953, p. 133). As a doctor at the camp, he witnessed the worst of the sick.

Finally, the couple was allowed to go home to Switzerland for a few days, but they were ordered to depart again. Eventually, they were released and allowed to return home for good. Schweitzer began writing down his recollections of Africa. Entitled *On the Edge of the Primeval Forest,* the book was published in English and in Swedish.

Schweitzer returned to Africa in 1924, where he found only the remains of his hospital. During 1924 and 1925, Schweitzer sent for two doctors and two nurses from Europe to treat the increasing number of patients suffering from dysentery. He moved his hospital and made it larger. In 1927 he returned to Switzerland to give lectures and organ recitals. He returned to Africa in 1929 and stayed.

Reflecting on his own life, Schweitzer realized that there were two perceptions that overwhelmed his existence. "One consists in my realization that the world is inexplicably mysterious and full of suffering; the other in the fact that I have been born into a period of spiritual decadence in mankind" (Schweitzer, 1953, p. 170). However, Schweitzer believed in the future of humankind. Ultimately, he felt that "whether we be workers or sufferers, it is assuredly our duty to conserve our powers, as being men who have won their way through to the peace which passeth all understanding" (Schweitzer, 1953, p. 188).

The Dalai Lama

The Dalai Lama fled his homeland of Tibet in 1959 and became a refugee in India at the age of twenty-four. He spent most of his youth studying Buddhist philosophy and psychology and continued these studies for the rest of his life. In his book, *Ethics for the New Millennium,* the Dalai Lama established the concept of "positive ethical conduct." He attempts to approach ethics on universal, as opposed to religious, principles. Therefore, the book appeals to a larger audience.

While the Dalai Lama was in India, he was brought into closer contact with modern society; however, he spent his formative years resisting the influences of the twentieth century. The Dalai Lama became a monk and continued his spiritual quest traveling and speaking to different people. He dealt with lost family members, people who were sick with cancer or AIDS, and fellow struggling Tibetans. Because of his encounters with all these people, he was reminded of "our basic sameness as human beings" (4). Whether rich or poor, black or white, everyone struggles to achieve happiness and avoid suffering. The Dalai Lama believed that this search for happiness is sustained by hope. "Everything we do, not only as individuals but also at the level of society, can be seen in terms of this fundamental aspiration [hope]" (4). He believed that a spiritual revolution would help achieve this happiness for the entire world.

This spiritual revolution, however, did not have to be religious. After years of confronting other religions as well as his own, he realized that all religions and philosophies are not less capable of helping people lead better lives. "What is more, I have come to the conclusion that whether or not a person is a religious believer does not matter much. Far more important is that they be a good human being" (19). In believing this, the Dalai Lama has made an important distinction between religion and spirituality. He approaches different religions in terms of their claims to salvation or the afterlife, connected to more specific rituals or traditions. Spirituality is more universal, concerning qualities of the human spirit such as love, compassion, forgiveness, and harmony. Therefore, his call for a spiritual revolution need not be religious. "Rather, it is a call for a radical reorientation away from our habitual preoccupation with self. It is a call to turn toward the wider community of beings with whom we are connected, and for conduct which recognizes others interests alongside our own" (24).

The Dalai Lama divides suffering into two larger categories: natural disasters and human disasters. Natural disasters include earthquakes, floods, and other events that inflict suffering upon humans but are out of our control. Human disasters, such as wars, crime, violence, corruption, and the like, are all sufferings that come from our own origin and can be controlled or even stopped, which is the ultimate goal. Everyone is responsible for this unhappiness. However, the Dalai Lama recognizes that the legal system cannot eradicate these problems. Instead, ethics must be imposed. "Since love and compassion and similar qualities all, by definition, presume some level of concern for others' well-being, they presume ethical restraint. We cannot be loving and compassionate unless at the same time we curb our own harmful impulses and desires" (26). This is fundamental to good ethics.

The Dalai Lama also explains the concept of individuals' "kun long." Literally, the phrase means "thoroughly" or "from the depths," but in principle it is understood to be that which drives our intentions and actions, which denotes a person's overall wholesomeness and state of mind. When a person's heart and mind are wholesome, so, too, are that person's actions. "The individual's overall state of heart and mind, or motivation, in the moment of action is, generally speaking, the key to determining its ethical content, [and] is easily understood when we consider how our actions are affected when we are gripped with powerful negative thoughts and emotions such as hatred and anger. In that moment, our mind and heart are in turmoil" (31). When we are in this state, we lose sight of the impact our actions may have on others and ignore their own rights to happiness. Therefore, the spiritual revolution can only be achieved through this sort of ethical revolution, in which our "kun longs" are realized and made better.

On a trip to Europe, the Dalai Lama went to the site of the Nazi death camp at Auschwitz. Although he had tried to prepare himself for the experience, it was overwhelming. "I was dumbfounded at the sheer calculation and detachment from feeling to which they [the ovens where the Jewish were burned] bore horrifying testimony" (63). After seeing Auschwitz, the Dalai Lama vowed to never take part in such horrors and take it as a reminder of what can happen when individuals and whole societies lose sight of their basic human feelings. The Dalai Lama believed that humans must empathize with each other and attempt to fully understand what those who are suffering are experiencing. In Tibet, they call this idea "shen dug ngal wa la mi so pa," which means "the inability to bear the sight of another's suffering." "It is what compels us to shut our eyes even when we want to ignore others' distress" (64). In addition to the empathy that humans need to feel for each other, they must also be kind. He feels that the human smile is especially important in being kind because a genuine smile touches us.

In order to develop happiness and compassion, the Dalai Lama wrote, "We need to restrain those factors which inhibit compassion" and "cultivate those which are conducive to it" (81). Characteristics conducive to compassion include love, patience, tolerance, humility, and many others. "What inhibits compassion is that lack of inner restraint which we have identified as the source of all unethical conduct" (81). Restraint and, more broadly, moderation are essential to a wholesome soul. Therefore, humans must cultivate a habit of inner discipline. He uses drugs as an example: We know drugs are bad and we know their consequences. Therefore, we practice self-restraint and refrain from doing such things. "The undisciplined mind is like an elephant. If left to blunder around out of control, it will wreak havoc" (82).

There are many more lessons to be learned in the Dalai Lama's book. The end of the book is particularly striking. The Dalai Lama speaks of life and how fleeting it is. He reminds us to live the present well, day in and day out, and not turn around and dwell on mistakes because we can't turn back time. "Therefore, if when our final day comes we are able to look back and see that we have lived full, productive, and meaningful lives, that will at least be of some comfort. If we cannot, we may be very sad. But which of these we experience is up to us" (Dalai Lama). Life could not be summed up any better.

References

Albom, Mitch. (1997). *Tuesdays with Morrie*. New York: Doubleday.

Anglin, Patty, with Joe Musser. (1999). *Acres of hope: The miraculous story of one family's gift of love to children without hope*. Uhrichsville, OH: Promise Press.

Dalai Lama. (1999). *Ethics for the new millennium*. New York: Riverhead Books.

Fuller, Millard. (1986). *No more shacks!* Waco, TX: Word Books.

Gandhi, Mahatma. (1962). *The essential Gandhi*. Ed. Louis Fischer. New York: Vintage Books.

Kalindi. (1994). *Moved by love: The memoirs of Vinoba Bhave*. Trans. Marjorie Sykes. Devon, England: Green Books.

King, Rev. Martin Luther Jr. (1963). *Strength to love*. Philadelphia: Fortress Press.

Noble, Christina, with Robert Coram. (1994). *Bridge across my sorrows: The Christina Noble story*. London: Corgi Books.

Schweitzer, Albert. (1953). *Out of my life and thought*. New York: Mentor Books.

Schweitzer, Albert. (1965). *Reverence for life*. New York: Philosophical Library.

CHAPTER 6

Religious Love at the Interface with Science

Thomas Jay Oord

T his book turns now from scientific studies and the narrative of human altruism to the dialogue among science, religion, and metaphysics. A growing number of scholars are not satisfied with this "either science or love" question. A field of interest and body of work are emerging based on the belief that theories of love, especially religious love, must take into account truths from scientific investigation and speculation in scientific theory. Exactly how scholars involved in this emerging discipline believe love and science should be related and/or integrated varies greatly. What those in this budding field share in common, however, is the belief that issues of love are of paramount importance and that the findings and theories in various scientific disciplines—whether social or natural—must be brought to bear upon how love is understood.

This annotated bibliography includes a variety of literature either directly related to science-and-love issues or supporting literature for those issues. This listing is by no means exhaustive, for such a list would be endless. Instead, it attempts to be representative of the works available.

What makes this annotated bibliography unique is that it approaches the love-and-science discussion from the perspective of religion. This means neither that all of the books listed are of a specific religious nature nor that these authors consider themselves religious, although most books and authors do reflect a religious orientation. Rather, these works should be considered especially significant for those who wish to address the love-and-science field from a decidedly religious perspective.

A cursory glance at the literature reveals that various classical expositions of love continue to influence contemporary scholars. For instance, Plato's work on *eros,* especially in his *Symposium,* provides material with which contemporaries still reckon. The work and words of Jesus Christ, Aristotle, St. Paul, Mo-

Tzu, Augustine of Hippo, Thomas Aquinas, Guatama, Dionysius, St. Francis of Assisi, Martin Luther, John Wesley, Jonathan Edwards, Sri Ramakrishna, Soren Kierkegaard, and Gandhi also exert influence upon contemporary minds.

The contemporary discussion of love in the West, however, was initiated by Anders Nygren's theological arguments in his classic *Agape and Eros* (1957 [1930]). Nygren championed a view heavily influenced by Martin Luther's theology, and he believed this view to be supported by Christian scripture. Prominent among those in the mid-twentieth century who reacted to his arguments were Martin C. D'Arcy, Reinhold Niebuhr, Paul Tillich, and Daniel Day Williams. Today, many scholars proffering a theology of love still engage Nygren's ideas.

Nygren and his respondents rarely if ever explicitly addressed how science affects or is affected by the issues of love. Sociologist Pitirim Sorokin is credited with authoring the classic work in the love-and-science discussion. In his mid-twentieth century tome, *The Ways and Power of Love,* Sorokin considers seven aspects of love, including its religious, ethical, ontological, physical, biological, psychological, and social aspects. While the book often cites spiritual and religious figures and ideas, the majority of the author's interests revolve around love's psychological and social aspects. In his latter years, Sorokin established the Harvard Research Center for Creative Altruism because of his convictions about the power and importance of love.

A major issue at the heart of the love-and-science field—and an issue that emerges often in the discussion—is the question of the nature and definition of love itself. Love is, as Mildred Bangs Wynkoop has said, a notoriously ambiguous "weasel word." "Love" in the English language conveys meanings that other languages employ a variety of words to convey. In addition, when some use "love," they mean for it to be taken exclusively as an unqualified good. This use derives from Hebrew heritage, and it might be called the "*hesed* love tradition" (*hesed* is a Hebrew word often translated "steadfast love"). Others use "love" to refer to either good or bad actions; this usage arises out of what might be called the "virtue and vice love tradition." In this latter tradition, one adds a qualifier to love such as "proper" or "appropriate" when referring to an unconditional good.

Not only is the definition of love up for debate, but a great deal of discussion arises about which type of love is best, most appropriate, or most valuable. In this deliberation, three classic Greek words, what might be called the "archetypes of love," take center stage: *agape, eros,* and *philia.*

Nygren's claims about the superiority of *agape* kicked off a modern debate about the meaning and legitimacy of the archetypes. Scholars of the Christian canon have convinced most today, however, that Nygren's claim to have grounded his *agape* convictions in scripture reflect his own theological orientation to a greater extent than what the biblical text actually supports. Many have also reacted against Nygren's theological and philosophical assumptions. For instance, many feminist scholars contend that *agape,* as Nygren conceives it, sustains harmful attitudes and ways of living; they prefer instead the value-affirming archetype *eros.* One of the more important contemporary partners in this debate, Edward Collins Vacek, argues that *philia* should receive honored status above the other two loves. Those active in the current debates often work carefully to persuade others that particular definitions of these three love archetypes are especially useful or significant.

In the love-and-science dialogue, *agape* is often mentioned as the love-type that must somehow be accounted for in scientific theory. A survey of the literature, however, reveals that participants in this dialogue attribute widely diverse meanings to *agape.* It has been equated with self-sacrifice, equal-regard, unlimited love, repaying evil with good, altruism, unconditional love, universal acceptance of others, divine love, gift-love, bestowal, the mutuality of God-self-others relations, religious love, and pure love, among other phrases. Because these definitions are significantly different, they generate or reflect widely divergent agendas, expectations, and religious orientations. What Robert Adams says of *agape* as it relates to the specifically Christian context applies to the love-and-science discussion: "'Agape' is a blank canvas on which one can paint whatever ideal of Christian love one favors."

The picture painted on the theoretical love canvas typically has a great deal to do with how the love-artist understands what it means to be human. Who humans are and of what they are capable obviously influences what can plausibly be said about their capacity for and motivation to express love. Not surprisingly, issues related to human nature arise to the fore in contemporary love-and-science discussions. Whether explicitly or implicitly, this influence can be observed in scholarship of such sciences as genetics, physics, medicine, psychology, biology, sociology, neurology.

One of the better volumes to illustrate these fruits and possibilities found in the love-and-science discussion is *Altruism and Altruistic Love: Science, Philosophy, and Religion in Dialogue,* edited by Stephen G. Post, Lynn G. Underwood, Jeffrey S. Schloss, and William B. Hurlbut. The volume specifically addresses a major focus in the love-and-science dialogue: the relationship between authenticity and origin of altruism and egoism. Among other things, essayists want to know whether humans and other complex organisms are inevitably egoistic if less-complex organisms are inevitably egoistic. And if humans are not inevitably egoistic, does this mean that less-complex nonhumans are not "programmed" to be selfish as well? Scholars wonder about the extent to which humans share traits and features with organisms that are typically not thought of as expressing give-and-take love. Especially prominent in this volume are the scientific disciplines currently most influential in setting the tone of the love-and-religion exchange: biology, psychology, and neurology.

The participant entering the love-and-science fray with religious concerns in mind will want to inquire into how science might shape what should be said about human nature. For instance, a Buddhist who agrees with the Dalai Lama that humans are essentially compassionate and good must reckon, in some way, with the claims by some scientists that all organisms, including humans, are invariably selfish. By contrast, a Christian who endorses the theological claim that humans are totally depraved and can only act lovingly if supernaturally enabled must reckon, in some way, with the claims by some scientists that organisms, especially humans, can act lovingly despite not witnessing divine action in their lives.

The scope of one's love interests is an issue that engenders diverse reflection. Some contend that love should be expressed to all and that preferences to those near and dear undermine the authenticity of genuine love. This approach, however, seems at odds with dominant theories in sociobiology, such as kin selection and group selection, which point toward evidence that supports the claim that creatures are more altruistic toward their genetic relatives or local communities. Others argue that love can only be expressed toward those with whom one is closely related. Perhaps the question to be answered is: Can a balance be achieved such that love can be simultaneously universal and preferential?

The idea that humans may properly love themselves has been debated throughout religious history. The love-and-science discussion often adds an evolutionary, a psychological, or a genetic twist to this old debate. Is self-love ever appropriate? Should self-love be regarded as morally equivalent with other-love? If altruism requires self-sacrifice, does this mean that regard for one's own interest is at odds with altruism?

Theory and research in the scientific realm also place into question the status of creaturely freedom. The vast majority of contemporary love ethicists contend that freedom is required for creaturely love. But this freedom-determinism debate has a long history in religion, and it appears that most scientists do not regard nonhumans as acting freely. Is human freedom a necessary illusion? Did freedom for love emerge at some point in the evolutionary adventure of life? Or do all organisms possess a degree of freedom, meaning that degrees of freedom exist even at the most basic levels of existence examined by physicists?

Earlier I noted that how one understands love says a great deal about how one understands human nature. But must humanity be the originator of how theists conceive of love? To put the question another way, should theologies of love that interface with science start from "above," by considering divine love, or "below," by examining creaturely love?

Karl Barth, one of the twentieth century's greatest theologians, would undoubtedly want any theological discussion with science to begin with divine love. Today, Barth's theological heirs and those called Radical Orthodox theologians would likely agree. From a different orientation, present-day Continental theologians often argue that one must set aside scientific questions related to ontology if one is to make progress in conceiving of love adequately. Those who argue that theology should begin from above are often reacting to "theologies" they believe both start from below and end up below. A crucial issue in the present love-and-science debate is how to decide which vision of God serves as the most adequate basis for speaking about love.

One reason Anders Nygren's notions of love have been so heavily criticized in the past half century is that the theory of *agape* he advocates presents a vision of a God who acts unilaterally, is not truly affected by others, and does not act in the give-and-take relations that we understand love to entail. A shorthand way many contemporary theologians critique this vision is to say that Nygren does not present a "suffering God." In the classical sense, suffering simply means being affected or influenced by another; in the contemporary sense, suffering typically has to do with feeling pain. Most contemporary love theologians argue that God suffers in both senses.

Although the idea that God is affected by creatures has been a dominant theme in religious piety, it was not until in the mid-twentieth century that Charles Hartshorne and other process theists, formulated sophisticated philosophical and theological formulations to account for a relational deity. Divine love was later to be dubbed "Creative-Responsive" by process theologians John B. Cobb Jr. and David Ray Griffin. One of the classic theological love texts to be considered by present-day love-and-science scholars is *The Spirit and Forms of Love* by process theologian Daniel Day Williams. The resources in the process tradition for conceptualizing love led George Newlands to write that "love has come to the fore particularly in process thought in America."

The notion that God relates with the world and thus suffers is no longer the exclusive domain of process theists, if it ever really was previously. What might be called kenotic theology, exemplified well in Jürgen Moltmann's writings, also supposes that God suffers. God loves from abundance, claims Moltmann, and through self-emptying and self-limitation God loves into being a partially independent world. A recent volume of essays edited by John Polkinghorne (2001) explores these kenotic themes. The key difference between process and the majority of kenotic theologies is that the latter argue that God's relations with the world are essentially voluntary, while the former contend that God necessarily relates with nondivine individuals.

The themes of divine relatedness and suffering are adopted by many whose orientations extend beyond process and kenotic theologies. Feminist theologians have argued that God is not only relational, but the deity also has desires concerning and finding value in creation. Trinitarian theologians place the locus of divine love relations within the Trinity itself, and God's interaction with the world somehow reflects intra-Trinitarian relationships. Openness theologians reflect many of these same themes while arguing that God's love entails divine openness to the world and to a partially unknown future. Many biblical scholars are suggesting that themes of divine suffering and relationality are strongly supported by the Christian/New and Hebrew/Old Testaments.

The relationship between divine love and divine power is also a perennial subject for discussion. In the love-and-science conversation, the topic arises especially in relation to two concerns: the creation of the universe and the problem of evil. It seems to many that a God with the power of creating a universe ought to have the power to prevent genuinely evil occurrences. If such a creative God fails to prevent genuine evil, can we plausibly say that this God is perfectly loving after all? However, to argue that God's actions toward the world are limited only to persuasive love seems to deny that God has the capacity to create something from nothing (or something from chaos). In these discussions, the topic of divine coercion arises.

How one believes God acts in and toward the world affects the ethical scheme one supposes is most adequate. To some the fact that existence has evolved a certain way suggests that humans ought to live and love a certain way. The question at the heart of this issue is often proposed in this way: Does "is" imply "ought"?

The literature on ethics examined in this annotated bibliography reflects a gamut of ethical approaches. Some love ethicists stress the paramount importance of developing virtues, especially love. Others turn to saints and role-models as the impetuses for loving action. Many stress the importance of the actor's context and what the actor expects will be the outcome of his or her actions. Others suggest that love simply arises out of the particular way lovers see the world. Some love ethicists urge their readers to follow the teachings of a particular religious leader, religious text, or religious community. Each of these basic theoretical assumptions is used in the love-and-science conversation to propose proper responses to issues such as marriage, friendship, abortion, euthanasia, cloning, genetic engineering, politics, and sex.

What follows is the aforementioned annotated bibliography. Written materials are placed alphabetically into one of three categories: representative theological texts; interfaced science texts; and primarily philosophical texts.

Representative Theological Texts

 Allen, Diogenes. (1992). *The path of perfect love.* Boston: Cowley Publications.

Allen, professor of philosophy at Princeton Seminary, wrote this book because he believed that academic theology was in a state of skepticism. He argues throughout that traditional doctrines of Christianity are best understood when grounded upon the doctrine of divine love. Humans perceive the presence of

God in both the natural and human environment, which means that humans experience love in ordinary daily life. This also means that the entire universe is conceived in love, sustained by love, and directed toward its consummation. In this sense, love has cosmic proportions.

In light of understanding Christianity as founded upon love, Allen argues that Christians must act in a certain way. Specifically, Christians must be attentive to academic and scientific disciplines, learn to see ourselves as the objects of perfect love, be aware of that which is beyond our present life, pay attention to Jesus and confess what we see in Him, and forsake the world. Death should be seen as the complete destruction of the self-centered life that we now have, and life after death as resurrection should be understood as possible because of divine love. The author sums up the book by saying that he has argued that the presence of God can be perceived indirectly by a person who is moving away from a self-centered stance and who has forsaken the world. "The more our life is disciplined by attentiveness to others, and the more we cultivate an awareness of the inability of the world to give us the fulfillment that we crave, the deeper and clearer is our awareness of God's presence" (103).

⮆   Dalai Lama. (2001). *An open heart: Practicing compassion in everyday life.* Ed. Nicholas Vreeland. Boston: Little Brown.

Material for this book is derived from the Dalai Lama's 1999 address in Central Park, New York, where he spoke insightfully about how one might live a better life. The book provides a variety of specific practices and techniques that can engender happiness.

Spiritual practice is a matter of taming unwanted emotions, which means becoming aware of how the mind works. Through time humans can develop helpful states of mind while eliminating harmful states. By doing this, we will cultivate compassion for others and happiness for ourselves. Following traditional Buddhist methods, the Dalai Lama points to the causes of suffering and then reflects upon how this suffering can be overcome.

⮆   D'Arcy, Martin C. (1964). *The mind and heart of love, lion and unicorn: A study in eros and agape.* Cleveland: World.

D'Arcy's work provides a classic Roman Catholic response to Anders Nygren's Lutheran-influenced classic, *Agape and Eros.* D'Arcy's quotation best sums up his thesis in *The Mind and Heart of Love:* "The simplest statement of the law which governs what is highest and lowest in the Universe can be called that of 'Give and Take'" (14). Because this law of giving and taking—which D'Arcy identifies with *agape* and *eros*—is at the heart of all living things God creates, both giving and taking are part of legitimate Christian love. D'Arcy explicitly supports this thesis by drawing from a variety of literature, a phenomenological philosophy, the notions of the *animus* and *anima,* and a metaphysics of essence and existence.

The bulk of *The Mind and Heart of Love* consists of D'Arcy's discussion of important works on love with special attention given to a phenomenological account of love's nature. "The notions of love and of the self are universal," concludes D'Arcy, "and most must have a fair idea of what they mean because they have their own experience to guide them and a long heritage of common sense and wisdom."

The backbone for D'Arcy's most basic claims concerning human love is his analysis of the human self. Each person has an *animus* and *anima,* and this composition contains the clues to the workings of love. The *anima* and the *animus* correspond with the archetypal loves *agape* and *eros.* Although the two loves of the self differ significantly, both *agape* and *eros* must live together in each person. This reveals why giving and receiving are inherent in all life.

The differing characteristics of a taking *animus/eros* and a giving *anima/agape* can be listed as such:

Animus (Lion)	*Anima* (Unicorn)
Reason	Will
Order	Irrational
Mind	Soul/Heart
Active	Passive
Self-regard	Self-sacrifice
Egocentric	Altruistic
Masculine	Feminine
To be for itself	To be for others
Life	Death
Possessing	Being Possessed
Taking	Giving
Eros	*Agape*

The self-regarding *animus* exhibits itself in the world of reason. It is set on self-realization and proceeds from the Aristotelian argument that humans necessarily love themselves even when loving others. The *animus* is a taking or receiving love. The self-denying *anima,* on the other hand, cares little for its dignity or rights. This love prefers mutuality and fusion with the beloved. *Anima* is giving, self-sacrificial, and altruistic. Its impulse is to seek to belong to another. The *anima* is a giving love. Each love makes itself felt to some degree in its bid to dominate the self, and each, whether *animus/agape* or *anima/eros,* "can be good or bad" (220).

The lives of humans involve a more-or-less successful attempt to harmonize these two elements of the self. This means that, according to D'Arcy, "the principle of give and take has to be harmonized in all phases of love" (83). In perfect love, the *animus* and *anima* rejoice together in an undivided act. "The animus and the anima give each together mutual assistance and love," which means that "*eros* and *agape* are not enemies, but friends" (344).

At its best, the natural union of *anima* and *animus* is short-lived. A supernatural act is needed to secure lasting harmony. Because the ideal harmony is not achieved naturally, humans experience existential angst. Christian theologians identify this lack of harmony with the Fall.

D'Arcy means for his phenomenologically based hypothesis to extend to creatures other than humans; animals share this twofold movement of giving and taking. As D'Arcy puts it, "To give . . . , as well as to take, is inherent in all living organisms" (243), a point said to be illustrated in the basic impulses of all things for self-preservation and contribution to the order of the whole. However, the striking difference that separates humans from animals, according to D'Arcy, is that human love has spiritual implications while animal love does not. "The difference can be best expressed in saying that the higher actions of man have an intrinsic value and that man has a personal dignity" (15).

After establishing his phenomenologically based hypothesis that love involves both giving and taking, D'Arcy turns to the classical philosophy of essence and existence to secure a metaphysical basis for this hypothesis. He draws upon philosopher Hunter Guthrie's work to fulfill this intention. The philosophy of essence and existence that D'Arcy appropriates supposes that, although all persons share a common essence as humans, they differ from one another in their unique existence.

The existential self, being contingent and unstable, seeks union with a necessary, stable absolute. The love of the human essence and the love of a human being's existence need each other. Without the essential love, the love of existence is without a backbone, and, without the movement of the existential love toward the Absolute, the essential love will substitute a pseudo-absolute for the true One. This means that the love of the essential self can only be subsidiary and find its role as a minor partner to the other love. "The two loves must implement each other," says D'Arcy, but "the essential one must be subordinated to the love which reaches up to the God whose name is, 'I am Who am'" (291).

From the preface to the final pages of *The Mind and Heart of Love,* D'Arcy speaks of creaturely love as essentially involving both give and take. D'Arcy expresses this theme when he claims that "perfect love is mutual giving and taking, possessing and being possessed" (263). More specifically giving and taking, claims D'Arcy, are necessary elements for love. If *eros* were to be eliminated, as Nygren had suggested, *agape* would wither away in its solitude. The theme that perfect love involves both give and take is also implicit in the most-quoted phrase from D'Arcy's book: "*Eros* and *agape* are not enemies, but friends."

& De Rougemont, Denis. (1983 [1940]). *Love in the western world.* Trans. Montgomery Belgion. (Rev. ed.) Princeton, NJ: Princeton University Press.

De Rougemont claims in this classic that the modern notion of romantic love originated in medieval courtly love. He further argues that this medieval notion of romantic love cannot form a proper basis for Christian marriage.

The author traces the tradition of courtly love from the twelfth century through the nineteenth century to modern day. He begins with the legend of Tristan and Isolde and notes the inescapable conflict between passion and marriage. Passion is grounded in an *eros* that is often spoken of by the poets. Such *eros* is implicitly selfish and finds its only consummation in death, which means that romantic love includes an unconscious death wish.

The selfishness of passion is at odds with the mature *agape* love found in Christian marriage. The author claims that his underlying belief is a phrase from Heraclitus, "opposites cooperate, and from their struggle emerges the most beautiful harmony." De Rougemont does not argue that passion should be eliminated from marriage; rather, marriage cannot be founded upon passionate love alone.

& Fiddes, Paul S. (1988). *The creative suffering of God.* Oxford: Clarendon.

The author surveys recent thought about the suffering of God and, along the way, develops his own ideas of divine suffering. Fiddes notes at the outset that theological statements throughout the history of the church have tended to support a view of God as unmoving, unchanging, and unsuffering. Today, however, at least academic theologians emphasize their strong conviction that God does suffer. The author attempts to offer a coherent notion of a God who both suffers and yet can fulfill divine purposes. The view he offers understands God as freely choosing to be self-limited, to suffer change, to be affected by time, and to experience death, while remaining the living God. The author is especially influenced by process theological conceptions, but, in the end, the position he takes is his own; it is not in line with "orthodox" process thought.

Four major contributions have been made to the present debate about whether God suffers. The first, represented by Jürgen Moltmann, understands the suffering of God as being derived from the theology of the cross. The nature of God is revealed in the cross of Jesus as God participates in human history. A second major contribution comes from American process philosophy. In this vision, every participant, including God, is bound in a network of mutual influences with others. This means that divine suffering becomes central to divine action. The third dominant contribution to the present debate on the suffering of God comes from the mid-twentieth century "Death of God" theological movement. Finally, those whose sympathies remain with classical theism continue to exert some influence in the debate. "A theology of a suffering God needs to weave all four of these strands into a pattern, or to use another image, it must stand where four ways cross" (15). The chapters in the book explore the four major contributors to the current debate upon divine suffering.

In a chapter Fiddes titles "Why Believe in a Suffering God," he proposes four reasons why this theme is especially important in contemporary theology. First, it is difficult to understand what it means to say that God is a loving God if God does not suffer. Second, if the cross of Jesus Christ is central to Christian theology, this implies a notion of a God who is affected by the world and its experiences. Third, the problem of human suffering, itself, calls for a Creator who suffers along with creatures in pain. Finally, the scientific and natural view of existence supports the idea of an interactive deity.

⊰⊱ Fretheim, Terence E. (1984). *The suffering God: An Old Testament perspective.* Philadelphia: Fortress Press.

Fretheim argues that the Hebrew Bible/Old Testament writings affirm that humans affect God by implying that God is not immutable or impassible: the actions, thoughts, and desires of creatures affect God. This work is especially important for theists in the Judeo-Christian-Muslim traditions who believe that a view of a static and unchanging deity cannot correspond with core implications of the claim that God is love.

God, according to the Old Testament witness, changes in light of what occurs in the creaturely realm. God is wounded by human disobedience (Jer. 3:19–20); God grieves because of human rebellion (Ps. 78:40–41, Isa. 63:7–10); God wails and mourns (Jer. 48:30–32, Amos 5:1–2); God becomes angry over sin (Hos. 8:5, Ezek. 16:42); God waits for human response (Jer. 13:27); God suffers with humans in compassion (Isa. 54:7–8, Judg. 2:18). Humans possess real power and real freedom, and their actions really affect both the future and God. Nearly forty references to divine repentance are found in the Old Testament, and most of these instances are the direct result of human activity. Even passages suggesting that God displays wrath are coherent only if humans truly affect God. The God described in the Old Testament is not immutable but mutates in give-and-take relationships with creatures.

⊰⊱ Fuller, Millard. (1994). *Theology of a hammer.* Macon, Ga.: Smyth and Helwys.

Fuller is the founder and president of Habitat for Humanity, an organization that builds homes for the poor. This book offers numerous anecdotes and illustrations concerning work in Habitat for Humanity since its inception. The author speaks from a Christian perspective and identifies core Christian convictions that undergird his ministry.

Fuller contends that the theology of the hammer means that Christian faith

demands more than just talk and singing. "We must put faith and love into action to make them real, to make them come alive for people" (7). This theology
is also about bringing together diverse peoples, churches, and organizations to
help build houses and establish viable communities. Even though those involved may have diverse political, philosophical, or theological preferences "we
can agree on the imperative of the Gospel to serve others in the name of the
Lord" (7). Fuller believes that sufficient resources exist for solving the problems
of poverty housing and homelessness. "Everybody made in the image of God,
and that's the whole crowd, ought to have a decent place to live and on terms
they can afford to pay" (17). Although his work consists mainly of stories of
practical work in building homes, Fuller acknowledges that, in addition to the
Bible, he has been influenced by such theologians as Walter Rauschenbush, Albert Schweitzer, Alan Durning, Henri Nouwen, and Dorothy Day.

Gilleman, Gerard. (1961). The primacy of charity in moral theology.
Westminster, Md.: Newman Press.

Gilleman's main purpose in writing this book is to reinstate charity as the
fundamental "nourishing substance" of all the virtues. He writes as a Roman
Catholic particularly influenced by the writings of Thomas Aquinas. Although
Gilleman's work is more than forty years old, it remains a valuable work for
those pursuing theologies of love and virtue ethics revolving around charity.

The author believes that the moral manuals have overstressed objective and
individualistic bearings of moral theology and placed law, rather than love, as
their dominant theme. Authentic Christian life is essentially the imitation of
Christ, which implies that moral theology should not be legalistic.

The contemporary theological tradition from which Gilleman is oriented
does not, according to him, place love as its central and fundamental concern.
When charity as the form of the virtues informs ethics and theology, Christian
thought is arighted. God must supernaturalize love in the Christian. This process makes possible the practical living out of love in one's life. In this way,
"moral life appears as the expression of that mysterious, ambivalent being that
is in incarnate spirit" (346). This entails the moral life as a distinct and actual
continuation of the action of Christ on the cross. "It is the love of the Trinity, it
is the intimate nature of God Himself, that we find at work in human activity—
under a very humble form, it is true, but ever so expressive" (347).

Gilman, E. James. (2001). Fidelity of heart: An ethic of Christian
virtue. Oxford: Oxford University Press.

The author's intent is to take two philosophical-theological trends in
Christian ethics, what he calls, "obediential dispositions" and "empathetic emotions," and weave them together into a theory of Christian ethics. By obediential
dispositions, the author refers to the tradition of character or virtue ethics. By

empathetic emotions, the author refers to the tradition of moral passions in ethics.

The word *heart* in the title is used by the author to refer to a quality of human character consisting of two dimensions, dispositions or habits on one hand, and emotions on the other. Dispositional habits invite or elicit certain emotional attachments that are commensurate with their particular character trait. If a given habit is operative, the emotions relative to it will manifest themselves.

The author draws upon theological ethicists Alisdair MacIntyre and Stanley Hauerwas, as well as philosophers Aristotle and Thomas Aquinas for basic notions in character ethics. However, Gilman believes that these theologians and philosophers typically overlook the emotional aspect of Aristotle's ethics. Gilman turns to philosopher Martha Nussbaum and theologian Edward Vacek for grounding to propose the emotional side of his Christian ethic of the heart. Emotions are powerful, moral forces that, when properly cultivated, function as reliable, moral guides. "This book aims to explicate the meaning of 'fidelity of heart,'" says Gilman, "by showing how both obediential dispositions and empathetic emotions are essential dimensions of any community devoting itself passionately, intimately, and single-mindedly to following, and not just admiring, Christ" (8).

After a chapter in which Gilman suggests that the heart needs to be "reenfranchised," he addresses in subsequent chapters three virtues of the heart: love, peace, and justice. The book concludes with an exploration of what it means to have a faithful heart in the public life. Gilman turns to the virtue of compassion in this regard. He suggests that loving God, self, and others requires the follower of Jesus Christ to embrace a joyful sorrow that transforms enemies into friends. To pursue peace, according to Gilman, requires not just making peace; it also requires affirming and acting by the ways of pacifism.

&⊘ Jackson, Timothy. (1999). *Love disconsoled: Meditations on Christian charity.* Cambridge: Cambridge University Press.

Jackson's book is comprised of fairly divergent essays addressing the role of *agape* love as he construes it in relation to various issues and texts. Chapter 1, "Biblical Keys to Love," reveals that Jackson's theology of love is based primarily upon his interpretation of *agape* in the New Testament. The story of Jesus Christ provides the key to understanding love in the Bible and also the content and rationale for Christian charity. Jackson defines *agape* as the New Testament Greek word for the steadfast love that God has for human beings, as well as the neighbor-love humans are to have for one another (11). "Only because God first loves us gratuitously," says Jackson, "are we commanded and enabled to love God unreservedly and to love fellow human beings as we ought to love ourselves" (12). *Agape* as found in scripture is characterized by three interpersonal features: "(1), unconditional commitment to the good of others; (2), equal regard for the well-being of others; and (3), passionate service open to self-sacrifice for the sake of others" (15). Jackson stresses that *agape,* as he under stands it, does not make self-sacrifice essential; however, openness to self-sacrifice, under the right circumstances, is definitive of the virtue of *agape.*

Jackson distinguishes between what he calls "strong *agape*" and "weak *agape.*" By strong *agape,* he means love as the primary human source and end that is indispensable for moral insight and power. Strong *agape* is a metavalue by which both individual integrity and social civility turn on a commitment to care for something larger than oneself or one's tribe. In contrast, weak *agape* understands love as a moral virtue or value among equals with which it competes. When addressing *eros* and *philia,* Jackson argues both are dependent upon *agape* for their beginning and their ordered continuing.

With regard to ethical theory, Jackson argues that *agape* is like a duty in that it is not merely an optional good deed. However, *agape* is more than a duty in that it is not merely obligation among others. Rather, *agape* is what Jackson calls "primal goodness, the impetus behind all ethical actions and principles" (28). Strong *agape* between human beings involves three dimensions of the moral life: traits of character, forms of action, and concrete social consequences. The ethic of strong *agape* insists "that we are always called to do the loving thing, but it does not deny the relevance of agent-character or action-consequence" (214).

In chapter 2, Jackson uses novels written by Ernest Hemingway and F. Scott Fitzgerald to wrestle with the question of whether *agape* should be understood as an instance of prudence or an instance of self-sacrifice. He concludes that neither view is adequate for the long-suffering love of *agape* as understood in the Christian gospel.

Chapter 3's discussion addresses *agape, eros, philia,* and self-love by looking at the works of Augustine, Sigmund Freud, Simone Weil, and Edward Vacek. Neither Freud nor Augustine has an adequate conception of Christian charity because, as Jackson sees it, *eros, philia,* and self-love grow out of *agape* as its proper fruits and are secondary goods in comparison with the priority of *agape* itself. *Agape* wills the good of others for their own sakes, but, in willing that good, *agape* may require sacrifice that outstrips the demand of strict justice and natural preference.

In the chapter from which the book takes its title, Jackson examines how Christianity's putting charity first among the theological virtues compares to a consoling, Boethian view of ethics. A chastened view of charity best serves Christian epistemology and ethics, but a denial of foundationalism in epistemology does not require the loss of moral realism. Christian theology's priority of love rises above the question of immortality as endless life. "Putting charity first implies that immortality is not the greatest good, nor probably a necessary means to the greatest good" (170).

Jackson concludes the book with thoughts on how love is expressed through the cross of Christ. Love must be weaned away from traditional claims to certainty, invulnerability, immortality, and irresistible grace. The strong agapist stands for the priority of love among genuine values and the steadfastness of love among real doubts.

King, Martin Luther. (1963). *Strength to love.* Cleveland: Collins World.

This classic text is comprised of fifteen sermons preached by the Reverend Martin Luther King Jr. The sermons provide a glimpse into the most fundamental notions driving King's social compassion and Christian witness. Sermon titles include "A Tough Mind and a Tender Heart," "On Being a Good Neighbor," "Love in Action," "Loving Your Enemies," and "Pilgrimage to Non-Violence."

In "Loving Your Enemies," King writes, "probably no admonition of Jesus has been more difficult to follow than the command to 'love your enemies'" (47). Jesus surely understood the difficulty inherent in the act of loving one's enemy. The responsibility of Christians is to discover the meaning of this command and seek to passionately live it out.

In answering the question, "how do we love our enemies," King says that we must first develop and maintain the capacity to forgive. Second, we must see the goodness in those who hurt us. Third, we must not seek to defeat or humiliate the enemy, but to win the enemy's friendship and understanding. "Jesus recognized that *love* is greater than *like*. When Jesus bids us to love our enemies, He is speaking neither of *eros* nor *philia;* He is speaking of *agape,* understanding, and creative, redemptive good will for all men" (50).

Lewis, C. S. (1960). *The four loves.* New York: Harcourt Brace.

C. S. Lewis is one of the most important theologians of the twentieth century, although his scholarly discipline was literature. He examines four main types of love, with special concentration on two types of love, "Gift-love" and "Need-love."

In his first chapter, Lewis identifies the humblest and most widely diffused of the loves, that is, the loves and likings at the subhuman level. Following an examination of subhuman love, he moves to discuss a love that he calls "affection." Affection comes from the Greek love word *storge*. The third chapter is devoted to friendship love, from the Greek work *philia*. This friendship love is the least of the natural loves, "the least instinctive organic, biological, gregarious, and necessary" (58). Friendship should be distinguished from community love because communities require cooperation. Friendship love by contrast is free from instinct, free from duty, and free from the need to be needed. Following an examination of friendship, Lewis addresses *eros*. By *eros* Lewis refers to "the love in which lovers are in," that is, romantic love.

In the book's final chapter Lewis addresses charity. Charity is "Gift-love" and the primal "Gift-love" comes from the divine energy. While Lewis claims that "to love at all is to be vulnerable" (121), he also claims that God is self-sufficient. "In God there is no hunger that needs to be filled, only plenteousness that desires to give. The doctrine that God was under no necessity to create is not a piece of dry scholastic speculation. It is essential" (126). Also, "God, who needs nothing, loves into existence, holy, superfluous creatures in order that He may love and perfect them" (127).

After God loves into existence holy, superfluous creatures, God implants in those creatures both the Gift-loves and the Need-loves. Gift-love comes by grace and we call it charity. God also gives a supernatural Need-love of God and a supernatural Need-love of other creatures. It is through these two gifts that creatures have a longing for God and a love for others.

๙๏ Marion, Jean-Luc. (1991). *God without Being.* Chicago: University of Chicago Press.

In this tome, heavily influenced by Continental theology and philosophy, the author argues that true love theology needs to abandon all metaphysics of the subject. It needs to embrace a revelation-based strategy for Christian love theology, not requiring any corelational stance between theology and modernity. God's revelation of love is a pure gift beyond reason and incomprehensible. Marion's conversation partners in this book include Nietzsche, Heidegger, Wittgenstein, and Derrida.

Theology is only proper when done within the horizon of God's own self-revelation as *agape*. While God exists, Marion does not believe that one ought to ascribe being to God. "Under the title, 'God Without Being,'" explains Marion, "I am attempting to bring out the absolute freedom of God with regard to all determinations, including, first of all, the basic condition that renders all other conditions possible and even necessary for us, humans, the fact of Being" (xx).

While for humans it is necessary to be in order to love, "God is love" comes before "God as Being." God's primary theological name is charity, and in this sense Marion's enterprise is postmodern and similar to Derrida's. Marion concludes by suggesting that what can be known about God comes only in so far as God gives Himself as a gift, the "gift gives only itself."

๙๏ Martin, Mike W. (1996). *Love's virtues.* Lawrence: University Press of Kansas.

Martin offers a philosophically rigorous yet highly accessible argument for the importance of developing the various virtues found in a robust notion of love. Martin argues that love encompasses a wide variety of virtue-structured ways in which persons value each other as having irreplaceable worth. In short, love is "a virtue-structured way to value persons" (1).

Although there is a variety of loves, Martin chooses to examine erotic love, defined as love involving sexual desires and monogamous marriage. By marriage, he means moral relationships involving sexual desires and long-term commitments to one's partner. His purpose in writing the book is to clarify the role of moral values in understanding this kind of love. This book provides internal justification for marital love by examining the moral dimensions of love that make it desirable insofar as love's virtues are embedded in marriage.

The book is divided into ten chapters, each of which, except the first, addresses particular virtues of love. The first chapter, "Love and Morality," is one of the most important because it frames the issues that the author highlights throughout the remainder of the work. Martin argues that love is internally related to morality: "Moral values define love as ways to value persons" (10). The notion of morality that he proposes is pluralistic insofar as he realizes that people have differing conceptions of moral ideals of goodness. These moral values enter into the very meaning of love by structuring love's relationships and shaping its experiences. In short, virtues and ideals enter into defining what love is.

Martin believes that moral philosophies and prominent ethical theories have failed to give love its proper place. Those moral theories that presuppose an impartiality paradigm give little attention to the preferential treatment that love often calls for. In proposing his own moral philosophy, Martin affirms an ethical pluralism that acknowledges objective value, affirms liberty and tolerance of diversity, and underscores the moral significance of personal caring relationships. "Love encompasses a variety of virtue-guided and virtue-structured ways to value persons. Understood within a pluralistic perspective, love makes possible morally creative forms of shared caring" (31).

In examining the particular virtues that shape and partly define love, Martin begins with the virtue of caring. According to him, caring is the central virtue that defines love. It is central partly when it has good motives and intended objects, partly because it tends to produce good consequences, and partly because of its connections with other virtues. The object of genuine love is the well-being of the beloved together with the shared well-being of two lovers. This means that love that interweaves altruism and self-interest; in fact, Martin claims that it fuses them. "Love transcends the dichotomy between *eros* and *agape* by creating motives to promote the shared good of two or more people" (39). The caring involved in genuine love is "directed toward persons in their full individuality, motivated in part by a concern for their well-being intending with any luck to produce good consequences" (42). Caring is "expressed in, conditioned on, enhanced or limited by, and in general interwoven with other virtues within a complex moral tapestry" (42).

For the remainder of the book, Martin examines by chapter the following virtues: faithfulness, sexual fidelity, respect, fairness, honesty, wisdom, courage, and gratitude. Regarding the virtue of fairness, Martin argues that neither mutual consent nor 50–50 distribution of benefits and burdens is adequate for understanding fairness in terms of love. Instead, Martin advocates the idea of equal autonomy as the primary love criterion of fairness. Martin notes, however, that "although love is never entirely selfless, love includes a willingness to make sacrifices on behalf of one's spouse" (116). Love intertwines the good of two people. Love contains elements of benevolence without being a disinterested altruism: it blends the self-interest of two persons so as to transcend the distinction between selflessness and selfishness.

With regards to the virtue of wisdom, Martin argues that wisdom is primarily understanding what love is, including love's requirements, constituent values, and contributions to meaningful life. Wisdom is "knowing how to care for the person we love and putting that knowledge into practice" (147). "Knowing how to love implies knowing how to be honest, how to be faithful by establishing mutual commitment and arrangements reasonably designed to protect love, how to find the courage to confront dangers to relationships, how to be fair in balancing benefits and burdens, how to show gratitude for love" (148). In sum, Martin's book is a top-notch book of moral philosophy concentrating upon love as the uniquely important touchstone for virtue ethics.

    ❧ Meilaender, Gilbert. (1981). *Friendship: A study in theological ethics.* Notre Dame, Ind.: University of Notre Dame Press.

This classic study in theological ethics is written to argue that *philia* deserves an honored place within Christian ethics. Meilaender notes that at one time *philia,* rather than *agape* or charity, was the common way to understand love. However, *agape* displaced *philia* in Christian thought, and the author attempts to think theologically about this displacement in this book. *Friendship* examines the tension between *philia* and *agape* and probes the significance of this tension for Christian thought experience.

Each chapter explores a way in which *philia,* as a preferential bond, is important for understanding theological ethics. While *agape* is to be shown even to the enemy, *philia* is a mutual bond marked by inner reciprocities. While *agape* is said to be characterized by the fidelity and changelessness of God in covenant, *philia* is recognized to be the subject of change. While *agape* has been used to designate the search for a suprahistorical resting place in God, *philia* is the noblest thing aspired to in civics. While *agape* understands one's vocation as the supremely important form of service to neighbor, *philia* emphasizes the bond of relationship toward those with personal significance.

In all of these contrasts, the author notes that the central element in their tension is the preferential character of friendship. "Whatever its dangers, friendship is surely a bond of great significance for human life. No adequate theological ethic can fail to make place for it. When Christ came into this world, he came to his own, John's Gospel tells us. And the divine love which Christ dis-plays—God's *agape*—cannot therefore be entirely alien to the needs and possi-bilities of our human nature" (105).

      Moffatt, James. (1930). *Love in the New Testament.* New York: Richard R. Smith.

Moffatt's work on love, although dated by nearly seventy-five years, is a classic and remains today perhaps the clearest and deepest analysis of love in the New Testament. In particular, Moffatt addresses the key Christian phrase, God is love.

After noting all of the passages in the New Testament pertaining to love, Moffatt concludes that the distinctiveness of Christianity is that Christians re-gard themselves as being loved by God. Furthermore, Christianity was initiated and finds at its center One who not only taught love, but lived it perfectly: Jesus Christ. Responding to Nygren and others who claim that the word "*eros*" is not in the great Corinthian love hymn because Paul meant to emphasize the differ-ence between *agape* and desire for God, Moffatt argues instead that Paul's intent was to refrain from using a word the Corinthians would identify with vulgarity.

Those in the science-and-love dialogue who privilege Christian scripture would do well to mine the deep resources of this classic biblical reference on love.

      Mollenkott, Virginia. (1983). *The divine feminine: The biblical im-agery of God as female.* New York: Crossroad.

This text is a classic in its arguments to reclaim biblical images of God as fe-male. The author believes that understanding the feminine image of God ulti-mately empowers both men and women. "I want to delve deeper into just one way in which the Bible supports human sexual equality and mutuality: the im-ages of God as female that sprinkle the sacred writings of Judaism and Chris-tianity" (7).

After surveying the history of what has happened to female imagery of God in scripture, Mollenkott focuses on a series of scriptural images and their impli-cations for twentieth-century society. These feminine images include God as a nursing mother, a midwife, a mother pelican, a female homemaker, a baker-woman, female beloved, mother eagle, and Dame Wisdom.

Mollenkott concludes the tome with suggestions for how the understand-ing of the divine feminine might be included in contemporary worship. "If our goal is pointed inclusion of females in the feminine in the language of worship, we may find ourselves utilizing female god-images and pronouns as frequently as possible" (115). She also urges for Christians to refer to God in terms of the language of love. Because love has traditionally entailed characteristics more commonly assumed to be feminine, referring to God as love in Christian theology would be helpful in reclaiming the images and language association with femininity found in the Christian Bible.

   ˢ❧ Moltmann, Jürgen. (1981). *The Trinity and the kingdom: The doctrine of God.* Trans. Margaret Kohl. San Francisco: Harper & Row.

As one of the most influential theologians of the contemporary period, Jürgen Moltmann has influenced a variety of theologies of love. His *The Trinity and the Kingdom* brings together many themes found in his other books (e.g., *The Suffering God* and *God in Creation*), including the notion that God truly suffers with creaturely pain and that God is present and active in the world.

What makes *The Trinity and the Kingdom* especially interesting for the science-and-love discussion is how Moltmann wrestles to explain how it is that God is essentially loving. He acknowledges the truth of what many other love theorists have claimed: "love cannot be consummated by a solitary subject. An individuality cannot communicate itself: individuality is ineffable, unutterable" (57). This implies that "if God is love, then he neither will, nor can, be without the one who is his beloved" (58). Furthermore, because love relations imply some degree of need, God cannot be, in all ways, self-sufficient: "If God is love, then he does not merely emanate, flow out of himself; he also expects and needs love" (99). Using "suffering" in its classical sense, which means to be affected by another, Moltmann argues that "if God were incapable of suffering in every respect, then he would also be incapable of love" (23).

The answer to many issues pertaining to divine love can be found when examining relations within the Trinity. God "is at once the lover, the beloved, and the love itself" (57). This intra-Trinitarian love is illustrated by the fact that "in eternity and out of the very necessity of his being, the Father loves the only begotten Son. . . . In eternity and out of the very necessity of his being, the Son responds to the Father's love through his obedience and his surrender to the Father" (58). Three notions *together*—divine persons, divine relations, and change in divine relations—provide the basis for conceiving of intra-Trinitarian love. Because love has everlastingly been expressed through intra-Trinitarian relations, love can be considered an essential attribute of God.

Moltmann entertains several hypotheses in *The Trinity and the Kingdom* for conceiving the correlation between the creation of the world and the Trinity. Sometimes he speaks of God creating from chaos, other times of God creating from nothing. He even places these apparently contradictory notions alongside each other; he speaks of divine creating as "creation out of chaos and *creatio ex nihilo*" (109). He claims that "creation [is] God's act in Nothingness and . . . God's order in chaos" (109). However, the evidence from his statements about God's love for the world being voluntary while the love between the Father and Son is necessary leads one to conclude that Moltmann ultimately affirms *creatio ex nihilo* rather than creation from chaos.

The creation hypothesis Moltmann proposes most vigorously, however, is based soundly upon intra-Trinitarian suppositions: "If we proceed from the inner-Trinitarian relationships of the Persons in the Trinity, then it becomes clear that the Father creates the one who is his Other by virtue of his love for the Son" (112). Because of this desire to communicate to nondivine individuals, it was through the eternal Son/Logos that the Father creates the world. In fact, "the idea of the world is inherent in the nature of God himself from eternity" (106). This means that "the idea of the world is already inherent in the Father's love of the Son" (108). Because God creates the world in his love for the Son and creates through the Son, the Son "is the divinely immanent archetype of the idea of the world" (112). The solution to how God and the world are related, then, is to suppose that the idea of the world has been eternally present to deity in the Son.

Moltmann has been at the fore in suggesting that kenosis, as God's self-emptying love, should be seen as the clue to God's loving creation and interaction with the world. "The divine kenosis which begins with the creation of the world reaches its perfected and completed form in the incarnation of the son" (118). This self-emptying kenosis provides the key for understanding how God can be, in essence, wholly omnipotent and yet completely loving. God, in free self-sacrifice, gives up power, knowledge, and presence to allow space for creatures to be.

ॐ Muhaiyaddeen, M. R. Bawa. (1981). *A book of God's love.* Philadelphia: Fellowship Press.

This book is a devotional book of sorts, published by a Muslim society in the United States. The author is a Sufi mystic from Sri Lanka. The author advocates compassionate love as an instance in the ray of God's infinite love. The author's intent is to "lighten your heart, a map to help you find the treasure hidden within you. That treasure contains the most valuable and elusive things in life which everyone seeks but very few ever find—unconditional love, everlasting youth, and unchanging truth" (ix).

Muhaiyaddeen suggests that the only kind of love that is truly beneficial is selfless love. "Unless love is connected to God, unless it is connected to truth, to compassion, to justice, and to grace, it is possible for it to breakdown" (7). God's love must take shape within humanity, which means that divine love must form in human hearts. Such love includes suffering with those who suffer and selflessly giving to those who are in need. "We must draw that grace and that treasure within us. This love is true love, the love borne of faith and trust, the love borne of brotherly unity, the love that comes from being one family, the love that comes from prayer, the love that comes from merging with God, the love which has no limit" (20). The author argues that love entails relationships with others. "Once you have God's love, God's qualities, and God's actions, everyone is connected to you, and therefore you will feel the suffering no matter whose it is" (24).

♠ Nygren, Anders. (1957 [1930]). *Agape and eros.* Trans. Philip S. Watson. New York: Harper & Row.

Anders Nygren's *Agape and Eros* is monumentally important for the contemporary dialogue between science and theologies of love. When examining Nygren's hypotheses pertaining to love, Gene Outka concludes, "whatever the reader may think of [*Agape and Eros*], one may justifiably regard this work as the beginning of the modern treatment of the subject" (Outka, 1972, p. 1). Nygren's work is not so important for its substantive contributions to this dialogue. He fails to consider the science of his day, and this work is almost exclusively theological in orientation. Furthermore, contemporary biblical and theological scholars have been almost uniformly rejected his particular *agape* and *eros* love hypotheses.

What makes Nygren's tome so important to the current science and theologies of love interface is the book's formal contribution: *Agape and Eros* implanted on the Western psyche the notion that when the word *agape* is used to speak of love, we refer to something distinctive. *Agape* has come to function as a kind of code word, although to what exactly is being referred varies dramatically from author to author. Although biblical scholars have almost unanimously rejected the claim that *agape* holds special status in Christian scripture and tradition, the perceived significance of *agape* persists today, thanks in large part to *Agape and Eros.*

Nygren states that his purpose in authoring the book is "to investigate the meaning of Christian love" and "illustrate the main changes it has undergone in the course of history" (27, 39). Such an investigation is important because love occupies the central place in Christian theology and piety. Furthermore, if one has access to "the distinctive character of the Christian conception of love," says Nygren, the contrasts between it and inauthentic Christian loves will emerge (29).

According to Nygren, *agape* is the only authentically Christian love: "nothing but that which bears the impress of *agape* has a right to be called Christian love" (92). "*Agape* is the center of Christianity, the Christian fundamental motif *par excellence*" (48). The other main type of love, *eros*, is not only non-Christian, it has also proven to distort authentic faith whenever Christian theologians have embraced it. *Agape* and *eros* originally had nothing to do with each other, because they belong to two "entirely separate spiritual worlds, between which no direct communication is possible" (31–32). In addition, each type of love suggests a different attitude toward life.

The author divulges what he means by *agape* when he lists what he believes are this love's essential aspects: 1) *Agape* is spontaneous and unmotivated; 2) *agape* is indifferent to value; 3) *agape* is creative; and 4) *agape* is the initiator of fellowship with God. The first two features of *agape* reveal that the explanation for God's love is not found in its object. Divine *agape* is spontaneous in that it does not look for something that, as Nygren says, could be adduced as its motivation. By the fact that divine love seeks those who do not deserve it and can lay no claim to it, *agape* is manifest most clearly in its spontaneous and unmotivated character. The third feature is, according to Nygren, the deepest reason for *agape*'s uniqueness; it indicates that love is God's creative activity. Love creates value in the one who is without inherent value. Fourth, *agape*, as the initiator of fellowship with God, discloses that God must come to meet humans and offer them fellowship.

Having explained what he means by *agape*, Nygren addresses the meaning of *eros*. Although he never gives a firm definition of this love, he identifies it both with the inclination toward the sensual expressed in mystery-piety and with the drive to transcend the sensual that Plato expresses in its highest form. *Eros* in mystery-piety is the vulgar *eros* of the sense-world; *eros* in Plato is the heavenly striving for the transcendent world of ideas. While Nygren finds no connection between vulgar *eros* and *agape*, heavenly *eros* is *agape*'s chief rival. In both its vulgar and heavenly versions, however, *agape* differs from *eros* in kind, not degree. Nygren argues that the negative consequences of Hellenistic thought in general, and *eros* theology in particular, have invariably led to a distortion of pure, Christian love theology. "When Christianity tried to express itself in Platonic terms," he contends, "the *agape* motif inevitably underwent a transformation" (54).

Nygren considers how the Christian church has appropriated the two love motifs in history. In his view, the history of Christian ideas proceeds in a rhythm, alternating between synthesis and reformation. A reformation in the history of Christian love occurs whenever *agape* shatters the synthesis constructed between it and *eros*. The two historical figures that illustrate this synthesis and reformation best, according to Nygren, are Augustine and Luther. Augustine constructed an illegitimate synthesis of *agape* and *eros;* Luther's Reformation set *agape* in its proper place as the only authentically Christian love.

One of the most important turning points in the history of Christian love occurred in Augustine's thought. In fact, Augustine's conception of Christian love is the most influential in all of Christian history, according to Nygren, surpassing even the influence of the New Testament. Augustine's theory of Christian love must be regarded as a continuation of the endless discussion of ancient philosophy about what is the highest good. The Christian command to love, according to Augustine, answers philosophy's question of how the highest good can be attained. This good, which is the eternal, transcendent, self-sufficient *eudaemonia,* is attained through a complete synthesis of *agape* and *eros*. The meeting of the *eros* and *agape* motifs produces a characteristic third love that Augustine calls "*caritas*," which is neither *eros* nor *agape*. Augustine's emphasis upon God's un-merited descent to humanity represents the *agape* element of *caritas*. His empha-sis upon the necessity of virtue in humanity's ascent to God represents the *eros* element of *caritas*. However, what makes *caritas* inauthentic Christian love, ac-cording to Nygren, is its inclusion of *eros* as ascent to God.

In the latter part of the book, Nygren turns to Luther as the one whose thought reestablishes the correct place of *agape* in Christian thought; the Protestant Reformation marked a time in history during which true Christian love (*agape*) was once again rightly elevated. Luther brought about this correc-tion by smashing Augustine's illegitimate synthesis of *eros* and *agape* in the doc-trine of *caritas*. Several factors were at work in this demolition. At the center was Luther's personal struggle against the upward tendency of *caritas*. This struggle resulted in his rejection of every idea of merit. He also rejected doctrines that implied the possibility of ascent to God by way of reason or mysticism. Luther ruthlessly rejected any attempt to ennoble and refine self-love, insisting it be an-nihilated.

Unlike Christian theologians who had come before, says Nygren, Martin Luther insisted upon a purely theocentric love. In doing this, Luther proclaimed that fellowship with God was possible on the basis of sin, not of holiness. In this regard, Nygren writes: "The deepest difference between Catholicism and Luther can be expressed by the following formula; in Catholicism: fellowship with God is on God's own level, on the basis of holiness; in Luther: fellowship with God is on our level, on the basis of sin. In Catholicism, it is a question of a fellowship with God motivated by some worth—produced, it is true, by the infusion of *caritas*—to be found in man; in Luther, fellowship with God rests exclusively on God's unmotivated love, justification is the justification of the sinner."

Nygren concludes by emphasizing Luther's belief that humans themselves do not produce Christian love for the neighbor; this love must come down from heaven. God employs humans as instruments so that, as Nygren says, "the Christian is not an independent center of power alongside God" (734). Luther thinks of the Christian as a tube that passes love received from above to the neighbor below. The tube/Christian makes no contribution to the character or shape of this love. Unlike Augustine's *caritas*, a love that can only use the neigh-bor to get to God, Luther's *agape* love addresses the neighbor *as* neighbor. In fact, Luther claims that love for God is none other than love for neighbor.

 Outka, Gene. (1972). *Agape: An ethical analysis.* New Haven: Yale Uni-versity Press.

Outka provides an ethical analysis from an analytic perspective of Chris-tian theological writing pertaining to *agape* from writers in the years 1930 to 1970. Among the central figures that he discusses are M. C. D'Arcy, Gerard Gilleman, Soren Kierkegaard, Reinhold Niebuhr, Anders Nygren, and Paul

Ramsey. This work is still one of the very best because of its rigorous analysis of love issues.

Outka is not so much interested in offering his own proposals about how best to understand *agape*, nor is he interested in proposing a particular theological scheme. Rather, he analyzes prominent texts with an eye toward how their authors understand *agape* as ethics. "I am convinced that many of the historic ethical concerns of the Judeo-Christian tradition have been encapsulated in the 'love language,' and one ought to try to understand more clearly just what has been meant within that language" (5).

In the first chapter, Outka addresses what love as a normative, ethical principle or standard means. His concentration is upon how one's understanding of *agape* affects how one understands neighbor-love. Outka contends that crucial aspects of *agape* include the fact that *agape* is independent and unalterable. "Regard is for every person qua human existent, to be distinguished from those special traits, actions, etc., which distinguish particular personalities from each other" (9). Furthermore, Outka contends that *agape* entails a basic equality whereby one's neighbors' well-being is as valuable as another's neighbors' well-being.

In chapters 2 and 3, Outka addresses how various authors understand *agape* as related to loving oneself and to acting for justice. Chapter 4 engages how *agape* is related to various dominant ethical schemes and what Outka calls "subsidiary rules." The author notes that almost all of the authors do not equate *agape* with a particular given moral code. Chapter 5 includes the author's assessment of how *agape* might be understood as a virtue or aspect of one's character. Chapter 6 entails an examination of how various authors justify or support their contention that persons ought to love with *agape*. In other words, these are justifying reasons for why someone might regard others with equal-regard. In the seventh chapter, Outka pays particular attention to the claims of Karl Barth with regard to *agape*. He notes that Barth understands *agape* as both equal-regard and self-sacrifice. Outka then addresses how Barth understands the major themes examined in the book's previous chapters.

In the book's final chapter, Outka explores various issues that have arisen in his examination of dominant texts on *agape*. He proposes what he believes to be the fundamental content of human *agape* and some unresolved issues related to that content. "The meaning ascribed in the literature to love, in general, and to *agape*, in particular, is often characterized by both variance and ambiguity" (257–258). This has to do, says Outka, with the particular wider beliefs and theological schemes espoused by the writers of the love literature. It also has to do with the many ways in which the word *love* is used in the English language.

Upon reflecting on the matters that have arisen in his examination of love texts, Outka comes to a tentative suggestion for the meaning of *agape* as "an active concern for the neighbor's well-being, which is somehow independent of particular actions of the other" (260). This means in part that the human must not let disparities and inequalities determine his or her basic attitudes toward others with whom he or she interacts.

Outka also notes that various problems arise when one understands self-sacrifice as the quintessence of *agape*. "Generally, therefore, I am inclined to think that instead of appraising self-sacrifice as the purest and most perfect manifestation of *agape,* the difficulties I have considered are voided if one allows it only *instrumental* warrant" (278). Regard of one's self ought to be based upon the fact that he or she is a creature of God who is more than a means to some other end. Outka also notes that *agape* involves certain social and personal relations thus entailing an overlap between regard of others and social cooperation.

<ES Pinnock, Clark H., Rice, Richard, Sanders, John, Hasker, William, & Basinger, David. (1994). *The openness of God: A biblical challenge to the traditional understanding of God.* Downers Grove, IL: InterVarsity.

Pinnock joins four other authors to provide one of the more hotly debated books on the doctrine of God among Evangelical Christians. At the root of the vision of deity they designate the "Open God" is their shared conviction that love is God's chief attribute, and all other divine attributes must not undermine the primacy of love.

In order to offer a coherent doctrine of God, essayists address issues of divine transcendence, immanence, power, omniscience, mutability, and passibility. At the core of his proposal is his account of divine loving activity that includes God's responsiveness, generosity, sensitivity, openness, and vulnerability. In fact, Clark Pinnock contends that "love rather than almighty power is the primary perfection of God" (114).

Essayists in *The Openness of God* argue that no doctrine is more central to the Christian faith than the doctrine of God. Laying out a coherent, livable, biblical doctrine is crucial for the practical and theoretical aspects of theology. Many Christians, however, observe an inconsistency between their beliefs about the nature of God and their religious practice. For example, Christians ask God to act in a certain way when they pray, although their formal theology may suppose that God has predetermined all things. A major factor in assessing the viability of a theological scheme, then, is the piety question: How well does this "live"?

"How can we expect Christians to delight in God or outsiders to seek God if we portray God in biblically flawed, rationally suspect, and existentially repugnant ways?" asks Pinnock (104). In his attempt to avoid rationally suspect hypotheses, Pinnock seeks to offer a coherent doctrine of God, that is, each divine attribute "should be compatible with one another and with the vision of God as a whole" (101).

The Openness of God authors share the basic conviction that love is the principal theme in Christian theology. Pinnock insists, for instance, that love is the primary perfection of God. Richard Rice, who assumes the task of offering biblical support for the open view advanced in the book, claims that the open view expresses two basic convictions scripture supports. First, love is the most important quality humans attribute to God. Second, love is more than care and commitment; it also involves sensitivity and responsiveness. Rice further notes that, from a Christian perspective, *love* is the first and last word in the biblical portrait of God. When one enumerates God's qualities, one must not only *include* love on the list, but, to be faithful to the Bible, one must put love at the *head* of that list. A doctrine of God faithful to the Bible must show that all God's characteristics derive from love. Rice concludes, "Love, therefore, is the very essence of the divine nature. Love is what it means to be God" (19).

Pinnock embraces the notion that God is like a loving parent when affirming these hypotheses. In this parental model God possesses "qualities of love and responsiveness, generosity and sensitivity, openness and vulnerability" (103). God is a person who experiences the world, responds to what happens, relates to humans, and interacts dynamically with creatures.

Essayists reject the classic conception of God described as "an aloof monarch" removed from the world's contingencies, that is, the entirely transcendent God. They reject the deity who is completely unchangeable, all-determining, irresistible, and does not risk. "The Christian life involves a genuine interaction between God and human beings," Pinnock contends. "We respond to God's gracious initiatives and God responds to our responses . . . and on it goes" (7).

Essayists also deny divine foreordination, divine foreknowledge of free creaturely actions, and the hypothesis that either divine foreknowledge or unilateral determination is compatible with creaturely freedom. God knows all things that can be known, but divine omniscience does not mean that God possesses exhaustive foreknowledge of all future events. Total knowledge of the future would imply that future events are fixed. "If choices are real and freedom significant, future decisions cannot be exhaustively known," Pinnock explains (123).

త్ర Post, Stephen G. (1990). *A theory of agape: On the meaning of Christian love.* Lewisburg, PA: Bucknell University Press.

This work is an innovative and creative endeavor in Christian love theology. The author proposes various doctrinal hypotheses concerning adequate notions of *agape* love. The author's intention is "to challenge various assumptions and settled orthodoxies in order to move the literature on love in a new direction" (9).

Among the claims made are the following: love should be understood as a communion or mutuality between God, self, and neighbor. This Christian love is found within the fellowship of Christian believers and informed by the Christian tradition. Love can involve a degree of self-fulfillment. Also, God is a suffering God who is affected by human responses to divine calls for love. "The western tendency to idolize selfless love devoid of even the slightest iota of self concern is an aberration from the valid ideal of unselfishness in fellowship" (12).

Post understands the chief purpose of neighbor love as raising the neighbor toward God and toward the fellowship of Christian believers who share a vision of divine love. He argues that *agape* should not be equated with strict self-denial; neither should *agape* be reduced to the universal love of humanity. Rather, because Christian love is participatory and occurs in fellowship, *agape* is nurtured and sustained in communities. This also means that the development and furtherance of the habits of love occurs best within the Christian family.

Post concludes the book by noting the necessary link between freedom and love. "In the absence of freedom no person will fully express his or her inmost self, and attempts to coerce this affective self revelation inevitably breed resentment" (117).

✎ Spohn, William. (2000). *Go and do likewise: Jesus and ethics.* New York: Continuum.

The author writes from a Roman Catholic Christian perspective and argues that adequate Christian ethics must place the words and actions of Jesus at its center. Spohn believes that Christianity confesses Jesus Christ to be the definitive but not exclusive revelation of God. "Morally, this confession means that Jesus Christ plays a normative role in Christians' moral reflection. His story enables us to recognize *which* features of experience are significant, guides *how* we act, and forms *who* we are in the community of faith" (2).

The first three chapters make the case for the sources and method that the author employs. The argument is that three particular sources shape Christian ethics: the New Testament, virtue ethics, and spirituality. The second half of the book addresses how one perceives God's reign and Jesus' compassionate vision, as well as exploring the emotions and dispositions of the Christian life. When explaining the importance of compassion in the ethical vision introduced by Jesus, the author writes, "Luke's parable of the Good Samaritan shows that compassion is the optic nerve of the Christian vision" (87). The author concludes that the Christian moral life is grounded in the person of Jesus, and this grounding is demonstrated through the regular Christian practices that shape the lives of committed believers.

⚘ Stone, Bryan P., & Oord, Thomas Jay (Eds.). (2001). *Thy nature and thy name is love: Wesleyan and process theologies in dialogue.* Nashville, TN: Kingswood.

This collection of essays brings together Wesleyans who are, for the most part, friendly to basic concepts in process theology. What makes the book especially attractive to those engaged in the science and love dialogue is that both of the theological traditions addressed herein, Wesleyan theology and process theology, affirm a vision of God whose essence is love. Both traditions emphasize the priority and universality of grace in ways that do not negate human responsibility. Both understand divine-human interaction in relational terms. And both theological visions are particularly amenable to evidence in theories and science. Both are interested in natural theology.

Essays particularly helpful for those considering the influence of love upon science are the following: "Process Theology and the Wesleyan Witness" by Schubert M. Ogden, "Process and Sanctification" by Bryan P. Stone, "Human Responsibility and the Primacy of Grace" by John B. Cobb Jr., "Seeking a Response-able God: The Wesleyan Tradition and Process Theology" by Randy L. Maddox, "Reconceptions of Divine Power in John Wesley, Panentheism, and Trinitarian Theology" by Tyron L. Inbody, "A Process Wesleyan Theodicy: Freedom, Embodiment and the Almighty God" by Thomas J. Oord, "Compassion and Hope: Theology Born Out of Action" by Mary Elizabeth Mullino-Moore, and "John Wesley, Process Theology, and Consumerism" by Jay McDaniel and John L. Farthing. This collection of essays provides evidence of the current trends in Wesleyan and process theologies, and it sets an agenda for scholars to address the nature of God and what it means to love.

⚘ Templeton, John. (1999). *Agape love: A tradition found in eight world religions.* Philadelphia: Templeton Foundation Press.

Templeton argues that *agape* love is not exclusive to any one religion, but it is an underlying principle in all major world religions. He defines *agape* love as unlimited, pure, and unconditional as well as altruistic.

Agape love expresses a unity of purpose that is common to all people. It holds within it the opportunity to transcend differences of religious beliefs and to live in joy and peace. *Agape* involves feeling and expressing pure, unlimited love for every human being, with no exception.

Templeton notes that all religions are not the same, and it is not his goal to convert persons from one religion to another. "Rather, the purpose is to point toward the possibilities and responsibilities of love. It is to awaken people to the realization that despite the differences, all religions share some very important, fundamental principles and goals, the highest of which is the realization of *agape* love—unconditional, unlimited, pure love" (5).

The eight religious traditions explored are Judaism, Christianity, Islam, Hinduism, Buddhism, Taoism, Confucianism, and Native American spirituality. The author concludes with these words: "The option to grow in *agape* is open to everyone on earth. It is an invitation to true happiness for you and others. May it become our aspiration, our expression of God's love radiating through us" (111).

🔖 Templeton, Sir John. (2000). *Pure unlimited love: An eternal creative force and blessing taught by all religions.* Philadelphia: Templeton Foundation Press.

Templeton offers this inspirational book on love as a brief explanation for what he considers the creative force in all religions. He defines pure, unlimited love as the "transcendent power of divine love that expresses itself through our hearts and minds when we are open and receptive to it."

Each short chapter answers the question posed in its title. For instance, in the chapter titled, "Can Unlimited Love Eliminate Conflict?," Templeton responds that it can because love enables one to ignore adversity, insults, loss, and injustice. The final chapter includes these words: "Whatever the need or circumstance, love can find a way to adjust, heal, or resolve any problem or situation" (56).

🔖 Tillich, Paul. (1963). *Love, power, and justice: Ontological analyses and ethical applications.* New York: Oxford University Press.

This preeminent twentieth-century Christian theologian argues in this small book that love, power, and justice all imply an ontology and must be understood in aspects of being itself. It is in this book that he famously defines love as "the drive toward the unity of the separated" (25). He also refers to love as the moving power of life and believes all love includes qualities of *eros* and *agape.*

Tillich does not believe that one can speak of self-love in anything more than a metaphorical sense. After all, if love is the drive toward the reunion of the separated, it is difficult to speak meaningfully of self-love.

In his exposition of the nature of power Tillich notes that love is the foundation, not the negation, of power. Love is the ultimate principle of justice, although justice preserves what love unites. "The basic assertion about the relation of God to love, power and justice is made, if one says that God is Being-itself" (109). However, everything that one says about Being-itself must be said symbolically.

The author's words about how divine love and power are related are also noteworthy. "Since God is love and His love is one with His power," contends Tillich, "He has not the power to force somebody into His salvation. He would contradict Himself. And this God cannot do" (114).

✧ Vacek, Edward Collins. (1994). *Love, human and divine: The heart of Christian ethics.* Washington, DC: Georgetown University Press.

Although this text was written fairly recently, it is fast becoming a classic work on love, one that those who wrestle with theologies of love must take seriously. Vacek is a Roman Catholic, but his hypotheses and conclusions are not characteristic of most Catholic thought. The author is well read and the topics covered are vast. "The central idea of this book is quite simple: (1) God loves us; (2) we love God; (3) we and God form a community; (4) we and God cooperate" (xv).

Vacek's main contention is that the love of God must be the center of Christian life and theology. To offer such a theology of love, Vacek undertakes a phenomenological orientation, which pays close attention to human experience. In particular, the author admits that Christian experience is privileged.

One reason this text offers such a rich resource to those in the love-and-science dialogue is that the author examines closely the three dominant forms of love: *agape, eros,* and *philia.* Vacek argues that Christians are mistaken to claim that *agape* is *the* Christian love. Rather, contends the author, *philia* represents the most complete Christian love; it "holds pride of place among Christian loves" (xvi). In fact, Vacek claims that "the central thesis of [my] book . . . is that communion or *philia* is the foundation and goal of Christian life" (280).

Chapter 1 argues that a love relation with God implies a distinctively Christian moral life, which entails certain emotions and values or what Vacek calls "orthokardia": "The ordered affections that unite us with God, ourselves, other people, and the world" (5). It is the Christian's relation with God that makes the Christian life distinctive.

The second chapter addresses the nature of love, and he notes that "most philosophical and theological writing, when it speaks of 'love,' does not analyze what love is, but rather assumes it has an evident meaning" (34). Avoiding this mistake, Vacek defines love as "*an affective, affirming participation in the goodness of a being (or Being).* Woven into this description are two strands. Any theory of love has to account for our experience of wanting to be with or have those we love, and delighting when we do so. Love unites. A theory of love also must account for our experiences of wanting for the beloved" (34; emphasis in original). He further defines love as an emotional, affirming participation in the dynamic tendency of an object to realize its fullness.

The doctrine of God that Vacek envisions includes a God who is truly related to creation. The author describes the Godworld relation as "love-as-participation" (95). This means that while God is free to create, God is also bound to that which is created.

God's identity is united, but not wholly so, with history. Humans have autonomy vis-à-vis God, but their freedom depends upon the deity. Vacek suggests that creaturely cooperation with the activity of God is required for the full expression of love in the world.

When addressing the extent and duration of love that should be expressed by lovers, Vacek argues that "love tries to enhance the well-being of the beloved, and it does so not only in the short term and for this or that person but in the long run for as many persons" (182). However, "because God loves not only us but others and also all of creation, we cannot . . . conclude that what God is doing in the world will always be entirely for our good. Some loss to our own well-being will be necessary" (188).

In chapters 5 through 9, Vacek addresses issues typically subsumed under an exploration of three kinds of love: *agape, eros,* and *philia.* He claims that we may love the beloved for the sake of the beloved, for our own sake, or for the sake of the relationship we have with the beloved. He calls these love relations "*agape, eros,* and *philia,*" which means that he distinguishes each by his phrase "for the sake of." In the chapter "*Agape,*" Vacek gives insightful critiques of the work of both Anders Nygren and Gene Outka. He argues that *agape* "is centered on the beloved's value and is directed toward the enhancement of that value. It is a faithful love that is spontaneous, generous, and willing to sacrifice" (191). In later chapters, Vacek also argues for a positive theological case for self-love.

In the final two chapters, Vacek addresses issues related to friendship love. Although his approach to Christian love is a pluralist one, in that he affirms the value of both *eros* and *agape,* Vacek notes in these chapters his central thesis that "communion or *philia* is the foundation and goal of the Christian life" (280). By *philia* he "means affectively affirming members of a community for the sake of the communally shared life" (287–88). It is this friendship love that constitutes a mutual relationship with God. "Philia creates, expresses, and enhances a mutual relationship. *Philia* fulfills us, but that fulfillment is not its primary consideration" (311). Vacek argues that theological focus on *agape* or *eros* without *philia* tends to promote individualism.

While duties to strangers are important for the Christian, they are not the paradigm for Christian living. Instead, Christians begin with the special relationships that they have with those who are near and dear, especially with God. "This book arises from the convictions that God relates to us in special relationships, that human selfhood begins in such relations, particularly in the family, and that the fullness of human personhood is possible only through deep *philia* relationships" (312).

    Vanhoozer, Kevin, Ed. (2001). *Nothing greater, nothing better: Theological essays on the love of God.* Grand Rapids, MI: Eerdmans.

This collection of edited essays is a decidedly theological work with little or no reflection on how scientific matters might affect theologies of love. Its value is that it represents the work of theologians, mostly from Reformed theological traditions, who wrestle with how to conceive of divine love.

The book's editor, Kevin J. Vanhoozer, begins his introductory essay—the best essay of the book—by noting that "it is exceedingly odd that Christian theologians have themselves been somewhat indifferent—inattentive, neutral with regard to the concept of the love of God" (1). It is no exaggeration to say that the defining and situating of divine love is the perennial task of Christian theology.

A growing number of Christian theologians believe that a major advance, even a revolution, in the understanding of the love of God has recently occurred. The traditional view of God entails that the deity metes out good but takes neither joy nor delight in the good that comes about. This classical God is immutable and impassable. Several developments in the twentieth century, however, have changed the way we understand divine love. Among the movements that have generated these developments are process philosophy, Trinitarian theology, liberation theology, feminist theology, and various postmodern thinkers, like Jean-Luc Marion.

Vanhoozer notes, "the concept of the love of God is both fundamental to the doctrine of God and, oddly, disruptive of it. There seems to be no place in a systematics in which the notion of the love of God neatly fits" (13). When discussing the structure of systematic theology, Vanhoozer observes that the love of God functions either "as a discrete doctrinal topic" or "as the structuring principle that provides a point of integration or thematic unity between individual doctrines." "Somewhat surprisingly," states Vanhoozer, "few theologians have chosen that latter option" (14).

In the second half of the opening essay, Vanhoozer briefly discusses how love affects issues such as divine sovereignty, reciprocal relations, divine control, divine suffering, and panentheism. After addressing these issues, he concludes that "we must say at least three things: the love of God is something that God has, something that God does, and something that God is" (23). Vanhoozer closes his introduction by claiming that "the moral of this introduction is that the love of God should occupy no one place in a theological system, but every place" (29).

The rest of *Nothing Greater, Nothing Better* includes a variety of essays of varying degrees of helpfulness. Gary Badcock looks at Anders Nygren's famous work, *Agape and Eros,* and concludes, like many others before him, that it is appropriate to speak of divine *eros.* On the basis of God's act in Christ, that is, creaturely response to divine initiative is something that God needs.

Geoffrey Grogan reviews a diversity of the biblical evidence pertaining to love. Lewis Ayres reflects upon Augustine's understanding of the love of God as it is expressed in St. Augustine's commentary on First John and in his work, *On the Trinity.* Trevor Hart considers the question of how we speak of God. Following Karl Barth, he concludes that the possibility of human speech about God rests entirely upon the incarnation. What we have in the incarnation is a God-given analogy. Alan Torrance also addresses analogical language, the incarnation, the Trinity, and other issues. Torrance wonders if love can be understood as God's essence, and, disappointingly, concludes that this question is unanswerable. He also rejects natural theology and argues that only those who have fellowship with Christ will allow their minds and language to become transformed as to speak adequately of God.

Tony Lane addresses the question of God's wrath in relation to God's love. Lane concludes that one must not affirm wrath as part of God's essence. Paul Helm addresses the question: Can God love the world? One of his conclusions is that God could not be equally benevolent to all human beings, but God can love all humans unequally. Helm also suggests, inaccurately from this reviewer's perspective, that the problem of evil is a matter of degree. David Fergusson addresses the issues of eschatology by asking the question, Will the love of God ultimately triumph? After all, if God's future is genuinely open, divine triumph over evil is not a foregone conclusion. Fergusson argues that those who affirm double predestination and those who affirm universalism ultimately remove human freedom by construing God's love as something that constrains human choice. Roy Clements concludes the book with a sermon on Hosea 11.

 ✎ Vanier, Jean. (1999). *Becoming human.* Mahwah, NJ: Paulist.

The book entails the material of five talks that its author, Jean Vanier, gave on the Canadian Broadcasting Corporation radio program. Vanier is the founder of L'Arche, an international network for people with intellectual disabilities in more than thirty countries.

The author comments that the book springs from his experience of humanness and not directly from his life of faith. In this sense the book is more about anthropology than about spirituality. "This book is about the liberation of the human heart from the tentacles of chaos and loneliness," writes its author, "and from those fears that provoke us to exclude and reject others. It is a liberation that opens us up and leads us to the discovery of our common humanity" (5). Among the subjects addressed in the chapters are loneliness, belonging, inclusion, freedom, and forgiveness. The author argues that by opening ourselves to outsiders we can achieve true personal and societal freedom, which includes the freedom to become truly human.

 ✎ Vanstone, W. H. (1978). *The risk of love.* New York: Oxford University Press.

In his struggles to understand the role of the church and what God requires, the author looks to a robust notion of love, including understanding the nature of God in a way that is amenable to the structure of love. The work in the initial segments is largely autobiographical as the author identifies his own journey to the theology of love that he eventually proposes.

In attempting to understand the purpose of the church, Vanstone wrestles with what it might mean for the church to glorify God. He comes to believe that God can be glorified only if God is truly interested in the work of the church. It is the importance of the church's work and his awareness of material reality that leads Vanstone to suppose that the whole of creation is a work of love.

After rejecting the idea that divine love is wholly dissimilar to creaturely love, the author argues that we must extrapolate from the authentic love that we see around us in the creaturely world. In his analysis of the phenomenology of love, Vanstone discovers three signs of authentic love. The first is that authentic love has no limitation, in the sense that it does not choose to love some people and hate others. This does not mean that love is not constrained by circumstances, however. The authenticity of unlimited love involves the totality of giving of oneself to the other. The second mark of authentic love is the giving up of control. Love becomes distorted when it attempts to possess or manipulate the other. This means that love is risky, for it cannot control the other and often fails in its attempt to benefit the other. The third mark of authentic love is that the other affects it. The love gives to the object a certain power over the one loving. The one loved affects the one loving. This means that lovers are vulnerable.

Upon examining a phenomenology of creaturely love, Vanstone turns to address divine love. He attributes to God a love that is limitless, vulnerable, and precarious. He appeals to the idea of kenosis, in the sense that God is self-giving in expression of love for creatures. The activity of God's love in creation is precarious, by which Vanstone means that it must not "proceed by an assured programme" (62).

The precariousness of divine love is especially evident in the fact that evil exists. The fact that evil occurs implies that there is an other that is not divine; it does not imply that evil is willed by the creator. Vanstone argues that the God who foreordains and predetermines cannot be a God who loves. "If the creation is the work of love, its 'security' lies not in its conformity to some predetermined plan, but in the unsparing love that will not abandon a single fragment of it, and man's assurance must be the assurance not that all that happens is determined by God's plan, but that all that happens is encompassed by His love" (66). When addressing the vulnerability of divine love, Vanstone contends that divine loving activity can result in either triumph or tragedy. Which of these two it will be is determined in part by creaturely response. This implies that God has need. For divine love to become complete, it must wait upon the understanding of those who receive it. This means that the creativity of God is dependent upon the responsive creativity of the creatures.

Trinitarian theology fulfills the requirement that God needs another. "Trinitarian theology asserts that God's love for His creation is not the love that is borne of 'emptiness' . . . it is the love which overflows from fullness" (69). "Of such a nature is the 'kenosis' of God is the self-emptying of Him Who is already in every way fulfilled" (69). It is God who awaits a response from creation, a response that issues in either triumph or tragedy. "Tentatively, but with growing assurance, theology may interpret the dynamic of nature as the activity of love" (85).

The proper human response to God amounts to the celebration of God's love, and that by which the love of God is celebrated may be called "the church." The church is wider than any recognized ecclesiastical structure; however, it includes the simplest action done out of awareness of God's love. The church, says Vanstone, is "the sum of all the structures and forms within which man expressed the recognition of the love of God" (97). In the visible church, humans aspire to create something that expresses their recognition of God's love. The church exists as the point in which the love of God is most profoundly exposed as the possibility for tragedy or triumph.

  Williams, Daniel Day. (1968). *The spirit and the forms of love.* New York: Harper & Row.

Williams's theology of love should be considered a classic expression of how someone inspired by the philosophical concerns of process philosophy and Christian faith might understand love, both human and divine. Given that process thought has proven especially helpful for many in the science and religion dialogue, one would do well to mine the chapters of *The Spirit and the Forms of Love* for gems to orient one's work in the interface between science and theology.

Williams reveals his purpose for writing *The Spirit and the Forms of Love* as his attempt to answer the question, "What is the meaning and truth of the Christian assertions that God is love, that love to God and the neighbor are the two great commandments, that fulfillment of human love depends upon God's action of reconciliation, and that the love of God is the ground of all hope?" (vii). When beginning to answer these questions, Williams turns to Christian scriptures. Although expressions of love in the Old Testament are diverse, Williams contends that the meaning of love therein is nothing other than the meaning of God's historical dealing with humanity. According to Williams, what Christians mean by love grows out of Jesus' history.

Williams offers three typologies to illustrate three major forms of love in the Christian tradition. The first is the Augustinian synthesis of the New Testament faith and the Neoplatonic vision. Its characteristic is the attempt to bring the various human and divine loves into an ordered structure. The second type is the Franciscan, which is expressed in the free, radical expression of love in a sacrificial life. The third type is the Evangelical way, which centers upon two notions: the loves of God and humans are to be understood within the affirmation of salvation by grace alone, and grace gives the individual a new sense of vocation to be a servant of God in the secular order.

Neoplatonic metaphysics have unfortunately often undermined Christian attempts to conceptualize Christian love adequately. When the main structure of Christian theology was formulated in the creeds, "the biblical faith in God became fused with the Neoplatonic doctrine of God as absolute being" (17). When Augustine sought to combine the biblical vision with Neoplatonic metaphysics, he ascribed to God all power and perfection (as completeness). This meant that temporality, change, becoming, and passivity were to be ascribed to God. Neoplatonic metaphysics denies the possibility that human determinations can alter God's experience, and the notion that God's experience is unalterable contradicts the broad biblical witness of God's interacting love.

"What would it mean," Williams wonders rhetorically as he transitions to proposing a process metaphysics to replace Neoplatonism, "to relate the Christian doctrine of God to a metaphysical outlook in which God's being is conceived in dynamic temporal terms?" (9). It would mean something very different something more intelligible and biblical. The "process" in process metaphysics designates this thought's indebtedness to a broad movement in modern thought that reconsiders metaphysical problems based on an evolutionary worldview and the temporal flow of experience. Williams avers that contemporary humanity is conscious of its radical historicity involving real freedom, possibilities yet unrealized, and an open-ended future that humans shape partly by their own decisions. Because of this and because the biblical God acts in a history where individuals have freedom, a philosophy should be championed that corresponds with general science, conceives of God in historical-temporal terms, and also accounts for creaturely freedom.

In broad terms Williams defines process theology as a perspective supposing that God is joined with the world in the adventure of real history where God and creatures have freedom to act and respond. Crucial to Williams's work is his insistence that similarities must exist between divine and human love. The analysis Williams performs is based upon this hypothesis: Whatever is present in the inescapable structures of human experience must be present in ultimate reality. After coming to a working hypothesis that accounts for the elements of those inescapable structures of experience—particularly the experience of love—one then asks about the implications this account has for a doctrine of God.

What, asks Williams, are the ontological conditions that human love requires and how are these conditions reflected in divine love? He suggests three conditions. First, individuals must be in relation. Love requires that real individuals each bring to relationship something that no other can bring and that those individuals possess the capacity to take into account another's unique individuality.

Second, love requires a degree of freedom in the one loving. All loves and lovers have a historical context and thus absolute freedom is impossible. Freedom is always qualified by the physical, emotional, and historical circumstances in which love exists. Furthermore, contends Williams, the very nature of love includes affirming and accepting the freedom of the other. "Nothing is more pathetic than the attempt to compel or coerce the love of another, for it carries self-defeat within it. That which is coerced cannot be love, hence in love we will that the other give his love freely" (116). If God wills to love, and, above all, if God wills to *be* loved, God cannot entirely determine the love of the other. God gives freedom to creatures in order that they may love.

Third, what has been said about freedom, action, suffering, and communication implies the categorical condition Williams calls "causality." According to him, love is meaningless without causality. Love "must be the kind of action, with whatever coercion is involved, which so far as possible leaves the other more free to respond" (120).

Fourth and finally, love requires that individuals—including the divine individual—be related. Loving not only requires a movement toward the other but also, says Williams, the capacity to be acted upon. Suffering is the language of feeling and of caring, and that is its importance for love. When humans love, they are a part of a history in which suffering is one condition of relationship. Divine love includes God "making himself vulnerable to receive into his being what the world does in its freedom," argues Williams, "and to respond to the world's actions." Process thought offers "a new metaphysical vision that embodies the conception of God as living, creative, and responsive to the world" (17).

The final chapters of the book are given to addressing particular issues that emerge in relation to the love scheme Williams proposes. Chapters address the incarnation, the atonement, self-sacrifice, sexuality, social justice, and the intellect.

๙๏ Wynkoop, Mildred Bangs. (1972). *A theology of love: The dynamic of Wesleyanism.* Kansas City: Beacon Hill.

This is a modern-day classic in Wesleyanism and love theology. The author offers this theological exposition as a defense of her thesis that John Wesley's theology provides the most adequate footing for a theology of love. "It is this author's considered opinion," contends Wynkoop, "that John Wesley has contributed a sound and usable approach to theology which is worthy of consideration in the solutions of the problems related to the theology-life syndrome. His 'hermeneutic' was 'love to God and man.' This theme runs throughout his works. At least when each doctrine of the Christian faith is identified and defined by him, the basic meaning invariably comes out 'love.' Wesley's thought is like a great rotunda with archway entrances all around it. No matter which one is entered it always leads to the central Hall of Love, where, looking upward toward the dome, one gazes into the endless, inviting sky. There is no ceiling to love" (16). Although the vast majority of the book is given over to John Wesley's theology, Wynkoop acknowledges her indebtedness to the process theology of Daniel Day Williams.

The thesis of the book is that the dynamic of Wesleyanism is love. Rather than representing Wesley's theology as a theology of holiness, the author believes that it is more faithful to call Wesley's thought a theology of love. Wesleyan theology has its roots in the major themes of the Bible, including the fact that God loves the world, Christ loved the church, Jesus demands total love to God and neighbor, the ethics of Christian life is summed up in love, and a right relationship with God is one based upon love.

The bulk of the work consists of the author's identification of love as the core to central theological doctrines. Topics addressed include the divine-human interaction, grace, faith, purity and a clean heart, Christian perfection, and sanctification. This statement stands as a summation of Wynkoop's argument: "The summarizing word—Wesley's ultimate hermeneutic—is *love*. Every strand of his thought, the warm heart of every doctrine, the passion of every sermon, the test of every claim to Christian grace, was love. So central is love that to be 'Wesleyan' is to be committed to a theology of love" (101).

Interfaced Science Texts

&❧ Browning, Don. (1987). *Religious thought and modern psychologies: A critical conversation in the theology of culture.* Philadelphia: Fortress Press.

The purpose of the book, as the author puts it, is to "uncover the ethical and metaphysical horizon of some of the major contemporary psychotherapeutic psychologies" (ix). To do this, the author analyzes implicit principles of obligation and what he calls "deep metaphors" embedded in and around conceptualities of psychology. Browning's work in this book has been vital reading for those engaging in issues related to psychology and religion.

Presuppositions and resources in the Jewish and Christian religious traditions inform Browning's critique. Among the dominant psychologies that the author addresses are those of Freud, Jung, behavioral psychology, humanistic psychology, and Erik Erikson. The dominant religious figures used to criticize and engage the psychologies include Reinhold Niebuhr, William James, and Paul Ricoeur.

The author believes that modern psychologies are indispensable for modern life and that they should be evaluated for the ways in which they play the role of religion in modern thinking. Clinical psychologies cannot avoid a metaphysical and ethical horizon. A major assumption made by the author is that "traditional religion and modern psychology stand in a special relation to one another because both of them provide concepts and technologies for the order-ing of the interior life" (2).

The author labels various contemporary psychologies as "cultures." He as-sociates Freud with, what he calls "the culture of detachment"; the culture of detachment sees the world as basically hostile and humans as largely self-absorbed creatures with only small amounts of energy for larger altruistic ven-tures. Humanistic psychologies and Jung are variations of what he calls the "cul-ture of joy"; the culture of joy sees the world as basically harmonious. Skinner's beliefs are an example of the "culture of control," which sees humans primarily as controlled and controllable by their environment. Erickson and Kohut sub-scribe to the "culture of care," which grasps the tensions and anxieties of life and gravitates toward an ethics that finds a place for both self-love and self-transcending love for the other.

Browning finds most affinities between Christian thought and the culture of care in the thought of Erickson. "It is my thesis that significant portions of modern psychologies, and especially the clinical psychologies, are actually in-stances of religio-ethical thinking" (8). "It is not only in theology but, to a sur-prising extent, in the modern psychologies as well, that the way we metaphori-cally represent the world in its most durable and ultimate respects, influences what we think and what we think we are obligated to do" (20). When addressing the Freudian-based modern psychologies, the author argues that psychoanalysis oscillates between ethical egoism and cautious reciprocity. By contrast, Chris-tianity celebrates the principles of self-giving love and justice.

The critical chapter of the book comes in chapter 6, "Making Judgments about Deep Metaphors and Obligations." In it, Browning addresses the central or deep metaphor of Christianity, namely that the ideal of human fulfillment comes from the notion of self-sacrificial love as *agape*. Browning looks at the works of Anders Nygren, Reinhold Niebuhr, and Gene Outka. Modern psy-chologies have put pressure on theology to build a greater place for self-regard into theology's model of human fulfillment. The *caritas* model found in the work of theologians such as Louis Janssens provide a model of *agape* that has a place for both self-sacrificial love and the mutuality of neighbor-to-neighbor love. This model also incorporates insights on the importance of self-regard without overemphasizing self-regard to the detriment of equal regard for the other. It is this *caritas* model to which the modern psychologies of Erickson and Kohut come closest.

    Cobb, John B., Jr., & Griffin, David Ray. (1976). *Process theology: An introductory exposition.* Philadelphia: Westminster.

This book serves as the seminal introduction to process thought written by two of the most important contemporary figures in this tradition. Because pro-cess thought has been drawn upon by so many in the science and religion dialogue, this text serves as a valuable resource for those wanting to become acquainted with the concepts that so many find valuable.

Perhaps the most important chapter of the book is titled "God as Creative-Responsive Love." The authors note that process theology, as they employ it, operates from the perspective of Christian faith on one hand and a metaphysical context provided by process philosophy on the other. The authors explore what the biblical phrase "God is love" means, and they begin with an exposition of what it means for God to express sympathy. Cobb and Griffin note that in classical theology divine sympathy was denied: "This denial of an element of sympathetic responsiveness to the divine love meant that it was entirely creative; that is, God loves us only in the sense that he does good things for us" (45). The authors note that the traditional notion of love as solely creative was partly introduced to deny that God is dependent upon creatures in any way and that God's independence implies perfection. Process theology, by contrast, understands God's emotional state as dependent upon creaturely existence. "Upon this basis, Christian *agape* can come to have the element of sympathy, of compassion for the present situation of others, which it should have had all along" (48).

The authors contend that the creative activity of God is no less essential to understanding divine love than is the sympathetic aspect of divine love. For instance, a loss of belief in the creative side of God's love would tend to undermine liberation movements of various kinds. The creative love of God, however, is persuasive only. Cobb and Griffin note that the idea that God can intervene coercively has led to a variety of problems, especially with regard to understanding the problem of evil and the science-inhibiting notion of "God of the gaps." By "persuasion" the authors mean that God does not have the ability to exercise controlling, unilateral power. "Process theologies understanding of divine love as in harmony with the insight, which we can gain both from psychologists and from our own experience, that if we truly love others we do not seek to control them" (53).

Cobb and Griffin note several advantages that their understanding of God as creative-responsive love entails. One notion is that God is understood as promoting enjoyment instead of as the cosmic moralist. "In traditional Christianity, morality and enjoyment were often seen as in fundamental opposition. In Process Thought, morality stands in the service of enjoyment" (57). Another advantage of understanding God's love as creative/responsive is that divine love can be understood as adventurous. A God's creative activity that is exclusively persuasive corresponds with a love that takes risks. This means that the deity is not the sanctioner of the status quo, but that God is still the source of the order that emerges in the world. God is the source of order because God offers possibilities to creatures to respond in ways that increase enjoyment and design. A third advantage of understanding God as creative-responsive love is that this entails that God's life is also on an adventure. Finally, the God that process thought envisions possesses qualities typically considered feminine. For instance, God is passive, responsive, emotional, flexible, patient, and appreciative of beauty.

ⵉ Davidson, Richard J., & Harrington, Anne (Eds.). (2002). *Visions of compassion: Western scientists and Tibetan Buddhists examine human nature.* Oxford: Oxford University Press.

Essayists examine aspects of Tibetan Buddhism as they relate to the views of western behavioral science. While western science has typically held a neutral or negative view of human nature, Tibetan Buddhism celebrates the positive human potential for compassion. *Visions of Compassion* is an extraordinary cross-cultural dialogue about human nature and its relation to the nonhuman world.

Structurally, the book is organized into two parts. The first draws upon Buddhist studies, anthropology, and the history of science to focus on cultural, historical, and metalinguistic challenges. The second part moves the reader to address some of the best of what western biobehavioral and social scientific tradition has to say about altruism, ethics, empathy, and compassion. One of the more interesting aspects of the volume is the conversations printed from the transcripts of the actual conference exchanges between the scientists and monks in Dharamsala.

In Buddhism coming to know reality is associated with an expansive sense of liberation, a feeling of connectedness to cosmic and living processes. However, modern scientific scholars often feel alienated from the reality that they seek to understand. Anne Harrington suggests that perhaps the western alienation from nature is partly a result of a secularized Judeo-Christian world that still believes in evil but has lost its faith in God. Philosopher-scientist Elliott Sober proposes that the ability to feel extended compassion beyond one's group is correlated with the ability to feel compassion with one's close relatives. In other words, "individuals well-attuned to the suffering of those near and dear have circles of compassion that potentially extend quite far afield" (63). In his own inspiring essay, the Dalai Lama argues that "with a will to change, confidence in our own positive potential, and a basic outlook on life that respects the profound interdependence of all things, we *can* and *must* secure a firm grounding for fundamental ethical principles" (80).

ⵉ Grant, Colin. (2001). *Altruism and Christian ethics.* Cambridge: Cambridge University Press.

This text comes in a series of books written to explore Christian ethics and various issues (e.g., family, priorities, power, and feminism). Grant argues that when ethics become separated from religion due to the influence of the social sciences, scholars end up seeing human beings as fundamentally self-interested. This book extends an analysis of secular and sacred literature with regard to altruism.

The key thesis "defended here is that altruism is a modern secular concept that betrays theological overtones, and the dismissal of the notion endangers the lingering theological sensibility it echoes" (xiii). Altruism becomes a parody of the self-giving love of Christianity. However, to dispense with altruism is to dispense with God and with the divine transformation of human possibilities. Altruism is a modern concept whose roots lie in a Christian understanding of *agape*, which is defined by the author as the self-giving love that is seen to be characteristic of God and in which human beings are called to participate.

In his chapter, "The Elusiveness of Altruism," Grant addresses the literature that attempts to define precisely what one means when one talks about acting egoistically and altruistically. He concludes that the notion of altruism corresponds with the emergence of the notion of self-consciousness. This modern notion of the individual provides the basis for the emergence of issues of self-interest and altruism. The work of C. Daniel Batson plays a prominent role as providing empirical evidence for the existence of altruism, in striking contrast to the notion of egoism in sociobiology.

The second part of the book, entitled "Ideal Altruism," addresses many of the philosophical and political notions of altruism. In "Contract Altruism," Grant addresses prominent versions of self-interest ethics and concludes that these versions suggest that ethics is either illusory, contradictory, or unnecessary. In "Constructed Altruism," Grant addresses Immanuel Kant's version of altruism as impartiality and John Rawl's political alternative to altruism. Grant's main point in this chapter is that each of these philosophers understands or adopts a view of what he calls "essential individualism." Grant wonders if humans are not finally isolated individuals but rather inherently social beings. The notion of social beings fits into the chapter, "Collegial Altruism." In this context, the notions of empathy and sympathy as understood by philosophers (e.g., David Hume and feminists) come into play.

Grant titles the final part of the book, "Real Altruism," because in this section he addresses more specifically how altruism is conceived of in Christian or theistic terms. Under the label, "Acute Altruism," Grant addresses the Christian notion of *agape*. His preference for the work of Anders Nygren becomes evident here; the author addresses criticisms of Nygren's classic *agape* theses. Grant concludes that "if proponents of *eros* make their case only by adopting something of the coloration of *agape*, and advocates of *philia* require the initiative of *agape* to achieve the mutuality they prize, this would seem to confirm Nygren's insistence on the indispensability of *agape*" (177). In, "Absolute Altruism," Grant explores the process notion of God as both altruistic and egoistic. He concludes that "as God may both give and receive, in ways appropriate to God, so self-fulfillment in other regard may both find expression in a wider, less deliberate, and less self-conscious sense of altruism" (217).

In the final chapter, "Actual Altruism," the author's own proposal comes forth. Altruistic behavior persists against the massive insistence that it is folly. And this persistence indicates that altruism, or something like it, is present in human life at a profound level. The term *altruism* tends to disappear in a context where a more relational, social view of life is assumed. Upon noting the many paradoxes that altruism entails, Grant concludes that *deliberate* altruism is impossible. Altruism is seen most profoundly in the lives of saints who direct their lives toward religious ends rather than altruism in itself. This means that "altruism is achieved best where it is least intended" (250). "Unintentional altruism is most natural for the transcendence sponsorship of the religious level where we are delivered from ourselves. It could be said that altruism is a test of the seriousness of religious vision" (250).

🔖 Hefner, Philip. (1993). *The human factor: Evolution, culture, and religion.* Minneapolis: Fortress Press.

Hefner's book is an enterprise in making sense of Christian faith in the context of contemporary scientific knowledge and experience. The author aims at a theological anthropology in the light of the natural sciences. In other words, the book wrestles with the question of *who* human beings are, *what* they are, and what they are alive *for*. Hefner positions himself in what he calls the Hebrew/Jewish/Christian stream.

The book's arguments are set before the reader in clear fashion. First, he argues that humans are thoroughly natural creatures having emerged from natural evolutionary processes. These processes have produced culture, and humans are members of culture. Second, the planet is in critical condition and it is the challenge of humans to fashion a viable system of cultural information to fulfill their human nature in this ecosystem. Third, myth and ritual, which emerged somewhere between 100,000 and 20,000 years ago, provide information to enhance human life in its present threatened conditions. And finally, we are required today to use science and myth to offer proposals for the direction, meaning, and purposes of humanity.

Hefner's influential theory of humans as "co-creators" is developed fully in this book. The theory of the co-creator involves three aspects:

[One,] the human being is created by God to be a co-creator in the creation that God has brought into being and for which God has purposes. Two, the conditioning matrix that has produced the human being—the evolutionary process—is God's process of bringing into being a creature who represents the creation's zone of a new stage of freedom and who, therefore, is crucial for the emergence of a free creation. Three, the freedom that marks the created co-creator and its culture is an instrumentality of God for enabling the creation (consisting of the evolutionary past of genetic and cultural inheritance as well as contemporary ecosystem) to participate in the intentional fulfillment of God's purposes. (32)

The author's proposals related to love, altruism, and morality come near the end of the book. Hefner is well aware of and critiques various theories related to altruism proposed by philosophers and scientists. He suggests that "our moral action of love for God and neighbor is our way of living in harmony with the way things really are" (191). In other words, the love that God has for us and our love for God and neighbor places us in the all-encompassing symbolic universe that drives the Christian tradition.

The Christian myth entails that "all morality presupposes and is response to the prior love of God for us, a love that seeks our well-being and the fulfillment of that for which we have been created" (194). Nature itself is an ambiance in which humans belong and that enables humans to fulfill the purpose for which they were brought into being. "The central reality that undergirds all concrete experience and to which we continually seek to adapt," claims Hefner, "is disposed toward us in a way that we can interpret as graciousness and beneficent support" (194).

The author devotes a chapter in his book to altruism and Christian love. He argues that the concepts of altruism articulated in evolutionary biology focus on the same phenomenon as the love command of the Hebrew/Christian tradition. The evolutionary, biocultural sciences approach beneficent behavior from the perspective of natural history of life. Myth and ritual, however, approach this phenomenon from the perspective of human culture. Christian theology should interpret beneficent behavior as an expression of the basic cosmological and ontological principles. In addition, Christianity should consider altruism to be an intrinsic value, rooted in the fundamental character of reality.

   ❧ Montagu, Ashley (Ed.). (1953). *The meaning of love.* New York: Julian.

Montagu edits this volume of essays on love, written by a variety of scientists, physicians, and a theologian in the early 1950s, including Abraham Maslow, Pitirim A. Sorokin, and James Luther Adams. The editor writes that these essays find their purpose in "helping to liberate the love that is within, to enable more people to understand, feel, and enjoy the great power that is within them, the need which they have to give and receive love" (v). Montagu believes that inquiring into the various meanings of love may give clues for understanding love and the capacity to express love more adequately.

❧ Murphy, Nancey, & Ellis, George F. R. (1996). *On the moral nature of the universe: Theology, cosmology, and ethics.* Minneapolis: Fortress Press.

The book is cowritten by Murphy, a professor of Christian philosophy, and Ellis, a professor of applied mathematics. Both are members of the Anabaptist Christian tradition, and their thought, especially as it relates to pacifism and ethics, reveal this connection to Christian tradition. One of the book's virtues is that its authors clearly lay out their proposals in a very accessible manner.

The overall argument for the book is that the fine-tuning of the cosmological constants that has produced a life-bearing universe calls for an explanation. The authors believe that a theistic explanation offers a more coherent account of reality than a nontheistic one. The pattern of divine action in the world, however, seems to indicate that God works with nature, "never over-riding or violating the very processes that God has created" (xv). The fact the God does not violate or override the processes leads the authors to believe that divine action entails refusal to do violence to creation. They link this with kenosis, a Christian New Testament word typically translated "self-emptying." God renounces self-interest for the sake of the other, no matter what the cost is to God, and the authors contend that this divine activity ought to be emulated by humans. The authors call for a new research program to explore the possibilities of this kenosis thesis in light of science.

The ethical core of the proposal is that self-renunciation for the sake of the other is humankind's highest goal. One of the more illuminating chapters in the book addresses the power of persuasion, nonviolent coercion, and violent coercion. The authors argue that persuasion is to be preferred and they speculate that "a consistent policy of using the least coercive means possible in each social situation will affect the character of the individuals involved such that less coercion will be needed in future resolution of conflict" (151). In sum, contemporary cosmology points ultimately to an ethic that centers on self-sacrifice and nonviolence.

❧ Polkinghorne, John, & Welker, Michael (Eds.). (2001). *The work of love: Creation as kenosis.* Grand Rapids, MI: Eerdmans.

In one of the best theoretical books pertaining to theologies of love at the interface with science, essayists in *The Work of Love: Creation as Kenosis* grapple with how to envisage divine love at work in creation. Those who contributed essays to this book should be commended for adopting a kenotic framework for talking about divine creative love at work in the world.

The title word, *kenosis,* derives from a New Testament letter to a group of Christians in ancient Phillipi (Phil. 2:7). Biblical scholars typically translate *kenosis* as "self-emptying" or "self-offering." Scholarly consensus does not exist, however, about how exactly to conceive of divine kenosis. In this book the authors explore how varying notions of kenosis might help when imagining divine action in the world.

The Work of Love begins with a helpful overview essay by Ian Barbour. In his usual irenic and explanatory form, Barbour notes five themes that advocates of kenotic theology believe their perspective addresses more adequately than other theological alternatives: the integrity of nature, the problem of evil and suffering, the reality of human freedom, the Christian understanding of the cross, and feminist criticisms of the patriarchal God. Barbour also identifies particular themes in process theology as they relate to creation, divine power, and love; among these are the adequacy of God's power, *creatio ex nihilo* and the Big Bang, eschatology and the Big Crunch, immortality, and resurrection.

Perhaps the most important issue Barbour highlights is the question whether, to display love, God is self-limited or limited due to metaphysical necessity. He notes that process theists affirm the metaphysical limitation of divine power because, among other reasons, that vision of God allows one to affirm unequivocally that God loves relentlessly even though evil events occur. "To say that the limitation of God's power is a metaphysical necessity rather than a voluntary self-limitation," cautions Barbour, "is not to say that it is imposed by something outside God. This is not a Gnostic or Manichean dualism in which recalcitrant matter restricts God's effort"(13). A question raised implicitly and to which I will return in my critique is this: Must divine kenosis be identified with voluntary divine self-limitation?

After Barbour's piece, the book gradually moves from essays that are more scientifically oriented to those that are more theologically oriented, although virtually all the contributors engage both scientific and religious issues. Arthur Peacocke contends that the evolutionary character of the actual process of creation justifies the notions that God creates by self-offering and God is self-limited. The data suggest that "biological evolution is continuous and evidences emergence of new forms of life" (22). The Hebrew conception of a living God correlates well with a God whose creative relation is dynamic, argues Peacocke, and this suggests that God is the "Immanent Creator." There is no need to look for God as an "additional nonscientifically accessible factor supplementing these creative processes" (24).

While God is the ultimate ground and source of both law and necessity and of chance, God took a risk by creating through DNA mutations and randomness. In addition, suggests Peacocke, significant natural trends and propensities are built into evolution, which favor selection for complexity, information-processing and storage, pain and suffering, self-consciousness, and language. This all means that there can be "overall direction and implementation of divine purpose through chance (mutations) operating in a rule-obeying context (the environment) without a deterministic plan fixing in advance all the details of the structure(s) of what eventually emerges with personal qualities" (33). Divine purposiveness need not be divinely manipulated by special providence. "There is a creative self-emptying and self-offering (a *kenosis*) of *God*," argues Peacocke. This entails "a sharing in the suffering of God's creatures, in the very creative, evolutionary processes of the world" (38).

Holmes Rolston III takes up the current sociobiological dogma that life inevitably entails maximizing short-sighted selfishness. Rolston wonders if this dogma depends "not so much on empirical evidence as on the choice of a general interpretive framework from which to view the phenomena" (44). Providing a quick overview of various biological theories that suggest that organisms are both selfish and unselfish, Rolston argues that the sharing and taking of genes themselves should not be considered in moral categories. Genes are, in the ethical sense, neither altruistic nor egoistic. Rolston even suggests that "there are no moral agents in wild nature. . . . Only humans are moral agents" (49).

The precursor of human kenosis begins in nonhuman emptying into species of larger populational and species lines. Such nonhuman, nonmoral kenosis emerges in an ecology of organisms that are interdependent and symbiotic. Kenosis occurs in life itself as the living order is perpetually redeemed in the midst of its perishing. "Death can be meaningfully integrated into the biological processes as a necessary counterpart to the advancing of life," suggests Rolston (59). "Creatures have been giving up their lives as a ransom for many. In that sense, Jesus is not the exception to the natural order, but a chief exemplification of it" (60).

Malcolm Jeeves focuses on recent evidence and theory in contemporary psychobiology which shed light on "the roots and fruits" of the self-giving component of kenotic behavior. Responding to the early twentieth-century work of psychologist William Sanday, Jeeves notes that many today view personhood, in general, and "soulishness," in particular, differently than Sanday did. For instance, recent studies point to characteristics of soulishness as present in nonhumans. In fact, claims Jeeves, "within the Christian tradition it is not necessary to deny the emergence of elements of kenotic behavior in nonhuman primates in order to defend the uniqueness of the self-giving and self-emptying Christ" (89). Also, recent work suggests that both "top-down" and "bottom-up" influence occur between brain and mind, which means that neurobiology places limits on our thoughts and actions.

In terms of self-giving as originating in self-determination, Jeeves reports that one's behavior is directly dependent upon genetic endowment, neural substrate, upbringing, and other factors. Jeeves concludes that the capacity for self-giving love may have polygenetic bases, and a kenotic community may be necessary for nurturing the development and expression of kenotic behavior.

The book's editor, John Polkinghorne, tackles the age-old question, "Why is there something rather than nothing?" Answering this question, he contends, "involves appeal to the divine love that has willed the existence of the truly other so that, through creation, this love is also bestowed outside the perichoretic exchange between the Persons of the Holy Trinity."

Polkinghorne turns to kenosis as an alternative to process theology's God. The process doctrine of God is "open to [the] question whether deity has not been so evacuated of power that hope in God as the ground of ultimate fulfillment has been subverted" (92). Kenosis offers a way other than, on the other hand, classical theology's God. The God of classical theism "is in total control and whose invulnerability is such that there is no reciprocal effect upon the divine nature of a kind that a truly loving relationship would seem to imply" (92).

Although affirming *creatio ex nihilo*, Polkinghorne believes that the evolutionary character of the universe requires that one combine creation out of nothing with *creatio ex continua*. Creation has been allowed to make itself, and "no longer can God be held to be totally and directly responsible for all that happens" (95). The doctrine also tempers somewhat the problem of evil by "maintaining God's total benevolence but qualifying, in a kenotic way, the operation of God's power" (96). "Of course, this is a self-qualification," adds Polkinghorne. Such self-limitation of divine power "is quite different from Process Theology's conception of an external metaphysical constraint upon the power of deity," because the kenotic vision maintains "that nothing imposes conditions on God from the outside" (96). The picture of divine action Polkinghorne offers involves God's interaction with, but not arbitrary interruption of, creation. Polkinghorne has "come to believe that the Creator's kenotic love includes allowing divine special providence to act as a cause among causes" (104); God acts energetically as well as informationally.

George F. R. Ellis presents in his essay "the virtues of kenosis as a unifying theme in the understanding of both human life and cosmology" (107). Because God expresses kenosis, we ought to "be tuned to the welfare of others and of the world," which entails self-sacrifice for the good of others. Divine kenosis is a voluntary choice whereby God exercises "total restraint in the use of God's power," suggests Ellis, "for otherwise a free response to God's actions is not possible" (114). The purpose of the universe is to make possible creaturely sacrificial responses to a sacrificial God. This requires a universe with some degree of order, creatures with freedom, impartial natural laws, a God whose nature and activity is largely hidden, yet a nature open to those who wish to discern some things about it.

Michael Welker offers a brief comparative essay on romantic, covenantal, and kenotic loves. Kenotic divine love "reveals that God turns lovingly to those who . . . in themselves do *not* have any potential to reveal the goodness of God . . . [and] who in themselves do *not* have any potential to help transform the world according to God's will" (134). God turns to creatures and gives them space in order to liberate them and to ennoble them to experience and enact divine love. In sum, "God's kenotic love, revealed in Christ's love and bestowed on creatures by the working of the Holy Spirit, draws human lives into the creative love that makes them bearers of God's presence and the incarnation of the new creation" (136).

Jürgen Moltmann proffers a theological vision that inspires many of the book's essayists. Moltmann argues that one must "ask about God's presence in the history of nature and in the chance events that herald a future which cannot be extrapolated from the past or present" (138). The heart of Moltmann's proposal is that God freely chooses to be the creator of a world. God does so in that "(1) out of his infinite possibilities God realizes this particular [world], and renounces all others" and "(2) God's self-determination to be Creator is linked with the consideration for his creation that allows it space and time and its own movement, so that it is not crushed by the divine reality or totally absorbed by it." God "distances himself" from the world, and the "limitation of his infinity and omnipresence is itself an act of omnipotence" (145). God "withdrew himself into himself in order to make room for the world" and "to concede space for the presence of creation" (146). But it is for the sake of love that God is self-limited, according to Moltmann.

Keith Ward begins his essay be explaining that theologians in recent centuries have turned to kenotic theology so that they may speak of divine relationship with the world. Ward's view of creation as kenosis includes the divine realization of possibilities eternally present in the divine being, which means that God enjoys values that would not have been enjoyable had a universe never been created.

Ward explores an idea that is a central issue to be addressed when seeking to advance an adequate conception of kenosis. "Perhaps some realization [of possibilities] is essential to the divine nature," speculates Ward, "so that God necessarily creates other personal agents. If one thinks that 'God is love' (1 John 4:16), that love is an essential property of the divine nature, and that love can only be properly exercised in relation to others who are free to reciprocate love or note, then the creation of some universe containing free finite agents seems to be an implication of the divine nature" (159). Ward is hesitant to take this position, however, stating that it is "a rather presumptuous exercise" to speculate about the divine nature.

Paul Fiddes explores the "both problematic and immensely illuminating" claims that God creates out of love and love is at the heart of the universe. The claim that love is the reason for creation carries certain consequences, however. For instance, the claim implies that God has needs to be satisfied. It also implies that nondivine beings exist capable of relating lovingly with God. These two implications entail that both *agape* and *eros* are types of divine love.

The claim that a loving God needs responses from creatures leads to a problem: If God, as love, is necessarily related to others, how can the world be contingent and God be free? The answer that Fiddes prefers starts with the divine will instead of the divine nature. This is the nominalist tradition, which entails that "God freely determines the kind of God that God will be" (181). Among other things, this position states that God freely chooses to give and receive love. The difficulties of this position are partly logical, however, for it seems illogical that one begin choosing prior to having a nature. Nevertheless, Fiddes prefers this position because it denotes God as a participatory event. Another difficulty with this position is that we no longer trust in God's love; instead, we must trust the divine will. Fiddes believes that he overcomes this objection by claiming that, although God's eternal nature is not love, we can only identify God as love from a finite perspective.

Sarah Coakley's essay concludes the book with a thesis that I noted early in this review: kenosis has been given a wide variety of meanings in different contexts in the Christian tradition. Coakley argues that decisions about theological starting points vitally affect the conclusions one reaches pertaining to how to conceive of kenosis. She notes that the self-sacrifice of kenosis has been a contentious theme in feminist theology, because it can be identified with the abasement that feminists seek to avoid.

◈ Pope, Stephen J. (1994). *The evolution of altruism and the ordering of love*. Washington, DC: Georgetown University Press.

Pope's work here is of the highest caliber with regard to how theologies of love might interface with biological science. In many ways, the author sets a standard that others would do well to follow, as he correlates core notions, theories, and research from both religious studies and modern sociobiology.

Pope sets as his task the correlation of biological science, especially altruism, with a Catholic understanding of the ordering of love. Succinctly: "I propose a contemporary biological interpretations of inter-human and human-natural interdependencies can be used to develop a more extensive and inclusive range of moral responsibility than is suggested by recent trends in catholic ethics" (8).

After surveying Roman Catholic writing on love in recent years, Pope notes that liberation theologians and those with personalist theological leanings have neglected central notions of love that connect with what is natural. Liberation theologians have insisted—to the neglect of other themes—that the church embrace a special regard for the poor, marginalized, and the oppressed. Personalist theologians have overemphasized the one-to-one interpersonal relationships of love. Pope turns to current scientifically based theories of human nature to inform a contemporary Catholic love ethics.

The ordering of love the author has in mind incorporates both universal love of neighbor and a prioritizing of love toward others. Pope contends that we must remain attentive to the periodic conflicts between these two realms of responsibility, which in turn requires that we prioritize various objects of love. Correct prioritizing is exactly what recent Roman Catholic authors have failed to do.

Pope turns to Thomas Aquinas's account of the order of love because this account includes features of human nature that must be considered if an adequate contemporary ethics of love is to be offered. For instance, Thomas overcomes the split between self-love and neighbor-love by speaking of proper and improper self-love and proper and improper neighbor-love. Although Thomas urged love for all, he also contended that the order of charity requires not only greater love, but also more intense affection, toward those nearest to the one loving.

Although not claiming a simple synthesis of Thomastic ethics with evolutionary theory, the author does point out several functional equivalencies between the two. Pope notes that evolutionary theory implies or explicitly affirms sociality or group-living, interaction with group members, communication, developing alliances with others, mating, and rearing offspring. For instance, kinship theory in contemporary evolutionary thought corresponds with Thomas's emphasis upon the priority of love for one's own family. Contemporary evolutionary theory also embraces the notion of reciprocity in its reciprocity and tit-for-tat theories. Sociobiologists argue that we have evolved to be intensely social beings. Evolutionary theory also claims, like Thomas, that self-love is based in human nature. This means that self-love is neither good nor bad—neither a virtue nor a vice—but simply an expression of what it means to be human. When considering the possibilities and resources of kin preference, reciprocity, and other social evolutionary characteristics, Pope claims that kin preference may be one of the most intuitively plausible claims of sociobiology. However, that reciprocity theory fails to grasp properly both the nature of trust and the nature of personal commitment engaged for the sake of another.

In a chapter entitled "Evolution and Altruism: An Interpretation and Assessment," Pope wades through some of the main issues in his analysis or altruism and love. He notes the sociobiological tendency to reduce all goods to the organism's inclusive fitness. This reductionism is neither empirically warranted nor morally justified. The author also notes that some sociobiologists promote determinism, but human love, though having a biological basis, implies that human reason, will, or choices are not genetically controlled. While human behavior reflects its genetic heritage, it is also true, says Pope, that culture profoundly shapes the norms of altruism and family loyalty in a given society.

Although the predominant assumption in sociobiology is that all organisms are fundamentally egoistic and altruism is illusory, Pope notes that this assumption is at odds with mounting evidence that supports genuine altruism. Theories contending that organisms are exclusively egoistic do not account for the genuine altruism that many experience at least some time in their lives.

In sum, Pope contends that contemporary evolutionary theory provides (1) an empirical basis on which to develop a contemporary restatement of the order of love, (2) an evolutionary basis for the claim that self-love is naturally prior to love for others, (3) a base for the claim that intimacy in shared life between spouses constitutes the greatest friendships with which human beings are capable, and (4) an evolutionary base for a debt of gratitude to one's parents. Pope argues that the determining of priorities among the various objects of love requires an exercise of moral discernment. The ordering of love is based in, but not determined by, nature.

&#x0001; Post, Stephen G., Underwood, Lynn G., Schloss, Jeffrey S., & Hurlbut, William B. (Eds.). (2002). *Altruism and altruistic love: Science, philosophy, and religion in dialogue.* Oxford: Oxford University Press.

This volume includes the work of some of the leading figures in the science and religion love dialogue. The essays are the product of a 1999 conference entitled "Empathy, Altruism and *Agape:* Perspectives on Love in Science and Religion." Major funding for this conference came from the John Templeton Foundation and John Fetzer Institute.

"It is in the context of the dialogue between science, philosophy and spiritual traditions that this book addresses various views of the roles of altruism and egoism," writes editor Stephen G. Post (5). "Our intent in this book is to grapple honestly with current scientific questions about the existence of genuine altruism and to explore the nature of human other regarding motives and acts" (6). Among the tasks that the book addresses is the effort to understand better the emergence of altruism and empathy and how these contribute a greater capacity to love.

The book is organized into five sections. In the first, four essayists wrestle with the definitions of altruism, *agape,* and love. Elliott Sober defines altruistic behavior as enhancing the fitness of someone else at some cost in fitness to the donor. Sober's own position on the emergence of altruism and egoism is a pluralistic one in the sense that he recognizes that humans and other organisms have both egoistic and altruistic inclinations. Edith Wyschogrod writes as a phenomenologist who claims that moral experience begins with a claim upon the self to engage in other regarding acts. In this sense ethical meaning arises in the encounter with another human. Psychologist Jerome Kagan asserts that the human being is utterly unique, in that only humans have emerged from evolution with a moral sense. It was with the evolution of the human brain that humans could evaluate vice and virtue. Stephen G. Post examines the tradition of *agape* in light of altruism and altruistic love. According to Post, altruistic love does not eclipse the care of the self, but it effectively affirms participation in the being of the other. "Altruism is other regarding, either with regard to actions or motivations; altruistic adds the features of deep affirmative affect to altruism; *agape* is altruistic love universalized all humanity as informed by theistic commitments" (56). Despite universalization, however, "*agape* forces us to honestly confront the ordering of our love and care with respect to both the nearest and the very neediest on the face of the earth" (59).

The second section of the book takes up the social scientific research and addresses this in this relationship to altruism and love. This group of essays notes that observing or measuring motivations with regard to love is very difficult. Lynn Underwood addresses data from selected studies and attempts to map a conceptuality of love from the social science perspective. She wrestles with basic notions of love, self, context, and freedom, among other things. C. Daniel Batson challenges the common assumption that all behavior is selfish. Batson's "empathy/altruism" hypothesis is that other-oriented emotional response evokes a motivational state with the ultimate goal of increasing the other's welfare. Batson looks at more than twenty-five experiments to distinguish between self-directed motives and truly altruistic motives. Batson says that the tentative conclusion from his studies is that feeling empathy for a person in need does evoke altruistic motivation to help that person.

Kristen Renwick Monroe defines altruism in terms of actions rather than motives. Monroe suggests that perception of the self in relation to others strongly affects decisions to be altruistic. Finally, Samuel Oliner analyzes altruistic behaviors of rescuers of Jews during World War II and volunteers working with the dying. He characterizes altruism as actions that are (1) directed toward another, (2) involve a high risk or sacrifice to the actor, (3) are accompanied by no external reward, and (4) voluntary. After examining data of the two groups, both the rescuers and those involved in hospice, Oliner concludes that there is no single motivating explanation that triggers people to behave compassionately for the welfare of others. However, gentile rescuers who risked their lives for Jews had learned compassion, caring norms, and responsibility for diverse others from parents and others in authority. Hospice volunteers exhibited a higher degree of intrinsic religiosity, despite a lower incidence of affiliation with mainstream religious traditions. Oliner suggests that social institutions, whether they be religious, educational, or in the workplace, need to reconsider their roles and responsibilities so that they might foster kind and loving acts.

The third section of the book takes up the debates within evolutionary biology and psychology with regard to egoism and altruism. Michael Ruse outlines the genecentric sociobiological perspective on altruism. He asserts that a Darwinian interpretation of social behavior and morality requires that organisms be reproductively beneficial. Stephen Pope addresses the varieties of love from the perspective of theology and biology and speaks of an ordering of loves. Pope suggests that appropriate altruism comes out of who we are rather than being an imposition that occurs contrary to our deepest native needs and desires. "I believe the goods valued by both the moral egoists and the moral altruists can be assimilated and properly coordinated within a balanced interpretation of the ordering of love" (170). David Sloan Wilson and Elliott Sober consider the history of altruism and evolutionary biology. They note the fluctuation that the history of altruism has had but hope that altruism will find a permanent place in dominant evolutionary thinking.

Melvin Konner reviews data from evolutionary biology, primatology, and anthropology. He describes obstacles to altruism and notes that evolutionary theory makes most disinterested forms of altruism problematic. In particular, aggression in both nonhumans and humans makes altruism problematic. Jeffrey P. Schloss surveys evolutionary approaches to human cooperative behavior and notes that the good news is that current theory is conciliate in its affirmation of that natural basis for genuine other regard within kinship or social groups. The challenging news, however, is that the counterpart of such affiliation is exclusion towards those outside those groups. There is no biological theory proposed for how outgroup sacrifice and "love your enemy" altruism can come about. "If the struggle for existence is the engine of natural selection and survival of the fittest is the direction of travel, then those organisms that sacrifice their biological well-being for the good of another will be kicked off the train" (214).

The fourth section of the book considers the emotional aspects of altruistic love by focusing on the role of empathy in both humans and nonhumans and discussing the evolutionary advantages of particular anatomical, physiological, and psychological developments. Essayists consider how developments in these fields provide a basis for varied forms of altruism. Neuroscientist Thomas Insel discusses his work in neurochemistry and neurophysiology in rodent species. His findings point to the possibility that in human beings subtle genetic variations may underlie individual differences in the capacity and inclination for attachment and other forms of altruistic behavior. Neurologist Antonio Damasio discusses evolutionary origins of emotions and feelings, their fundamental adaptive value, and the extension in the empathetic processes that allow human sociality and altruism. He notes that the emotions use the body as their theater. The foundational processes of emotion and feeling, coupled with an individual's ability to know of the existence of such emotions and feelings in the self and others, are the basis of what is best in humans, including conscience, ethical rules, and the codification of law. Hanna Damasio discusses case reports of patients with damage to the portion of the brain that appears critical in the foundational processes of altruism. She concludes that there is a system in certain sections of the prefrontal cortex that is critical for the learning and maintenance of certain aspects of social behavior that pertain to interpersonal relationships. Damage to this results in defective decisions regarding altruism. Her work underscores the claim that the capacity for altruism has a physical foundation.

Primatologists Stephanie Preston and Frans de Waal consider the behaviors and linkage between humans and nonhumans. They report on what appears to be a degree of cognitive empathy among the great apes. Empathy is a general class of behavior that exists across species to different degrees of complexity. The data from primatology warns against drawing demarcation lines between humans and other animals with respect to emotional aspects of empathy. The basis in emotional and social connectedness is crucial to an understanding of empathy and altruism because it creates the bridge between ultimate and proximate explanations and between philogeny and ontogeny. William B. Hurlbut concludes the section with his own chapter on empathy, evolution, and altruism. He claims that the beginnings of sociality are seen even in the most primordial configurations of living matter. "Among the earliest lifeforms, organisms drew information from one another to pattern and coordinate such basic biological functions as reproduction and nourishment" (310). Empathy is a form of intersubjectivity in which the observer actually participates in the feelings of the other. Hurlbut notes that the idea that the human life has a moral dimension and that it is in some sense a product of the universe is at odds with prevailing scientific culture. To assert an objective ethical order within nature would be to affirm teleology, the reality of human freedom, and the unique status of our species. Hurlbut argues that "for all the controversy concerning the possibility of genuine generosity and altruistic love, at the levels of life, amid the sounds of the street and the strivings and struggles, there is everywhere, in small or greater degrees, the evidence of love. Many people, perhaps most, in some way give the effort and energy of their lives from a belief in love and the desire to build a better world. If there is a natural sentiment and hope, it is that love is real" (325).

The fifth section looks at altruistic love from a religious context. Don S. Browning suggests that evolutionary biology is moving religious thinkers toward a synthesis model in which love is understood as having both altruistic and egoistic aspects. Browning argues that the moral theologian "would finally ground the sacrificial element in love on the Christian's belief in the infinite value of the other and on the sense that some acts of self sacrifice are both willed and empowered by God, even though self-sacrifice, as such, might not be seen as the central goal of Christian love" (344). Gregory L. Fricchione interprets human religious expression as an outgrowth of evolutionary developments centered around separation and attachment theory. Fricchione claims "separation/attachment is a common referent conferring extensional identity across different conceptual levels of complexity" (354). *Agape* is a healthy synthesis of self-affirming/self-realizing love with self-giving love. Reuben L. F. Habito concludes the volume by speaking of compassion and love from a Buddhist perspective. The compassionate life from a Buddhist perspective is an outflow of the wisdom that truly sees the way things are, the view of reality that overcomes the separation of self and other. Habito suggests that Buddhism offers a valuable contribution in forging a common future as the earth community.

   🐾 Post, Stephen G. (2000). *More lasting unions: Christianity, the family, and society.* Grand Rapids, MI: Eerdmans.

More Lasting Unions is a sequel to Post's earlier work, *Spheres of Love To-ward a New Ethics of the Family.* This sequel covers the history of Christian thought and practice and then applies this history to contemporary issues of so-cial importance. "This book examines the deeper spiritual foundations of last-ing unions in the context of western culture as it was shaped by Christianity," explains Post, "and shows a continuing need for spirituality of marriage and family life that encourages us all to see the tremendous value in a deeper form of commitment than contemporary culture appears able to encourage" (1).

The author begins by providing a general interpretation of the data point-ing to the adverse effects of the divorce culture; marriage and the family are at a crossroads in contemporary society. Christianity offers an alternative to this culture, because it powerfully endorses the overall value of the family and faith-ful marriage. "This endorsement is a profoundly essential one to Christianity," claims Post, "and must inform its endeavor to positively affect culture and soci-ety" (8). He argues that as a culture we seem to have forgotten that family life is the foundation upon which society rests. Monogamy is consistent with the Christian ethical norm of *agape* as equal regard.

The Judeo-Christian notion of prophetic ethics involves three principles, says Post. The first principle is that we are to give greater protection to the most vulnerable. The second is that fidelity in marriage ensures for all children the benefit of having both a caring mother and a caring father. And third, women must be treated with equal regard within a marriage covenant.

The author examines marriage and family as understood in the teachings of Jesus. He concludes that Jesus endorsed one's love of parents, spouses, chil-dren, and friends—although this endorsement is relativized under crisis condi-tions. Jesus was critical of the family only when the family became an obstacle to His salvific mission.

The family is strengthened by participation within the community of the church. *Agape,* argues Post, "must be fully appreciated as providing a strong moral underpinning for family life and therefore is providing a powerful locus that should inform the spiritual and moral tone of the Christian family" (66). While the Christian tradition is complex, somewhat contested, and pluralistic, it holds that those who marry are bound by God and the common good to in-tend and to realize stability for the future of children and society.

More attention has recently been paid to homosexuality, abortion, and pre-marital and extramarital sexual relationships than to marriage and family as community and institutions. Unfortunately, Post says, western culture seems to esteem passion more than social stability. In response to the need to pay atten-tion to the family, Post constructs a contemporary theology of the family. He ar-gues that marriage should be seen as a covenant rather than a contract, insofar as a contract implies that one serves the love of the self and not the mutual love of both partners. "A socially responsive Christianity," claims Post, "must construct a new ethics of marriage and family that, informed by equality between men and women, thinks deeply about what spouses owe each other, their children and outsiders near and far" (113). While love is manifested in solicitude for the welfare of the self and the other, ultimately this love is sustained by the conviction that a caring, parental God exists at the center of the universe. It is wrong, declares Post, "for any Christian to think that formlessness in marriage and family is perfectly reasonable or theologically sound" (2).

Post breaks new ground in offering theological reflection in the context of society's understanding and practice of adoption. Christian ethics support the bonding and covenant love of adoptive families. While affirming the evolutionary argument that creatures have a biological investment as parents to continue their genealogy, Post suggests that Christian ethics suppose that the ties of nature are important but not absolute. "Christian community legitimizes families created purely by *agape* rather than begotten biologically" (133). When birth parents simply cannot raise a child, the child's best interests, coupled with an appreciation of the circumstances of the parents, require recourse to adoption. The relinquishment of a child by a woman who cannot care for it can be an expression of *agape*. Post concludes his chapter on adoption by arguing that Christianity needs to create a pedagogy for all oppressed adopted persons. This pedagogy would include liberation from social stereotypes that such adopted persons internalize and even sometimes self-impose.

In examining the contemporary challenge of giving care to those who suffer from severe disabling conditions, Post notes that honoring the commandment to honor thy father and thy mother requires more of us now than it did when parents died much younger. The fastest growing segment of today's population is the elderly. Post claims that it is possible for people with progressive dementia to experience emotional, relational, esthetic, and spiritual well-being.

The final chapter addresses the tension between love for family members and love for all of humanity. While *agape* includes love even for enemies, persons have a natural inclination to love the near and dear. Christianity points toward a love of neighbor in a manner consistent with impartiality, but there also must be some rough ordering of love to allow for special considerations with respect to the family. There is no simple formula, says Post, for discerning to what measure one loves the near and dear as opposed to the stranger. A theory of justice that fails to strike a reasoned balance between the family and the common good, however, is an inadequate theory. Post concludes that "the challenge facing the family is to nurture familial bonds in loyalty while simultaneously caring for the neediest neighbors" (196).

࿊ Rolston, Holmes. (1999). *Genes, Genesis and God.* Cambridge: Cambridge University Press.

This text is the product of Rolston's Gifford Lectures of 1997. His basic task is to relate cultural genesis to natural genesis and understand how value in culture has its links to value in nature. While Rolston argues for a continuity of culture and biological nature, he also contends that culture exceeds and emerges out of biology, so that genuine novelty occurs. In fact, the author believes that science, ethics, and religion are emergent phenomena in culture. He uses these three domains "for the generating, conserving, and distributing of values as test cases, demanding their incorporation into the larger picture of what is taking place on our planet" (xiii).

Much of the first third of the book addresses genetic theory, and Rolston surveys a wide variety of literature in this field. Perhaps one of the strengths of this book is the author's command of the wide literature pertaining to the subjects he addresses.

The final third of the book addresses issues related to ethics, love, and religion. Although Rolston affirms value in nature, he does not believe that there is any ethics in nature. He examines and critiques various biological theories related to egoism and altruism. In the model he promotes, "one needs value naturalized as well as ethics humanized; then ethics will require appropriate respect for value, whether human or non-human" (280).

Rolston argues that ethics arise out of evolutionary natural history. It is a history in which values have already been arising. "Such genesis of ethics, distinctive to the human genius, testifies both to human uniqueness, emergent from natural history, and to the creative power evidenced in the spontaneous genetics, the primal source now transcended with the appearance of genuine and universal caring and altruism" (280).

From ethics emerges religion, and the capacity to be religious evolved within or emerged out of natural systems where there was no such capacity in non-humans. Rolston advocates a naturalizing of religion, by which he does not mean that religion can be explained away naturalistically. Rather the naturalizing of religion means that religion is generated by the human confrontation with the forces of nature. This means that religion comes as a response to prolific Earth.

While religion involves more than altruism, Rolston argues that altruism plays an important part in a variety of religious traditions. Religion functions to generate innovative ethical behavior, which in turn makes possible the human spirit. This spirit cannot exist outside a social covenant, however. Religion, then, is an emergent property from complex biodiversity through evolutionary history. In this emergence, God plays a role.

◆ Sorokin, Pitirim. (2002 [1954]). The ways and power of love: Types, factors, and techniques of moral transformation. Philadelphia: Templeton Foundation Press.

The Ways and Power of Love is a classic work in the science-and-love dialogue. Although Sorokin is known for his work in sociology, he also established the Harvard Research Center for Creative Altruism out of his conviction about the power and importance of love. This review refers to the 2002 edition published by the Templeton Foundation Press; the book was originally published in 1954.

Sorokin begins this large volume by considering seven aspects of love: religious, ethical, ontological, physical, biological, psychological and social. While the book often cites spiritual and religious figures and ideas, the majority of Sorokin's interests revolve around the psychological and social aspects of love.

In his chapter, "The Five-Dimensional Universe of Psycho-Social Love," Sorokin provides a heuristic device for understanding various dimensions of love. One dimension is love's intensity, whereby love is considered to have low- or high-intensity forms. The second dimension is extensivity, by which Sorokin means to denote the scope of love from love of oneself only to love of the whole universe. The third dimension of love is its duration, which refers to the time during which love is expressed—from a moment to an entire lifetime. The fourth is purity, by which Sorokin means that the love that is free from egoistic motivation is purest. The fifth is love's adequacy, by which Sorokin means the objective consequences of one's action in comparison to one's subjective goals. Using this five-dimensional theme, Sorokin explores the varieties of love by characterizing them as exemplifying certain types. For instance, some love may have low intensity but very high extensivity. Or love may have great high purity but a very short duration.

Sorokin considers love to be a type of energy, and he believes that the increase in the production of love energy to be of chief concern in our times. Love, as a commodity that can be produced, might be increased through a variety of ways. "Love, its properties, its empirical dimensions, the relationships between its dimensional variables, and, finally, the problems of the efficient production, accumulation, and distribution of love energy—all of these open a vast, little known, and desperately field of exploration. At the present time mankind perhaps needs to explore this field more than any other" (46). In a chapter exposing the benefits of love, Sorokin lists the following: love stops aggression, love begets more love, love increases human vitality and longevity, love is an element in curing disease and sickness, love integrates the psyche of an individual, and love becomes a creative force for good in social movements.

In the second part of the book, Sorokin addresses basic mental and personal structures of humans as the relate to love. "The ultimate task of these studies is to find out the efficient ways of making persons more creative and altruistic.

In order that this purpose may be fruitfully advanced, one has to have an adequate theory of the mental structure of the human personality and of the energies generated in operating through the human organism" (83).

Sorokin's own theory of human personality is that humans have four energies: the biologically unconscious or subconscious level, the biologically conscious level, the socioculturally conscious, and what he calls the "supraconscious." The author is most interested in the supraconscious of an individual, by which he means that which manifests the greatest creative victories and what is most typically linked in humans with the divine. Theistic individuals often attribute this supraconscious as either God working through them or God inspiring them to do some particular activity. It is this supraconscious intuition that informs the highest human creativity in virtually all the fields of inquiry, from religion to science. Sorokin appeals to the ideas and saints in a variety of religious traditions as evidence of those who acknowledge this supraconscious in the world. The perfectly integrated creative genius most in touch with the supraconscious is one in whom the five aspects of love operate at a high level. This means that "supreme love can hardly be achieved without a direct participation of the supra-conscious and without the ego-transcending techniques of its awakening" (125).

In the book's third section, Sorokin addresses various ways in which altruism might grow by examining logical arguments, empirical evidence from various individuals throughout history, and testimonials. Sorokin places the great altruists of history in a threefold typology.

The first, what he calls "fortunate altruists," are loving and friendly from childhood. The most important factor to understanding fortunate altruists is that these individuals were raised in a good family that loved them and expected them to be loving. "It is much easier to grow in the family garden a large crop of creative altruists from newborn babies than it is to transform a grown-up egoist into an altruist" (205).

The second type of altruists, whom Sorokin calls "late altruists," become altruistic because of a sharp turning point later in their lives. It appears that a deep inner war in the mind and values of the late altruist becomes the driving force that brings them to decide to act altruistically. Sorokin also finds that, although altruists participate in a variety of living situations, the overwhelming majority of outstanding altruists were born and raised in ordinary sociocultural environments.

The third type, what Sorokin calls the "intermediary type," turns to altruism at various points in life, and these turnings reflect milder transition periods.

Sorokin argues that merely accepting the truth of certain values as important is not enough for an individual to become an altruist. Rather, altruists are deeply permeated by the value of altruism; this is evident in their ideas, emotions, feelings, volitions, and actions. When altruism is purely intellectual and when it does not permeate one's heart, emotions, and volitions, it does not produce loving results.

In part 4, the longest section, Sorokin notes various techniques for the altruistic transformation of persons and groups. "The altruistic formation and transformation of human beings is an exceedingly delicate, complex, and difficult operation. There is no single magic procedure that can successfully perform it . . . to be effective, the methods must vary in accordance with the many conditions and properties of the individuals and groups" (287). Several chapters are given to listing what comes to be twenty-six different techniques for enhancing altruism. Subsequent to examining these techniques, Sorokin offers a chapter on various techniques of yoga, followed by the techniques of the monastics. He concludes with the techniques of "contemporary free brotherhoods," such as Mennonites, Hutterites, and others.

In the fifth and final part of the book Sorokin addresses the questions of ingroup and outgroup altruism. Unfortunately, ingroup altruism tends to generate an outgroup antagonism. "The more intense and exclusive the in-group solidarity of its members," argues Sorokin, "the more unavoidable are the clashes between the group and the rest of humanity" (459). The universal or more extensive aspect of love ends up clashing with the narrow tribal ingroup love. What is preferred is the universalization of altruism. "The universal sublime love is the supreme value around which all moral values can be integrated into one ethical system valid for the whole of humanity" (486). This means that tribal solidarities must be transcended if interhuman warfare is to be eliminated from the world.

Sorokin ends the chapter and the book with this quote: "By the mysterious forces of destiny, mankind is confronted with a stern dilemma: either to continue its predatory policies of individual and tribal selfishness that lead to its inevitable doom, or to embark upon the policies of universal solidarity that bring humanity to the aspired-for heaven on the earth. It is up to everyone of us which of the two roads we prefer to choose" (489).

The Ways and Power of Love is an essential text for those engaging in the dialogue between theologies of love and science. Stephen G. Post writes in the introduction that this is Sorokin's greatest work and "a classic text that transcends the limits of any particular era" (xxvii). The strengths of the text are many; the insights are vast. Unfortunately, however, some of the work is unsystematic and often the sections seem disconnected. The reader is left with the impression that, although Sorokin's insights ring true intuitively, there is a great deal more work to be done in carefully arguing and scientifically testing the various hypotheses he forwards.

◈ Walsh, Anthony. (1991). *The science of love: Understanding love and its effects on mind and body.* Buffalo, NY: Prometheus.

Walsh is a sociologist who investigates the current scientific research and what it entails for how we understand various forms of love. The author intends to understand love in all its particulars, including its scientific basis. He defines love as that which "satisfies one's need to receive and bestow affection and nurturance; to give and be given assurances of value, respect, acceptance and appreciation; and to feel secure in a unity with, and belonging to, a particular family, as well as the human family" (9). Walsh laments that even social scientists who explore behavior have infrequently studied love. He is convinced, however, that humans must probe the nature of love and learn how to generate it and sustain it.

The book is divided into three sections. The first, "Skin Love," deals with the importance of love in early infancy. Included in this section are chapters exploring the importance of touch and tenderness upon infants in their first experience of love. Walsh also addresses how messages of love affect the structure and function of the infant's developing brain. A chapter is devoted to the differences between male and female parental love upon children. The impact of loving care upon the triune nature of the brain is also examined. It is Walsh's contention that "love is not merely theologically or philosophically desirable, but it is also a biological and psychological necessity" (37).

In the second section, Walsh examines what he calls "kin love," by which he means the loving ties with one's fellow human beings. In examining kin love, the author investigates the psychological and physical problems associated with the absence or deprivation of love. He notes that children suffering from psychosocial dwarfism are severely retarded in physical growth. Walsh notes the negative effects upon the immune system and the susceptibility to disease that those experience who have not been loved adequately. He also points out that love deprivation may interact with social and biological correlates of schizophrenia. Research details the importance that love plays in prevention of suicide; love also is a deterrent for drug and alcohol abuse. In a chapter devoted to criminology, Walsh shows the disturbing statistics by detailing the correlation between lawlessness and the lack of giving and being given love. In the section's final chapter, he argues that some social forms are conducive to love and some are inimical.

The book's third segment, "In Love," deals with romance and how romantic love is generated and sustained. The origin of sex is addressed, as well as the way chemicals in the brain and body effect one's romantic inclinations. Walsh looks at the different ways in which humans—both males and females—choose partners and what each finds attractive in the other. Included in this section are Walsh's thoughts about scientific evidence for monogamy, promiscuity, and orgasm. Throughout all three sections, the author relies heavily upon scientific data and the theories of prominent scientists to unravel theories of love that correspond with the work of science.

Primarily Philosophical Texts

❖ Adams, Robert Merrihew. (1999). *Finite and infinite goods.* Oxford: Oxford University Press.

Metaphysician and moral philosopher Robert Merrihew Adams, offers an elaborate framework for ethics based upon divine love as the ultimate good. Adams understands God as the Good itself, which means that the Good is a concrete personal individual. In Adams's metaphysics, God plays the part of the form of the beautiful in Plato's thought. God as the supreme Good transcends all other goods.

Adams believes that God's existence is metaphysically necessary, and those properties that fit God follow necessarily from the divine nature. The supreme Good is one aspect of the divine nature. This means that the only limits upon God are those that follow from God's own nature. Love is a necessary aspect of the divine nature, but God's preferences and actions as expressions of love are contingent. "The freedom ascribed to God does not include, as ours does, a possibility of desiring or choosing those ends that are rightly counted as bad" (48). This means that the standard of goodness is defined by the divine nature and thus is good for all possible worlds.

According to Adams's theory, what counts as good is not reducible to any human view about what the good is. The good is not fully accountable by any empirical test. Rather, the realm of value is organized around a transcendent good that is God. This means that the nature of value cannot be confined to the horizon of the physical or human world.

Adams makes a distinction between well-being and excellence. He notes that most contemporary thought focuses mainly upon well-being, or what is good for a person. Adams's own theory places primary importance upon excellence. Excellence implies a goodness in itself rather than goodness for another. Interest in well-being is secondary to the greater interest in excellence. What is good for a person is the living of a life characterized by the enjoyment of that which is excellent.

In the second segment of the book, Adams addresses what it means for individuals to love the good. The appropriate ethical relation is to be for the good, which entails loving it. God expresses *eros* in that God loves the good. Instead of understanding divine love as pure benevolence, Adams entertains seriously the notion that God desires relationship with creatures. This noninstrumental interest in relationships and excellences is part of what it means for both God and creatures to love. Adams considers what divine grace entails, arguing that it is a fundamental aspect of divine love. "Grace is love that is not completely explained by the excellence of its object" (151). While Adams claims that it would be absurd to suppose that all love excludes instrumental interest in the beloved, he also claims that love requires an interest in the beloved that is not merely instrumental. "Even divine love would be the richer rather than the poorer for finding value in the beloved" (165). Ideal love finds its reasons in the noncomparative appreciation of an object. This means that God's love is directed to things that are good, but it is not dominated by caring about whether these things are the best. Adams concludes this section with chapters on devotion, idolatry, and the value symbols.

Adams labels the third part of the book, "The Good and the Right." According to him, the good provides a proper framework for thinking about what is right and not the other way around. What is good has a fundamentally social aspect. Adams incorporates his theistic vision by arguing that only the commands of a definitively good God are candidates for defining what is human moral obligation. A main advantage of divine command theory of the nature of moral obligation is that it satisfies the demand for objective moral requirements. There are many possibilities for how these commands are communicated or revealed by God, including scriptural texts, utterances of prophets, requirements of human communities, individual intuitions, and so on. Signs that occur in time and place note these commands.

After examining the story of Abraham and Isaac, Adams concludes "that in any cultural context in which it is possible to worry about Abraham's Dilemma, it will hardly be credible that a good God has commanded the sort of sacrifice that is envisaged here. . . . I think it is the part of religious as well as moral wisdom to dismiss all thoughts of our actually being commanded by God to practice something as horrible as human sacrifice. The question whether God commands such a thing should stay off our epistemological agenda as long as it possibly can, which I expect will be forever" (290–291).

The question of love and obligation leads to an inquiry into vocation. Adams defines vocation as "a call from God, a command, or perhaps an invitation addressed to a particular individual, to act and live in a certain way" (301). Direct and unambiguous commands from God are extremely rare, argues Adams, which means that conflicting values and obligations in any situation need to be thought about critically before interpreting these as communicating a divine command. The concept of vocation helps to solve the issue of whether or not creatures can love all other creatures. A divine call to love some persons and some kind of goods provides a way of understanding one's vocation. These questions of vocation lead naturally to the concluding part of Adams's book, which addresses the epistemology of value.

ᴄᴏ Goicoechea, David, Ed. (1995). *The nature and pursuit of love: The philosophy of Irving Singer*. Amherst, NY: Prometheus.

This volume is a collection of twenty exploratory and critical essays concerning the philosophy of love propounded by Irving Singer. Singer is one of the greatest latter twentieth-century philosophers on romantic love. His distinctive contribution is his contention that love should be understood as bestowal, a notion that overcomes what Singer believes are deficiencies in Anders Nygren's notion of *agape.*

The book begins with two interviews on Singer by Robert Fulford. The printed transcripts give the reader an insider's view to the various topics that Singer addresses in his life's work. At the conclusion of the edited text, Singer offers his reply to the volume's essays, which are written by critics and friendly commentators. Most of the essays in the text were originally delivered in a three-day colloquium. They reflect Singer's broad interests while focusing on his key distinction between love as appraisal and bestowal as elements in the definition of love.

ᴄᴏ Hartshorne, Charles. (1941). *Man's vision of God and the logic of theism*. New York: Willett, Clark & Company.

One of the twentieth century's greatest philosophers offers a rational and empirical defense for the existence of God based upon reason and love. The ground for the book is "a conviction that a magnificent intellectual content is implicit in the religious faith most briefly expressed into three words, 'God is love,' which words I sincerely believe are contradicted as truly as they are embodied in the best known of the older theologies, as they certainly have been misunderstood by atheists and skeptics" (ix).

Hartshorne offers a solution to the problem of evil that is based upon a notion of divine power in harmony with creaturely power. "In their ultimate individuality things can only be influenced, they cannot be surely coerced" (xvi). Hartshorne's understanding of God as both absolute and relative provides a fundamental thesis for process theology's doctrine of God. In some respects, God is unchanging; in some respects, God changes. Because God is unchanging love, God's experiencing of love and gift of love must change in moment-by-moment existence.

Hartshorne's understanding of love plays a pivotal role in the development of the book's themes. He argues that "love is the desire for the good of others, ideally all others" (14). Divine love includes social awareness and action from that awareness. It includes both selfish and unselfish acts by God. "In God there is a perfect agreement between altruism and egoism" (161). He argues that theologians went through many contortions to show that God's love both was love and nothing of the kind. "They sought to maintain a distinction between love as desire, with an element of possible gain or loss to the self, and love as purely altruistic benevolence; or again between sensuous and spiritual love, *eros* and *agape*. But benevolence is a form of desire" (116).

"The whole idea of religion," says Hartshorne, "is that we can know God as He is in Himself, though vaguely, for we know Him through love. We know ourselves and everything else in relation to a dim but direct sense of God's love. Love of God is the norm of creaturely love; for religion, all other human love is deficient" (127). In words that sound poetic but that Hartshorne takes seriously, he writes, "the divine as love is the only theme adequate to the cosmic symphony" (216).

Hazo, Robert G. (1967). *The idea of love.* New York: Praeger.

A philosopher offers a philosophical analysis of the love suppositions of numerous major theologians, psychologists, and philosophers of the western world. The purpose of the book is to discover what unites and divides thinkers of the past and present who have written about human love in particular. "We are concerned, primarily, with determining what any given author's core conception of love among human beings is, and only secondarily shall we deal with the additional characteristics, traits, or properties he may employ to distinguish the various loves with which he is concerned" (7).

The book is divided into two basic parts. The first discusses critical notions and controversies about human love as understood by the various authors. Hazo argues that all of the literature on love reveals that love is understood as either tendential or judgmental. By "tendential," Hazo refers to feelings, emotions, or desires that imply that love is not an act of thought or attitude of mind. By "judgmental," the author refers to love as a matter of cognition whereby the lover admires, respects, or values the object of love. Tendential love is further subdivided into acquisitive and benevolent desire. Judgmental love is divided into two types, esteem and valuation. Esteem signifies a person's judgment that someone is good in his or her self. Valuation has to do with a person's judgment that someone is good for the one judging. Hazo notes that most of his authors place love entirely within the sphere of tendency. Those who include an element of cognition differ on their belief about whether cognition comes prior to, along with, or following tendential love.

After disclosing the various types of love that emerge from a study of dominant literature on love, the author explores various controversies about natural human love. Hazo claims that whether love is tendential or judgmental, the authors he examined have minimum agreements as to what love is. First, the respect in which a lover loves the beloved is the respect in which the lover is interested in the beloved. Second, love always involves some preference. Third, love points toward action. Fourth, all authors speak of love as either good in itself or as pointing toward some good. These characteristics form what Hazo believes is the nucleus of the idea of love.

The second chapter includes discussions of more than twenty-five questions about what love is. The questions that Hazo proposes expose the controversies in the literature about the nature and types of natural human love.

After examining controversies about natural human love, Hazo turns to controversies in the literature about supernatural human love. All authors examined in this segment believe that a supernatural realm exists and that the religious experience of love by humans is impossible without supernatural aid. The intent is not to examine the nature of divine love but only to deal with God's love to the extent that one must to make intelligible the particular author's conception of how God inspires or instigates love in humans.

Hazo begins with a general note that there seems to be an important difference in the general conceptions of love held by Roman Catholics and Protestants. He believes that the dispute about the character and relationship of *eros* and *agape* within the Christian tradition is at the very core of how one understands supernatural human love. He notes that "with some qualifications, all agree that God's love for man is purely benevolent, since God is, by definition, perfect and in need of nothing" (101). The authors addressed in this chapter include Augustine, Aquinas, Fenelon, Bernard of Clairvaux, Anders Nygren, Soren Kierkegaard, Denis De Rougemont, Reinhold Niebuhr, Paul Tillich, and C. S. Lewis.

Hazo concludes from the literature that the controversy of supernatural human love focuses on the question of self-interestedness versus disinterestedness. He also notes that the difference between how one understands self-interest in relation to supernatural human love is directly related to how one understands the effects of original sin. This leads him to conclude that "the idea of love or, rather, human love, is less fundamental than the idea of man" (160).

The fourth chapter addresses the unity and diversity among literatures and among authors proposing theories of natural and supernatural human love. Hazo is especially impressed by the similarities of characteristics between natural love and supernatural human love. Among those similarities are the agreement that love is (1) a constructive, unifying, or good thing, (2) a key to human happiness, and (3) primarily a relational concept, one in which the notions of self and other are pivotal.

The remaining chapters of the book provide documentation and analysis of the specific views of specific authors as they relate to love. Those authors discussed include Plato, Augustine, Aristotle, Cicero, Thomas Aquinas, Dante, Leone Ebreo Castiglione, Bernard of Clairvaux, Soren Kierkegaard, Immanuel Kant, Max Scheler, Pitirim Sorokin, Sigmund Freud, Karl Menninger, Carl Jung, William James, Plotinus, Marsilio Ficino, Giovanni Pico della Mirandola, Pietro Bembo, Ibnsina, Andreas Capellanus, Marie-Henri Boyle Stendahl, Arthur Schopenhauer, Denis De Rougemont, George Santayana, Charles Darwin, Jean-Jacques Rousseau, Benedict de Spinoza, Gottfried Leibniz, Adam Smith, G. W. F.

Hegel, Georg Simmel, Nicolai Hartmann, C. S. Lewis, Jose Ortega y Gasset, Theodor Reik, Erich Fromm, Rene Descartes, David Hume, John Locke, Vladimir Solovyev, and Blaise Pascal.

    ⬧ Norton, David L., & Kille, Mary F. (Eds.). (1971). *Philosophies of love.* Totowa, NJ: Rowman and Littlefield.

This tome provides a wide variety of readings on love and philosophy. The editors believe that love is a profound measure of human life and that a person's philosophy of love permeates his or her philosophy of life. The text includes more than forty contributions, mostly classic essays with regard to love. "Developing a philosophy of life is not something we can relegate to others to do for us, like house building or plumbing repair, but something each of us must do for himself. There is no escaping it, each of us is required to be something of a philosopher" (1).

The editors divide the book into six parts. "Romantic Love: Madness of a Normal Man" has eight readings on romantic love. "*Eros:* Love as Aspiration toward the Ideal" includes ten essays on *eros*. In part 3, "*Agape:* The Divine Bestowal," *agape* love is addressed. The final three sections are "Tristanism and Chivalric Love," "Friendship: 'Because It Was He, Because It Was I,'" and "Fellow Feeling: Universal Bond of Humankind."

    ⬧ Nussbaum, Martha. (2001). *Upheavals of thought: The intelligence of emotions.* Cambridge: Cambridge University Press.

Philosopher Nussbaum argues in this book, the product of her Gifford Lectures, that emotions shape who we are, and they must form part of a system of ethical reasoning as intelligent responses to the perception of value. A part of emotions is judgments that can be true or false, and good or bad guides the ethical choice. "A central part of developing an adequate ethical theory," claims Nussbaum, "will be to develop an adequate theory of the emotions, including their cultural sources, their history in infancy and childhood, and their sometimes unpredictable and disorderly operation in the daily life of human beings who are attached to things outside themselves" (2). Emotions have a complicated cognitive structure in relation to objects that we cherish and this relationship extends over time. This means that without emotional development, a part of our reasoning capacity's political creatures will be missing.

Nussbaum's Neo-Stoic inspired project is to construct an analytic framework for thinking about emotions in general. Emotions "involve judgment about important things, judgments in which, appraising external objects are salient for our own well being, we acknowledge our own neediness and incompleteness before parts of the world that we do not fully control" (19).

In her first chapter Nussbaum sets out the basis for her argument about the intelligence of emotions. Emotions view the world from the perspective of one's own scheme of goals, the things to which one attaches value for what it means to live well. In short, emotions are valuative appraisals of the world.

Continuity exists between humans and nonhumans in that both display emotions. Studies of animal emotions underscore Nussbaum's claim that cognitive appraisals need not all be objects of reflexive self-consciousness. Although all individuals feel emotions, both human and nonhuman, this does not mean that individual histories and social norms do not shape emotions. In fact, they do. A path should be steered between those at one extreme who argue that emotions are totally constructed by society and those at the other extreme who argue that society plays no role in the shaping of emotions.

Emotions "bear the traces of a history that is at once commonly human, socially constructed, and idiosyncratic" (177). This means that adult human emotions cannot be understood without understanding their history in infancy and childhood. Nussbaum rejects theories calling individuals to bring every emotion into line with the dictates of reason, or the dictates of one's ideals, whatever they may be.

In the second part of this 700-page book, Nussbaum focuses on the emotion of compassion, which she defines as "a painful emotion occasioned by the awareness of another person's undeserved misfortune" (301). Compassion includes cognitive aspects, including (1) the belief or appraisal that the suffering one encounters is serious rather than trivial, (2) the belief that the person does not deserve the suffering, and (3) the belief that the possibilities of the person who experiences the emotion are similar to those of the sufferer.

Compassion involves a significant quasi-ethical achievement in that it values another person as part of one's own circle of concern. One should not depend upon the vicissitudes of personal emotion but should build emotion's insights into the structures of ethical rules and institutions. Furthermore, compassion and social institutions are related in that compassionate individuals construct institutions that embody what they imagine and institutions influence the development of compassion in individuals.

In the third part of the book, Nussbaum addresses various traditions of erotic love, hoping to show that erotic love can be part of morally acceptable life. Erotic love "involves an opening of the self toward an object, a conception of the self that pictures the self as incomplete and reaching out for something valued" (460). This means that erotic love is based on unequal concern not explained by reason alone. It is love that is partial.

The literature that Nussbaum explores in section three is part of the ascent tradition of love. Authors who write of this love offer ways to reform or educate erotic love "so as to keep its creative force while purifying it of ambivalence and excess, and making it more friendly to general social aims" (469). The authors that Nussbaum addresses in the final part of the book include Plato, Spinoza,

Proust, Augustine, Dante, Emily Brontë, Mahler, Walt Whitman, and James Joyce. This literature presents (1) a tradition that sees *eros* love as fundamentally the contemplation of the good and beautiful, (2) a Christian account of the ascent that investigates the role of humility, longing and grace, (3) a romantic account that strives for love's transcendence, and (4) the reverse ascent or the descent of love in which human desire sets out its task of embracing the imperfect human world with love.

The Neo-Stoic theory of emotions that Nussbaum develops entails that while love is an emotion, it is also a relationship. Given this, Nussbaum critiques the authors' writings in the third section of her book using three normative criteria. The first criteria is compassion by which she asks, "Does this view of love deny the constituent features of compassion, including the seriousness of various human predicaments, one's responsibility for these predicaments, and the proper extent of concern." The second criteria is reciprocity. By reciprocity Nussbaum means the idea that relationships of concern are established in which people treat one another as agents and ends, not as things. The third criteria, individuality, means that love recognizes that human beings are separate and qualitatively distinct individuals.

৵৵ Singer, Irving. (1984). *The nature of love: Plato to Luther* (vol. 1, 2nd ed.). Chicago: University of Chicago Press; (1984). *The nature of love: Courtly and romantic* (vol. 2). Chicago: University of Chicago Press; (1999). *The nature of love: The modern world* (vol. 3). Chicago: University of Chicago Press.

In this monumental, three-volume work, Irving Singer explores vast expressions and theories of love from ancient times to the present. His intent is not to present his own philosophy of love; rather, the author attempts to be investigative in his approach. The first volume, *Plato to Luther,* traces the ideas of love from ancient times up through the middle ages. In addition to his study of Judeo-Christian love, Singer addresses love in the works of Plotinus, Aristotle, and Plato.

In his introductory essays of volume 1, Singer analyzes love as both an ideal and a psychological state. It is in this volume that Singer uses the words *appraisal* and *bestowal* to delineate two different kinds of love. Singer believes love involves a way of valuing in that what one finds valuable in the other one embraces. But love also creates value in the other. The history of love in the western world is a history of new ways of bestowing and acquiring values.

Singer argues that the Bible and Greek philosophy are the two sources from which the dominant philosophies of love stem. He also contends that "what distinguishes Christianity, what gives it a unique place in man's intellectual life, is the fact that it alone has made love the dominant principle in all areas of dogma. Whatever Christians may have done to others or themselves, theirs is the only faith in which God and love are the same" (159).

Singer believes that it is the ideas of love that have developed throughout history that have inspired love. This is a philosophical work in the phenomenological tradition. Singer's works are instructive resources for those wanting to address the wide history of love.

Soble, Alan. (1989). *Eros, agape, and philia.* New York: Paragon.

Soble provides this collection of primary writings dealing with the subject of love as a companion volume to an earlier volume of readings on the philosophy of sex. He does so believing that love is "such a rich phenomenon provoking questions in ontology, epistemology, the philosophy of mind, theology and philosophy of religion, and that to restrict the investigation of its many forms and dimensions to the ties between love and sexuality is to commit a painful, conceptual truncation" (ix). The book is divided into four main sections: "Where We Are"; "Classical Sources"; "Exploring the Classics"; and a contemporary analysis of love. Throughout the book, Soble often relates the word *love* to its various romantic implications.

Soble's method in compiling the volume is to provide three or four primary writings prefaced by a summary of the reason these writings are important. He introduces the entire book, however, by asking, "What is love?" "The complexity of this question compare it to, What is a chair? is reflected in the fact that so many different answers to it exists and debates about the nature of genuine love seem impossible to resolve" (xix). Love can be compared to art, for each is equally a difficult domain to describe.

One of the reasons love is so difficult to explain is that the word refers to many different things. Often, however, the attempt to conceptualize love is framed with regard to the Greek love words *eros, philia,* and *agape.* Soble believes that the general characterization of "*eros*-style" love arises in this way: *x* loves *y* because *y* has attractive or valuable qualities. "*Agape*-style" love is understood as *x* loving *y* independently of *y*'s merit. This book offers original formulations of the theories of *eros, agape,* and *philia,* and then attempts to explain more generally what these love types might mean for contemporary thinking.

Solomon, Robert C. (1981). *Love: Emotion, myth, and metaphor.* Garden City, NY: Anchor.

Solomon attempts to construct a philosophical set of arguments for a contemporary conception of romantic love. He attacks what he believes are nonsensical, common expressions and notions of love that have been perpetrated in praise of love as an emotion. The author looks at empirical evidence and tangible facts of collective experience to separate wishful thinking about love from the nature of experiencing love itself.

Solomon writes in a very entertaining way using expressions and metaphors, literature and common experiences of life. Topics addressed include emotions, feelings, *eros,* feminism, fantasies, illusions, commitments, honesty, intimacy, sex, and self-esteem. The author defines love essentially as an emotion that is surrounded by myths and metaphors and motivated by hopes and desires.

அ Solomon, Robert C., & Higgins, Kathleen M. (Eds.). (1991). *The philosophy of (erotic) love.* Lawrence: University Press of Kansas.

This volume is one of the very best for its presentation of the wide varieties of writings about erotic love. The text is divided into four parts. The first includes classic writings on erotic love from authors living prior to the twentieth century, including Plato, Sappho, Theno, Ovid, Augustine, Heloise and Abelard, Andreas Capellanus, Shakespeare, John Milton, Spinoza, Rousseau, Hegel, Schopenhauer, Stendahl, and Nietzsche.

The second part of the book includes classic writings on love from those in the twentieth century, Sigmund Freud, Carl Jung, Karen Horney, Rainer Maria Rilke, Emma Goldman, Denis de Rougemont, D. H. Lawrence, Jean-Paul Sartre, Simone de Beauvoir, Philip Slater, and Shulamith Firestone.

The third section of the book offers contemporary essays that advance theories and notions proposed by authors of antiquity, Irving Singer, Martha Nussbaum, Jerome Neu, Louis Mackey, Emelie Rorty, Elizabeth Rappaport, and Kathryn Pauly Morgan.

The fourth part of the book includes essays that are more theoretical, including a number of new attempts to define and understand love. Authors in this section include Robert Nozick, Annette Baier, William Gass, Laurence Thomas, Ronald de Sousa, and Robert C. Solomon.

அ Taylor, Charles. (1992). *Sources of the self: The making of modern identity.* Cambridge: Harvard University Press.

The author offers a grand-scale history of modern, western identity. By "identity" he means the ensemble of understandings of what it means to be a human agent, including the sense of inwardness, freedom, individuality and, being embedded in nature. The text is a largely historical piece intended to allow the reader to grasp the richness and complexity of the modern understanding of the self as it developed out of earlier pictures of human identity.

In his preface the author sums up his approach. "I focus on three major facets of this identity: first, modern inwardness, the sense of ourselves as beings with inner depths, and the connected notions that we are 'selves'; second, the affirmation of ordinary life which develops from the early modern period; third, the expressivist notion of nature as an inner moral source" (x).

Taylor concludes that the modern identity of humans is richer in its moral sources than many contemporary skeptics suppose. Disengaged instrumental modes of thought and action have steadily increased their hold on modern life, argues the author. One important insight in this book is that modern subjectivity has its roots in ideas about what is the human good.

⤳ Wyschogrod, Edith. (1990). *Saints and postmodernism: Revisioning moral philosophy.* Chicago: University of Chicago Press.

The author's basic argument is that ethics in a postmodern age must not look to normative structures of moral theories; ethics must look instead to the lives of saints as a basis for understanding how to live. What marks the saint as the model for ethics is the fact that saints recognize the primacy of the other person and dissolve any self-interest that they might have. This means that ethics is "the sphere of transaction between 'the self' and 'Other'" (xv). The ethics of saints emerge in their life habits.

Wyschogrod argues that saints exhibit a particular altruism. This altruism is reflective, and negation and ambiguity mark saintliness. Saints who are altruistic reject any self-empowerment in their total regard for the Other. This means that the Other is not only different from the one acting but also carries the moral weight. The Other's needs include the needs of his or her material body.

Saints should not be imagined as emanating from some specific religious community. Rather, saints are found across a broad spectrum of belief systems and institutional practices. "A saintly life is defined as one in which compassion for the other, irrespective of cost to the saint, is the primary trait" (xxiii).

Wyschogrod does not find dominant and traditional moral theories to provide adequate bases for ethics. Most moral theories treat the Other as another kind of self. Most moral theorists begin an understanding altruism with the action of the self. Wyschogrod advocates understanding altruism by beginning with the Other as its starting point. In short, the author argues that a theoretical ethic must be supplanted by an ethic grounded in narrative and hagiography. She argues from the standpoint of phenomenological and postmodern thinkers such as Martin Heidegger, Emmanuel Levinas, Jacques Derrida, Georges Bataille, and Maurice Blanchot.

Contributors

Giacomo Bono is a postdoctoral fellow at the University of Miami, where his research is broadly focused on interpersonal forgiveness and gratitude. He recently completed his Ph.D. in applied social psychology at Claremont Graduate University, where he also completed his M.A. in psychology. His dissertation examined group and cultural factors relevant to commonplace forgiveness. For the past three years Bono has taught a variety of courses (social cognition, social psychology, experimental research methods, introductory psychology, history of psychology, and critical thinking) at universities in Southern California. Currently, he is conducting research on intrapersonal and interpersonal processes and various mental/physical health outcomes associated with forgiveness and gratitude with the ultimate goal of applying forgiveness to the prevention of interpersonal and interethnic conflict.

Lia Fantuzzo is a doctoral student in political science and research associate at the Center for Research on Religion and Urban Civil Society (CRRUCS) at the University of Pennsylvania in Philadelphia. As an undergraduate at Penn, she studied English and French. Fantuzzo has been an intern in Washington, D.C., for several foundations and spent one year as a research assistant for the CRRUCS. She recently published a study on how religious organizations are rescuing America's at-risk kids. Fantuzzo is committed to studying urban communities and the opportunities that exist for effective partnerships between and among local institutions.

Byron R. Johnson, Ph.D., is director of the Center for Research on Religion and Urban Civil Society (CRRUCS) and distinguished senior fellow in the Robert A. Fox Leadership Program at the University of Pennsylvania. He is also senior fellow in the Center for Civic Innovation at the Manhattan Institute and a senior scholar at the Vanderbilt Institute for Public Policy Studies. Before coming to Penn, Johnson directed the Center for Crime and Justice Policy at Vanderbilt University, Nashville.

Professor Johnson's research focuses on quantifying the effectiveness of faith-based organizations to confront various social problems. Recent publications include studies on the efficacy of the "faith factor" in reducing crime and drug use among at-risk youth in urban communities, and the role of religious programming to reduce recidivism rates of former prisoners. Along with other research intermediaries, Johnson and CRRUCS colleagues are launching a ground-breaking study of faith-based mentoring to Philadelphia's most disadvantaged and at-risk population—the children of prisoners. Recent journal publications have appeared in *Criminology, Justice Quarterly, Journal of Research in Crime and Delinquency,* and the *Journal of Quantitative Criminology.*

Kevin Kniffin is a doctoral student and research assistant at the State University of New York at Binghamton, where he studies evolutionary biology with Dr. David Sloan Wilson.

Michael E. McCullough, Ph.D., is associate professor of psychology at the University of Miami in Coral Gables, Florida. He received a B.S. from the University of Florida in 1990 and a Ph.D. in psychology from Virginia Commonwealth University, Richmond. His scholarly work focuses on religion, spirituality, and the virtues, how these aspects of people's lives unfold, and how they are linked to health and well-being. In 2000 McCullough was awarded the Margaret Gorman Early Career Award from Division 36 (Psychology of Religion) of the American Psychological Association. In 2001 he received third prize in the American Psychological Association/John Templeton Foundation award program for research in positive psychology. Dr. McCullough has written over seventy peer-reviewed journal articles and book chapters. He has also authored or edited four books, including *Forgiveness: Theory Research and Practice* (Guilford Press, 2000), *Handbook of Religion and Health* (Oxford University Press, 2001) and an upcoming volume on the psychology of gratitude (Oxford University Press). His work has been funded by a variety of private foundations.

Thomas Jay Oord, Ph.D., is professor of theology and philosophy at Northwest Nazarene University and former philosophy department chair at Eastern Nazarene College. Oord has written and/or edited several books, the latest *Thy Nature and Thy Name Is Love.* Oord serves on the executive councils of several academic societies, including the Open and Relational Theology group and the Wesleyan Theological Society. He also serves as academic correspondent for *Research News and Opportunities in Science and Theology.*

Emma Y. Post is a student at Bucknell University, where she majors in English literature and political science. She is a contributor to *The Bucknellian,* and to *Research News & Opportunities in Science and Theology.*

Stephen G. Post, Ph.D., is professor and associate director for educational programs, Department of Bioethics, School of Medicine, Case Western Reserve University, as well as Senior Research Scholar in the Becket Institute at St.

Hugh's College, Oxford University. Post is serving as president of the newly formed Institute for Research on Unlimited Love, which studies phenomena such as altruism, compassion, and service. His most recent book is *Unlimited Love: Altruism, Compassion, and Service* (Templeton Foundation Press, 2003). He received his Ph.D. in philosophical and religious ethics from the University of Chicago (1983), where he was an elected university fellow. His work is in three major areas: cognitive disabilities and dementia; *family* caregivers and the ethics of the family; and altruism and compassionate love in the context of scientific research, philosophy, religion, ethics, and the professions.

Post is editor-in-chief of the definitive *Encyclopedia of Bioethics*, 3rd edition (Macmillan Reference, in preparation), and the author of more than 120 articles in leading peer-reviewed journals representing the sciences and humanities, as well as six books and ten edited books.

Jeffrey P. Schloss, Ph.D., received his undergraduate degree in biology from Wheaton College and his Ph.D. in ecology and evolutionary biology from Washington University. He has taught at the University of Michigan, Wheaton College, Jaguar Creek Tropical Research Center, and is currently professor and chair of biology at Westmont College in Santa Barbara. He has been awarded a Danforth Fellow, a AAAS Fellow in Science Communication, and serves on the editorial and advisory boards of numerous journals and organizations relating science and religion, including *Zygon, Journal of Theology and Science, Science and Christian Belief, Science and Spirit,* and the John Templeton Foundation.

Schloss's interests are in evolutionary theories of human nature, and recent projects include a collaborative volume, *Altruism and Altruistic Love: Science, Philosophy and Religion in Dialogue* (Oxford University Press, 2002), and co-editing a two-volume series of the *Journal of Psychology and Theology* focusing on biological and theological perspectives on human nature.

Marc Siegel is a research assistant for the Center for Research on Religion and Urban Civil Society (CRRUCS). He is a recent graduate of the University of Pennsylvania with a B.A. in economics. While at Penn, Siegel was the recipient of the Glory of Missouri award for charity issued by the Missouri House of Representatives. He was also awarded the Gentleman, Leaders, Innovators scholarship and named a finalist for two Ivy Day Awards issued for dedication to school service. Siegel spent three summers as an intern in the U.S. Attorney's Office and was one of two students nominated by Penn to work with Governor Tom Ridge to design an internship program to help keep students in Pennsylvania upon graduation.

David Sloan Wilson, Ph.D., is an evolutionary biologist who studies a broad range of subjects relevant to humans, in addition to nonhuman species. He is best known for his work on multilevel selection theory in which altruism and other prosocial behaviors evolve by benefiting whole groups. He has published widely in biology, philosophy, psychology, and anthropology journals. With philosopher Elliott Sober, he is the author of *Unto Others: The Evolution of Unselfish Behavior* (Harvard Press, 1998). His most recent work is *Darwin's Cathedral* (University of Chicago Press, 2002).